THE PSYCHOLOGY OF ATTENTION, SECOND EDITION

Research on attention has evolved dramatically in recent years. There are now many new ways of studying how we are able to select some aspects for processing, while ignoring others and how we are able to combine tasks, learn skills and make intentional actions. Attention is increasingly seen as a complex process intimately linked with perception, memory and action. New questions are continually being addressed, for example in the areas of crossmodal attention and the biological bases of attention.

After an initial consideration of what attention might be, this book charts the development in the ideas and theories that surround the field. An entirely new chapter addresses the nature of auditory attention and the question of how visual and auditory attention are combined across modalities. The problems of task combination, skill acquisition and automaticity are also considered, as well as the selection and control of action and conscious and unconscious processing.

The Psychology of Attention, Second Edition provides a comprehensive and accessible introduction to this fascinating and rapidly developing field.

Elizabeth Styles is Lecturer in Psychology at St Edmund Hall, Oxford.

The Psychology of Attention, Second Edition

Elizabeth A. Styles

Psychology Press
Taylor & Francis Group

HOVE AND NEW YORK

First published 2006 by Psychology Press
27 Church Road, Hove, East Sussex BN3 2FA

Simultaneously published in the USA and Canada
by Psychology Press
270 Madison Avenue, New York, NY 10016

Psychology Press is an imprint of the Taylor & Francis Group, an informa business

© 2006 Psychology Press

Typeset in Palatino by RefineCatch Limited, Bungay, Suffolk
Printed and bound in Great Britain by TJ International Ltd., Padstow, Cornwall
Paperback cover design by Sandra Heath

All rights reserved. No part of this book may be reprinted or reproduced or utilised in any form
or by any electronic, mechanical, or other means, now known or hereafter invented, including
photocopying and recording, or in any information storage or retrieval system, without
permission in writing from the publishers.

This publication has been produced with paper manufactured to strict environmental standards
and with pulp derived from sustainable forests.

British Library Cataloguing in Publication Data
A catalogue record for this book is available from the British Library

Library of Congress Cataloging in Publication Data
Styles, Elizabeth A.
     The psychology of attention / Elizabeth A. Styles. – 2nd ed.
         p.   cm.
     Includes bibliographical references (p. 295) and index.
     ISBN 1-84169-396-0 (hardback) – ISBN 1-84169-397-9 (pbk.)
  1. Attention. I. Title.
     BF321.S85 2006
     153.7′33 –dc22   2005030585

ISBN13: 9-78-1-84169-396-5 (hbk)
ISBN13: 9-78-1-84169-397-2 (pbk)

ISBN10: 1-84169-396-0 (hbk)
ISBN10: 1-84169-397-9 (pbk)

To the memory of my father Gilbert Howell

Contents

List of figures

Preface

I know from my students that cognitive psychology fills some of them with dread. They see it as the "difficult" side of psychology, full of facts that don't quite fit any theory. Cognition does not have the immediate appeal of social or developmental psychology, to which, they say, they can relate more easily through personal experience. However, towards the end of a course, they begin to see how the pieces of the jigsaw fit together and exclaim: "This is interesting, why didn't you tell us this to start with?" The trouble is that, until you *have* put some of the pieces together, it is difficult to see even a part of what the overall picture is. Next, the parts of the picture have to be put in the right place. With respect to the topic of attention, no one yet knows exactly what the picture that we are building looks like; this makes work on attention particularly exciting and challenging. We may have some of the pieces in the wrong place or be thinking of the wrong overall picture. In this book, I hope you will find some pieces that fit together and see how some of the pieces have had to be moved as further evidence is brought to light. I hope you see, from the everyday example of attentional behaviour in the introduction, that we can relate to cognitive psychology just as well as social psychology. Attention is with us all the time.

The initial motivation for this book came from the fact that my undergraduates were unable to find a suitable text on attention to back lectures, tutorials and seminars. My second motivation was that most chapters in general cognitive psychology texts tend to concentrate on the original early work on selective attention done in the 1960s, dual task performance work from the 1970s and feature integration theory from 1980. These aspects are important, but research on attention includes far more than this, in fact so much more, that the possibility of gathering it all into an undergraduate text is impossible. As cognitive neuroscience moves ahead, bringing together traditional experimental work, neuropsychological studies and computational modelling, the prospect for a better understanding of attention is coming nearer. At the same time, the range of evidence that needs to be considered has increased far beyond that which was accounted for by the original theories. However, I believe that in the end there will be a "simple" solution. As we understand more about the brain and the way in which it works, we are beginning to see how attentional behaviour may emerge as a property of complex underlying processing.

Since the publication of the first edition of this book research into attention has changed in several exciting ways. First, there has been an increase in the availability of brain-imaging techniques that allow researchers to link brain activity to attentional behaviour. Second, there has been a resurgence of interest in auditory attention and how attention in different sensory modalities interact. In this sense attention research is becoming more closely related to how attention is used in the real world. Third, researchers are now finding close links between attention perception and memory.

In choosing what to include, I have necessarily been selective and am sure to have omitted some work that others would see as essential. There has not been room to include the burgeoning amount of data available from brain imaging and neuroscience, so although I have included some examples, I have largely restricted the content to experimental cognitive psychology and evidence from cognitive neuropsychology. Posner (2004a) covers the cognitive neuroscience of attention, including chapters by experts on imaging studies, synaptic and genetic studies, together with developmental aspects and attentional deficits. This is an advanced book, but will be of interest to those who wish to pursue the contribution of neuroscience to current views on attention.

The selection of work I have chosen is bound to be biased by the time I spent as a student and then, as a colleague, of two great thinkers in attention: Alan Allport and Donald Broadbent. Their energy, enthusiasm, wisdom and kindness inspired my own interest in attention. I acknowledge my debt to them here. I am also grateful to the staff and students at Buckinghamshire Chilterns University College at High Wycombe and St Edmund Hall Oxford, for good company, encouragement and the use of resources.

Liz Styles
Oxford 2005

Introduction 1

What is attention?

Any reader who turns to a book with the word "attention" in the title might be forgiven for thinking that the author would have a clear idea or precise definition of what "attention" actually is. Unfortunately, attention remains a concept that psychologists find difficult to define. William James (1890) told us that: "Everyone knows what attention is. It is the taking possession of mind in clear and vivid form ... it implies withdrawal from some things in order to deal effectively with others." However, it would be closer to the truth to say that "Nobody knows what attention is" or at least not all psychologists agree. The problem is that "attention" is not a single concept, but an umbrella term for a variety of psychological phenomena. Shiffrin (1988, p. 739) provides a more precise definition: "Attention has been used to refer to all those aspects of human cognition that the subject can control ... and to all aspects of cognition having to do with limited resources or capacity, and methods of dealing with such constraints." However, "all" is used twice here, suggesting that, even within this definition, there are many aspects of attention involved. There is, however, some agreement that attention is characterised by a limited capacity for processing information and that this allocation can be intentionally controlled. Desimone and Duncan (1995, p. 193) capture the properties of visual attention, and say that: "The first basic phenomenon is limited capacity for processing information. At any given time only a small amount of the information available on the retina can be processed and used." Certainly, we have the subjective feeling that although we may be able to choose what we attend to in vision, there is a severe limitation on the amount of information that we can attend to at any one moment. We can only look in one direction at a time and only take in part of the visual scene. These are central characteristics of human performance, with which we are all subjectively familiar and for which there is a large body of empirical evidence. So, in this sense, we do know what attention is. Does this capture all varieties of attention? What if, while you look in one direction, you also listen to a conversation behind you? Can you choose to look in one direction but attend to something else "out of the corner of your eye"? To what extent can attention be allocated according to behaviourial goals? In Shiffrin's definition, the subject is given the role of control. This is not a very scientific explanation and as we shall see in the chapters that follow, the nature of attentional control is the subject of some debate.

It is evident that "attention" is a term used to refer to different phenomena and processes, not only by psychologists, but also in common usage of the word. This seems to have been the case throughout the history of psychology. The same word is applied to different aspects of situations and experiences in everyday speech and defined differently by different psychologists. One of the reasons for the rise of the behaviourist movement in psychology was the difficulty psychologists at the turn of the 20th century were having in formulating precise definitions of terms such as "attention" and "consciousness". Psychology had grown out of mental philosophy to become the "science of mind", but unless it was clear what was meant by the terms used in explanations, psychology could not be truly scientific. The famous behaviourist J. B. Watson (1919) wrote:

> If I were to ask you to tell me what you mean by the terms you have been in the habit of using I could soon make you tongue-tied. I believe I could even convince you that you do not know what you mean by them. You have been using them uncritically as a part of your social and literary tradition. (p. 6)

Behaviourism aimed to purge psychology of its use of everyday psychological terms and provide a true science of behaviour without recourse to any intervening variables in the "mind". The problem for psychologists of the behaviourist tradition was that the "mind" was not so easy to banish from explanations of human performance. Behaviour could be scientifically observed and stimulus–response relationships discovered, but unobservable internal mechanisms such as "attention", however poorly defined, which evidently allow adaptive goal directed behaviour could not be experimented on. They were not amenable to explanation in terms of simple stimulus response associations.

Treisman (1964d), who was one of the most important contributors to the development of theories of attention, started her paper "Selective attention in man" by saying:

Fifty years ago psychologists thought of attention as "the focalisation of consciousness" or "the increased clearness of a particular idea". But these and other definitions in terms of mental faculties or subjective experience proved sterile for empirical research and ended in a series of inconclusive controversies. Recently interest in this problem has revived.

She goes on to identify the practical need to understand attention, the development of the information processing approach to psychology, which provides a metaphor for modelling internal processes and advances in understanding the neurophysiological bases of attention as important factors in this revival. Behaviourism fell from favour and the cognitive approach, in which humans were seen as information processors, took over as the predominant metaphor of mind. The cognitive approach provided a scientific way of modelling the intervening variables between stimulus and response. So, where are we after nearly another 50 years? This is what this book is about.

Varieties of attention

Attention is not of one kind, so rather than searching for a single definition, we need to consider attention as having a number of different varieties. Perhaps we cannot understand what attention is until we accept this. Allport (1993, p. 203) points out the problem that the same term "attention" refers to a wide range of situations:

It seems no more plausible that there should be one unique mechanism, or computational resource, as the causal basis of all attentional phenomena, than there should be a unitary basis of thought, or perception or of any other traditional category of folk psychology.

Let's use a scenario from everyday life to illustrate the problem. We are out walking in a wood and I tell you that I have just noticed an unusual variety of butterfly land on the back of the leaf in a nearby tree. I point out the tree and where about the leaf is and tell you to pay attention to it. Following my instruction, you select one tree from many. You then "attend" to a particular leaf, rather than the tree itself, so presumably you and I share some common understanding of what attention is. You continue to look carefully, hoping you will see the butterfly when it moves out from behind the leaf. Now, you will try and keep your attention on that leaf so as not to miss the butterfly when it appears. In addition, you will have some expectation of what the butterfly will look like and how it may behave and be monitoring for these features. This expectation and anticipation will activate what psychologists call top-down processes, which will enable you to be more ready to respond if a butterfly appears, rather than some dissimilar animal, say, a caterpillar.

However, if while you are selectively focusing attention on the leaf an apple suddenly falls out of another part of the tree, you will be distracted. In other words, your attention will be automatically captured by the apple. In order to continue observing the leaf, you must re-engage your attention to where it was before. After a time you detect the beautiful butterfly as it flutters round the leaf, it sits a minute and you watch it as it flies away.

In this example, we have a variety of attentional phenomena that psychologists need to understand, and if possible explain, in well-defined scientific terms. We will see that no single term is appropriate to explain all the phenomena of attention and control even in this visual task. Let's look at what you were asked to do. First of all, you translated the spoken words into an intention to move your eyes in the direction of my pointing finger. You then were able to search among the branches and leaves to attend to a particular leaf. In order to do this "simple" task, there had to be some kind of setting up of your cognitive system that enabled one tree, then the leaves rather than tree, to become the current object of processing. Finally, one particular leaf was selected over others on the basis of its spatial location. Once you are focusing on the leaf, you are expecting butterfly-type shapes to emerge and may occasionally think you have detected the butterfly if an adjacent leaf flutters in the breeze. Here the perceptual input triggers, bottom up, one of the attributes of butterfly, fluttering, that has been primed by your expectations and for a moment you are misled. The idea of "mental set" is an old one. Many experiments on attention use a selective set paradigm, where the subject prepares to respond to a particular set of stimuli. The notion of selection brings with it the complementary notion of ignoring some stimuli at the expense of those that are selected for attentional processing. What makes selection easy or difficult is an important research area and has exercised psychologists for decades. Here we immediately run into the first problem: Is attention the internal setting of the system to detect or respond to a particular set of stimuli (in our example, butterflies) the same as the attention that you "pay" or allocate to the stimulus once it is detected? It seems intuitively unlikely.

Which of these kinds of attention is captured by the unexpected falling apple? We already have one word for two different aspects of the task. A second issue arises when the apple falls from the tree and you are momentarily distracted. We said your attention was automatically drawn to the apple, so although you were intending to attend to the leaf and focusing on its spatial location, there appears to be an interrupt process that automatically detects novel, possibly important, environmental changes outside the current focus of attention and draws attention to themselves. An automatic process is one that is defined as not requiring attention although, of course, if we are not certain how to define attention, this makes the definition of automatic processes problematic. Note now, another problem: I said that you have to return attention to the leaf you were watching, what does this mean? Somehow, the temporary activation causing the apple to attract attention can be voluntarily overridden by the previously active goal of leaf observation. You have remembered what you were doing and attention can then be directed, by some internal process or mechanism, back to the original task. To say that you, the subject, can voluntarily control this, as Shiffrin (1988) did in his definition, tells us nothing, we might as easily appeal to there being a little-man-in-the-head, or homunculus, on which many theories seem to rely.

To continue with the scenario, if you have to sustain attention on the leaf, monitoring for the butterfly for more than a few minutes, it may become increasingly difficult to stop your attention from wandering. You have difficulty concentrating, there seems to be effort involved in keeping to the task at hand. Finally the butterfly appears, you detect it, in its spatial location, but as soon as it flies away, you follow it, as if your attention is not now directed to the location that the butterfly occupied but to the object of the butterfly itself. The question of whether visual attention is spatially based or object based is another issue that researchers are interested in.

Of course, visual attention is intimately related to where we are looking and to eye movements, so perhaps there is nothing much to explain here, we just attend to what we are looking at. However, we all know that we can "look out of the corner of the eye". If while you fixate your gaze on this *, you are able to tell me quite a lot about the spatial arrangement of the text on the page and what the colours of the walls are, so it is not the case that where we direct our eyes and where we direct attention are one and the same. In vision, there appears to be an obvious limit on how much information we can take in, at least from different spatial locations, simply because it is not possible to look in two directions at once. Although even when attending to one visual location, the question arises of how we selectively attend to one attribute from a number of sources of spatially coincident information, it is possible to attend to either the colour or the shape of the butterfly.

Auditory attention also seems to be limited. However, unlike our eyes, we cannot move our ears to select a location or search the environment. Of course, some animals can do this, you only have to watch an alert cat to know this. However, even though we do not physically move our ears to allow one sound source to be focused on, and therefore all sounds will be picked up, we can select what to listen to. In fact, when there are several different streams of sound emanating from different locations around us, the traffic outside, the hum of the computer on the desk, the conversation in the room next door, we do not appear to be able to listen to them all at once. Our inability to direct the auditory sensory apparatus mechanically cannot be the reason we cannot listen to two things at once. There must be another reason.

We all know that we can selectively listen to the intriguing conversation on the next table in the restaurant, even though there is another conversation, continuing on the table we are sitting at. This is an example of selective auditory attention and a version of the "cocktail party problem". Somehow, internal processes can allow one set of auditory information to gain precedence over the rest. Listening to a conversation in noise is clearly easier if we know something about the content. Some words may be masked by other noises, but our top-down expectations enable us to fill in the gaps, we say that there is redundancy in language, meaning that there is more information present than is strictly necessary. We make use of this redundancy in difficult conditions. If the conversation were of a technical nature, on some topic about which we knew very little, there would be much less top-down expectation and the conversation would be more difficult to follow. Although we may be intent on the conversation at the next table, a novel or important sound will capture our attention, rather like the visual example of the apple falling out of the tree. However, as in vision, we are not easily able to monitor both sources of information at once, if we are distracted, we must return our attention back to the conversation.

Now we have another question: Is the attention that we use in vision the same as that that we use in audition? While it is difficult to do two visual or two auditory tasks concurrently it is not necessarily difficult to combine an auditory and a visual task. Of course, this is evolutionarily sensible. We need to know that the face we see moving in front of our eyes is the source of the words we are hearing or not, as the case may be. Attending to the moving lips of a speaker can help us disambiguate what is being said, especially in noise. We like people to look at us when they are speaking to us. While most research has been involved with vision and hearing, we can, of course, attend to smells, tastes, sensations and proprioceptive information. To date we know far less about these areas but we all know that a painful stimulus such as a bee sting will capture attention and a nagging headache cannot easily be ignored. The very term "nagging" suggests this constant reminding of its presence. Attention to pain is important for self-preservation and survival, but people with chronic pain can be compromised in performing other tasks because the pain demands attention. The question of why some tasks interfere with each other, while others seem capable of being performed independently, and how we are able to share or divide attention, may crucially depend on the modality of input and output as well as the kind of information processing that is required in the two tasks.

So, why do some tasks or kinds of processing require attention but others do not. While you were looking for butterflies, we may have been walking and talking at the same time. It is possible to continue eating dinner in the restaurant at the same time as listening to a conversation. Walking, talking and eating seem to proceed with-out attention, until the ground becomes uneven, a verbal problem is posed or your peas fall off your fork. At these moments, you might find one task has to stop while attention is allocated to the other. Consider learning a skill such as juggling. To begin with, we seem to need all our attention (ask yourself which kind of attention this might be) to throw and catch two balls. The prospect of ever being able to operate on three at once seems rather distant! However, with practice, using two balls becomes easy, we may even be able to hold a con-versation at the same time. Now introduce the third ball, gradually this too becomes possible, although to start with we cannot talk at the same time. Finally, we can talk and juggle three balls. So, now it seems that the amount of attention needed by a task depends on skill, which is learned over practice. Once attention is no longer needed for the juggling we can attend to something else. However, if the juggler goes wrong, the conversation seems to have to stop while a correction is made to the ball throwing. It is as if attention is being allocated or withdrawn according to the combined demands of the tasks. In this example, attention seems to be either a limited "amount" of something or some kind of "effort". Accordingly, some theorists have likened attention to resources or effort, while others have been more concerned with where a limiting attentional step operates within the processing system to select some information for further processing.

Memory is intimately related to attention. We seem to remember what we have attended to. "I'm sorry I was not paying attention to the colour of her dress, I was listening to what she said." Although you must have seen the dress, and, in fact, assume that she was wearing a dress, you do not remember anything about it. If we want to be sure someone remembers what we are telling them, we ask them to pay attention. How attentional processing affects memory, as well as how a concurrent memory task affects attention, are other important issues. However, there is evidence that a considerable amount of processing is carried out without attention being necessary and without the subject having any memory of the event. Although the subject may not be explicitly able to recall, at a conscious level, that some particular information was present, subsequent testing can demonstrate that the "unattended" stimuli have had an effect, by biasing or priming, subsequent responses.

Note that for a stimulus to be apparently "unattended" it seems to have to be "unconscious". This brings us to another thorny question: What is the relationship of attention to conscious experience? Like attention, consciousness has a variety of meanings. We usually say we are conscious of what we are attending to. What we are attending to is currently in short-term or working memory. What is in short-term memory is what we are consciously thinking about at that moment in time. Here, I hope you see the problems of definition, if we are not careful we find ourselves ensnared in circularity. Memory and attention are also closely interwoven when planning and monitoring day-to-day activities. Have you ever gone to make a cup of tea and poured the tea into the sugar bowl? The correct actions have been performed but not on the correct objects. This sort of "slip of action" often arises when we are "not paying attention" to what we are doing. When we engage in a complex sequentially ordered set of actions to achieve a goal, like making a cup of tea, not only do we have to remember the overall goal, but we must also monitor and update the steps that have been taken towards goal completion, sometimes updating goal states as we go. In this example, we may have to stop and wash out the sugar bowl before continuing, but will not have to go right back to the beginning of the goal sequence where we filled the kettle. Attention in the control of action is an example of another kind of attention, driven by goals, or what we intend to do. The question of the intentional, voluntary control, where behaviour is planned according to current goals and instructions is a growing area of research in the attention literature.

Rather than labour the point further, let us accept that to try and define attention as a unitary concept is not possible and to do so would be misleading. Perhaps the best approach is to look at experimental situations that we all agree involve one or another application of some sort of "attention" and from the data obtained, together with what we now know about the organisation of the underlying neurophysiology and the breakdown of normal function following brain damage, try to infer something about the psychological processes or mechanisms underlying the observed behaviour.

Is attention a causal agent or an emergent property?

From the way I have been talking about "attention", it might sound as if it is a "thing" or a causal agent that "does something". This is the problem of the homunculus to which I have already referred. Of course, it might well be that "attention" is an emergent property, that is, it appears to be there, but plays no causal role in information processing. William James (1890) pointed out this distinction when he queried: "Is attention a resultant or a force?" Johnston and Dark (1986) looked at theories of selective attention and divided them into cause theories and effect theories. Cause theories differentiate between two type of processing, which Johnson and Dark call Domain A and Domain B. Domain A is high capacity, unconscious and passive and equates with what various theorists call automatic or pre-attentive processing. Domain B is the small-capacity, conscious, active processing system and equates with controlled or attentive processing. In cause theories, Domain B is "among other things an attentional mechanism or director, or cause of selective processing" (p. 66). They go on to point out that this kind of explanation "betrays a serious metatheoretical problem", as, "if a psychological construct is to explain the intelligent and adaptive selection powers of the organism, then it cannot itself be imbued with these powers" (p. 68). We shall meet many examples of cause theories as we move through the chapters, for example: Broadbent (1958, 1971), Kahneman (1973), Posner and Snyder (1975), Shiffrin and Schneider (1977), Norman and Shallice (1986). However, as I said, it might just be the case that attention is an "effect" that emerges from the working of the whole system as inputs interact with schemata in long-term memory, an example of this view is Neisser (1976). Johnson and Dark think that it would be "instructive to see how much we can understand about selective attention without appealing to a processing homunculus" (p. 70). As has already been argued, attention seems so difficult to define, that it is intuitively likely that these different forms of "attention" arise from different effects rather that reflecting different causal agents.

Preview of the book

There is a familiar joke about asking someone the way to a destination and getting the reply, "Oh, if you want to go there, you don't want to start from here!" The trouble is, you can't change where you start from. If we were to begin to research attention today with all the knowledge that has accumulated along the way, then we might ask questions that are rather different from those initially posed. Allport (1993) has eloquently put all these points before.

Today, cognitive psychology is part of a joint venture, often called cognitive science, that aims to understand how the brain enables us to attend effectively. Together with evidence from biological and neuropsychological studies, computational modelling, physiological studies and brain imaging there has been considerable progress in understanding attention. When attention research began in the 1950s, cognitive psychology did not even have a name. Since this initial work on attention, research has taken a long and winding road, sometimes going down a cul de sac, sometimes finding a turning that was missed. Posner (1993) divides work on attention into three phases. Initially, in the 1950s and 1960s, research centred on human performance and on the concept of "the human as a single channel processor". In the 1970s and early 1980s the field of study had become "cognition" and research was mostly concerned with looking for and studying internal representations, automatic and controlled processes and strategies for focusing and dividing attention. By the mid-1980s "cognitive neuroscience" was the name of the game and psychologists were taking account of biology, neuropsychological patients and computing. Posner points out that although there has been a shift of major emphasis, all the strands of research continue, and are represented in the 1990s. Looking forward to the future, Posner proposed that advances in understanding the underlying neuroanatomy and the use of computer simulations in neural networks will accelerate our understanding of attention if used in conjunction with experimental studies. Allport (1993) suggested that the uses of the term attention are too many to be useful, but Posner (1993) believed that if we think of attention as a system of several brain networks, the concept is valid. The development of sophisticated techniques such as PET and FMRI now allow researchers to observe brain activity during cognitive tasks that involve varieties of attention. Posner (2004a, 2004b) reviews the achievement of brain imaging in aiding our understanding of the link between psychology and neuroscience. He points out that many of the experiments conducted today would have been unthinkable 15 years ago, because the techniques were not available. Information about the different brain areas involved in different tasks is increasing on an almost daily basis and the challenge is to interpret and understand the implications of these data for theories of attention. One of the central themes to emerge is that attention is involved in resolving conflict at a neuronal level both within local brain areas and among more distant brain areas, e.g. Desimone and Duncan (1995). The brain has numerous networks that feed information back and forth in the brain and because modern neuroimaging methods allow researchers to observe the brain in action, it is becoming possible to see how these networks are activated in different "attentional" tasks. It is evident that different tasks recruit different brain areas and different networks. There is not room in a book such as this to cover the neuroanatomical evidence on attention, but we must be aware that all attentional behaviour emerges from a very complex system – the brain.

Structure of the book

We have seen that attention is a complex area of research and that the term "attention" is applied to and implicated in a variety of rather disparate situations and whether there are many or just a few kinds of "attention", there is certainly not this one. It is difficult to know how to make this complex field of study digestible. I have chosen to follow the development of ideas. So, to a large extent the chapters follow the chronology of research on attention because the design of new experiments is usually driven by the outcome of previous ones. If different experiments had been done first, different questions might have been asked later and the whole picture taken on a different complexion.

We start, in Chapter 2, with some of the initial studies of auditory and visual attention and models, proposed by Broadbent (1958), Treisman (1960), Deutsch and Deutsch (1963). These models and others shaped the argument on the "early–late" debate, which came to dominate psychology for many years. Generally these models assumed a single, limited capacity, general purpose processing channel, which was the "bottleneck" in processing. Prior to the bottleneck, processing was parallel and did not require attention, but after the bottleneck, processing was serial and required attention. Theorists argued about where in the processing continuum the bottleneck was located.

The following four chapters are all concerned with selection, mainly from visual displays. In Chapter 3, issues centre on the nature of visual attention and how it is controlled and directed. We consider the evidence for a spotlight of visual attention and work by Posner and others on attentional cueing effects. The importance of neuro-psychological studies is demonstrated by considering how visual neglect can help us to understand both normal attentional orienting and attentional deficits. We also examine experiments aimed at discovering how visual attention moves and if it is more like a zoom lens than a spatial spotlight. A major question asks whether attention is directed to spatial locations or to objects that occupy those locations. We find that object-based attention is important, which leads us to ask how objects are constructed from their independently coded components.

In Chapter 4, we consider search and selective report from visual displays. We shall review evidence that the brain codes different attributes of the stimulus, such as identity, colour and location in parallel and address the question of how these different codes are accurately combined. Here, Treisman's feature integration theory is introduced and again the question of whether visual attention is spatially based or object based continues. Evidence for and against Treisman's view is evaluated and alternate theories and computational models are introduced such as Duncan and Humphreys' (1989) attention engagement theory.

Chapter 5 introduces recent work on auditory attention and then moves on to consider how information arriving from different senses has been shown to work together or interact in studies involving crossmodal attention. This is a relatively new and exciting area of research on attention and demonstrates an increasing appreciation of how attention involves multiple components across different brain areas. Also in this chapter we discuss the role of attention in pain.

Moving on from selectivity, Chapter 6 addresses the question of how attention is divided when tasks are combined. Resource theory is evaluated and the importance of stimulus response compatibility between tasks is illustrated. Although in many cases tasks can be combined provided the input/output relations do not demand concurrent use of the same subsystem, we shall see that recent work suggests that there remains a fundamental limit at the final stage of processing, when responses are selected. Attentional blink and change blindness are related to the division or diversion of attention and recent experiments in these areas are discussed.

Chapter 7 continues the task combination theme, with a discussion of experiments about automaticity, skill and expertise. Here automatic and controlled processing is explained in terms of Shiffrin and Schneider's (1977) two-process theory. However, Neuman's (1984) critique, reveals that the distinction between automatic and controlled processing is at best blurred. We attempt to explain how expertise and skill emerge with practice. By the end of these chapters it will be clear that a very large amount of information processing is carried out automatically, outside conscious control. Not only does this raise the problem of how to distinguish between tasks that do or do not need "attention" for their performance, but also raises the question that if there is a distinction, how is "attentional" or "conscious" control implemented?

This is the question we turn to next, when theories of selection and control of action are debated in Chapter 8. Much of the evidence presented in this chapter is taken from visual selection experiments, but the central question we shall be concerned with now is "What is attention for?" Seminal ideas put forward by Allport (1987) and Neuman (1987) are used to illustrate the role played by selective attention in guiding actions. Then, starting with an examination of the breakdown of normal intention behaviour exhibited by patients with frontal lobe damage, we try and explain both normal and abnormal behaviour in terms of Duncan's (1986) theory of goal directed behaviour and Norman and Shallice's (1986) model of willed and automatic behaviour. The intentional control of attention and the ability to switch between tasks is now widely studied experimentally on normal subjects. We shall discuss early work by Allport, Styles, and Hseih (1994) and Rogers and Monsell (1995) and evaluate the current state of theory.

Finally, our discussion of conscious control leads on, in Chapter 9, to a consideration of what is meant by the term "consciousness", what processing can proceed without it and how it might be defined. We shall look at a variety of arguments about the nature and purpose of consciousness. Each chapter includes, where appropriate, data from neuropsychological patients, something on the neurophysiology of the brain and computational models of attentional behaviour.

Summary

Attention is not a unitary concept. The word is used to describe and sometimes, which is more of a worry, explain, a variety of psychological data. Although we all have some subjective idea of what we mean when we say we are "attending", what this means is different in different situations. As research has progressed, old theories have been modified or abandoned, but as science is driven by testing theories, the path followed by the psychology of attention has been strongly influenced by the initial assumptions. Today, account is taken of biological, neuropsychological, computational and functional considerations of attentional behaviour that will, we hope, bring us closer to finding an answer to the question "What is attention?"

Further reading

- Allport, D. A. (1993). Attention and control: Have we been asking the wrong questions? A critical review of 25 years. In D. E. Meyer, & S. Kornblum (Eds.). *Attention and performance, XIV: A silver jubilee.* Hillsdale, NJ: Lawrence Erlbaum Associates, Inc.

    This chapter, as its title suggests, reviews the direction of research on attention and is very critical of the assumptions that have driven research for so long. It is, however, quite a difficult work, incorporating a lot of neurophysiology and neuropsychology, which we shall meet later in this book.

- Posner, M. I. (1993). Attention before and during the decade of the brain. In D. E. Meyer, & S. Kornblum (Eds.). *Attention and performance, XIV: A silver jubilee.* Hillsdale, NJ: Lawrence Erlbaum Associates, Inc.

    This chapter is really an overview of the chapters on attention contained within the book, but provides a brief history of the development of attentional research. The series of books called *Attention and performance* began in 1967 and have been published every two years ever since. They contain within them the history and evolution of work on attention by major contributors of the time.

- Richards, G. (1996). *Putting psychology in its place.* London: Routledge.

    For those interested in the history of psychology, this book provides a clear overview.

The rise of attention research: A cognitive approach 2

Beginnings

During the Second World War it had become clear that people were severely limited in their ability to act on multiple signals arriving on different channels. Pilots had to try to monitor several sources of concurrent information, which might include the numerous visual displays inside the cockpit, the visual environment outside the plane and auditory messages coming in over the radio. Ground staff confronted difficulties when guiding air traffic into busy aerodromes and radar operators suffered from problems in maintaining vigilance. Psychology had little to say about these problems at the time, but researchers were motivated to try and discover more about the limitations of human performance.

Welford (1952) carried out an experiment that showed that when two signals are presented in rapid succession and the subject must make a speeded response to both, reaction time to the second stimulus depends on the stimulus onset asynchrony (SOA) between the presentation of the first and second stimulus. When the second stimulus is presented after only a very short SOA, reaction time to the second stimulus is slower than when there is a long SOA between stimuli. Welford called this delay in response to a second stimulus in the short SOA condition the "psychological refractory period" (PRP). Welford was able to show that for every millisecond decrease in SOA there was a corresponding increase in reaction time to the second stimulus.

Welford argued that this phenomenon was evidence of a "bottleneck", where the processing of the first stimulus must be completed before processing of the next stimulus can begin. At long SOAs, the first stimulus will have had time for its processing to be completed before the arrival of the second stimulus and so no refractoriness will be observed. We will examine more recent research on PRP when we discuss dual task performance in Chapter 6. For the present we will note that at the time Welford's work seemed to provide good evidence for a central limit on human processing capability.

Early experiments on selective auditory attention: Dichotic listening

Almost all the early experiments on attention used auditory stimuli. Apart from the fact that multi-channel tape recorders became available at the time and provided an elegant way of presenting stimuli, Broadbent (1971) explained that there were very good reasons for investigating audition rather than vision. We cannot move our ears in the same way as we move our eyes, neither can we close our ears to shut out unwanted inputs. Although we said in the introduction that our attention is not necessarily directed to where we move our eyes, this is usually the case. With auditory stimuli any selectivity of processing must rely on central or neural, rather than peripheral or mechanical processes.

A popular experimental paradigm was the dichotic listening task. This involved presenting two simultaneous stimuli (usually, but not always, different) to the two ears via headphones and asking the subject to do one of a variety of tasks. In a selective attention task, the instruction is to attend to the message presented to one ear and to ignore the other message, which is simultaneously presented to the other ear. This mimics the "cocktail party" situation, where you selectively listen to one speaker rather than another. In ordinary life, the speech message we attend to will be in a particular voice (with its own characteristic physical quality) and be coming from a different direction to other voices. Under laboratory conditions, it is possible to present two different voices or two messages in the same voice to the same spatial location, i.e. to the same ear, or to deliver two messages in the same voice, or two messages in different voices to the two ears etc. In a divided attention experiment, the subject would be required to attend to both messages at the same time.

Most of the first studies were of selective attention. Results from studies by Broadbent (1952, 1954), Cherry (1953) and Poulton (1953, 1956) showed that both the physical acoustic differences between voices and the physical separation of locations were helpful for message selection. The most effective cue was physical separation. These results were taken to confirm that a listener can selectively attend to stimuli that possess some common physical feature and can reject stimuli that do not possess that feature. Cherry (1953) also showed that performance was better when subjects were told beforehand which channel was to be responded to, rather than when they were given instructions about which channel to report afterwards. Further, it was discovered that when selective listening is forced by requiring the subject to repeat the relevant message out loud as it arrives (this is called "shadowing") subsequent recall tests revealed that subjects had virtually no memory for the information that had been presented to the unattended ear. Although there was very little memory for the content of the ignored message in terms of its meaning, or language in which it is spoken (subjects did not notice if the unattended message changed from English to German), subjects did notice if the speakers voice changed from that of a man to a woman or if a bleep or tone was presented.

Taking all the evidence into account, Broadbent (1958) interpreted the data as demonstrating that stimuli that do not need response are, if possible, discarded before they have been fully processed and that as physical features of the input are effective cues for separating messages, there is a filter that operates at the level of physical features, allowing the information characterised by that feature through the filter for further processing. In unattended messages, only physical properties of the input seemed to be detected and it is these properties that can guide the setting of the filter.

Broadbent's (1958) book, called *Perception and communication*, turned out to be extremely influential. With its publication, research into "attention" was resurrected, having been virtually ignored for many years. Part of the problem of investigating something like attention is that it is hard to observe. Attention is an internal process and, as such, had been abandoned to philosophy when the behaviourist tradition dominated psychology. Part of Broadbent's contribution was to provide a means of conceptualising human performance in terms of information processing. Based on his own research and other contemporary evidence, Broadbent proposed a new conception of the mind, in which psychological processes could be described by the flow of information within the nervous system. Broadbent's model was to prove the starting point for modern theorising on attention and the structure and underlying assumptions of the model have shaped the pattern of subsequent work. He drew three main conclusions. First, he concluded that it was valuable to analyse human functions in terms of the flow of information through the organism. He believed it was possible to discuss information transmission in the abstract, without having to know the precise neural or physical basis of that transmission. This conception of the nervous system as an information processor was an extremely important and influential idea and signalled the beginning of the information processing approach to psychology. (See Eysenck & Keane, 2000 for an introduction to approaches in psychology.)

The concept of information had arisen from communication theory (Shannon & Weaver, 1949). Information can be described mathematically and not all signals carry the same amount of information. As uncertainty increases so does the amount of potential information. Fitts and Posner (1973) provide an accessible introduction to the topic and give the example of tossing a coin. The statement "it will be either heads or tails" does not contain any information because knowing this does not reduce our uncertainty over which way the coin will come down. However, if we are told "it is tails" we have no uncertainty and have gained information. So, what information does is reduce the amount of uncertainty present in a situation. Fitts and Posner use another everyday illustration to explain how the amount of information in a statement varies with the degree of uncertainty. If we are told which way a die has fallen, we gain more information than when we are told which way a coin has fallen. This is because there are six possible outcomes for rolling the die, but only two possible outcomes for tossing the coin.

Broadbent was concerned with the transmission of information within the nervous system. Information transmission is maximal when a given stimulus always gives rise to the same response. When this happens, there is no uncertainty between the stimulus input and the response output. However, if a different response were to occur on some occasions, the amount of information transmitted would be reduced. If the amount of information transmitted is calculated and divided by the time taken to make the response, then the rate of information transmission can be found. The attraction of this information processing approach to studying human performance is its ability to provide measures of otherwise non-observable internal processes.

Related to these measures of information is the measure of redundancy. In any situation where there is less than the maximum amount of information, there is redundancy. A good example is English spelling because there are different transitional probabilities between letters in legal words. When reading poor handwriting, our prior knowledge allows us to disambiguate the letters we find difficult to read. Thus, the presence of some letters predict, or reduce, the possible letters that might follow. The most obvious example is that "q" is always followed by "u", here the "u" is redundant because it is predicted by the "q". When redundancy is high, information is low and vice versa. Redundancy in language is also useful when we try to listen to something in a noisy situation because even if we hear only part of the input there is enough redundancy for us to understand the message. (Noise can also be mathematically expressed in information-processing terms.) Later, when we consider some results of experiments on dual task performance and unconscious processing, we shall see how the amount of information, or redundancy, there is in the messages can affect performance.

Broadbent borrowed the idea of the transmission of information within a telecommunications channel and this brought with it a number of corollary assumptions, which led to Broadbent's second conclusion, that, as a communications system, the whole nervous system could be regarded as a single channel that was limited in the rate at which information could be transmitted. Third, for economy of mechanism, Broadbent concluded that the limited capacity section of the nervous system would need to be preceded by a selective filter, or switch, which protected the system from overload and only passed on some small, selected portion of the incoming information. All other information was blocked. These major conclusions were largely accepted, together with the necessity for a short-term buffer store that preceded the selective filter. This buffer was a temporary memory store in which the unselected information could be held, in parallel, for short periods of time. The model became known as Broadbent's "filter theory". It is important to note that in this model, although information enters the system in parallel, it is only held temporarily in the buffer memory. Unless information is selected to pass through the filter for further processing, that information is lost. Only when information passes through the filter into the limited capacity channel, which is a serial processor, is it identified. This means that selection from the parallel input is made at early levels of processing and is therefore an "early selection" model. Note also that this model is structural, in that it posits a sequence of information flow through a series of stages and transformations that are limited by structural properties of the proposed system.

If we digress for a moment, let's just look at what has been suggested. First, Broadbent has made the tacit assumption that if a cue aids selection, the nature of the cue represents the level of analysis that has been achieved by the information that is selected. There is, in fact, no real reason to suppose that, because physical cues are effective in guiding selection of one message over another, the messages have only been processed to the physical level. It is perfectly possible that there is much fuller processing of all inputs, but physical cues happen to be the best way of selecting channels. The assumption that an effective cue tells us about the degree of analysis of what is selected was not seriously challenged until van der Heijden (1981, 1993, 2004), whose ideas will be considered in Chapter 3.

Second, almost all the studies at this time were limited to studying selection of information within a single sensory modality, i.e. audition. Although the problems encountered by aviators were often in situations where information was coming in via both visual and auditory modalities and responses were having to be made as either motor outputs to control the plane, or spoken responses to given messages, the first model of attention is concerned with a very simple situation, like "repeat the message in one ear and ignore the other". Nothing else has to be done. In daily life we routinely find ourselves in far more complex situations than the dichotic listening task and should pause to consider how safely we can generalise the results of these experiments to life in the real world. In fairness, most psychology experiments have to be concerned with small-scale, well-controlled experiments, because otherwise it is difficult to know which variables are affecting behaviour and performance. However, to build a general theory of attention on "attention" in one modality might be judged as dangerous. We shall, however see to what extent selection in audition experiments is like selection in vision experiments a little later in the chapter.

Going back to Broadbent (1958). Here, then, was an elegantly simple model. The human information-processing system needed to be protected from overload and was therefore preceded by a selective filter that could be switched to whichever channel was required on the basis of some physical characteristic of the sensory input. Exactly how this switching was achieved is not clear. If attention needed to be divided, say between both ears to monitor both messages at once, then the filter was said to be able to switch rapidly between channels on the basis of the spatial location or physical characteristics of information in the sensory buffer.

Broadbent (1954) experimented on the division of attention using simultaneous, dichotic presentation, in what became known as the "split span" technique. The listener is presented with six digits, arranged into three successive pairs. In each pair, one digit is heard through a headphone to the right ear, with the other digit presented simultaneously to the left ear. When all three pairs, i.e. six digits, have been presented the subject is asked to recall as many digits as they can. The interesting finding here is that when all digits are reported correctly, it is usually the case that the subject reports the three items from one ear before the three items from the other ear. Thus, Broadbent argued, selection is ear by ear, and the second set of digits is waiting in the buffer store, to be output when the channel is switched. Even in this simple task it seemed that people could not simultaneously attend to both channels, i.e. ears, at once.

One of the most important contributions made by Broadbent was that he was one of the first people to produce a diagram of the flow of information through the nervous system. If we look at Figure 2.1, we see there is parallel processing, indicated by multiple arrows, through the senses and short-term store as far as the selective filter. All processing beyond the selective filter is strictly serial. Broadbent believed that only information that passes through the limited capacity channel becomes conscious and can modify or become part of our long-term knowledge. In this way, he believed that the filter controls what we "know" at a conscious level about the perceptual input. Our ability to apparently do two things at once can be explained by time sharing, or multiplexing.

According to the theory, which allows only strictly serial processing, combining tasks that require continuous parallel processing is not possible. We only seem to be able to do two tasks at the same time, when those tasks can proceed momentarily without attention, allowing time for rapid switching between them. As the evidence stood at the time, the theory seemed to be perfectly plausible.

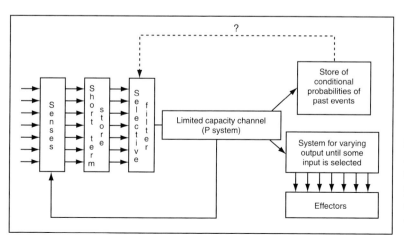

Figure 2.1. Diagram of the flow of information within the nervous system, as conceived by Broadbent (1958).

Reproduced from Broadbent (1971), *Decision and Stress* with permission of Elsevier and author's widow. Copyright 1971.

Challenges to filter theory

One of the good things about a rigid theory is that it generates strong predictions. In the new decade of the 1960s, the search was on for experimental results that challenged Broadbent's original theory. Note that many of the original assumptions were retained, such as the notion of some limit on computational capacity of the brain and the notion of a selective filter at which there was a "bottleneck" in processing. In general terms, much of the new research was concerned with the search for the bottleneck. Research still continued with auditory stimuli using the tried and tested split span and shadowing techniques.

An immediate challenge to the 1958 version of filter theory came from a series of studies by Moray (1959). Using shadowing experiments, Moray showed that when the same small set of words was repeated on the unattended ear, recognition memory for those words was very poor, even a few seconds after presentation. If the unshadowed words had received attention, they should have been easily recognisable. This result is predicted by filter theory and appears to support it. However, some of Moray's results were not consistent with the predictions of Broadbent's theory. For example, Moray found that listeners often recognised their own name when it was presented on the unshadowed and, in theory, unattended ear. This was quite contradictory to the notion of a selective filter that only allowed input to the serial, limited capacity channel on the basis of physical attributes. Remember, it is only when information gains access to the limited capacity system that the subject becomes consciously aware of its occurrence. Moray's results suggest that there is more analysis of unattended information than Broadbent thought. In particular, there must be some parallel semantic processing prior to conscious identification. We should note however, that in Moray's experiment subjects were not generally able to recognise words from the unattended message, only particularly relevant words, like the subject's name, were likely to "break through" the filter. Wood and Cowan (1995) have replicated Moray's original experiment under much more tightly controlled conditions and found very similar results. Wood and Cowan found that 34.6% of subjects recalled hearing their name on the unattended channel (Moray's result was 33.3%) and that subjects who detected their name monitored the irrelevant channel for a short time afterwards. So, although some of the early experiments may have had methodological flaws their results still appear robust.

Breakthrough of the unattended was studied in more detail by Anne Treisman (1960). Treisman has continued to work on attention right up to the present day and we shall examine her feature integration theory of visual attention in Chapter 4. Just remember that when people talk about Treisman's theory of attention, you need to know which one they are referring to. Back in the 1960s Treisman provided more experimental evidence that was inconsistent with original filter theory. She showed that even if a subject is attending to the stream of events on one channel, there may be information breakthrough from the unattended message, especially if there is a meaningful relation between what is currently being attended and what is coming in on the unattended channel. Subjects were told to shadow a story (story 1) on one ear and to ignore the other story (story 2) that was concurrently presented to the other ear. While the subject was shadowing story 1, story 1 was switched to the other, presumably unattended, ear. Story 2 ceased to be presented to the unattended ear and a new story (story 3) came in to replace story 1 on the attended ear. According to Broadbent's initial theory, subjects would have their selective filter set to the attended ear, or channel, and would have no knowledge about the meaning of information on the channel that was blocked off. So when the stories were switched, they should have immediately carried on, shadowing the new story, story 3. However, Treisman found that as soon as the stories were switched, subjects shadowed a few words from story 1 from the unattended ear before picking up story 3 from what should be the attended ear.

The difficulty of selecting one message on the basis of its content, when two messages in the same voice were presented to the same channel, initially studied by Cherry (1953), was further examined in a series of studies by Treisman (1964a, 1964b, 1964c). She asked her subjects to shadow one message and ignore the other. The relevant message was always a female voice reading a passage from a novel and the irrelevant message was sometimes in the same voice, sometimes in a different voice. In one condition, Treisman compared performance when the unattended message was a passage from the same novel with the case where the unattended message was a technical passage about biochemistry, a message in a foreign language or nonsense syllables. The subjects' ability to shadow the attended message was significantly affected by the content of the material in the unattended message, with the most difficult condition being when the same voice was reading two passages from the same novel. Shadowing the passage from a novel was easier when it was concurrently presented with the biochemical passage. When the unattended passage was in a foreign language, it made a difference whether the subject knew the language or not. Overall, these experiments showed that a difference in the semantic content of the two messages could be used to aid selection, but that a content difference is much less effective than a physical difference. These results are inconsistent with a strict filter that only operates on the physical characteristics of the input and are in accordance with the previous experiment by Moray. It was now clear that selection from the parallel stages of processing could be much later or further along the processing continuum than Broadbent had initially thought. This new evidence led Deutsch and Deutsch (1963) to propose a rather different view of selective attention that could account for semantic effects of the "unattended" message.

Is selection later rather than earlier?

This theory from Deutsch and Deutsch has been interpreted as the first "late" selection theory. Here the bottleneck was still present but the limit on parallel processing was much nearer the response stage than the identification stage. Collecting together evidence from experiments such as those by Moray (1959) and from studies that showed electroencephalogram (EEG) changes during sleep to the presentation of a subject's name, they suggested "that a message will reach the same perceptual and discriminatory mechanisms whether attention is paid to it or not; and such information is then grouped or segregated by these mechanisms" (p. 83). They suggested that incoming signals were weighted for importance and in some way compared to determine the currently most important signal. At the time they felt that any comparison mechanism that had to compare every possible incoming signal with all other possible signals would make decision times extremely slow, if not impossible.

Connecting every possible incoming signal to all other possibilities seemed out of the question. Today, with the advent of connectionist, parallel distributed computational methods, this multiple comparison process is no longer considered difficult, but in the early 1960s the brain was likened to computers that were serial limited capacity devices. Deutsch and Deutsch, therefore, suggested a simple analogy. Imagine you wanted to find out which boy in the class was the tallest. You could measure each one individually, but this would take time. However, if you gathered all the boys together and placed a board over their heads, then the boy whose head touched the board would be the tallest and he would immediately know that fact. If you took that boy out of the group, then the board would come to rest on the next tallest boy's head. The same system could compare signals. If, as each signal arrived, it pushed up some "level" that reflected its own "height" or importance, then any other signal that would be of less importance would be below this level. However, if the most important signal ceases, then the level will fall to that of the next most important signal. Thus the level is determined by the signals present and Deutsch and Deutsch suggested that only the most important signals switch in other processes like memory storage and motor output.

The model assumes that all sensory messages are perceptually analysed at the highest level. When the subject is at normal levels of arousal, the signal that is at the highest level will enter memory or evoke a response. However, if the individual is drowsy or asleep a signal will only evoke a response if it crosses the current level of a fluctuating arousal system. Thus Deutsch and Deutsch (1963) propose that, in all cases, the signal of the highest importance will be responded to, or the subject alerted by it, provided its activity is above the current arousal level. In this way the most important message will have been selected not at an early level, but after *full processing*.

Additional evidence consistent with the idea that selection could proceed on the basis of meaning was supplied by a modification of the split span experiment, done by Gray and Wedderburn (1960). Remember, that when Broadbent had presented pairs of digits to both ears simultaneously, preferred order of report was ear by ear. Gray and Wedderburn presented the following kind of stimulus pairs "mice", "one", "cheese", to the right ear, while simultaneously presenting "four", "eat", "two" to the left ear. Subjects in this experiment did not preferentially report ear by ear, but grouped the information by meaning, so they reported, "Mice, eat, cheese" and "four, one two".

The early–late debate begins

Although Treisman provided some of the evidence that led to the Deutschs' proposing their late selection view of attentional selection, she herself considered that a modification to Broadbent's original theory was more appropriate. Breakthrough of the unattended only happened occasionally, in fact rather infrequently. In 1960 Treisman showed that on 6% of trials subjects reported a word from the unattended channel if that word was highly probable. Put another way, this shows that on 94% of trials there is no breakthrough at all. If all incoming information were processed fully, it seemed unlikely that there could be so little breakthrough. Treisman (1964a) proposed that the filter was not such an all-or-nothing affair as Broadbent had said.

Rather than blocking out all information that does not meet the selection criterion for attention, the filter "attenuated" or reduced the strength of the unattended channels. If incoming information were not totally blocked off, then partial information that was consistent with current expectations, e.g. the continuation of the stories in Treisman's shadowing tasks, or personally relevant, e.g. the subject's name in Moray's (1959) study, might be sufficient to raise the activation of those words above the threshold of consciousness. (See Figure 2.2.)

Treisman (1960, 1969) put forward ideas that are similar to those best-known as Morton's logogen model (Morton, 1969, 1979), which is concerned with interactive processes in reading. Morton (1969) proposed that word recognition was mediated by "logogens". Each word that we know has a logogen, which collects both perceptual and semantic evidence. When there is sufficient evidence to raise

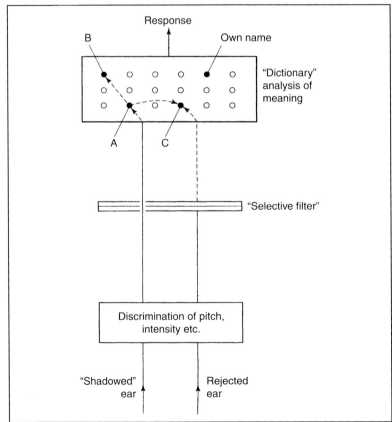

Figure 2.2 The modified theory of attention introduced by Treisman (1960). Following occurrence of word A, the "thresholds of words B and C are lowered because they are very probably following word A. If word C is activated by the "attenuated" signal from the rejected ear, it may be heard.

Reproduced from Broadbent (1971) *Decision and Stress* with permission of Elsevier and the author's widow. Copyright 1971.

the logogen above its threshold, the logogen "fires" and becomes available for response, in some sense we "know" about it. When we listen to a sentence, the words at the beginning of the sentence will lead us to expect certain other words to follow. These expectations, based on semantic knowledge "prime", or raise the activation level of, the logogens for the most likely words. For example "The cat sat on the ——?" If "rainbow" is the next word, you will be slower to read it than if "mat" were the next word. "Mat" is quite clearly written here but if the writing were indistinct, or had coffee spilt over it, the perceptual input would be degraded and top-down processes would help disambiguate the bottom-up input making it more likely that you could read "mat" than "rainbow".

Rather than logogens, Treisman initially proposed that the nervous system contained a set of dictionary units, each of which corresponded to a word. Different words have different thresholds depending on their salience and probability. If the attenuator has the effect of reducing the perceptual input from the unattended channels, then only when words are highly probable or salient, will their thresholds be sufficiently low for the small perceptual input to make the dictionary unit fire. Thus the attenuator can account quite neatly for breakthrough of the unattended at the same time as providing almost perfect selection most of the time.

Early experiments on selective visual attention

The work we have discussed so far has been concerned with auditory attention, but around the same time that Broadbent published his filter model, other psychologists, most notably Sperling (1960), were beginning to try out new methods of studying selective visual attention. Unlike auditory information, which is a pattern of frequencies distributed in time, visual information is distributed in space and usually endures over time. In visual experiments, the whole display can be presented simultaneously in parallel, which allows different kinds of experiment. Not only can we measure the accuracy of selective visual attention, but we can control the time for which a stimulus is available and manipulate the physical and/or the semantic relationship between targets and distractors.

Sperling's experiments

In a classic series of experiments, George Sperling (1960) investigated people's ability to selectively report items from very brief visual displays. Sperling presented stimuli using a tachistoscope. The tachistoscope was invented in the 1880s, but modern ones are essentially the same except they are automatically, electronically controlled. In essence, a tachistoscope is a lightproof box. The subject looks in one end and the stimulus is placed in the other end. However, as the box is lightproof and dark inside, the subject cannot see the stimulus until a light is switched on. Using special lighting tubes, which onset and offset extremely quickly, the duration of the light, and hence exposure duration, can be carefully controlled to an accuracy of a few milliseconds. By using half-silvered mirrors, a number of viewing "fields" can be added to the box, each field having its own lighting control. The most usual tachistoscope has three fields, one for the stimulus, one for a fixation point, where the subject looks in preparation for the stimulus, and the third field can have a probe that marks the stimulus position to be reported or a "mask", which functions to disrupt, degrade or terminate stimulus processing. For an accessible review of masking, see Humphreys and Bruce (1989).

Sperling (1960) found that when subjects were presented with visual arrays lasting 50 msec, containing 12 letters, they were only able to report about four or five items. However, subjects said they could "see" the whole display for a short time after the display was terminated. The data suggested that although all items were initially represented in a brief visual memory, there was some limit on the rate at which items could be retrieved from this store before they had decayed. Sperling believed the pattern of results was evidence for a high capacity, fast decay visual memory store that faded over a short time and that unless this rapidly fading memory for visual information were transformed into another, more permanent state, it was lost. This brief visual information store was subsequently named iconic memory by Neisser (1967) and is analogous to the sensory store located between the senses and the selective filter in Broadbent's model.

Sperling then introduced an important modification, instead of asking the subject to report the whole display, he gave them a "cue" immediately after display offset, which indicated which row they were to report. (See Figure 2.3.) When the cue was a tone (three different pitched tones corresponded to the three rows) subjects could report virtually all the items from the cued row. Note that the subjects had no idea which row would be asked for. This showed that they must have perceived all 12 items in the display.

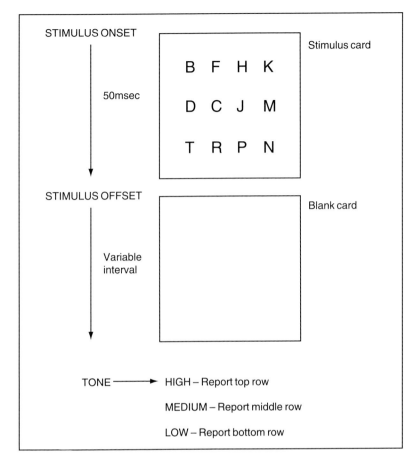

STIMULUS ONSET

50msec

B F H K

D C J M

T R P N

Stimulus card

STIMULUS OFFSET

Blank card

Variable
interval

TONE ⟶ HIGH – Report top row

MEDIUM – Report middle row

LOW – Report bottom row

Figure 2.3 Diagram of the sort of display used by Sperling (1960). In whole report the subject reports non-selectively from the display, in partial report the row indicated by the cue is to be reported. In both conditions report is after the display has terminated.

The partial report superiority effect

Next, Sperling investigated what happened if he delayed presenting the tone. As the delay between display offset and tone presentation increased the proportion of items that could be reported decreased, until after a delay of 500 msec, subjects' performance was no better than in the whole report (WR) condition, as presumably, iconic memory had completely decayed away. The advantage that cueing gives is called the partial report (PR) superiority effect and suggests that the cue, in this case a tone, can be used to allow a subset of items to be selectively transferred to a later stage of processing. In effect, this is the same as using a physical location cue, such as left or right ear to select one auditory message from another. Although Sperling was investigating the nature of what we now call iconic memory, his results are of importance in studies of attention, because they can tell us something about which cues are, or are not, effective for guiding selective attention among a complex display of visual stimuli. In the partial report condition, selective attention allows the stimuli indicated by the cue to be preferentially reported. (See Figure 2.4.)

As the PR advantage was found when a tone indicated which row to report, it seemed evident that the spatial locations of the items in the display must have been represented in iconic memory. Subsequent experiments have shown that other cues such as colour (Dick, 1969; Von Wright, 1969, 1970), size or shape (Turvey & Kravetz, 1970) will also allow selective processing. A bar marker, or probe, can also be used to indicate visually which location in a row is to be reported. Avebach and Coriell (1961) carried out a similar experiment to Sperling's, but they presented only two rows of letters, followed at varying intervals by a bar marker to probe a given location in the row. They found that when the probe was presented immediately after display offset, report of the probed letter was very good, but as the probe delay increased, there was a corresponding decrease in the probability of the correct letter being reported. This result is analogous to the PR advantage declining with cue delay.

Rather like auditory filtering experiments, it seems as if physical cues are effective in allowing selective report. Another potential cue for selection is the category of the item, for example, whether the target is a letter or a digit. However, Sperling found that if item category was given as the post-exposure cue there was no PR advantage and hence argued that the representation from which

Figure 2.4 Schematic description of results from a partial report experiment showing the partial report superiority and the loss of this advantage as the stimulus–cue interval increases.

Reproduced from Humphreys and Bruce (1989) with permission of the publisher and the author. Copyright Lawrence Erlbaum Associates.

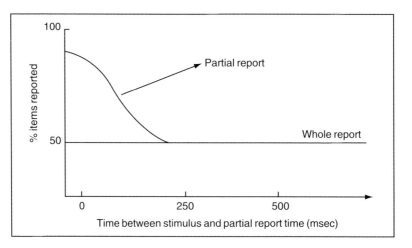

selection was made was pre-categorical, i.e. before category membership had been determined. If category membership was not represented in iconic memory, then, of course, it could not act as a basis for selection. This is the same assumption made by Broadbent (1958) in his auditory selection experiments. We shall see, however, that this assumption may, in fact, be false.

An interesting experiment was done by Mewhort (1967) who presented his subjects with two rows of letters and used a post-exposure tone to indicate which row to report. Sometimes the information in the uncued, irrelevant, row was just a string of letters, like YRULPZOC, and sometimes the row was more like a word, for example, VERNALIT. Mewhort found that the content of the irrelevant row had an effect on the number of letters reported from the cued row, so that when the row was VERNALIT, subjects reported more from the cued row than when the uncued row was not like English. This result shows that subjects must have been processing the uncued row, otherwise it could not have affected performance. Subjects could not have been completely ignoring the irrelevant row, just as we saw that subjects were affected by information on the ignored or unattended channel in dichotic listening experiments. Mewhort's data indicated that the meaning of unattended items can "breakthrough" to influence processing of attended information. Thus, iconic memory could not be a purely visual store containing solely the visual properties of colour and location, for if it were, semantics should have no effect. The puzzle here is that while there is evidence of semantics influencing processing, subjects cannot use semantics as a PR cue.

We now do have evidence that semantic and categorical properties of the stimulus can act as a basis for selective report. Dick (1974) reviewed the usefulness of various cues for selective report from iconic memory. If a cue declines in efficiency over time, the assumption is that its representation fades and is lost with time. Partial report for colour and location decline with instruction delay, but a category cue (letters or numbers) does not show this decline. Further, Dick (1971) analysed a number of experiments using partial report, in terms of accuracy as a function of response position. He found that when order of report was scored, full report accuracy was always greater than partial report accuracy, for all response positions. Graves (1976) investigated whether more items were identified than could be reported from a tachistoscopic array and found that when position of report is required, the number of items identified together with their correct position was no greater in partial report than in full report. Item identity and the position of the item in the display seemed to separate out.

Experimental evidence for separate identity and location coding in vision

Eriksen and Rohrbaugh (1970) performed a bar probe experiment. They found that accuracy of report declined with cue delay, as had Avebach and Coriell (1961), but, the important finding was that as the probability of reporting the correct letter in the correct position declined, the probability of reporting an item adjacent to the true target increased. When subjects made an error, they were most likely to report another item that had been present in the display – we call this type of error a mislocation error. Note here that subjects were not simply reporting "any old" letter that was in the array, which might be expected if they opted to select a location at random, rather they reported a close neighbour, not an item from further away at the end of the row. If the store from which subjects were making their selection was some kind of fading image of physical information, we would have expected subjects to begin to make intrusion errors, that is reporting an item that was not in the display. Perhaps reporting "F" rather than "E", or "O" rather than "G". So Eriksen and Rohrbaugh's results suggest that both identity information and location information were available, in parallel, at the time of selection.

This idea is consistent with a model of processing that assumes parallel analysis of all inputs to the level of identification, with serial selection for response. The problem for selection seems to be that more identities are available than can be reported and a decision must be made to determine which of the competing responses corresponds to the target. Townsend (1973) proposed that the problem is not *what* the target is but *where* it is. Again this points to the possibility that positional information decays, but identity information does not.

Selective masking experiments reported by Mewhort, Campbell, Marchetti, and Campbell (1981) show that different properties of a stimulus are selectively disrupted by different types of mask. Their results provide further evidence for the independent coding of identity (what the stimulus is) and stimulus location (where the stimulus is). Styles and Allport (1986) reported a series of experiments in which subjects reported the identity of the central letter from a group of five stimuli and also if they saw any other letters they were to write these down as well in the appropriate position on the response sheet.

The duration of the display was manipulated by pattern masking and the semantic and featural and categorical relationship between the target and distractors was manipulated in a variety of ways. With this procedure we were able to watch the time course of selectivity of report and the development of location information in each condition. A target letter was presented in the centre of a group of four distractors, with the group appearing either above or below fixation, so that the target was not preferentially processed because it was at fixation. Feature level distractors were simple groups of lines; letter-like flankers were made up from components of letters but not representing any actual letter, so had no meaning; digit flankers offered meaning but from a different category; letter flankers from a different response set to the target and, last, letter flankers from the target set. (See Figure 2.5.)

In the last condition, when a target is surrounded by other letters from the target set, the only way to distinguish a target from a non-target is by knowing not only what the identity is, but also where that

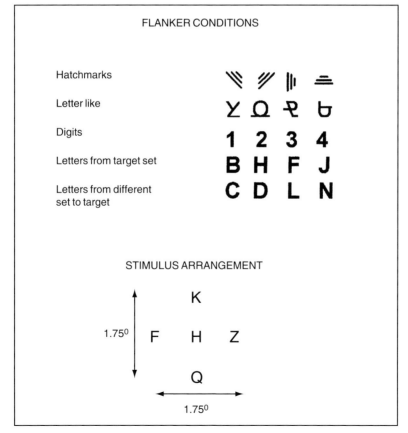

Figure 2.5 Examples of the stimuli used by Styles and Allport (1986). In each condition, apart from hatchmarks there were nine stimuli in each set.

identity is. All the other conditions could have been performed by priming the target set and selecting the letter most strongly activated by the display. We found a hierarchy of interference effects. Any distractor causes interference, as indicated by a reduction in accuracy by the line features, digits produced less interference than the lines, while letter-like features and letters from the non-target set were more disruptive, but not different from each other. Letters from the target set were most interfering. In all conditions, except where the target was flanked by distractors from the target set, the target could be selected by simply reporting the most active member of the primed, target, set. In these conditions targets began to be accurately reported at a short stimulus onset asynchrony (SOA) well below 100 msec. However, in the last condition, when both identity and location were needed for accurate report we found that at SOAs below 100 msecs, although target letters could be reported they were put in the wrong position, i.e. most errors were mislocations. As more time became available accuracy of reporting the correct letters at their correct location increased. This is evidence for the independent representation of "what" something is and its other attributes like location. The results of this experiment also bear on the question of the level in processing at which interference takes place. If interference were at the level of feature extraction then any letter features should have caused equal interference. This was not the case. The interference effects from letter-like shapes was no different from that caused by non-target letters, but letters from the target set were significantly more disruptive. Despite all these conditions having distractors that comprised letter features, it was the identity of the distractors that caused differential interference. It appears that the identities, or categorial information about letters, rather than their featural components that interfere with response to the target.

In summary, there is a good deal of evidence that although subjects say they have "seen" all the items from a brief display, they are severely limited in their ability to accurately report them all. However, it is the case that more items can be reported than can be accurately integrated with their position in the display. Only when partial report is of identity alone, does it exceed whole report. Physical attributes such as colour or location act as efficient cues for selection and as such would seem to support an "early" selection account of visual attention. The question of how attention is involved in accurately combining the separable features of objects with their location is a topic of Chapter 4. However, with respect to the early late debate, a number of results show that, as in auditory experiments, in vision too, there is "breakthrough" of categorical information that affects selection, suggesting a "late" interpretation of selective attention.

Pertinent and unattended information

Norman (1968) believed that sensory inputs were extensively processed automatically and unconsciously before we consciously "know" about them. He believed that this processing relied heavily on the permastore of information in long-term memory. Sensory features of the input automatically addressed their location in semantic memory so that if the input matched some stored representation, the meaning would be accessed. If the input were a nonsense word, i.e. had no pre-existing representation, no meaning would be found, telling you that the input was not a word. In Norman's model, selection comes after semantic memory has been accessed and both attended and unattended sources of information have automatic and effortless access to semantics. Once semantics have been activated, pertinence values are assigned to those activations according to current ongoing cognitive activities.

Pertinence is determined by the context of the inputs and activates nodes, or locations, in semantic memory. Selection is then based on the summation of activation in semantic memory from both sensory input and context. This account may seem rather like Treisman's attenuator, in that highly probable inputs are more likely to be selected because of an interaction between priming and input. However, Treisman placed the attenuator at the beginning of the system, prior to the place where long-term knowledge is stored whereas Norman placed the selective, attentional process after parallel access to semantic memory. Also, Norman's model has some aspects in common with that of Deutsch and Deutsch (1963), but rather than complete analysis of all inputs to the highest level, Norman allowed attention to be a matter of degree. Pertinence values are assigned at all levels of processing and the pertinence value may change with further processing. A message that initially seems of low pertinence may be found to be more pertinent following further processing. Finally, most messages will have been rejected, leaving only the most pertinent to become most deeply processed. Norman's model can easily account for the effects of semantics that were troublesome for original filter theory. Highly probable words that are presented to the unattended ear will be attended because of the effect of context determined pertinence. Lewis (1970) did an experiment that showed how the relation between the shadowed or attended message and the unshadowed or unattended message affected shadowing rate. Words presented to the unattended ear were semantically related, associatively related or unrelated to the message being shadowed. Although subjects were unable to remember anything from the unattended ear, the time it took them to say the shadowed words was greater when there was a semantic relation between the two. This effect is predicted by Norman's model, as the unconscious semantic processing slowed the processing of the attended words.

A number of other experiments were devised to measure the effects of unattended semantic information. For example, Corteen and Wood (1972) and Corteen and Dunn (1973) did some intriguing experiments using galvanic skin response (GSR). When subjects expect to get a small electric shock, their skin resistance changes. This is what GSR measures. Corteen and colleagues conditioned subjects to expect a shock in association with a particular set of words, in this case, words to do with the city. These subjects were then given a dichotic listening task and asked to attend to one ear while ignoring information on the other ear. Every so often, one of the shock-associated words was presented on the unattended channel and the subjects showed a clear GSR, although they claimed that they did not detect any of those words. Interestingly, these subjects also showed a GSR to other city words that had not been included in the training set. This result suggests that not only was there semantic access of the unattended words, but there was also semantic generalisation. Other experimenters have found similar results. Lackner and Garrett (1972) demonstrated that the interpretation of an ambiguous sentence could be biased by the presentation of an unattended sentence that suggested one particular interpretation of the sentence. McKay (1973) presented ambiguous sentences in a dichotic listening task. Subjects shadowed sentences such as: "They threw stones at the bank yesterday." Here bank was ambiguous, in that the sentence would have been equally sensible if you were thinking of a riverbank or a high street money bank. McKay found that if the word "river" was presented on the unattended channel, subjects did not remember having heard "bank", but interpreted the sentence in terms of riverbank rather than money bank. Experiments like these can be interpreted as providing more evidence that the selective processes in attention come after the meaning of words has been accessed. We shall review much more work on the semantic activation of the unattended in Chapter 9. Here we need to note that the increasing evidence for semantic processing prior to selection posed a serious challenge to Broadbent's theory.

More models of selective attention

Other proponents of late selection put forward their own versions of attentional theory. These theories are still structural and are concerned with the location of a bottleneck, where parallel processing stops and serial processing begins. Johnston and Heinz (1979) allow the bottleneck to move in a flexible way, so that selection will take place as early as possible in processing, but exactly where selection happens will depend on current task demands and prevailing circumstances. They suggest that the more stages of processing that are required prior to selection, the greater will be the demands on processing capacity. Duncan (1980) suggested that selection involved passage between two levels, where that passage is controlled by a "selector". Only information passed through the selector gains awareness or the ability to control a response, but all stimuli are fully identified at the first level. The limit in Duncan's model is entry to level 2, where awareness can only deal efficiently with one stimulus at a time.

Modifications to filter theory

Broadbent (1971, 1982) modified his original theory somewhat, although he said that as the 1958 model was so general, the changes were not major. To meet the challenge of the data since 1958, he expanded the role of the filter and added two new selection processes: pigeonholing and categorising. Filtering was seen as grouping the input on the basis of simple characteristics and this information passes to higher levels. The results of filtering represent "evidence" for the stimulus, rather than the providing determinate evidence from the outside world. So, although the evidence may suggest that one state of the environment, or stimulus, is more likely than another, this is not certain. However, although there may be ambiguity over the state of the outside world, the output of the limited capacity channel must be either one state or the other. Broadbent named this the "category state". To determine which category state is best fitted to the evidence, a decision is required and rather than information theory, which was the basis for the 1958 model, Broadbent (1971) frames his explanation in terms of statistical decision theory. This allows for the concept of noise, or uncertainty, to be incorporated into the system.

So, first, selective filtering links the stimulus states to states of evidence. Rather than the all-or-nothing filter of the 1958 model, Broadbent accepted Treisman's modification of the original filter theory, which allowed some stimuli to be responded to on the basis of less evidence than others. Now, as he explained in his 1982 paper, the filter was seen as a strategy to allow performance under conditions where interference would otherwise occur. Filtering did not block out everything about the unattended, some features could breakthrough and other features could trigger other later processes. Another concept introduced in 1971 was "pigeonholing". This refers to the process that relates the evidence from the filter to a category state. Pigeonholing alters the number of states of evidence that lead to any particular category state. Broadbent (1982) says pigeonholing is rather like filtering, except instead of selecting on the basis of features, selection operated by biasing the threshold of a category state, which has the effect of allowing some categories to be triggered by less evidence than would normally be needed. So, for example if you were asked to listen out for the name of an animal, then you would very rapidly respond to animal words irrespective of the voice in which they were spoken and you would be more responsive to animal words than words to do with, say, fruit.

Bundesen (1990) put forward a unified theory of visual recognition and attentional selection in which he explicitly modelled these two attentional mechanisms, filtering and pigeonholing, proposed by Broadbent (1971). Bundesen's paper is rather mathematical and contains detailed mathematical modelling of many visual attention tasks. However, the maths need not concern us here, we shall simply consider the concepts of filtering and pigeonholing. Bundesen defines filtering as the selection of elements from the visual field and pigeonholing as a the selection of categories. The filtering mechanism increases the probability of elements from the target category being selected "without biasing perception in favour of perceiving the elements as belonging to a particular category" (p. 525). This is achieved by using attentional weights derived from pertinence values. Selection of elements belonging to one category are favoured over elements belonging to other categories by increasing the attentional weights of elements belonging to the pertinent category. For example, Bundesen explains that in a task where red digits are to be selected in favour of black digits, the pertinence values of the perceptual category "red" would be high and the pertinence values of "black" would be low. The difference in pertinence values has the effect of speeding the perceptual processing of red elements and is a filtering process, in that it changes the probability that a red element is detected. However, to recognise the identity of the red digits, pigeonholing is necessary to bias the system to recognise identity rather than another attribute of the stimulus, such as size. According to Bundesen, pigeonholing is "a pure categorical bias mechanism, complementary to filtering" (p. 525). So, to identify a red digit, perceptual bias parameters would be set high for digits and low for all other pertinence values. This biasing speeds the categorisation process for digit relative to other attributes. In this example, the categorisation "digit" is favoured by the categorical bias mechanism. Bundesen's (1990) theory of visual attention (TVA) is incorporated by Logan (1996) into another mathematical theory of attention, CTVA, which is covered later.

Broadbent (1982) was still in favour of the attenuation alternative to the all-or-none filter and held to the view that selection was early, saying that late selection models "are driven by the need to explain breakthrough and have not developed explanations for these other phenomena" (p. 261). These other phenomena included problems of task combination, the question of why unattended events do not provide context for attended events and why false percepts are provoked by unattended information. Broadbent believed that if all unattended events were fully analysed these problems should not arise.

However, increasing evidence for at least some parallel processing up to higher levels of analysis led experimenters to try to distinguish more clearly the precise location of the rate-limiting stage or bottleneck. Psychologists at this time were deeply entrenched in their belief that the nervous system was, indeed, as Broadbent had suggested a serial processor, of limited capacity and that some processes were logically "earlier" or "later" than others. These kinds of assumption have been challenged by Allport (1980a, 1993) who pointed to the increasing volume of evidence that the brain computes information in parallel over multiple specialised processing systems and argued that we should be considering what attention is designed to achieve in the control of coherent human behaviour. For the moment, you should also note that what might have started out as rather general questions about attention, such as what causes some messages to be difficult to select, seems to have become crystallised into a single question about where, in some kind of structural system, the change from parallel to serial processing happens. This question is, of course, important. Parallel processes proceed "automatically" without the need for attention, whereas attentional processing appears limited. Psychologists wanted to be able to characterise those processes that were "attentional" and those that were not and so the search for the processing bottleneck continued. Remember, though, that discovering precisely where selection occurs is only one question among the issues surrounding attention and finding where selection takes place may not help us to understand why or how this happens. Nevertheless, any theory has to account for the experimental results and, in the search for the bottleneck, psychologists certainly collected plenty of data!

It began to seem as if the "bottleneck" metaphor were wearing thin. As soon as the bottleneck can be moved around, or can be hypothesised to be located at either end or almost anywhere in the processing continuum, perhaps it ceases to be a bottleneck after all. However, remember Welford's (1952) evidence on the psychological refractory period (PRP)? This clearly showed some limit on simultaneous processing. Another phenomenon called attentional blink and repetition blindness also suggest a severe limit on attentional processing. We shall meet these effects in later chapters. We shall also discover that there is evidence that the level of processing at which selective attention operates might depend on the task being performed. Lavie, Hirst, de Fockert, and Viding (2004) have put forward load theory of selective attention and cognitive control, which, they argue resolves the early–late debate. This theory is based on evidence that the level at which selective attention operates is dependent on perceptual load, working memory load and the amount of control required in a task. We shall cover this theory in the next chapter, after we have learnt more about what has been discovered on the nature of attention.

At the time it was beginning to look as if a different metaphor to the single channel processor was needed. Norman proposed that there was no fixed, structural point where the system was limited, rather, the system is limited by having only a fixed amount of processing "resources". The concept of resource limitation began to gain popularity, psychologists began to experiment on the limits of task combination and examine how these "resources" could be shared between tasks. We shall cover resource theory in Chapter 6.

Summary

Initial research suggested that the human information-processing system was limited in its ability to perform multiple tasks. Broadbent (1958) proposed that the human could be likened to a single channel for processing information. The single channel selected information to be passed through a protective filter on the basis of physical characteristics. Only this selected information was passed on to be identified. In auditory experiments evidence for semantic processing for material presented on the unattended auditory channel led to the suggestion that all information was pre-attentively analysed for meaning, but only the most important signals were passed on to the response stage

(Deutsch & Deutsch, 1963). Treisman (1960) introduced a compromise theory in which the unattended signals were able to break through the filter. Evidence from experiments on selective visual attention from brief visual displays also showed that physical cues were an effective basis for selective report (Sperling, 1960), but careful analysis suggested that more was processed than could be reported (Dick, 1971). Townsend (1973) thought that report was limited by the problem not of *what* something was, but *where* it was, and experiments provided support for the separability for identity and location information in vision (Styles & Allport, 1986). In both auditory and visual experiments, semantic and categorical information appeared to be activated, but could not be reported. Different theories were proposed that suggested the serial bottleneck between pre-attentive parallel processing and serial attentive processing could move according to task demands (e.g. Johnston & Heinz, 1979; Norman, 1968). New ideas (to be dealt with in Chapter 6), which viewed attention as a pool of processing resources, began to gain popularity. Lavie et al. (2004) has proposed a load theory, which attempts to resolve the early–late debate, covered in the next chapter.

Further reading

Every introductory book on cognition has a section on early attention experiments and theory. Here are a few examples:

- Eysenck, M. W., & Keane, M. T. (2005). *Cognitive psychology: A Students' handbook*, 5th ed. Hove, UK: Psychology Press.
- Hampson, P. J., & Morris, P. E. (1996). *Understanding cognition. Basic psychology*. Oxford: Blackwell.
- Styles, E. A. (2005). *Attention perception and memory: An integrated introduction*. Hove, UK: Psychology Press.

A useful review of selective attention including early work and subsequent developments is:

- Driver, J. (2001). A selective review of selective attention research from the past century. *British Journal of Psychology, 92*, 53–78.

The nature of visual attention 3

Introduction

Usually, we move our eyes to an object or location in space in order to fixate what we are attending to. However, as early as 1866, Helmholtz noted that attention and fixation were not necessarily coincident. In the introduction, we noted that if you fixate in one place, for example on the asterisk here *, you are able to read nearby words without shifting fixation to the location occupied by those words. Further, if you are attending and fixating in one place, you may find your attention drawn to a familiar word, like your name or home town, elsewhere on the page, or by a movement in peripheral vision. It is as if there is some kind of breakthrough or interrupt mechanism caused by information outside fixation.

One of the most popular metaphors for visual attention is that it is like a spotlight that allows us to selectively attend to particular parts of the visual environment. William James (1890) described visual attention as having a focus, a margin and a fringe. We have already seen in the previous chapter, that there is disagreement over the degree of processing that stimuli receive with and without attention. To some extent, the same arguments will continue through this next chapter, but we will mainly be concerned with the question of whether a spotlight is a good metaphor, how it knows where to go, to what it can be directed and what kinds of processing go on inside and outside the spotlight.

Selective filtering and selective set

Kahneman and Treisman (1984) made an important distinction between two broad categories of visual attention task: selective filtering and selective set. They point out that most of the early experiments involved tasks where subjects have to select a message or stimulus from a quite complex environment and select a response from a wide choice. For example, when shadowing an auditory message the words to be spoken might come from a wide vocabulary, rather than having to say simply "yes" or "no", or reporting all the letters in the cued row from a brief visual display rather than detecting whether a particular letter was present or not. Accuracy of report is generally taken as the dependent measure. From about 1970 onwards, a rather different kind of experiment became the norm; Kahneman and Treisman call these *selective set experiments*. Here, the stimulus set is usually small, the stimuli are simple and require a response from a small set of possibilities. In these experiments, the usual measure of performance is reaction time. The differences in the task requirements of the two paradigms might explain some of the conflicting evidence that emerges from them.

Selective set experiments

The Eriksen paradigm

In 1974 Eriksen and Eriksen introduced an experimental paradigm that has been widely adopted by many later experimenters as a useful selective visual attention task. We shall encounter the Eriksen task several more times with respect to interference effects and selective attention. Eriksen (1995) provides a short review of the usefulness of his task for investigating a variety of cognitive problems. According to Kahenman and Treisman's definition, the Eriksen task is closer to a selective set experiment than a filtering experiment. Subjects are presented with only a few items, which have well-defined responses from a small set and performance is measured by reaction time. Remember, a filtering experiment usually involves many items, a large response set and accuracy is the dependent measure. In the original version of the Eriksen task, subjects are instructed that there are two sets of letters that are to be responded to by moving a lever in either one direction or another. For example, H and K are mapped onto one direction, but S is mapped onto the other. The subject's task is to respond as quickly as possible to the central letter of a row of five. In these experiments, there was no mask following the display. Eriksen and Eriksen (1974) showed that when two letters (H and K) are assigned to the same lever response, a target H is responded to more slowly in displays like SSHSS, where lever responses are incompatible, than in KKHKK displays where lever responses are compatible. This effect is called the flanker compatibility effect (FCE). The data clearly implicate response competition as the source of interference between the letters in the display, for unless the distractors had been analysed to the point where their responses were available, no response level differences in interference should arise. Here, then, we have further evidence that identity information from the to-be-ignored, response-irrelevant stimuli is available to the processing system, even though in some selective report conditions, e.g. Sperling's selective filtering experiment, this identity information cannot control selective report. Of course, there is another difference between the two studies. Sperling showed the display for a very short time; in the partial report condition subjects did not know which row they would have to report until after the display had terminated and would not have had time to make eye movements around the display to search each location. In the Eriksen experiment, subjects know where the target will appear and what they have to do before stimulus onset. Clearly, these tasks place very different demands on the subject and therefore may be tapping quite different kinds or levels of attentional operation. We will return to this point later.

Eriksen and Eriksen (1974) also discovered that interference from response incompatible distractors was dependent on the distance of the distractors from the target and that once the distractors were within one degree of visual angle of the target, they could not be ignored. As selective attention seemed unable to exclude distractors within this region, the notion of a minimum width "spotlight" emerged, with stimuli falling under the spotlight being fully processed. We shall review a variety of evidence regarding the nature of the attentional spotlight and what processing goes on within it shortly. For the present we continue the debate on the level of processing achieved by attended and unattended stimuli in visual displays.

Completely contradictory to Eriksen and Eriksen's (1974) results Bjork and Murray (1977) showed that the best inhibitor for a target letter is another example of the same letter. For example, if the target is "B", the strongest inhibition is found when the flanker is another "B". Let's call this the "BB" effect. According to the Eriksen experiments, as B and B have the same response there should be no interference between them. However, Bjork and Murray argue that, in this case, interference is due to feature-specific interference between signal and noise elements in a display, which results in competition at an early level of feature extraction. Bjork and Murray's (1977) feature specific theory of interference effects in visual attention is an extension of Estes (1972, 1974) theory, in which it is assumed that there are separate feature detectors for separate features and that associated with each feature detector are a number of input channels distributed over the visual field.

Of course, it is very often the case that the featural and the categorical properties of an item are confounded. Say, for example, you ask your subject to respond as quickly as they can to a letter that is flanked by either digits or other letters. If the result shows that subjects are slower to respond to a letter when it is surrounded by other letters is this because, at the featural level, letters are more similar to each other and so compete at an early level or is it because the responses to letters are from the same category and so compete for response at a later level? Jonides and Gleitman (1972) did a clever experiment to try to separate out these factors. Jonides and Gleitman presented two, four or six items for 100 msec. Subjects were asked to search for a letter embedded in either letter or digit distractors (or vice versa). The most interesting manipulation was to use O as either a letter or a digit. So, while the featural properties remained exactly the same, the category membership could be changed. Previous experiments had shown that there appears to be a parallel search (i.e. no RT cost for increasing display size) for between category search, but a linearly increasing cost for within category search (Egeth, Jonides, & Wall 1972). Jonides and Gleitman found that depending on whether subjects were told to search for an "oh" or "zero" the physically identical figure behaved either as a letter or a digit. This provides strong evidence that all array items are categorised prior to selection. If the effects were featural, the ambiguous O should behave the same in both conditions. Clearly these results are in conflict and the resolution must require consideration of other aspects of the task and the task environment.

Recent work on flanker compatibility: The argument continues

We have seen that when subjects must respond to a relevant letter that is flanked by irrelevant items, the nature of the information in the flankers produces a response compatibility effect. Many experiments have been done and theories proposed but still there is basic disagreement about the mechanisms and locus of attentional selection.

Two contradictory but well-established findings are in direct contradiction. The first, which we called the "BB" effect, where the encoding of features from the display is inhibited by adjacent, featurally similar elements and second, the "HHH" effect, which suggests that the featural encoding of display items is independent of adjacent featurally similar items. Santee and Egeth (1980, 1982) review the conflicting evidence and attempt to resolve the conflict in terms of experimental differences. Their conclusions are that when a mask is used perceptual interactions between features will be found, but when the location and the identity of the target are required as the response, there will be interference related to the identity of the distractors. In one of their experiments, they found that if target location was not required, there was no effect of interletter separation in the range 0.2–1.8 degrees of visual angle.

Miller (1991) has reviewed the evidence on the flanker compatibility effect and conducted experiments to determine the boundary conditions under which the effect could be found. Miller summarises the evidence. Eriksen and Eriksen (1974) found that when a subject must attend to the central letter that is flanked by letters having either a compatible or incompatible keypress response, the flanker letters produce large response compatibility effects, showing that the flankers have been identified even though they are unattended. The FCE can also be found in cueing tasks, where a bar marker is presented, before display onset, to direct the subjects' attention to the relevant location (Eriksen & St James, 1986). Eriksen and Rohrbaugh (1970), Mewhort et al. (1981) and Styles and Allport (1986) found mislocations. These data among others provide evidence for the identification of unattended letters prior to selection and so support a late selection account of visual attention.

Miller (1991) manipulated five factors that he thought might be responsible for the processing of unattended stimuli. These were:

1. poor spatial resolution of attentional focus
2. inability to hold attentional focus on a fixed location
3. inability to focus completely on an empty display location
4. inability to filter out stimuli that onset during the task (we shall see later that objects that onset somewhere else in the visual field have the tendency to "grab" attention)
5. inability to prevent analysis of all stimuli when there is insufficient demand by the attended items.

Miller found that he was unable to eliminate the FCE by manipulating any of these factors. His conclusion was that "early selection rarely, if ever, completely excludes unattended stimuli from semantic analysis". He also concluded that spatial separation is especially important in visual selective attention. However, the separation may depend on the target distractor relationship. Eriksen, Pan, and Botella (1993) showed that the interfering effects of incompatible distractors were inversely proportional to their distance from the attended area and suggested this reflected an inhibitory field surrounding the attended area. Laberge, Brown, Carter, Bash, and Hartley (1991) argued that a gradient of attention around a target, and hence the area within which interference would or would not be found, varied with the attentional demand of the task. Further, Yantis and Johnston (1990) were also able to manipulate the distance over which flanking distractors had an effect on response to the target.

The distance over which distractors interfere within the visual field is an important consideration when trying to determine if visual attention is a spotlight of fixed or variable width or more like a zoom lens. We shall return to this evidence later in the chapter. For the present, we will stay with the question of the level of processing achieved by both target and distractors in these experiments.

Perceptual load and selective attention

It is now becoming increasingly clear that the degree of processing achieved by information in visual displays is dependent on a variety of factors and that a clear-cut distinction between "early" selection and "late" selection may be inappropriate. Recall the differences between selective filtering and selective set experiments pointed out by Kahneman and Treisman (1984) who concluded that these different paradigms may require different attentional mechanisms. In a typical filtering task, the subject has a large target and response set and has to select one stimulus from a subset of many. The response measure is usually accuracy. Here, the memory load is high and results suggest early selection with very limited processing of unattended stimuli. A typical example of this kind of filtering task is that of Sperling (1960), which we discussed at the beginning of the chapter. In a selective set task, the subject usually makes a speeded response to a target from a small set and chooses from a restricted response set by pressing a button. The response measure is usually reaction time. Here, the memory load is low and results suggest that selective attention speeds response to expected targets: late selection. A typical example of a selective set task is the Eriksen and Eriksen (1974) experiment. Thus these two experimental paradigms are very different in terms of the demand made on the information-processing system and Kahneman and Treisman (1984) believe it is unlikely that the same type of perceptual processing is required in the two tasks.

Picking up on Kahneman and Treisman (1984) and point 5 in the Miller's (1991) paper discussed earlier, Lavie (1995) reviews evidence for the effect of load on performance in a variety of selective attention tasks. Lavie (1995) and Lavie and Tsal (1994) proposed that whether attention is early or late depends on the demands of the task. Basically, if the attentional demand of the task is low, irrelevant distractors will be processed, as there is still some attentional capacity left over. Therefore, so long as the task of selecting the target does not use all available attentional resources there will be interference. Contrariwise, when target selection requires full use of all attentional resources, there will be no possibility of distractors being processed. Although we have not yet covered resource theory, note here, that attention is being discussed in terms of a limited resource that must be shared across tasks, rather than a structural limitation as in Broadbent's filter model. Resource theory of attention is most widely applied in dual task situations and is covered in detail in Chapter 6. In the experiments here, the attentional resource is seen as being distributed across items in the display or among processing components of the overall task. Kahneman and Chajczyk (1983) demonstrated that the Stroop effect is "diluted" when other information is presented in the visual array. The argument is that the irrelevant information draws on attentional resources so reducing the amount available for processing the irrelevant distracting information. In a series of experiments using versions of the Eriksen and Eriksen (1974) task, Lavie (1995) systematically manipulated perceptual load to gauge its effect on interference from irrelevant distractors.

First, Lavie varied the set size of possible targets from one to six and found that interference effects from a distractor with an incompatible response to the target was only significant in the low load condition. In another experiment, processing demands were manipulated by requiring two different forms of processing for a coloured shape presented next to the target. Depending on combination of the colour and shape the subject was to respond or not to the target, in what is called a "Go, No-go" situation. In the low load conditions subjects were to respond if the shape was blue but not if it was red. In the high load condition, "Go" was signalled by either a red circle or a blue square and "No-go" by either a red square or a blue circle. Assuming attention is needed to correctly integrate the colours and shapes in the display, as well as there being a memory load, Lavie (1995) predicted that the high load condition would reduce interference from an incongruent distractor also present in the display. Results confirmed that interference from incompatible distractors is only found in the low load condition.

Lavie (1995) claimed "that perceptual load plays a causal role in determining the efficiency of selective attention" (p. 463). The experiment by Eriksen and Eriksen (1974) was a low load experiment and so there was attentional capacity left over to process the distractors, leading to the appearance of late selection. In Sperling's (1960) experiment the load was high and hence all the attentional capacity was required for target processing, leading to the necessity for early selection. This argument might account for the discrepancy and debate over whether selective attention is early or late being resolved. But there is a problem. Remember Bjork and Murray (1977) used displays that were as low in load as those of Eriksen and Eriksen (1974); how can the difference in results be accounted for? Lavie concedes that the "load" hypothesis does not really bring us any closer to solving this discrepancy in the data and has to assume that in certain conditions feature level interference will occur. Other problems arise out of the difficulty in defining exactly what "load" and "perceptual capacity" are. These are also problems associated with dual task experiments and divided attention, which we address more fully in Chapter 6. Lavie's work offers a promising compromise between a strict "early" or "late" selection theory and recently a fully articulated load theory has been proposed by Lavie et al. (2004). According to the load theory of attention (LTA), the degree to which attention can be selective, and hence the degree to which distractors will be processed, depends on the level and type of load involved in the processing of any particular task. Lavie et al. (2004) review the data on distractor processing, including that which we have reviewed here, and conclude that late selection is typical in tasks where perceptual load is low and early selection typical in conditions where perceptual load is high. However, for a full account of selective attention, they say that cognitive control must also be taken into account in those situations where perceptual load is low and therefore competing distractors are vying to control response. Attentional control and selection for action is dealt with in Chapter 8, but for the purpose of this discussion it is important to know that both everyday slips of action, such as pouring tea into the sugar bowl, or taking the usual route home when you meant to go somewhere else, are evidence for loss of intention control over actions. Further, patients with frontal lobe damage have difficulty completing sequential tasks and are easily distracted. Lavie et al. point out that this kind of evidence demonstrates the importance of frontal brain areas in cognitive control.

In normal people, the frontal lobes are also involved in working memory and dual task coordination and Lavie et al. propose that when these frontal processes are loaded up with, for example, a list of digits to remember, performance on a selective attention task would suffer. Previous work by de Fockert, Rees, Frith, and Lavie (2001) revealed that concurrent maintenance of a working memory load damaged performance on a selective attention task involving classifying written names according to occupation (e.g. popstar or politician) while ignoring faces. When working memory load was high there was greater interference between the name, e.g. Mick Jagger and an incongruent distractor, e.g. Bill Clinton's face, than when memory load was low. In addition, concurrent neuroimaging showed activity in the fusiform gyrus (a face-processing area) was significantly greater in the high load condition, showing that the face was indeed being processed.

Other evidence for a role for working memory in selective attention comes from work on individual differences. For example, individuals with a low memory span were more susceptible to interference from distractors in an auditory shadowing experiment than individuals with a high span (Conway, Cowen, & Bunting, 2001). On the basis of this kind of evidence, Lavie et al. (2004) carried out a series of experiments to test the hypothesis that the level of distractor processing in flanker tasks depends not only on perceptual load, but also on concurrent working memory load as well as the dual task load imposed by doing both tasks together. They also investigated the effect of having to switch between a selective attention flanker task and a memory task. In this case, although the tasks were not concurrent, there is still the need for control processes. (See Chapter 8 for a discussion on task switching.) Perceptual load was manipulated by increasing set size of distractors, working memory load was manipulated by requiring one or six digits to be memorised on each trial. Following previous experiments, perceptual load was predicted to decrease distractor effects while memory load was predicted to increase distractor effects. The results of their third experiment confirm this prediction, and "clearly establish within the same study, that perceptual load and working memory load have opposite effects on selective attention" (p. 348).

To test the effect of engaging cognitive control mechanisms in a task, and measure the consequences of this type of load, Lavie et al. (2004) conducted further experiments. They compared the effect of a one-item memory load and a six-item memory load in a task that required alternately doing the probe-digit memory task and then the distractor task. Now the two tasks were being carried out in close succession rather than concurrently, the authors reasoned that the requirement to monitor and update task goals would still require control, but that as the memory load was not being held during the selective attention distractor task the cost would be the same for both memory loads and only reflect the cost of task sequencing and shifting. Performance was compared with that of a single distractor task. Results showed that the need to perform the tasks alternately produced greater distractor interference and that there was no interaction with the size of memory load.

In conclusion, Lavie et al. (2004) argue that the dissociation between perceptual load and memory load suggest two mechanisms: one a passive perceptual mechanism that can allow distractors to be excluded in conditions of high perceptual load and a second mechanism that is more active and controls behaviour according to task priorities, excluding irrelevant stimuli even when they are seen and because perceptual load is low. It appears that a resolution to the early–late debate can be found if it is accepted that the extent to which distractors can be prevented depends not only on perceptual load, but also on the way attention is allocated by cognitive control.

Attention as a spotlight: Spatial cueing

Clearly visual attention can be directed to a spatial location. In the experiments by Eriksen and Eriksen (1974) and Lavie et al. (2004), for example, participants could direct attention to the target location in the display. In Sperling's experiments participants could selectively report the letters from one or another row in the display, but, in this case, attention was directed to the memorial trace in iconic memory, rather than a currently visible display. Also, there is evidence from flanker effects that there is a finite limit beyond which attention is unable to close down its focus sufficiently to exclude processing of adjacent items. Many experiments have used spatial markers prior to display onset to indicate the position of the upcoming target and these can apparently be used to direct the focus of attention.

The effects of cueing a position in retinal space where a visual target might appear has been studied by many psychologists including Posner (1978, 1980) and Posner, Snyder, and Davidson (1980). Posner's technique is elegant and simple. Subjects are asked to make a speeded response as soon as they detect the onset of a light in their visual field. Just before the target is presented, subjects are given a cue, which can be one or other of two types. The first type of cue, called a central cue, is an arrow that points either towards the left or the right, indicating that the target will appear to the left or the right of fixation. A central cue, although usually presented centrally on fixation, is also central in the sense that it is a symbol representing direction and as such requires central processing by the cognitive system for its interpretation. The alternative type of cue, called a peripheral cue, is presented outside, or peripheral to, fixation and involves a brief illumination of one of a number of box outlines that mark the possible locations at which a target may appear. A peripheral cue is not symbolic in the same way as a central cue, because no interpretation is needed to determine its location, a peripheral cue indicated position directly.

Posner manipulated the validity of spatial visual cues to determine the manner in which such cues could be used to summon or direct attention. Validity is the probability that the cue does, in fact, indicate where a target is to be presented. That is, although the cue could be a valid indicator of where the target would appear, on some trials the cue was invalid, indicating a location different from that at which the target would be presented. In order to compare the costs and benefits of valid and invalid cues, Posner included a baseline control in which a central cross was presented to indicate that a target was about to be presented, but did not provide any information about where the target was going to appear.

When the cue was valid, subjects were faster to respond to the target than in the control condition. It seemed as if subjects were able to use the cue to direct, or orient, attention because when the cue was invalid, their response was slower than control, suggesting that attention had moved in the wrong direction. These results were the same for both central and peripheral cues.

Further experiments have shown that there are differences between the cueing effects of a central cue, such as a directional arrow, and a cue such as a flash of light that appears in the periphery. When the cues are only valid on a small proportion of trials, it would be advantageous for the subject to ignore them, as most of the time they would be misleading. However, Posner has shown that while central cues can be ignored, peripheral cues cannot. If the subject believes that the central arrow is pointing in the invalid direction, they can ignore it. By the same token, even if the subject has good reason to believe that a peripheral cue is invalid, a response time cost still occurs, showing that, despite intention, attention is directed to the cued location. (See Figure 3.1.)

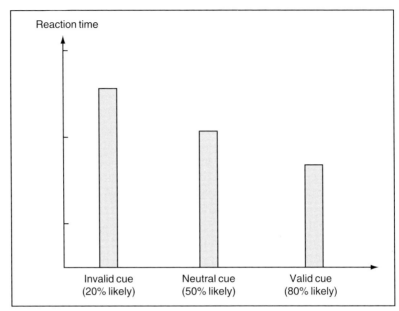

Figure 3.1 Response times to visual targets according to the likelihood of a spatial cue correctly indicating the spatial location of the target.

Endogenous and exogenous orienting of attention

Posner (1980) showed that directing attention to a valid stimulus location facilitates visual processing and led him to suggest that "attention can be likened to a spotlight that enhances the efficiency of the detection of events within its beam" (Posner et al., 1980, p. 172). It is important to note here that attention is not synonymous with looking. Even when there is no time to make an eye movement to the cued location, facilitation is found. Thus, it seems, visual attention can be covertly directed to a spatial location other than the one we are fixating. Posner (1980) proposed two ways in which attention is oriented to a stimulus that are dependent on which of two attentional systems are called on. He distinguished between two attentional systems: an endogenous system, which is intentionally controlled by the subject, for example, when an arrow cue is believed to be informative or not; and an exogenous system, which automatically shifts attention according to environmental stimuli, is outside the subjects control and cannot be ignored.

Neurological bases of directing visual attention

Further evidence from neurophysiological studies on monkeys, studies on normal subjects using positron emission tomography (PET) and cerebral blood flow and experiments with brain-damaged patients, led Posner and Petersen (1990) to propose two independent but interacting attentional systems. The posterior system is involved in directing attention to relevant locations using the operations of engaging, shifting and disengaging. Three areas of the brain show enhanced response when a monkey attends to the location of a stimulus rather then some other spatial location: the parietal lobe (Mountcastle et al., 1975), part of the pulvinar (Petersen, Robinson, & Morris, 1987) and the superior colliculus (Goldberg & Wurtz, 1972). Using PET studies, similar activity has been observed in humans (Corbetta, Meizen, Shulman, & Petersen, 1993; Petersen, Fox, Miezen, & Raichle, 1988). Lesions in these areas produce symptoms of attentional neglect, which we shall consider a little later. The posterior system is specialised for covert orienting to location information, but not for other features of the stimulus, such as colour. When subjects must select on the basis of these other cues, different areas of the anterior part of the brain are involved. This difference between the brain circuits involved in selectivity to different stimulus attributes may, according to Posner (1993), account for the finding that location is a more effective cue for visual selection than cues such as colour or form. Experiments showing the differential effectiveness of cues were discussed earlier, for example, Sperling (1960).

Posner and Petersen (1990) note there are strong connections between the posterior parietal lobe and parts of the prefrontal cortex. When a task requires monitoring for targets that may be presented in any input modality or during a Stroop task, the anterior cingulate gyrus is active (Pardo, Pardo, Janer, & Raichle, 1990). The pattern of connectivity between these anterior areas of the frontal lobes that are involved in planning and the posterior attentional system suggest the anterior system is involved in controlling the posterior system. Posner and Petersen (1990) suggest there is a "hierarchy of attentional systems in which the anterior system can pass control to the posterior system when it is not occupied with processing other material" (p. 10).

In a more recent review, which includes evidence from magnetic resonance imaging, Posner and Badgaiyan (1998) summarise the role of the posterior attentional system "in terms of cognitive theories, this network mediates disengagement, engagement and amplification of the attended target" (p. 64). The second, anterior network, is involved in overt, intentionally controlled orienting: "It is involved in attentional recruitment and it controls the brain areas that perform complex tasks. It exerts general control over the areas involved in target detection and response . . . and . . . is also responsible for anticipation of the target location" (p. 65). Posner and Dehaene (2000) discuss PET data that support the asymmetric involvement of the hemispheres in attentional functions. Blood flow increases are evident in right parietal lobe for attention shifts in both fields, but blood flow in left parietal only increases for right field shifts. There are other interpretations of the neurological underpinnings of visual orienting. For example, Laberge (2000) suggests that amplification of neural activity in cortical columns produces the selective property of attention. This amplification can be controlled "bottom up" by the stimulus or "top down" by intention. Laberge identifies numerous triangular circuits in the brain. These triangular circuits involve a direct pathway between the parietal areas where attention is expressed and frontal areas involved in control and an indirect pathway between parietal and frontal areas via the thalamus, which is involved in amplification. The direct pathway is involved in selecting parietal areas in which attention will be expressed while the indirect pathway modulates the intensity of attentional expression in the selected areas. Laberge assumes that an abrupt onset initiates, bottom up, brief parietal activity, which is the orienting of attention, but if this activity is to be prolonged, then top-down activity is necessary.

Overt and covert orienting: One system or two?

In experiments using normal subjects, Jonides (1981) showed that although covert orienting to peripheral cues is unaffected by a secondary memory task, voluntary orienting to central cues is affected by a secondary task. As already mentioned, a central cue needs interpretation by central mechanisms to ascertain the direction in which attention should be moved and requires controlled processing, whereas peripheral cues provide direct information on the to-be-attended location and orient attention automatically. A memory load competes with the interpretation of a central cue but not with a peripheral cue. (For a discussion of the distinction between automatic and controlled processing, see Chapter 7.)

Like Posner, Jonides (1981) interpreted these two varieties of attentional orienting as reflecting two different modes of controlling the same attentional orienting system. However, Muller and Findlay (1989) and Muller and Rabbitt (1989), argued that this might be the wrong interpretation. They termed exogenous orienting "reflexive" and endogenous orienting "voluntary". Muller and Findlay (1989) (reported in Muller and Rabbitt, 1989) found that there were different time courses for the costs and benefits produced by peripheral and central cues. Peripheral cues produced a fast automatic orienting response, which was strongest between 100 and 300 ms after cue onset, peaking at 150 ms. Central cues took 300 ms to reach their maximum effect, but last longer. At a stimulus onset asynchrony (SOA) of less than 300 ms the costs and benefits for peripheral cues were greater than for central cues, but after 300 ms peripheral and central cues had the same effect. Muller and Findlay had argued that as the effects of the different cues had different time courses this could be evidence for two separate orienting mechanisms.

Muller and Rabbitt (1989) did a series of experiments aimed at refining and clarifying the question of whether there was only one attentional orienting mechanism controlled in different ways, as Posner had proposed, or whether there were two distinct mechanisms, one reflexive and the other voluntary. Their experiments pitted peripheral and central cues against each other to determine the difference in their time courses and if they were equally susceptible to interruption. Results were consistent with an automatic, reflexive mechanism that is strongly resistant to competing stimuli and a second, voluntary mechanism that can be interfered with by the reflexive orienting mechanism. In their second experiment, Muller and Rabbitt found that when peripheral and central cues were compatible, facilitation of cued locations was greater than when the cues were incompatible and that the inhibitory effects of peripheral cues were lessened when they were in unlikely locations. It appeared that voluntary orienting to central cues could modify orienting in response to reflexive, peripheral cues. Muller and Rabbitt (1989) claim: "This pattern is consistent with the idea that the reflexive and the voluntary mechanism can be active simultaneously" (p. 328).

The fact that the "automatic" reflexive orienting can be modified by voluntary control processes, suggests that reflexive orienting is less than truly automatic. (Automatic processes cannot be voluntarily controlled, see Chapter 7.) However, according to the two-mechanism model of attentional orienting this can be explained. Reflexive orienting is triggered and proceeds automatically and, if both reflexive and voluntary orienting mechanisms are pulling in the same direction, they have an additive effect. However, if they are pulling in different directions, their effects are subtractive.

Symbolic control of visual attention

An arrow presented at fixation in Posner's experiments is a symbolic cue, in that it stands for a direction rather than marks it explicitly.

Pratt and Hommel (2003) discuss a variety of experiments that show how different types of symbolic information can control the allocation of attention to locations in the visual field. For example, Friesen and Kingstone (1998) found that participants directed their attention according to which way the eyeballs in schematic faces pointed. When the eyeballs shifted from looking straight ahead to looking to one side or the other participants were faster to detect peripheral targets that appeared on the side to which the eyeballs were "looking". Driver, Davis, Ricciarelli, Kidd, Maxwell, and Baron-Cohen (1999) replicated the effect using real faces and argued that perception of eye gaze triggers reflexive or involuntary visuospatial orienting. Langton and Bruce (1999, 2000) found similar effects when participants observed others pointing gestures. Pratt and Hommel (2003) believe these studies suggest that when we observe another person orient attention by a shift of gaze or by pointing, this can produce reflexive changes in the orientation of attention in the observer. Although not symbols in the same way as an arrow, the movement of eye gaze or a hand gesture do indicate direction rather than precise spatial location. Hommel, Pratt, Colzato, and Godijn (2001) demonstrated that not only arrows but overlearned directional words such as up, down, left and right can also produce involuntary shifts of attention, despite being irrelevant to the ongoing task. Participants were explicitly instructed that any arrows or words were irrelevant to their task, yet were unable to ignore them. Pratt and Hommel (2003) point out that if attention was always shifted in response to all visual signals capable of directing attention activities such as driving or walking among all the signs in the road would be very difficult. They give the example of seeing a sign at a junction that has two arrows, one for straight ahead and another for turn left. Or signs that says "merge left", "exit 200 yards right". As a visual attention shift cannot be made in two directions simultaneously, there must be a system that selects which shift to make. This shift is most likely related to current goals. The importance of goals in controlling behaviour and the ability to shift between goals will be discussed in detail in Chapter 7. Here we will mention some issues specific to orienting visual attention in an environment that presents conflicting orienting cues.

Can attention and selection dissociate?

Folk, Remington, and Johnston (1992) and Folk, Remington, and Wright (1994) have conducted a variety of experiments that have revealed the importance of goal-directed control or task requirements.

For example, onset cues capture attention when the task is to detect onset targets, but not when the task was to identify target colour and vice versa. This finding suggests that only task-relevant features of a stimulus capture attention. Remington and Folk (2001) argue for a dissociation between attention and selection. We have seen that orienting attention to a spatial location facilitates processing of visual stimuli and also that separating flanker letters from a target aid selectivity. Awh, Matsukura, and Serences (2003) review data showing that greater levels of distractor noise from irrelevant stimuli or from masked stimuli result in larger spatial cueing effects. Desimone and Duncan (1995) suggest that this evidence supports the view that spatial attention is an emergent property of competitive interaction in the visual system. According to this view stimuli in multi-element displays compete for limited processing resources by inhibiting the processing of other stimuli. Attended stimuli are therefore processed better because they are affected less by adjacent stimuli. This account suggests that the nature of the visual display determines the extent to which spatial selection affects visual processing. In a display with many distractors, spatial selection will have a large effect, but in sparse displays, spatial selection will have less effect. These studies relate to the flanker interference effects discussed earlier. Awh et al. (2003) showed by manipulating the probability of distractor interference that both intentional, top-down and stimulus-driven, bottom-up factors biased competition. These results led Awh et al. to suggest that the likelihood of noise distractors led to participants implementing top-down biasing, which resulted in better accuracy in reporting targets, and that "a complete model of biased competition should acknowledge strong interactions between top-down and bottom-up factors" (p. 61).

In a number of flanker interference tasks similar to those of Eriksen and Eriksen (1974) discussed earlier, it has been shown that interference effects of flankers are limited to task relevant features of the flankers, e.g. Maruff, Danckert, Camplin, and Currie (1999), who argue that behavioural goals constrain the selection of visual information. Remington and Folk (2001) report a study in which participants made speeded responses to either the identity or the orientation of a target character, which appeared in one of four locations arranged around fixation. The target was a red T or an L rotated 45°. A symbol was presented at the start of each trial to indicate which dimension was to be responded to. On orientation trials, participants were told to ignore the letter identity and on letter identity trials, they were told to ignore orientation. In addition to the red target letter, each target display contained three white non-target characters: the neutral letters E and F and one foil character, T or L. The foils were rotated so that they were only distinguishable from the target characters by colour. This arrangement meant that both targets and foils contained values on both relevant and irrelevant dimensions. Spatial attention was controlled by the presentation of a cue prior to target onset that would draw attention to one of the four possible target locations. It was arranged that on 25% of trials the character at the cued location was a target (red T or L), on 25% the character at the cued location was a foil (white T or L) and 50% of trials contained a neutral stimulus (white E or F) at the cued location. Responses were mapped onto the index or middle finger and involved pressing a button. The responses to the relevant and irrelevant dimensions of foils and targets were crossed with compatibility and task. This meant that task irrelevant responses, if triggered, would interfere with target responses.

Results showed that responses were significantly faster when the cue was at the target location than when at invalid locations. Response compatibility effects were evident for both the irrelevant target dimension and the relevant foil dimension and these effects interacted. There was significantly greater interference for incompatible values of the relevant foil dimension when the foil location was cued. Incompatibility on the irrelevant dimension of a foil had no effect on target response time, while incompatibility on the irrelevant target dimension did interfere. This difference cannot be explained by attention alone, as in both cases attention was cued to the stimulus position. Remington and Folk argue that these results are evidence that "access to response mechanisms can be restricted to task relevant dimensions of a visually attended object. This finding is inconsistent with the assumption that all dimensions and associated responses of an attended object are potentiated, whether relevant or not" (p. 513). In summary, they suggest that their results demonstrate that given a stimulus is attended the automatic extraction of stimulus dimensions is mediated by top-down goals. This means that while the attentional spotlight might facilitate processing within its beam, there are additional processes involved in selecting the dimensions relevant to the current task environment and instructions.

It is another question as to how an instruction can give rise to the setting of the information-processing system to preferentially process one dimension rather than another. This is the subject of selection and control of action addressed in Chapter 8.

Inhibition of return

Although a valid cue usually facilitates processing, there are conditions in which inhibition can arise. If there is a delay of 300 mscs or more after a peripheral cue, target detection at that location is slowed down. That is, the normally facilitatory effect has reversed to become inhibitory. This effect is called "inhibition of return" and although Wolfe and Pokorny (1990) failed to replicate the effect, inhibition of return (IOR) has been demonstrated several times, e.g. Posner and Cohen (1984), Maylor (1985). A plausible suggestion for why the visual system might require this kind of inhibition, is that it allows efficient visual search (Klein, 1988). Once attention has been directed to a location, that location is "tagged" so that there is no need to return to search that place again. Without such a record, the search process would be in danger of revisiting the same places over and over again. Inhibition of return can be observed in a variety of tasks, for example, inhibition of return can be associated with an object's colour; Law, Pratt, and Abrahams (1995) and to moving objects; Tipper, Weaver, Jerreat, and Burak (1994b). The issue of whether it is the spatial location or the object that occupies the location that is tagged will be discussed in more detail a little later when we consider whether attention is directed to objects or the space they occupy.

The question of how many successively cued spatial locations can be tagged for inhibition of return is the subject of some debate. Pratt and Abrahams (1995) found that IOR is only associated with the most recently cued location and they suggested that IOR has a very limited memory. However, Tipper, Weaver, and Watson (1996) claimed to find IOR for as many as three successive locations and argued that Pratt and Abraham's experiment was inappropriate, as it only included two possible target locations. Pratt and Abrahams (1996) replied that, in fact, Tipper at al. (1996) had only tested a special case in which subjects could segregate the display into two spatial regions and, as such, did not capture the complexity of real-world environments. When Pratt and Abrahams made the display more complex, they again found that only the most recently cued location was inhibited. There appears to be no resolution to this debate at present, but it is clear that factors such as expectation and perceptual grouping have marked effects on IOR.

In the preceding section, we saw that symbolic cues and task requirements can affect the direction of visual attention. Pursuing the idea that human behaviour is goal directed here, it is interesting to consider another experiment by Hommel, Pratt, Colzato, and Godjin

(2001). Participants were to respond to spatially unpredictable targets, but just prior to display onset they were presented with task-irrelevant arrows or directional words indicating either the correct target location (compatible cues) or an incorrect location (incompatible cues). It was made clear to the participants that the cues were not good predictors of the upcoming target, and that they should be ignored. However, the experimenters expected that the meaning of the symbols would capture attention and direct it to the described location. In their second experiment, they investigated the effect of these cues on IOR. Participants detected stimuli to the left or right of central fixation, having seen an immediately prior peripheral cue at the same or opposite location. As we know RTs are slower when attention must return to the previously attended location. However, in this experiment the target was preceded by a symbolic cue presented centrally in addition to the usual peripheral cue. The experimenters reasoned that if the symbolic cues worked against the IOR produced by the peripheral cues, they would cause a reduced IOR when they correctly indicated target location. Results showed that the direction represented by the central cue did interact with the peripheral cue to affect reaction times. There was less IOR when the word cue was valid than when it was invalid. Therefore the to-be-ignored symbolic cues were automatically processed and moderated the effect of the peripheral cue. This finding blurs the distinction between peripheral and central cues, as the automatic orienting effect usually attributed to peripheral cues can in some cases also occur with symbolic cues.

Movement of the spotlight

Given that cues can direct attention, another question arises. How does attention move over the visual field: Is it an instantaneous shift or does it take time? Is it initially spread over the whole field, narrowing down when the cue indicates a location or does a small spotlight travel to the cued location? Experiments by Posner and his collaborators have been taken to suggest that the spotlight takes time to move over visual space. When the cue indicates only the direction in which the target is likely to appear, rather than the precise location, it is better to have a longer time interval between cue and target when the target is distant from the currently attended point. Tsal (1983) showed that reaction time to a target gets faster as the interval between the cue and the target increases, suggesting that it takes time for the spotlight to travel to the cued location. It appeared as if there was a point of maximum selectivity moving through space, as if it were indeed a spatial spotlight. In a similar experiment, Shulman,

Remington, and McLean (1979) obtained data on near and far, expected and unexpected targets. It was found that response times to targets at far cued locations was equal to near uncued locations. This result is not consistent with the concept of an attentional spotlight moving through space.

Rather than time being used for spatial movement of the spotlight, this time might be better explained by the difference between early visual processing on the fovea and in the periphery. Downing and Pinker (1985) investigated the effect of cueing targets that were presented to different regions of the retina. Subjects were given cues at 10 positions, distributed over peripheral, parafoveal and foveal regions. Downing and Pinker discovered that when the cues were closest to fixation, response times for a valid trial were fast but on invalid trials, there were rapid increases in costs as the target appeared further from the cued location. When cues were presented at more peripheral locations, the costs and benefits were less sharply graded. These results are consistent with the notion that the attentional spotlight can be focused more sharply at foveal locations than in the periphery and that when subjects know in advance where a target will appear, and have time to make an eye movement that allows the target location to be foveated, interference from adjacent distractors will be minimal. At the fovea, we are able to focus attention much more narrowly than in the periphery, so the size of the spotlight is larger or smaller, depending on whereabouts in the visual field the stimulus appears. This ties in with the lateral masking effects we covered earlier. As targets are presented further into the periphery they are interfered with by flankers at a greater distance than targets on the fovea (Bouma, 1970). These effects are related to the size of receptive visual fields, which are larger in the periphery than in the foveal region. Supporting evidence from Humphreys (1981) showed that when subjects fixate a target, distractors as near as only 0.5° of visual angle from the target could be successfully ignored. However, the evidence from Awh et al. (2003) already discussed suggests that the probability of detecting a target also depends on the amount of distractor noise expected in the display.

Variable spotlight or a zoom lens?

If there was only a single spotlight, then dividing attention in the visual field would be difficult. Eriksen and Yeh (1985) were interested to see if subjects could attend to more than one position in a visual display. They used a cueing experiment, with letters distributed around a circle, or "clock face", as the targets. Some positions could contain target letters and the other positions were filled with distractor letters. Stimulus displays were shown for only 150 msec, which is too short for any re-fixation during the lifetime of the display. The cue indicated where the target would appear with a given probability. On some trials, the cue indicated the target position, but, on other trials, the target would appear directly opposite the target. There were three cueing conditions. One where there was an equal probability that the target would be at the cued position on 40% of trials or opposite it on 40% of trials. In the second condition, it was more likely that the target would be where the cue indicated (70%) than opposite the cue (30%). For the third condition, the cue reliably indicated the position of the target on all trials (100%). The control condition had no pre-cue at all.

When there was a pre-cue for the target, subjects responded more quickly than the no-cue control. Also, as the probability that the target would be at the cued location increased, so did the benefit of cueing, but only for the primary cue location where the cue actually appeared. Responses to the secondary location, which was opposite the actual cue, did not show the same benefit, and were slower, even when there was an equal probability that the target would appear in that location (in the 40%:40% case). However, there was a benefit for the secondary location, over the other non-cued location. Eriksen and Yeh interpreted their results as demonstrating that the spotlight could not be divided between the two equally probable locations, but could be rapidly moved from one location to the next. However, Castiello and Umilta (1992) have shown that subjects can split focal attention and simultaneously manipulate two independent attentional foci when objects are located in opposite hemi-fields.

There is also evidence that the "spotlight" can change the width of its focus depending on the task to be performed. Laberge (1983) used a probe to indicate which letter in a five-letter word was to be reported. Subjects "spread" of attention was manipulated. In one condition, they had to categorise the central letter in the row, which was expected to make them focus attention in the middle of the word. In the other condition, they were to categorise the word, which was expected to encourage them to distribute attention over the whole word. Laberge found that response to a probe was affected by whether the subject was attending to the central letter or the whole word. When attention was focused on the centre letter, responses to that letter was faster than any other letter, but when the whole word was attended, responses to any letter position were as fast at that to the centre letter in the focused condition. This result seems to show that the beam of the spotlight can be adjusted according to the task and is not of a fixed size.

Broadbent (1982) summarised the data on the selectivity in visual displays and suggested that we should "think of selectivity as like a searchlight, with the option of altering the focus. When it is unclear where the beam should go, it is kept wide. When something seems to be happening, or a cue indicates one location rather than another, the beam sharpens and moves to the point of maximum importance" (p. 271). Evidence consistent with this view came later, from an experiment by Eriksen and Murphy (1987). In this experiment subjects were to decide whether the underlined target letter was an "A" or a "U". The target and the distractor could be the same or different, e.g. AA or AU and the separation between target and distractor was varied. We know from all the work on flanker compatibility effects discussed already, and especially the work of Eriksen and colleagues, that when the target and distractors have incompatible responses, there will be interference unless the separation between target and distractor is more than about 1°. In Eriksen and Murphy's (1987) experiment, on some trials subjects were given a pre-cue indicating where the target would appear, but on other trials there was no pre-cue. When subjects were given a pre-cue, a response incompatible distractor close to the target caused more interference than one further away, as we would expect, because near incompatible distractors usually do cause interference. However, when there was no pre-cue, incompatible distractors interfered whether or not there were near or far. Eriksen and Murphy (1987) proposed that a better metaphor for visual attention would be a "zoom lens". Initially, attention is widely distributed with parallel processing of all elements in the display. In this case, all distractors will activate their responses. However, with a pre-cue, the lens, or attention, can be narrowed down so that only the elements directly in the focus of the lens will activate their relevant responses. Incompatible items outside this area do not, therefore interfere. However, we have already mentioned recent experiments by Lavie (1995) and Awh et al. (2003) that suggest the size to which the spotlight closes down could depend on the perceptual load of the whole task and the distractor environment. So, a number of task factors can influence the nature of selective visual attention.

Local and global processing

In everyday life, we sometimes want to attend to a whole object or to a small part of a larger object. We can attend to a tree, a branch on a tree or a leaf on a branch, but do we have to attend to the tree before its local details? Navon (1977) presented subjects with large letters, made up of small letters. (See Figure 3.2.) The large letter is the global shape and the small letters are the local shapes. With such stimuli it is possible to arrange for the local and global properties to be congruent, for example an E composed of small Es, or incongruent, an E composed of small Ss.

Navon showed that in the incongruent condition response to the small letters was interfered with by the global letter identity, but local letter identity did not interfere with global letter identification. This result was interpreted as showing that attention is directed to the coarse-grain global properties of an object before it is directed to analysis of fine-grain local properties. However, Martin (1979) manipulated the sparsity of the local elements in the global shape and discovered that in some cases it is possible for local processing to take precedence. Evidence seems to suggest that perceptual factors are important in determining whether local or global properties take precedence in attentional processing. Whichever is the case, there are data to indicate that it is difficult to divide visual attention between the local and global attributes of an object. Sperling and Melchner (1978) showed that subjects found it more difficult to divide visual attention between large letters surrounding small letters than between large letters surrounding degraded large letters. Shiffrin (1988) suggests attention focuses on one size or another and time is required to switch between size settings. Shiffrin views the data regarding global or local precedence as equivocal and thinks that although both levels are generally processed in parallel precedence may vary with experimental conditions.

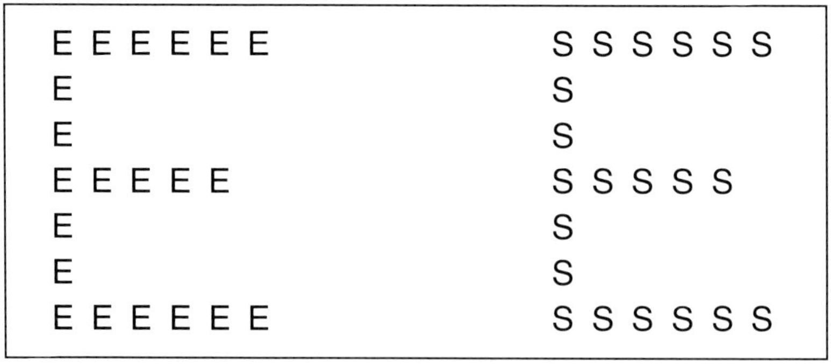

Figure 3.2 Examples of compound figures with local and global properties. In the congruent stimulus the global property, large E is the same as the local property small E. However, in the incongruent stimulus the global property "E" is incongruent with the local property "S".

```
E E E E E          S S S S S
E                  S
E                  S
E E E E            S S S S
E                  S
E                  S
E E E E E          S S S S S
```

Stoffer (1993) examined the time course of changing attention between the local and global levels in compound stimuli. He proposed that attention not only has to change spatial extent, but also has to change between representational levels. Clearly, if attention changes from operating on the global shape to a local element, there will have to be a zooming up or down of attentional focus. Stoffer compared the RT–SOA function in two conditions where subjects were to attend to either the local or global property. In one condition, involuntary shifts were cued by an abrupt onset that specified the spatial extent of the area to be attended and, in the other, voluntary changes were indicated by a symbolic instruction. Thus the task is analogous to Posner's (1980) spatial cueing experiments using a peripheral or central cue. Validity of the cues was manipulated and a cost–benefit analysis was performed. Results showed that attentional zooming and attention shifting are similar at a functional level in that they can both be controlled either involuntarily (exogenous cue) or voluntarily (endogenous cue). However, zooming to the local level took longer than zooming to the global level. Stoffer suggests that the global level is usually attended to first and this additional time reflects an additional step that is required to reorient to the local level of representation. There are many studies directed to discovering the variables involved in local and global processing. Luna, Marcos-Ruiz, and Merino (1995) review the evidence to that date.

Hemispheric differences in attention

Studies of patients have shown that the right cerebral hemisphere is biased toward global processing, while the left hemisphere is biased toward local processing. Robertson, Lamb, and Knight (1988) demonstrated that patients with right hemisphere lesions found attention to the global level most difficult while patients with left hemisphere lesions had most difficulty processing local attributes of a stimulus. Posner and Petersen (1990) argue that the hemispheres are individually specialised in the level of detail to which attention is allocated. Further specialisation is reviewed by Posner (1993), who points out that unilateral visual neglect, which we discuss in detail in the next section, is much more likely to follow right rather than left parietal lesions. This finding has led to the assumption that the right hemisphere controls attention to both sides of space. Corbetta et al. (1993) studied visual attention using PET. They found that the right superior parietal cortex is activated when attention is shifted to both the right and to the left. However, the left parietal cortex is only active during shifts to the right. It is also believed that in spatial cueing experiments, not only does the cue serve to orient attention, but also acts as a warning signal that increases the efficiency of, or enhances, signal processing. The right hemisphere is thought to be involved in maintaining enhancement, because patients with right-sided lesions have difficulty maintaining alertness during sustained attention tasks and vigilance tasks. Robertson and Manly (1999) suggest that the right hemisphere is more important for sustaining attention than shifting it and that deficits such as neglect, extinction and simultanagnosia, which we are about to cover, may result from a more general effect of arousal, impaired spatial attention and reduced attentional capacity.

Visual neglect

Evidence for the importance of orienting visual attention has come from studies of neuropsychological patients who have difficulty with the normally simple orienting task. Imagine a patient who bumps into objects in the left-hand side of visual space, who only eats the food from the right-hand side of the plate. It would be easy to imagine that this person is blind to one side of visual space and that there is a visual defect underlying the problem. When asked to copy a picture or draw an object, patients only draw one half of the picture or objects within the picture. (See Figure 3.3a.) Given a page of lines to cross, they only cross lines on one half of the page (Albert, 1973). (See Figure 3.3b.) The intriguing thing about patients with neglect is that they do not notice anything "odd" about their drawings or performance on crossing-out tasks.

If it can be shown that such a patient is not blind in the neglected region of space, there has to be another reason why they do not acknowledge the presence of objects placed there. These patients are not visually blind, but act as if they have not perceived one side of visual space. The very term "neglect" suggests that the explanation may lie in the patients' inattention to the contra-lateral side of space. If inattention is the explanation then theories of attention should be able to account for the behaviour observed in these patients.

Earlier we discussed Posner's work on endogenous and exogenous attention. We saw that attention can be facilitated by a cue that appears to automatically orient attention to the cued side of space, e.g. Posner (1980). Posner and his colleagues carried out a number of experiments on patients with unilateral visual neglect using the cueing technique. It was demonstrated that with valid cues, i.e. those

Figure 3.3a Copying performance of a flower and spontaneous drawing of a clock that a typical neglect patient might produce.

TARGET

COPY

SPONTANEOUS DRAWING

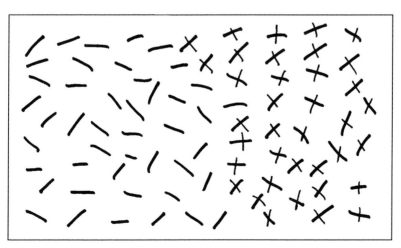

Figure 3.3b Idealised performance of a neglect patient on the lines cancellation test.

that reliably predicted where the target would appear, there was no great difference between targets presented in the neglected or non-neglected side. However, when the cue was invalid, i.e. appeared on the opposite side to where the target was presented, performance was very much more severely impaired than in normal subjects. Posner, Walker, Friedrick, and Rafal (1984) proposed that three components of visual attention were needed to explain these results. First, the ability to engage visual attention on a target; second, the ability to disengage attention from the target and, third, the ability to shift attention to the new target. As there was no difference in effect of a valid cue in either visual field, Posner argued that patients with neglect have no problem with the engagement of attention. Patients also seem to be able to shift attention, but when the cue is to the neglected side and the patient had previously been engaged on the non-neglected side, it appeared that visual attention could not be disengaged to move into the neglected area of space. Further studies have tested patients with thalamic lesions, specifically the pulvinar nucleus, who appear to have difficulty engaging attention to the side of space contra-lateral to the lesion, e.g. Rafal and Posner (1987). This belief is supported by PET studies by Laberge and Buchsbaum (1990), which indicated increased activity in the pulvinar nucleus during attention tasks in which ignoring a stimulus is important. Therefore, the pulvinar is not only involved in engaging attention, but also in preventing attention from being directed to other unwanted stimuli.

Another deficit often associated with unilateral visual neglect is visual extinction. Patients with this problem have parieto-occipital lesions and have no difficulty in identifying a single object presented visually. However, if two objects are presented simultaneously, they do not seem to "see" the object presented contra-lateral to the lesion. In this condition, patients can name an object presented to their visual field contra-lateral to the lesion, but only when there is nothing presented to their good side. When two stimuli are presented concurrently to both the good and bad side, the patient is only able to report the stimulus appearing in the good side of visual space. It is as if the presence of a stimulus in the good field extinguishes the response to the stimulus in the damaged field. However, Volpe, LeDoux, and Gazzaniga (2000) provide evidence that patients who exhibit extinction do not have a visual deficit but are experiencing a higher order attentional problem. Even when two objects are presented simultaneously, for example, an apple to the good field and a comb to the damaged field so that the patient only reports seeing the apple, the patient can make accurate judgements about whether the two objects are the same or different. When questioned about the basis for their judgement, the patient cannot give any verbal description of the extinguished stimulus; they claim not to know what the stimulus was although they know it is not the same as the stimulus that they are able to report from the good field. Of course, it might be possible if this comparison is made on basic perceptual properties if the pair of objects, an apple and a comb have different shapes. A simple shape discrimination judgement would support accurate performance. However, Berti, Allport, Driver, Deines, Oxbury, and Oxbury (1992) have shown that same/different judgements can still be made in conditions where "same" is two different photographic views of the some object. As the photographs have different perceptual properties but the same *conceptual* properties, it seems clear that extinction is affecting high-level representations of the objects rather than earlier perceptual levels. Volpe et al. (2000) suggest that patients are able to reach a level of processing for the extinguished stimulus that allows comparison between objects to be made, but does not support conscious awareness. This evidence suggests that despite "inattention" to an object its semantics are available but do not allow overt response. We shall discuss these findings again in Chapter 10 when we consider the nature and possible functions of consciousness.

Neglect of imagined space

So far, we have considered neglect in terms of what the patient "sees", either in terms of high- or low-level representations, based on analysis of a visual input from the external environment. What about internal representations of the imagination? Bisiach and Luzatti (1978) argue that neglect is the result of the subject failing to construct an internal representation of one side of visual space. They asked two patients with neglect to describe a scene that they knew very well, the Piazza del Duomo in Milan. When asked to report the scene as if they were standing on the steps of the cathedral, the patients reported only one side of the piazza, not mentioning any of the buildings that lay on their neglected side. Then the patients were asked to imagine that they had crossed the piazza and report what they could see when facing the cathedral. Now they reported all the buildings they had omitted from the other perspective and omitted all those previously reported. This demonstration is clear evidence against visual neglect being a result of a visual deficit. Further evidence for neglect operating at different levels of representation are found in patients with neglect dyslexia, to be covered shortly.

Objects groups and space

Some psychologists have suggested that attention is directed to perceptual groups according to Gestalt principles. Prinzmetal (1981) looked at how people grouped features in simple displays. He tested two hypotheses. First, that features from the same or neighbouring locations in space are likely to be joined and, second, that features from the same perceptual group are likely to be joined. In all his experiments, he found that the perceptual group principle predicted performance best. Merikle (1980) showed that perceptual grouping can influence the partial report superiority effect in an iconic memory experiment. Merikle suggested that spatial cues like a particular row or a cue-like colour were effective for partial report because they formed a perceptual group that was easily selected. There is no partial report superiority on the basis of a category distinction, he argued, because a category difference does not produce a perceptual group. Merikle found that when categorically different items in a display also form a perceptual group, they can act as an effective cue for selective report.

Driver and Baylis (1989) thought that distractors that are close to a target may cause interference, not simply because they are close to the target, but because items that are close together form a good perceptual group. They did an experiment to distinguish between the spatial spotlight and perceptual grouping hypotheses. The task they chose was a version of that used by Eriksen and Eriksen (1974) in which we have seen that response compatibility effects are found for flankers near the target, but not for flankers more distant than one degree of visual angle. Driver and Baylis's manipulation involved grouping distractors with the target by common movement. It is a well-established Gestalt principle that items that move together are grouped together. The task was to respond to the central letter in a horizontal display of five letters, where the central letter moved with the outer letters of the array, but the intermediate letters remained stationary. Two alternative predictions are made by the two hypotheses. A spotlight account predicts that distractors nearer the target will cause most interference, whereas the grouping hypothesis predicts that flankers grouped with the target will interfere most although they were farther away.

Results supported the perceptual grouping hypothesis, in that distant distractors that moved with the target produced more interference than stationary distractors that were close to the target. (Unfortunately, Kramer, Tham, and Yeh (1991) were unable to replicate this result.) Driver and Baylis believe that it is better to think of attention being assigned to perceptual groups rather than to regions of contiguous space, because in the real world we need to attend to objects moving in a cluttered environment. Imagine watching an animal moving through undergrowth. Here we can only see parts of the animal distributed over space, but we see the animal as one object because we group the parts together on common movement.

There is increasing evidence that we do attend to objects rather than regions of space. Duncan (1984) showed that subjects found it easier to judge two attributes that belonged to one object than to judge the same attributes when they belonged to two different objects. The stimuli in Duncan's experiment were a rectangle with a gap in one side over which was drawn a tilted line. Both the rectangle and the line had two attributes. The rectangle was long or short with the gap either to the left or the right of centre. The line was either dotted or dashed and was tilted either clockwise or anticlockwise. Duncan asked subjects to make one or two judgements on the possible four attributes. When two judgements were required, say gap position and tilt of line, subjects were worse at making the second judgement. However, when both the judgements related to the same object, say gap position and the length of the box, performance was good. Duncan proposed that we attend to objects and when the judgements we make are about two objects, attention must be switched from one object to another, taking time.

Object-based inhibition of return

Object-based attention is clearly very important. But if you remember, Posner (1980) showed that the attentional spotlight could be summoned by spatial cues and covertly directed to locations in space. An associated effect, inhibition of return, was hypothesised to result from the tagging of spatial locations. What if you were searching for an object, found it, but then the object moved? If attention were spatially based, you would be left looking at an empty location! Tipper, Driver, and Weaver (1991) were able to show that inhibition of return is object based. They cued attention to a moving object and found that the inhibition moved with the object to its new location. Tipper et al. (1991) propose that it is objects, not space, that are inhibited and that inhibition of return ensures that previously examined objects are not searched again.

Object-based visual neglect

The attentional explanation for unilateral visual neglect given earlier, assumed that it was space that was neglected rather than objects.

However, there is an increasing body of evidence in favour of the suggestion that attention can be object based. Indeed, the amount neglected by a patient will depend on what they are asked to attend to. In Bisiach's experiment, the object was the Piazza del Doumo; what if the object had been the Doumo itself? or if the patient had been asked to draw a single window? Then the patient would have neglected half of the building or half of the window. Driver and Halligan (1991) did an experiment in which they pitted environmental space against object-centred space. If a patient with visual neglect is given a picture of two objects about which to make a judgement and that picture is set in front of the patient so that both the environmental axis and object axis are equivalent, then it is impossible to determine which of the two axes are responsible for the observed neglect. Driver and Halligan (1991) devised a task in which patients had to judge whether two nonsense shapes were the same or different. If the part of the one shape that contained the crucial difference was in neglected space when the environmental and object axes were equivalent, the patient was unable to judge same or different. (See Figure 3.4.)

Driver and Halligan wanted to discover what would happen when the paper on which the stimuli were drawn was rotated so that the crucial part of the object moved from neglected space, across the environmental axis into what should now be non-neglected space. Results showed that patients still neglected one side of the object, despite the object appearing in the good side of environmental space.

Figure 3.4 Stimuli used by Driver and Halligan (1991). In (a) the object-centred axis and midline are identical and therefore confounded, but in (b) the feature distinguishing the two shapes lies to the left of the object-centred axis, but to the right of the midline.

From Driver and Halligan (1991). Copyright (1991) Erlbaum (UK) Taylor and Francis, Hove, UK. Reprinted with permission from the publisher and the author.

(a)

(b)

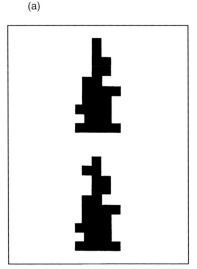
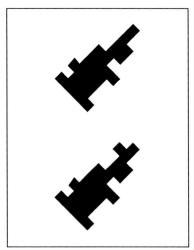

This experiment demonstrates that neglect can be of one side of an object's principal axis, not simply of one side of the space occupied by that object.

Behrmann and Tipper (1994) and Tipper and Behrmann (1996) have recently demonstrated the importance of object-based attentional mechanisms in patients with visual neglect. In their experiments, they presented the subjects with an outline drawing of two circles connected by a horizontal bar, a "barbell", which was arranged across the midline of visual space. A target might appear in either ball of the barbell, so that it was in either neglected or non-neglected space. As expected, patients with neglect showed very poor performance when targets appeared on the left, in their neglected field. Control patients were able to do the task equally well in either visual field. The question that Behrmann and Tipper were interested in was this: What would happen to patient's performance when the barbell rotated? If attention is object based rather than environmentally based, would visual attention move with the barbell if it was rotated? In the rotating condition, the barbell appeared on the screen, remained stationary for a short while and then rotated through 180°. This rotation took 1.7 seconds. The experimenters predicted that if attention were directed only to the left and right of environmental space, then performance in the rotating condition would be exactly the same as in the stationary condition. However, if attention is directed to the left and right of the object, then as rotation moves the left of the object to the right of space and vice versa, performance in the rotating condition should be the reverse of that when the barbell was stationary. Although not all patients showed exactly the same effects, it was discovered that in the rotating condition there was an interaction between condition (static versus moving) and the side on which the target appeared. For controls, there were no differences in target detection rates in the static and rotating condition and no left–right asymmetries. Two patients failed to detect the target on 28% of trials despite its arriving on their "good" side. Two other patients showed equivalent performance for both left and right targets, but overall, patients were slower to detect the target when it ended in the right-hand position (that is, the good side!) and four showed significantly better performance on the left side (the neglected side) in the moving condition. Remember that, in the static condition, all patients showed poorer performance for the left (neglected) side. The results show that when the object of attention moves, target detection can be better on the "neglected" than the "good" side of visual space. If the basis for visual neglect was environmental space, then irrespective of any movement of the object, targets falling in neglected space should be detected far less well than those falling in attended space. Behrmann and Tipper's results cast doubt on this explanation of visual neglect. The performance of these patients might be explained by an attentional cueing effect. As discussed earlier, Posner et al. (1984) have argued that neglect patients have difficulty disengaging their attention from the right side of space. Possibly, when the barbell rotates patients have difficulty disengaging from the right side of the object and attention is drawn into left-sided neglected space, so when a target appears there, response is faster. Behrmann and Tipper (1994) argue that while this explanation may hold for improved performance in the neglected field, it cannot account for impaired performance on the "good" side, as attention should always be biased to right-sided space in these subjects. Instead, Behrmann and Tipper propose that attention access both environmental- and object-based representations of space. In the static condition, both reference frames are congruent, with good attention directed to the right and poor attention to the left. However, when the barbell moves, attention is drawn with the object so that the "poor" attention that was directed to the left of the object moves to the right and the "good" attention that was directed to the right of the object moves to the left. This explanation could account for both left-side facilitation and right-sided inhibition in the rotating condition. As in the experiment by Driver and Halligan (1991), these data demonstrate that neglect may be based on different frames of reference in different conditions.

While there does seem to be some evidence for visual neglect having an object-based component, Behrmann and Moskovitch (1994) point out that object-based effects are not always found. They suggest that environmental space is usually the dominant coordinate system and that object-based effects may only be found under conditions where stimuli have handedness or asymmetry in their representations that require them to be matched in some way relative to the object's main axis.

Other theoretical accounts of disorders of visual attention

Some theoretical explanations of both normal vision and visual disorders involve the argument that attentional behaviour is the outcome of an integrated brain state. Duncan (1999) puts forward the view that attentional functions are distributed over a number of brain areas and systems:

Generally attention is seen as a widely distributed state, in which several brain systems converge to work on different properties and action implications of the same selected object. (p. 126)

The hypothesis is that multiple sources of information activating different brain systems responsive to visual input are subject to competitive processing. If one source of information is enhanced, then another is inhibited and the most active pattern of activity gains dominance or control. We have already met a similar argument from Desimone and Duncan (1995) applied to visual selection from among distractors. With respect to neuropsychological patients, Duncan (1999) proposes that the attentional bias observed in unilateral neglect and the phenomenon of extinction can be explained in terms of damaged areas losing the competition to dominate processing. Duncan suggests that a lateral bias is the consequence of lateralised brain injury and that right parietal lesions are not the only predictor of bias in neglect, simlutanagnosia and extinction.

Balint's syndrome

Patients who exhibit Balint's syndrome usually have posterior parietal lesions. A classical description was given by Balint (1909) but up-to-date evidence can be found in Jeannerod (1997). Patients have severe deficits in spatial tasks. Not only do they have difficulty orienting to visual stimuli, but they fail to orient their arm and hand correctly when reaching and do not make normal adjustments to finger shapes when grasping. They may also fail to orient in other modalities, such as hearing. When eye–hand coordination is required in a task, the deficit in these patients is most pronounced. Optic ataxia, as this difficulty is called, has been discovered to follow damage to the superior parietal lobule (Perenin & Vighetto, 1988). Patients often have difficulty judging length, orientation and distance and may have lost the ability to assemble parts into a whole. Generally, object-oriented actions are severely impaired. We have already discussed neglect and extinction in the preceding sections, but will now add another two patients with Balint's syndrome, studied by Humphreys, Romani, Olson, Riddoch, and Duncan (1994).

In this study, patients were presented with either two words or two pictures simultaneously, above and below fixation. Both patients showed extinction when presented with two words or two pictures, but when a picture and a word were presented, pictures tended to extinguish words. In another condition, stimuli were presented in the same location so that they were overlapping. When a single stimulus was presented, the patients were, as expected, always correct, but one patient, GK, reported both the picture and the word on 16/40 trials and only the picture the rest of the time. In their second experiment, Humphreys et al. (1994) presented stimuli in a vertical arrangement, with the target on fixation and the other stimulus either above or below it. Spatial selection should have favoured the fixated word, but again, although a word on its own could be reported, when a picture was simultaneously presented, GK showed extinction of the word by a picture.

Humphreys et al. conjectured that pictures might dominate words because they are "closed" shapes. Displays were constructed in which the shapes of a square and a diamond differed in their degree of closure. This was achieved by drawing only parts of the shapes. In the good closure condition, the corners specified the shapes but the sides were missing, while in the other, weaker closure condition, the lines of the sides specified the shape, with the corners missing. The task was to detect whether a square was present. Results showed that both patients showed a preference for squares with good closure, i.e. those made up from the corners. However, the patients were at chance when asked to decide if the square had been presented above or below fixation. Despite detecting the square, its spatial location was unknown to the patients. Humphreys et al. argue that extinction can be based on properties of the object, in this case, closure. Pictures have shape closure but words do not, hence pictures dominate words. Further, even when spatial selection and localisation are poor, these object properties can mediate selection from the visual display.

These patients had suffered damage to the brain areas in the parietal lobes that are normally involved in spatial perception. However, there was no damage to those areas in the occipito-parietal region that process the properties of objects. Humphreys et al. suggest that closed shapes dominate over open shapes and without spatial information to guide a shift between objects, extinction occurs. In an intact system, they suggest:

> There is normally coordination of the outcomes of competition within the separate neural areas coding each property, making the shape, location and other properties of a single object available concurrently for the control of behaviour. (p. 359)

Explicit in this quote is the next question we have to address: How are the multiple sources of information pertaining to an object brought together in order for us to perceive a world of unified objects and how is the visual environment segregated into those objects? We shall meet Balint's patients again to help us answer this question in the following chapter.

Summary

Visual attention has been likened to a spotlight that enhances the processing under its beam. Posner (1980) experimented with central and peripheral cues and found that the attentional spotlight could be summoned by either cue, but peripheral cues could not be ignored whereas central cues could. Posner proposed two attentional systems: an endogenous system controlled voluntarily by the subject and an exogenous system, outside the subject's control. Muller and Rabbitt (1989) showed that exogenous, or in their terms *automatic* "reflexive", orienting could sometimes be modified by voluntary control. Symbolic information can also produce involuntary shifts of attention Pratt and Hommel (2003). Although a cue usually facilitates target processing, there are some circumstances in which there is a delay in target processing (Maylor, 1985). This inhibition of return has been interpreted as evidence for a spatial tagging of searched locations to help effective search. Inhibition of return can also be directed to moving objects (Tipper, Weaver, and Houghton, 1994a). Other experimenters have tried to measure the speed with which the spotlight moves. The apparent movement of the spotlight might be more to do with the speed with which different areas of the retina can code information. Other researchers asked if the spotlight could be divided but concluded that division was not possible. It was suggested that a zoom lens might be a better analogy than a spotlight as its seems that the size of the spotlight depends what is being attended (Laberge, 1983). Lavie (1995) argued that the size to which the spotlight could close down depended on the perceptual load of the task. Load theory of attention appears to resolve the early–late debate by explaining how selective attention may operate at different levels depending on two selective attention mechanisms: one that operates when perceptual load is high to reduce distractor processing because the perceptual load has exhausted perceptual capacity; another cognitive control mechanism that reduces interference from perceived distractors in conditions where perceptual load is low, as long as cognitive load is low enough to maintain current task priorities. The right cerebral hemispheres are specialised for global processing and the left for local processing and attention can shift between these levels. The hemispheres are also specialised for orienting (Posner & Petersen, 1990), with the right parietal area able to orient attention to either side of space, but the left parietal area only able to orient to the right. Thus, right parietal lesions often give rise to visual neglect of the left side of space. The right hemisphere is also involved in maintaining arousal. Posner et al. (1984) believed there are three components of visual attention: disengage, shift and engage. Patients with visual neglect have no difficulty engaging or shifting attention, but if attention is cued to the neglected side they have difficulty disengaging from the non-neglected side. It has been demonstrated that patients can make judgements about stimuli in neglected space, even when the stimuli can only be judged on a semantic property. Despite no awareness of the stimulus on the neglected, or extinguished side, and visual "attention" not being directed there, semantics on the neglected side have been processed. Neglect can also be on one side of imagined, or representational, space. Rather than space per se, psychologists are becoming increasingly interested in object-based effects in attention. Driver and Tipper (1989) showed that objects that formed a group by common movement were attended to despite not being spatially contiguous. This is evidence against a purely spatial spotlight account of visual attention. Further, neglect can be to one side of object-centred space and inhibition of return can apply to objects rather than their spatial location. Extinction in patients with Balint's syndrome, who have severe spatial deficits, was shown to be based on the perceptual property of closure. As these patients have no location information, the coordination of perceptual codes that normally allows selection was not possible and the perceptually stronger representation dominated, leading to extinction (Humphreys et al., 1994).

Further reading

- Allport, A. (1989). Visual attention. In M. I. Posner (Ed.). *Foundations of cognitive science. A Bradford book.* Cambridge, MA: MIT Press.

  A review of the biological, neuropsychological and psychological evidence at the time.
- Parkin, A. J. (1996). *Explorations in cognitive neuropsychology.* Oxford: Blackwell.

  A good introduction to studying patients. Chapter 5 is on visual neglect.

- Posner, M. I., & Dehaene, S. (2000). Attentional networks. In M. S. Gazzaniga (Ed.). *Cognitive neuroscience: A reader*. Oxford: Blackwell.

    An overview of orienting and underlying brain mechanisms.

Combining the attributes of objects and visual search 4

One object but many attributes: The binding problem

There is overwhelming experimental, neuropsychological, anatomical and physiological evidence that the visual system analyses difference dimensions of the visual environment over multiple specialised modules and pathways. What we have not yet considered is how the separate codes are combined so that we perceive unified objects. Clearly, this is crucial. We do not inhabit a world of fragmented colours, shapes and meanings, but interact with meaningful objects that are segregated such that the correct attributes of individual objects are combined. The question of how this is achieved is called the "binding problem". Of course, we do not usually see one object in isolation. In a cluttered visual environment with many objects present, not only do the features of a single object need to be bound together, but also the features that belong to different objects must be segregated. In addition, when we experience objects in real life, they have not only visual properties such as colour and shape, they also have other sensory properties such as what they sound like or feel like. So, not only is there the problem of binding visual properties, there is also the problem of binding across sensory modalities. We shall discuss auditory and crossmodal attention and how crossmodality binding might be achieved in the next chapter. For the present, we shall limit our discussion to vision.

Experimental evidence for the separability of identity and location information

In Chapter 2, we reviewed studies that showed that the colour, identity and location of objects can dissociate and in Chapter 3, we have seen that there is conflicting evidence on the level of processing achieved by object attributes prior to selection. Numerous studies demonstrate that early in the lifetime of a brief visual display colour, identity and location are available, but are not stabilised together to allow accurate report. Sometimes identity or categorised information can influence selection, sometimes not. Participants make frequent mislocation errors, incorrectly reporting a letter adjacent to the target, apparently knowing "what" the letter was, but not exactly "where" it was. The interference effects that occur appear to differ according to task demands and provide conflicting evidence on what information combined prior to selection. We have also noted in the previous chapter that in Balint's patients there is a problem in making the properties of objects concurrently available for the control of behaviour. Here, we shall introduce more evidence for separate codes in the brain and then consider how all this information might be recombined into integrated objects to allow selective report and control actions.

Attentional dyslexia

Further evidence for the separability of "what" and "where", as well as for categorisation prior to selection, is reported by Shallice and Warrington (1977). Two patients with tumours in the left parietal lobe were tested for reading ability. Shallice and Warrington found that these patients could read whole words perfectly well, but were very inaccurate when asked to selectively report single letters from a specified letter position within a word. However, the letters that the patients did report were not random errors, but mislocations, i.e. patients reported a letter that was present in the display, but from the wrong location. These patients seemed to be performing in a similar way to normal subjects doing bar probe tasks, where errors were most likely to be reports of letters adjacent to the target, e.g. Eriksen and Rohrbaugh, 1970. The letter identities were available for report, but not accurately integrated with their correct location. Attentional dyslexic patients also show behaviourial similarities to normal experimental subjects engaged in lateral masking experiments, e.g. Eriksen and Eriksen, 1974, in that when there is a categorical difference within the display, so that the letter to be reported is flanked by digits, performance is almost perfect. The categorical difference between the target and distractors, allows selection on the basis of the "most active letter" and does not require the integration or stabilisation of location and identity. Another finding was that when several word were presented simultaneously, these patients mixed words together. So, for example, given "WIN FED" the patient might report "fin fed". Again, a similar effect can be found in normal subjects, when words are briefly presented and followed by a pattern mask, e.g. Allport, 1977. Letters are not mixed up randomly, but keep their word position. These errors are called "migration errors". There would appear to be some conflict between the finding that when report of a single letter is required, the attentional dyslexic has difficulty making a within category discrimination on the basis of location, but when given multiple words, letters migrate according to their position in the word. Yet the errors of an attentional dyslexic patient can be produced in the normal subject under experimental manipulations. Within words, higher level knowledge can constrain letter position so although the letters migrate they do so to preserve "wordness", producing migration errors. When selection is required from within the word, on the basis of an external verbal cue, accurate selection demands accurate localisation to coordinates outside the word. The underlying reasons for the pattern of impairment is not clear, but the fact that similar results can be found in both patients and normals supports the view that categorical information is available prior to attentional selection.

Neurophysiological evidence for independent codes

Advances in neurophysiology have revealed quite clear specialisations in cells, pathways and regions of the brain. Evidence from cognitive neuropsychology points to a variety of quite specific deficits of attentional processing. For example, there is good evidence for two streams of visual information analysis in association cortex. One, a ventral stream that projects from V1 to V4, TEO and TE and is responsible for analysing "what" an object is in terms of colour, shape and other features early in the stream and combined objects further on. A second, dorsal stream, projects to parietal cortex and is responsible for analysing "where" an object is (Posner & Petersen, 1990; Ungerleider

& Mishkin, 1982; Zeki, 1980; Zeki, Watson, Leuck, Friston, Kennard, & Frackowiak, 1991). Goodale and Milner (1992) proposed that the main function of the dorsal stream of the visual cortex is to guide actions. They believed that rather than a "what" and a "where" stream, the streams should be considered as a "what" and a "how" stream. Recently, Rizzolatti and Matelli (2003) have proposed that the dorsal stream is concerned with how to make actions, but can be further differentiated into two distinct functional systems, the dorso-dorsal stream, which is involved in the online control of actions, and the ventro-dorsal stream, responsible for action organisation. The ventro-dorsal stream is also hypothesised to play "a crucial part in space perception and action understanding" (p. 146). The relation between perception and action will be covered in Chapter 6.

Examination of the abilities of neuropsychological patients with localised brain damage are also consistent with specialisation of function. For example, achromatopsia is a selective loss of colour vision, but such patients can still perceive shape and motion. Conversely, the ability to perceive motion can be lost independently in patients suffering akinetopsia (Zeki et al., 1991). In intact participants, modern scanning techniques such as FMRI and PET reveal different brain areas when a response is required to different features, such as colour, shape or motion in the same display.

Putting it all together

All this evidence emphasises the importance of understanding and explaining how different attributes belonging to the same object in a visual display are accurately combined to control response. Even before all this information was gathered, by 1980 cognitive theories were beginning to be developed to approach this issue, e.g. Allport, 1977 and Coltheart, 1980a, who were considering the problem of combining multiple codes and how an understanding of this process might help us to understand why "early" attributes were good selective cues while, despite all the evidence for its availability, "late" semantic codes were poor selective cues. Also, in 1980, the first version of feature integration theory (FIT) was proposed by Treisman and Gelade. According to Quinlan (2003): "It is no exaggeration to say that FIT was one of the most influential and important theories of visual information processing in the last quarter of the twentieth century" (p. 643).

Coltheart's proposal

Coltheart (1980a) proposed a cognitive theory of iconic memory that would predict the result of response interference like the "HHH" effect found by Eriksen and Shultz (1979) and the "oh", "zero" effect found by Jonides and Gleitman, discussed in Chapter 2. It also accounts for the differential effectiveness of position and identity in selecting information from brief visual display. Coltheart suggested that the identity of an item is stored early in the lifetime of the display and this representation is relatively stable, decaying more slowly than the physical attributes of the letter such as colour and location. The physical or episodic information is unstable and will decay rapidly unless processed further. Although the precise nature of this further processing is not clearly specified by Coltheart, it involves the integration of the semantic and episodic information, i.e. what and where, by something called the "lexical monitor". The lexical monitor coordinates the episodic and semantic memories relating to a particular item. Unless these two sources of information are stabilised together, the identity information, which is considered to be rather like the activation of a lexical entry or logogen, dies away and cannot be reported. However, the fact that the lexical entries have been accessed, and hence activated, means that residual unconscious activation can still lead to semantic facilitation or interference effects.

In a partial report experiment, the lexical monitor can stabilise a subset of the array on the basis of the physical information tagged to the identities, but as the lexical monitor can only stabilise four or five items before the physical information has decayed, this limits whole report performance. Coltheart's model explains the effect of category differences on report, in that when the lexical entries are semantically close, from the same category, there are several competing entries vying for the attention of the lexical monitor, which must decide on the basis of physical information which is the target letter and therefore which lexical entry to stabilise. When there is a category difference between the target and distractors, the decision is much easier, because as the subject is primed to detect a letter and as only one letter is activated from the display, the lexical monitor has no choices to make. According to Coltheart, patients with attentional dyslexia have a faulty lexical monitor, which means when selection necessitates integrating physical and lexical information, in the case where one letter must be reported from among other letters, the patient cannot do the task. However, when a category difference in the display allows selection on the basis of the most active member of the target set, selection is possible. Migration errors are also a result of poor integration between where the letters are and what they are. When the only constraint is top-down lexical knowledge, letters will move to appropriate word positions, but not necessarily in the correct word.

Here we have a model within which all letters are processed to a post-categorical stage, but selection is based on physical information. It does not have to assume that an effective selection cue is a reflection of the degree of processing that has been achieved by what is selected. This is an important conceptual point and a similar view was put forward by Allport (1977). If letters are categorically processed prior to selection, but selection is effected by physical information, then these different sources of information must be combined or bound together in some way. Coltheart's lexical monitor is not very concrete, but, as we shall see the means by which the brain binds different attributes of the same object together is a topic of much current research.

Van der Heijden (1981, 1993) has called the process by which categorised information is selected on the basis of "early" perceptual information "post-categorical filtering". If we accept this view of selection to be correct, the "early–late" debate could be resolved. Items are fully processed to a "late" stage, but selection can be based on "early" physical features, like position or colour, which as we have seen, need to be coordinated or bound together with the identity. Can this model also explain why there are, under certain conditions, interference effects that suggest feature level interference? Like the "BB" effect of Bjork and Murray (1997). Presumably, here, the lexical monitor has two similar responses that are also closely similar at a featural level. In this case only spatial separation or location can be used to distinguish the target from the non-target and a fine, time-consuming discrimination will be required to determine which is which, so increasing reaction time.

Visual search with focal attention

Coltheart's lexical monitor was proposed to account for performance in tasks involving brief, pattern masked displays that relied on iconic memory. However, visual information usually persists in time and we can search the visual scene by making eye movements. Therefore, there is another question concerning visual search. How does attention find a designated target in a cluttered visual field? It is to this question that we now turn.

Feature integration theory

Feature integration theory (FIT) is a model for the perception of objects. The theory is constantly being updated but was originally proposed by Treisman and Gelade (1980). Treisman (1988, 1993, 1999) provides useful summaries of the status of FIT at those dates. Feature integration theory is in a state of constant evolution, frequently being updated to take account of fresh data and new ideas are constantly being tested in new experiments. There is therefore an enormous volume of work that would need a book to itself for a complete review. However, here we shall look at how feature integration theory started out to chart its evolution and summarise the position as seen by Treisman in 1999. Quinlan (2003) provides a detailed and critical review of the development of FIT. The initial assumption of the model was that sensory features such as colour, orientation and size were coded automatically, pre-attentively, in parallel, without the need for focal attention. Features are coded by different specialised "modules". Each module forms a feature map for the dimensions of the features it codes, so for example the distribution of different colours will be represented in the colour map, while lines of different orientations will be represented in the orientation map. Detection of single features that are represented in the maps takes place pre-attentively, in parallel. However, if we need to know if there is a line of a particular orientation and colour in the visual scene, the separately coded features must be accurately combined into a conjunction.

Conjunction of separable features can be achieved in three ways. First, the features that have been coded may fit into predicted object "frames", according to stored knowledge. For example, we expect the sky to be blue and grass to be green, if the colours blue and green are active at the same time, we are unlikely to combine green with the position of the sky. Second, attention may select within a "master map" of locations that represents where all the features are located, but not which features are where. Figure 4.1 is an illustration of the framework, as it stood in Treisman (1988). When attention is focused on one location in the master map it allows retrieval of whatever features are currently active at that location and creates a temporary representation of the object in an "object file". The contents of the object file can then be used for recognising the object by matching it to stored knowledge. Treisman (1988) assumes that conscious perception depends on matching the contents of the object file with stored descriptions in long-term visual memory, allowing recognition. Finally, if attention is not used, features may conjoin on their own and

Figure 4.1 Framework
proposed to account
for the role of selective
attention in feature
integration.

Reprinted from
Treisman (1988).
Copyright (1988)
reprinted by
permission of
Erlbaum (UK) Taylor
and Francis, Hove,
UK, and the author.

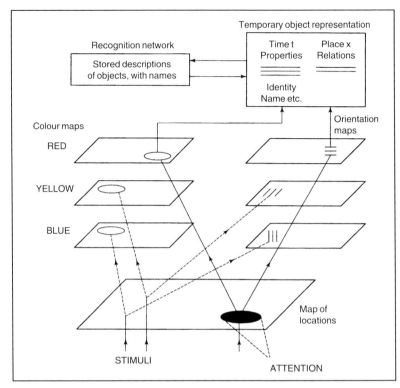

although the conjunction will sometimes be correct it will often be
wrong, which produces an "illusory conjunction".

Evidence for feature integration theory

Early experiments by Treisman and Gelade (1980) have shown that
when subjects search for a target defined only by a conjunction of
properties, for example a green "T" among green "X"s and brown
"T"s, search time increases linearly with the number of non-target or
distractor items in the display. When search is for a target defined by
a unique feature for example a blue "S" set among green "X"s and
brown "T"s, search time is independent of the number of distractors.
This difference in search performance was taken as evidence that in
order to detect a conjunction, attention must be focused serially on
each object in turn, but detection of a unique, distinctive feature could
proceed in parallel. Treisman suggests that the unique feature can
"call attention" to its location. This is sometimes called the attentional
"pop-out" effect.

As distinctive features automatically "pop out", there is no need for an attentional search through the display to find the target and display size will have no effect on search time. When the display does contain a target and that target is defined by a conjunction, the very first or the very last object conjoined may contain the target, but on average half of the items in the display will have been searched before a target is detected. Contrariwise, when there is no target present, every possible position must be searched. If we plot search times for present and absent responses, against display size, we find that there is a 1:2 ratio between the search rates for present:absent responses. Data of this kind are shown in Figure 4.2. Results like these suggest that conjunction search is serial and self-terminating and is consistent with the idea that in conjunction search, focal attention moves serially through the display until a target conjunction is found. Conversely, targets defined by a single feature are found equally quickly in all display sizes, which fits with the idea of a parallel pre-attentive search process. If activity for the relevant feature is detected in the relevant feature map a target is present, if not there is no target.

Treisman and Schmidt (1992) presented subjects with brief visual displays in which there was a row of three coloured letters flanked by two digits. The primary task was to report the digits and then to report the letters and their colours. As the display was very brief, there was insufficient time for serial search with focal attention on the

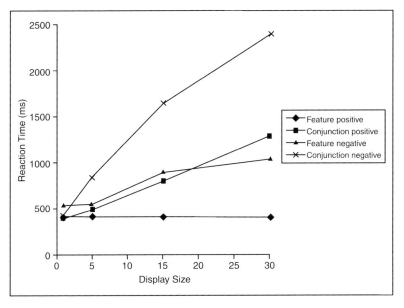

Figure 4.2 Typical performance in a detection task plotting response time to detect a target as a function of target definition (conjunctive versus single feature) and display size.

letters. Treisman and Schmidt found that subjects made errors in the letter task, but these were not random errors, rather they were "illusory conjunctions". Subjects reported letters and colours that had been present in the display, but assigned the wrong letters to the wrong colours. This seems to provide evidence that when focal attention cannot be directed to the locations occupied by the coloured letters, the features detected are combined in some arbitrary way.

Treisman (1986) examined the effect of pre-cueing target location. She argued that if attention is necessary for detecting a conjunction, then a pre-cue that tells attention where to go first should have eliminated the need for serial search of any other display locations. In contrast, as feature search does not require serial search by location, a location cue should provide no benefit. Cue validity was manipulated with the expectation that invalid cues would lead to response time costs, while valid cues would be beneficial. We looked at Posner's studies of cueing effects in visual attention in the previous chapter, but will note here that when attention is directed to the location of a target, processing is facilitated, but if attention is directed away from the target, location by an invalid cue processing is slowed down. In Treisman's experiment, results showed that for conjunction targets there was a substantial benefit of a valid cue but feature targets were hardly affected. This supports the idea that search for a conjunction uses attention directed to locations in the display. There was, however, a much smaller difference between the costs of an invalid cue on the two search conditions.

In the cueing experiment just described, Treisman used a similar technique to that used by Posner and his associates, but as the tasks used were rather different it could be that they were tapping different varieties of attention. Recall the suggestion by Kahneman and Treisman (1984) that there is an important difference between selective set and selective filtering experiments. In the kind of task typically used by the Posner group, there is usually only one target and so there is no need for the target to be selected from among distractors. This is more like a selective set task. Search for a conjunction target in Treisman's experiments is a selective filtering task. Kahneman and Treisman (1984) suggest that: "Different processes and mechanisms may be involved in these simple tasks and in the more complex filtering tasks." This suggestion is supported by experiments reported by Lavie (1995), which were discussed earlier.

Briand and Klein (1987) wanted to test if the kind of attention that Posner describes as a "beam" is the same as focal attention, described as "glue" by Treisman. They used a "Posner" spatial cueing task to orient the subject's attention to a "Treisman"-type task. When the cue was an arrow at fixation (that is, a central cue requiring endogenous attentional orienting by the subject), Briand and Klein found no costs or benefits associated with valid or invalid cueing on either a feature detection or on a conjunction task. However, when the cue was a peripheral cue to the location of the targets, a valid cue improved performance for conjunctions. Briand and Klein suggest that exogenous attention is important for conjoining features and that endogenous attention is important for later response selection processes.

Attentional engagement theory: Visual search and visual similarity

Duncan and Humphreys (1989, 1992) put forward a different theory of visual search and visual attention, which stresses the importance of similarity not only between targets but also between non-targets. Similarity is a powerful grouping factor and depending on how easily targets and distractors form into separate groups, visual search will be more or less efficient. Sometimes targets can be easily rejected as irrelevant, but in other displays targets may be much more difficult to reject. Part of the reason for this is that the more similar the targets are to the non-targets, the more difficult it is for selective mechanisms to segregate, or group, the visual display. Experiments by Beck (1966) have shown that subjects found it easier to detect a visual texture boundary on a page printed with areas of upright letter Ts and Ts that were rotated by 45°, than to detect a boundary between Ts and Ls. The difference in orientation between the two kinds of T meant that they shared no features, whereas the letters L and T contain the same features. So, shapes that are more similar in their features are more difficult to group together. Duncan and Humphreys (1989) did a series of experiments in which subjects might, for example have to search for a target such as an upright L among rotated Ts. The Ts might be homogeneous, i.e. all rotated the same way, or might be hetero-geneous, i.e. all at different rotations. By manipulating the hetero-geneity of distractors and their relation to the target, Duncan and Humphreys were able to show large variations in the efficiency of visual search that were not predicted by feature integration theory (FIT). Remember, FIT said that the elementary features are coded pre-attentively in parallel over the visual display and conjunctions of features, presumably necessary for determining if the features are arranged to make a T or an L require serial search with focal attention.

Duncan and Humphreys' experiments showed that although, in some conditions, conjunction search was affected by display size, in other conditions, display size effects were reduced or absent. In fact, in conditions where all the distractors were homogeneous, absent responses could be even faster than present responses. Duncan and Humphreys (1989) called this selection at the level of the whole display and suggested that visual search for the target is, in this case, based on rapid rejection of the distractor group.

Although it might be possible to try to redefine exactly what is meant by a feature in particular discriminations, for example, the corner of an L could be a distinctive feature of an L or junction of the horizontal and vertical components of a T join could be a feature of a T, this is clumsy and Duncan and Humphreys have evidence to suggest that this is not the case.

Duncan and Humphreys' (1989) results led them to propose that search rate is so variable depending on tasks and conditions as to make a clear distinction between serial and parallel search tasks difficult to sustain. As the difference between targets and distractors increases, so does search efficiency. Also, as the similarity between distractors increases, search for a target becomes more efficient. These two factors, i.e. target/non-target similarity and non-target/non-target similarity, interact. Thus efficiency of target search depends not only on how similar or different the target is from the distractors, but also on how similar or different the distractors are to each other. This theory is more concerned with the relationship between targets and distractors and the way in which the information in the visual field can be segregated into perceptual groups than spatial mapping. The computer model SERR described a little later, models this theory.

In feature integration theory the spatial mapping of attributes is very important. Van der Heijden (1993) reviews theories of attention with respect to whether they propose that position is "special" or not. Van der Heijden classes Duncan and Humphreys' theory as a "position not special" theory along with that of Bundesen (1990) and Kahneman (1973), but classes FIT as a "position special" theory. According to van der Heijden (1993), position is special and he has his own theory in which he sees spatial position as very closely related to attention, as, he claims, there is so much evidence in favour of position information both facilitating selective attention and being involved in the breakdown of attention, for example, in visual neglect.

Filtering on movement

Driver and McLeod (1992) provide evidence that is inconsistent with a purely spatial account of perceptual integration. In their experiment, they tested the ability of normal subjects to perform selective filtering tasks on the basis of conjunction of form and movement. They argued that as cells that are sensitive to movement are less sensitive to form and vice versa, there should be an interaction between the difficulty of form discrimination (a difference in line orientation) and whether the target was moving or not. Driver and McLeod discovered that search for a moving target was easier than for a stationary target provided the discrimination of the form of targets from non-targets was easy. However, when form discrimination was difficult, search was easier for a stationary target. McLeod and Driver (1993) argue that their data establish an important link between predictions based on our knowledge of physiology and observable behaviour. Their results show that subjects can selectively attend to the moving objects in order to make simple form discriminations, but this ability is no help if the task requires a more difficult discrimination of form. Thus different properties represented by different cells in the visual system can help to explain our ability (or inability) to selectively attend to different stimulus attributes. However, experiments by Muller and Maxwell (1994) have failed to replicate McLeod and Driver's results. It had subsequently been found that display density influences search rate for conjunctions of orientation and movement. To follow the debate, the interested reader should see Muller and Found (1996) and Berger and McLeod (1996).

FIT: The position in 1993

In her 1993 review, Treisman addresses a number of issues and up-dates her views. First, she considers what features are. Behaviourally, features can be defined as any attribute that allows "pop-out", mediate texture segregation and may be recombined as illusory conjunctions. Functionally, features are properties that have specialised sets of detectors that respond in parallel across the visual display. It has now been shown that there is also a "feature hierarchy". Treisman distinguishes between surface-defining features such as colour, luminance, relative motion, and shape-defining features like orientation and size. Shape is defined by the spatial arrangement of one or more surface defining features. Treisman (1993) gives the example of creating a horizontal bar whose boundaries are defined by changes, or discontinuities, in brightness or colour. She has shown that several shape-defining features can be detected in parallel within the surface defining media of luminance, colour, relative motion, texture and stereoscopic depth.

There is also evidence that some three-dimensional properties of objects pop out of displays. For example, Ramachandran (1988) showed that two-dimensional egg shapes, given shape from shading, would segregate into a group that appeared convex and a group that appeared concave. Only the shading pattern defined the target. The concave/convex attribution is given to the shape because the perceptual system assumes that light always comes from above. According to the original FIT, shape and shading would need to be conjoined. Yet there is increasing evidence that not all conjunctions require focal attention. Treisman (1993) suggests a possible solution lies in the distinction between divided attention and pre-attention. In her initial statement of FIT Treisman proposed that pop-out and texture segregation was carried out pre-attentively, but now considers that pre-attentive processing is only an "inferred stage of early vision" that cannot directly affect experience. As for conscious experience, some form of attention is required to combine information from different feature maps. Now she proposes that pop-out and texture segregation occur when attention is distributed over large parts of the visual display, with a broad "window" rather than a small spotlight. When the window of attention is large, feature maps are integrated at a global level, for accurate localisation and for conjoining features, the window must narrow down its focus. In an experiment like Ramachandran's with the shaded eggs, attention is divided over the whole display and can support global analyses for direction of illumination and orientation. Treisman (1993) also considers what happens to the unattended stimuli. If attention is narrowly focused on one part of the display, then stimuli in the unattended areas will not even be processed for global properties, as this only occurs under divided attention conditions.

We saw in the discussion of Duncan and Humphreys' (1989) experiments, that target detection times depend on the similarity of distractors to the target and the similarity of distractors to each other. Original FIT could not handle these data. More recently, Treisman has suggested that there are inhibitory connections from the feature maps to the master map of locations. The advantage of having inhibitory connections is that if we know we want to find a red circle, we can inhibit anything that is not red or a circle to speed search time. Also, if we know the distractors are blue and square, we can inhibit blue and square. However, the more similar the targets are to the distractors and the more dissimilar the distractors are from each other, the less efficient the inhibitory strategy becomes.

Some of the increasing evidence that visual attention is object based, discussed earlier, is accounted for by Treisman (1993). Briefly, she sees object perception and attention depending on the interaction between feature maps, the location map and the object file. She claims that for object-based selection, attention is initially needed to set up the file, but once it is set up the object can maintain attention on the location that it occupies. Another effect that FIT has to account for is negative priming (Tipper, 1985), which is evidence for a late selection account of attention. Generally, FIT has been interpreted as an "early" selection model, however, Treisman (1993) thinks that selection will be at different levels depending on the load on perception. When perceptual load is low, selection for action, or response, is the only kind needed. So selection may be early or late depending on the circumstances. (See Figure 4.3.)

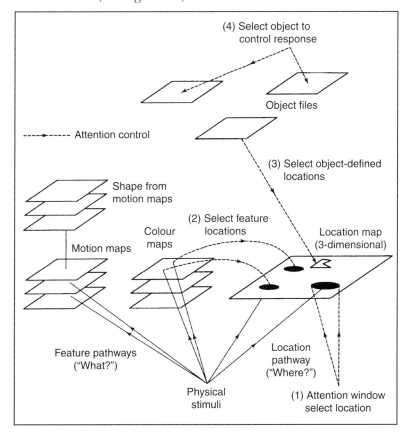

Figure 4.3 Figure illustrating four forms of attentional selection mediated by interactions between the location map, the feature maps, an object file, and a late-selection stage determining which objects should control response.

Reprinted by permission of Oxford University Press, from Treisman 1993).

Lavie (1995) reported some experiments showing that the amount of interference from irrelevant distractors in the Eriksen task is inversely proportional to the load imposed by target processing. So, now Treisman (1993) allows for four levels or kinds of attentional selection on the basis of location, features, object-defined locations and a late selection stage where attention determines which identified object file should control response. It is now evident that selectivity may operate at a number of levels depending on task demands. A strict bottleneck is therefore ruled out.

The position in 1999

In Treisman's (1999) paper she considers, among other things, the behavioural data from patient RM who suffers from Balint's syndrome, as a consequence of two strokes that destroyed both his parietal lobes. As explained in Chapter 3, the unilateral damage to one parietal lobe, particulary the right, often results in neglect of the left side of visual space or the left side of an object. This implicates the parietal lobes in spatial attention. Following loss of both parietal lobes, RM suffers from a severe deficit in combining or binding features and Treisman hypothesised that the master map of locations depends on parietal function. Despite his strokes, RM has normal acuity, contrast sensitivity, colour vision, stereopsis and visual fields; evidence for the specialisation of visual functions.

RM was shown simple displays comprising two coloured letters from the set T, X and O in red, yellow or blue. The letters were displayed for durations between one half and 10 seconds. He was asked to report the first letter he saw. RM made many binding errors; even in displays lasting 10 seconds he would report one letter in the colour of the other. Although he made 38% binding errors, he only made errors in which a letter or colour was not in the display on 10% of trials. Treisman concluded that RM "had lost the ability that we all rely on to see stable well-integrated objects and he now lives in a troubling world in which the binding problem is one he must constantly confront" (p. 95). If the master map of locations depends on the parietal lobes as Treisman suggested, then RM could be predicted to have a number of deficits. Treisman (1999) makes four predictions. First, he would have severe difficulty with conscious access to spatial information and so would be unable to point, reach for or verbally label locations. Second, if individuating objects (separating out from each other) depends on binding them to separate locations, then only one should be visible at once. Third, if space is the medium in which attention binds features, then if space representation is compromised there will be a risk of an illusory conjunction whenever more than one object is present. Fourth, conjunction search should be difficult or impossible, but feature search should be possible, even in the presence of many non-targets.

We have already seen the initial evidence for the third prediction: RM makes many illusory conjunctions when more than one object is present. Treisman points out that the first two predictions are classic symptoms of a Balint's patient as first described by Balint (1909) and are evident in RM. To test the fourth prediction, Treisman tested RM on conjunction and feature search tasks. He had no difficulty with feature search but was not able to do conjunction search even with very small displays of three or five objects. He was slow, up to 5 seconds and made 25% errors. When selection of a target can be made on the basis of a single distinctive feature, spatial information is irrelevant and the selective attention can be controlled from the relevant feature map. However, when a conjunction is required, selective attention is controlled through a serial scan by a spatial window. Most diagrams of FIT show only a few feature maps over which features need to be integrated. However, Treisman (1999) explains that there is now evidence for at least 50 possible features, which is far too many to illustrate clearly in a diagram. In her 1999 paper, she provides a number of approaches to explaining RM's performance. Treisman (1999) concludes with the view that binding features requires moving the attentional window over the map of locations and selecting from the feature maps those features linked to the attended location. The retrieval of these connections allows "what" and "where" to be combined.

Thus, Treisman concludes that when a master map of locations is not available as in the case of bilateral parietal loss binding is not possible. The evidence from both normal participants and RM "suggest that attention is needed to bind features together, and that without attention, the only information recorded is the presence of separate parts and properties" (p. 108).

A neurophysiological explanation of the binding problem

Singer (1994) considers the "binding problem" in neurophysiological terms. He suggests that any representation of a sensory pattern or motor program needs a mechanism that can bind the individual components together while preserving the integrity of the relationship between the components. The simplest way to do this would be to have a hierarchy in which neurons responsive to specific components of a pattern are mapped onto neurons responsive to specific patterns, which, in turn, are mapped onto a single higher order neuron.

From what we have seen about the specificity of coding within the visual system, this idea may seem promising. However, although at low levels of analysis we have evidence for colour, orientation, movement etc. being uniquely coded by neurons, at higher levels cells tend to become less specialised. Apart from a few exceptions, such as face sensitive cells found by Rolls and Baylis (1986) there is little evidence for specific higher order neurons that are sensitive to complex patterns. It is implausible that we could have a neuron for every pattern we might experience and unlikely that responses to novel stimuli could proceed effectively in such a system. Instead, Singer believes that *cell assemblies* must be involved.

It was Hebb (1949) who first suggested the idea of cell assemblies. This idea has grown in popularity recently (for example, Crick, 1984; Grossberg, 1980; Singer, 1994, 2004; von der Malsburg, 1985). The advantage of coding information in assemblies is that individual cells contribute at different times to different representations, so sometimes a cell will be part of one assembly of concurrently active neurons and sometimes part of another assembly of coactive neurons. Thus the significance of any individual neuronal response will depend on the context within which it is active. Singer (1994) sets three basic requirements for representing objects in assemblies. First, the responses of the individual cells must be probed for meaningful relations; second, cells that can be related must be organised into an assembly; and third, once the assembly is formed, the members within it must remain distinguishable from members of other assemblies. Most suggestions for how this is achieved assume that the likelihood of cells being recruited to an assembly depends on connections between potential members and that there are reciprocal excitatory connections that prolong and enhance the activation of cells that get organised into the assembly. One way in which neurons could be formed into assemblies would be by a temporal code. Von der Malsburg (1985) suggested that distributed circuits that represent a set of facts are bound together by their simultaneous activation. If discharges of neurons within an assembly are synchronised, their responses would be distinguishable as coming from the same assembly. Assemblies coding different information would have different rhythms, allowing different assemblies to be distinguished. Evidence has been found for the synchronised firing of neurons. Gray and Singer (1989) showed that neurons in cat cortex produce synchronous discharges when presented with a preferred stimulus. Singer (1994) says that activity of distributed neurons has to be synchronised in order to become influential, because "only coherent activity has a chance of being relayed over successive processing stages" (p. 99). This notion of binding by synchronous discharge has been proposed as a possible mechanism for integration over modalities (Damasio, 1990), attention (Crick, 1984) and consciousness (Crick & Koch, 1990).

Singer (1994, 2004) examines the consequences of the synchronised activity of distributed neurons for attention and performance. For example, the attentional pop-out effect, in which a single "odd" feature draws attention to itself from among the rest of the field, could result from the fact that neurons responsive to the same features are mutually inhibitory, producing a relative enhancement of the activity to the "odd" feature (Crick & Koch, 1992), which then pops out. Singer applies the same argument to assemblies. He says that assemblies that are effective in attracting attention are those whose discharges are highly coherent. This is because the tight synchrony allows the information of such assemblies to be relayed further in the information processing system than other less well-synchronised assemblies, so influencing shifts of attention. Of course, pop-out is mainly a bottom-up effect, but Singer proposes a similar effect could occur top down if it were assumed that feedback connections from higher to lower levels could bias the probability of assemblies becoming synchronised. Shifts of attention between modalities could be achieved by selectively favouring synchronisation in one sensory area rather than another. Following Crick and Koch, he conjectures that only those patterns of activation that are sufficiently coherent reach a level of conscious awareness.

Singer's ideas are highly theoretical and may offer a promising explanation for code coordination. They are at present somewhat unclear on the nature of the top-down attentional biasing or how higher levels might bias the probability of cell assemblies becoming synchronised.

Some connectionist models of visual search and visual attention

If we want to produce realistic models of human behaviour we would ideally have a computer that was very like the brain itself. This is the attraction of a variety of systems called connectionist networks, artificial neural networks or parallel distributed processing (PDP) models. Connectionist networks have characteristics that are close to those of the brain, in that they are composed of a large number of processing elements, called nodes or units, that are connected together by inhibitory or excitatory links. Each unit produces a single output if its activity exceeds a threshold and its own activity will depend on the weighted sum of connections onto it. Representations are held in the strength of the connections between units and the same units may be involved at different times in different representations. Quite clearly this is very similar to what we know of the structure and activity of the brain. Another interesting property is that these systems learn to associate different inputs with different outputs by altering the strength of their interconnections. In this way, the system learns and begins to exhibit rule governed behaviour without having had any rules given to it.

McClelland, Rumelhart, and Hinton (1986) point out that people are good at tasks in which numerous sources of information and multiple constraints must be considered simultaneously. PDP offers a computational framework within which simultaneous constraint satisfaction can be accommodated. Because all units influence all other units, either directly or indirectly, numerous sources of information, together with what the system already "knows", contribute to the pattern of activity in the system. All the local computations contribute to the global pattern that emerges after all the interactive activation and inhibition has resolved. In this way, a best-fit solution is arrived at, which takes into account all the information and constraints on the system. Connectionist models have layers of units, for example, input units and output units, between which are, depending on the type of model, hidden units that are important for computational reasons. They may also have units dedicated to coding particular features or properties of the input, for example, colour and position. We know the brain does and maps this information onto higher order units of the network, for example object recognition units or a motor program. (A good introduction to connectionist modelling in psychology can be found in Ellis and Humphreys, 1999.)

SLAM

The selective attention model (SLAM) was devised by Phaf, van der Heijden, and Hudson (1990) to perform visual selective attention tasks. Their definition of attention is as follows:

> Attention is the process whereby an abundance of stimuli is ordered and integrated within the framework of current tasks and activities; it integrates ongoing activity and newly arriving information. This integration results in the apparent selection of information. (p. 275)

According to their analysis, two processes are required in order to model attention. First, attribute selection and, second, object selection. Their model is based on the interactive activation model of letter identification by McClelland and Rumelhart (1981), in which processing is hierarchical but parallel at all levels in the hierarchy with both top-down and bottom-up interactions. Within each level, there is mutual inhibition between nodes. This means that at any given level, the most active node will inhibit all others and there can only be one "winner". Nodes from different levels whose representations are compatible have excitatory interconnections, whereas those representations that are incompatible have inhibitory interconnections. Rather than letters and words, SLAM is designed to process position (left and right), colour (red and blue) and form (square and circle), which we know are coded separately by the brain but need coordinating if a target is to be accurately selected. SLAM is particularly concerned with modelling the way in which these codes are coordinated in selective attention tasks.

At the first level in the model, representations consist of three modules that code combinations of the features. These are a form position module (e.g. square in the left position), a colour position module (e.g. red in the right position) and a form colour module (e.g. blue circle). At the next level, single features are represented, colour, form and position, and at the third level are the representations of the six possible motor responses and a biasing mechanism called the pre-trial residual activity. (See Figure 4.4.)

Phaf et al. (1990) ran numerous simulations of selective filtering tasks through the model. Of course, human subjects can be given an instruction, such as "name the colour" or "name the position". In the model, an instruction is set up by activating an "attribute set", either colour or position at the first level. This has the effect of priming either all positions or all colours. However, if the instruction is "name

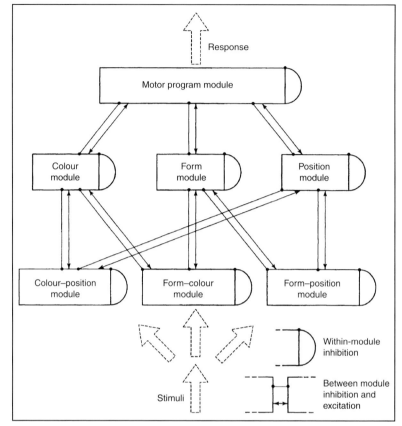

Figure 4.4 Schematic view of SLAM for the modelling of filtering tasks.
From Phaf, van der Heijden and Hudson (1990). Reprinted from *Cognitive Psychology*, 22, p. 286. Copyright (1990), with permission from Elsevier and the author.

the colour on the left", priming a single attribute set will not allow selection, as both attributes of the object are required to determine response. Phaf et al. assumed that this task requires activation at the second layer of the system and changed the weights in the model accordingly. The selection cue "enhances" one of the objects and the attribute set selects the response to the stimulus. Response times from the simulations were taken as measures of how long the system took to "relax", where relaxation is considered to be the outcome of a multiple constraint satisfaction process. Presenting different stimuli and giving different instructions perturbs the stability of the system resulting in different relaxation patterns that, essentially, provide the answer, or response to a particular task. Further, according to the task, relaxation may take more or less time, so increasing or decreasing "reaction time". The authors claim that SLAM behaves very much like a human subject, in that it only needs a stimulus and an instruction to reach a decision. The initial "simple" model was extended to examine Stroop performance by adding word colour and word form modules for some simulations. The results of their simulations are impressive in that there is a high correlation between experimental and simulation data for both selective filtering and Stroop tasks.

SERR

Humphreys and Muller (1993) developed search via recursive rejection (SERR), which is a connectionist model of visual search. Their model is based on the attentional engagement theory proposed by Duncan and Humphreys (1989) and Duncan and Humphreys (1992), discussed in the previous section. Remember, according to Duncan and Humphreys, search efficiency is affected by the strength of grouping effects between distractors compared with the strength of grouping effects between the target and distractors. Grouping can be based on the similarity of simple conjunctions and search will be parallel when the target and distractors form separate groups. As the strength of grouping that differentiates the target from distractors reduces, so does the efficiency of visual search. One particularly crucial finding that is important for the theory is that with homogeneous displays target absent responses can be faster than target present responses, which led to the suggestion that the ease with which perceptual groups could be rapidly rejected was important for visual search efficiency.

SERR is explicitly designed to model attentional processing. It, too, is a hierarchical connectionist network similar to the interactive activation model by McClelland and Rumelhart (1981). In SERR, the units at the first level are responsive to simple line segments at a particular orientation. These units feed onto units at the next level, which correspond to simple form conjunctions of line segments such as L or T conjunctions. Units are organised into "maps" arranged topographically, so that multiple items can be processed in parallel.

Figure 4.5 shows the basic architecture of the model.

Compare this to Figure 4.3 which represents FIT. Superficially, these figures look quite similar in conception. Both involve a number of interconnected "maps", which compute different properties of the stimuli, including features and locations. SERR is only concerned with simple lines and conjunctions of lines whereas FIT also has motion and colour maps and an attention window. In SERR motion and colour are not included, although presumably it could be modified to do so. However, although SERR does not have an attention window in the diagram, Humphreys and Muller (1993) suggest this

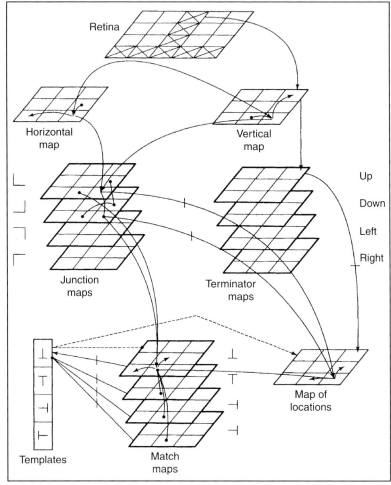

Figure 4.5 The basic architecture of SERR. Major connections are shown for units activated by an inverted T on the model's retina: → indicates an excitatory two-way connection; —• indicates an inhibitory two-way connection; →→ indicates an excitatory one-way connection; – – → indicates a fast excitatory connection used after a template's threshold is exceeded; and – – —• indicates a fast inhibitory connection used after a template's threshold is exceeded.

From Humphreys and Muller (1993). Reprinted from *Cognitive Psychology*, *25*, p. 52. Copyright 1993, with permission from Elsevier and G. Humphreys.

"window" is rather like the spatial area over which grouping takes place. "When distractors group separately from targets . . . selection operates across a broad area; when there is competition for grouping between different distractors and targets . . . selection operates over increasingly small perceptual groups" (p. 102).

There are other differences. SERR encodes simple conjunctions of form over spatially parallel units, but FIT does not. In SERR, distractor locations are rapidly rejected before the target reaches threshold and the area rejected varies according to the number of competing groups.

Of course, a major difference between these figures is that one, FIT, represents a theoretical model and the other, SERR, is implemented in a working computer simulation.

In SERR, the retinal array codes the stimulus pattern that excites features in the vertical and horizontal single feature maps, which feed onto units in the eight combined-feature maps (four for the end terminators, up, down, left and right, and four for each orientation of an L-junction). Each of the four match maps samples an area on the combined-feature maps for evidence for or against a particular target or distractor at that location. The match maps produce grouping by inhibiting units in other match maps that code competing stimuli at the same location. If the network is simulating search for Ts at particular orientations, the match map is tuned for T-conjunctions. There is a match unit for coding T in each orientation and each matching unit receives excitation from all junction and terminator units compatible with its orientation and inhibition from all junction and terminator units incompatible with its orientation. The map of locations is made up of units that are on if there is no bottom-up input. As input from the combined-feature maps increases, their activity decreases the activation in the map of locations so that when there is sufficient input, a location unit will go off, which has the effect of removing strong inhibition from the matching units. When a location unit is off, there is a mechanism that produces an inhibitory surround for a unit that is on.

Template units sample the whole array for evidence of a compatible match and accumulate evidence over time. Recursive rejection of non-targets is achieved by strong negative connections between the templates and the match map units, which can be rapidly deployed when a template fires. Templates have excitatory connections from their corresponding match map units and inhibitory connections from incompatible match map units. Once a template has accumulated enough evidence so that it fires, the model is designed to exclude all location units that contain no corresponding active match map units from search. If a template fires, all corresponding match map units are rapidly inhibited. At the same time, strong excitation is sent to all location units for which there are no active match map units other than the one inhibited. This has the effect of preventing search of any location maps that do not have at least one active compatible match map unit.

Humphreys and Muller (1993) tested SERR on a number of the search tasks used by Duncan and Humphreys (1989, 1992), for example, to find an inverted T among homogeneous or heterogeneous distractors. It produced flat search functions and faster absent than present responses with homogeneous distractors, but with heterogeneous distractors was not so good. SERR produced many more misses than humans in heterogeneous displays. A checking process was introduced, essentially by rerunning the network on a number of target absent trials, as human subjects might well be expected to include checking before making a target absent decision. With the checking mechanism in place, SERR's performance was much closer to that of human subjects with heterogeneous displays. SERR also has an impressive ability to predict some human search data. In this model, attentional behaviour emerges as a consequence of the search operations.

Search in SERR is based on objects rather than space, as it can select groups that are in different areas of the visual field. Selection is not restricted to one part of SERR's retina. The experiments by Duncan (1984) and Driver and Baylis (1989), which we discussed earlier in this chapter, showed the importance of perceptual groups for selection. SERR is clearly compatible with these results and the notion of object-based attention and not with the fixed size spatial spotlight metaphor of attention.

MORSEL

Mozer (1987) developed a connectionist net to model word processing. MORSEL has three components: first, BLIRNET, which is the central component, whose function in the model is to **b**uild **l**ocation **i**ndependent **r**epresentations of multiple words in a **net**work; second, the pull-out net (PO); and third, an attentional mechanism (AM). Although specifically designed for reading, the inclusion of an attentional mechanism means it is of relevance to theories of attention. BLIRNET is an artificial retina with six independent layers of units, the first of which code letter strokes, the next layer "coarse codes" (roughly, codes) the information from layer 1, the third layer course codes the information from layer 2, etc. By layer 6, letter clusters are represented. There were a number of severe problems with the model's capability for dealing with more than one word at a time, which resulted in the addition of the second and third components: a pull-out net (PO), which acts to clean up the perceptual input using top-down knowledge of words, and the attentional mechanism (AM), which is another layer of units isomorphic with those in layer 1. This layer of AM units was set up to bias the probability that activations in layer 1 would reach layer 2.

In essence, the AM units act as an attentional spotlight of the sort proposed by Posner (1980) and Treisman and Gelade (1980), whereby attention has the effect of enhancing the activation of the information under the beam or increasing the probability it will be selected. Following current evidence, Mozer allowed the spotlight to be focused on just one retinal location at a time. In BLIRNET, attention can be captured by stimulus attributes or controlled by higher level cognitive processes. As the AM unit receives input from both the "retina" and "higher level" processes, there will sometimes be conflict, which is resolved by constraint satisfaction. This means that, theoretically at least, attentional processing could be affected by both current goals and perceptual input, i.e. endogenous and exogenous attention could emerge.

MORSEL has been used to model neglect dyslexia by Behrman (1996). Kinsbourne and Warrington (1962) report a study of six patients who neglected the left half of visual space and also neglected the left-hand side of words. This neglect would occur even when the whole of the word was presented in the good field. It appears as if neglect dyslexia is based on the "object" of the word rather than environmental space. Ellis, Flude, and Young (1987) report another patient VB. When reading, she would only read the right half of each line of print and made errors on some words in the line. With single words she tended to misread "RIVER" as "liver" or "LOG" as "dog". Interestingly, although VB did not read the initial letter of words, sometimes she gave responses that reflected a simple deletion of the first letter, for example reading "CAGE" as "age", there were a number of occasions on which she was clearly reacting to the presence of the neglected letter. Given words like "ELATE" or "PEACH", she produced "plate" and "beach". Were she to have no knowledge of a letter being present in the neglected area, a response of "late" or "each" would have been expected. VB also tended to substitute the same number of letters as she had neglected. At some level of representation, then, it seems that the reading system had knowledge about, at least, the number of letters being neglected. Ellis et al. (1987) suggest that VB's performance reflects a greater deficit in the encoding of letter identity than in the encoding of letter position; she seems to know that positions are there that need to be filled but not what those letters are.

Carramazza and Hillis (1990) studied patient NG who also suffered unilateral neglect. In contrast to VB, whose errors were made on the left part of the word, errors made by NG were independent of the orientation of the word. That is to say, whether the word was horizontal, vertical or mirror reversed, errors were made at the same relative position in the word. Carramazza and Hillis suggest that these two forms of neglect dyslexia provide evidence for a dissociation between two different levels of visual word recognition. At the level disrupted in VB, the representation is viewer centred, whereas in NG, the word-centred level of representation is disrupted. These two cases are good evidence for different levels of representation at which attention can be neglectful.

Neglect dyslexia can also be material specific. For example, Patterson and Wilson (1990) report a patient who was able to name the left-hand side of an array of geometric figures, but was unable to name the left-hand side of a string of alphanumeric characters. Behrmann (1996) reviews neglect dyslexia and highlights the difficulty faced by theories of attention when trying to explain the variety of symptoms displayed by patients. Attentional neglect appears to occur in a variety of spatial frames and representational levels.

MORSEL has been used by Behrmann (1996) to simulate neglect dyslexia. Three properties of AM are essential for explaining the variety of symptoms in neglect patients. First, attention selection is by location and takes place early in processing. Second, attention tries to select a single item using early segmentation of the display without higher order knowledge. Third, attention gates the flow of activity through BLIRNET. MORSEL also employs a top-down system called the pull-out (PO) net, which cleans up degraded or noisy input using word knowledge. For the simulation, damage to AM was arranged in such a way that the bottom-up connections from the input feature map was graded so that the probability of a feature being transmitted was 90% at the right edge and only 48% at the left edge. This attentional gradient also had the effect of reducing the probability that AM will focus attention at the location of an undetected feature, since, unless a feature is detected, AM will not focus on that location.

When the lesioned model was presented with a pair of words, selection was strongly biased toward the word on the right; although the region occupied by the word on the left was also active, this activation was much weaker, or attenuated. The lesion also affected the distribution of attention over the word, so that the left side of each word was weaker than the right. This simulation shows how lesions to bottom-up connections affect the direction of AM not only over the whole retina, but also within a word. The lesion also produced higher order effects. When two words, such as COW and BOY were presented, the word BOY, on the right, was usually selected, but because BLIRNET has some ambiguity over precise letter position information, clusters representing slight re-ordering of the letters are weakly activated. In the example of COW and BOY there could, therefore, be complete activation of the word COWBOY. Now, if both BOY and COWBOY are active, the pull-out mechanism can read out either BOY or COWBOY. In contrast, if the two words did not form another word, for example SUN and FLY, FLY extinguishes SUN. This pattern of results mimics that found in patients and shows how top-down processing interacts with bottom-up processing to produce neglect at a different, higher order of representation. Evidence from the simulation suggests that neglect dyslexia is determined by the interaction between degraded input and top-down processes. Although the input is degraded, the complete input can be recovered by top-down activation. Once the complete input has been recovered, neglect may operate within the word frame, at a higher order of representation. In this way, damage at a low, perceptual level can give rise to higher order neglect within an object-centred reference frame. Examples such as this demonstrate the power of models in clarifying mechanisms of attention. The generalisability of MORSEL is supported by Mozer and Sitton (1998), who demonstrated that MORSEL can also be used to simulate other effects found in attention experiments such as visual cueing and distractor interference effects.

SIAM

Humphreys and Heinke (1998) and Heinke and Humphreys (1999, 2003) developed the selective attention for identification model (SIAM) to try to solve the problem of how we are able to recognise objects irrespective of their positions in the visual field. Models such as SLAM solve this problem by having multiple units for each spatial position. A more economical solution is to have a model that incorporates a unit that can act like the focus of attention and be shifted across different positions of the retina. Based on ideas proposed by van Olshausen, Anderson, and Van Essen (1993), SIAM acts on the output from retinal units. It has one set of units that map through an attentional window, or "focus of attention" (FOA); these units are called the "contents network". A second set of units corresponds to stored memories of objects or "the knowledge network". The incorporation of a knowledge network allows SIAM to use stored knowledge about objects to directly influence selection in a top-down direction. In this respect, it is different from other models mentioned here. The third set of units modulate the activation in the contents network and form the "selection network".

Working together in parallel, these three networks are able to achieve translation invariant object recognition, that, is the objects can be recognised whatever their position by the same system.

In order to be translation invariant, the contents of the visual field must only be mapped once into the FOA and the contents of the FOA must only cover neighbouring areas in the visual field. To meet these constraints, SIAM is a network of competitive and cooperative interactions. The selection network determines which retinal locations pass activation into the FOA. The selection network has a number of control layers, with one unit in each control layer linked to one unit on the retina. There are as many units in the control layers as there are possible mappings between retinal locations and FOA locations. Inhibitory connections ensure that only one location in the visual field is mapped onto one location in the FOA. When more than one object is presented, there is competition between the activations they set up in the selection network. In the absence of any top-down activation, the object that is selected first tends to be the one whose local parts produce most local support. If the object has a representation in the knowledge network then the template unit that is the best fit to the input is maximally activated and inhibits all other units in the knowledge network. This top-down activation tends to bias selection toward familiar rather than unfamiliar objects.

SIAM also incorporates a mechanism for shifting attention from the currently selected object to another object in the display. This is achieved by activating another set of units corresponding to the position occupied by the selected object in a "location map". Once activated a location unit inhibits all other positions corresponding to its location in the selection network and the knowledge network. This has the effect of preventing any further activation passing activation through the FOA and so the object at that location can no longer win the competition for selection and a different object wins. As a consequence of this location-specific inhibition, if the system were to try to return to the previously selected location before inhibition had dissipated, the effect would be the equivalent of inhibition of return (IOR), which we discussed in Chapter 3. Another advantage of a model such as SIAM is that the stored object knowledge in the knowledge network means it can account for a variety of object-based attentional effects.

A model for "attention"?

Although this chapter contains several theories and models of "attention", not one of them provides a general theory. Each model or theory is concerned with explaining or modelling only a small part of the data. There is so much to explain that it seems unlikely that there could ever be a single "unified theory". Not only is there a huge amount of data but also the data are concerned with attention at different levels. Some theories consider attention at a neurophysiological level, others at a cognitive level and, as we shall see in a moment, at a mathematical level. Computational models are also confined to simulating specific problems or behaviours. Recently, however, there have been attempts to provide wider ranging theories, for example, Schneider (1995) proposed a neurocognitive model for visual attention (VAM) and the following mathematical theory by Logan (1996).

Formal mathematical models

Both Bundesen (1990) and Logan (1996) have developed formal mathematical theories of visual attention. We mentioned Bundesen (1990) with respect to pigeonholing and categorisation in Chapter 2. Here we will briefly consider Logan's (1996) CODE theory of visual attention and (CTVA), which integrates van Oeffelen and Vos's (1982, 1983) contour detector (CODE) theory for perceptual grouping with Bundesen's (1990) theory of visual attention (TVA). Logan attempts to integrate theories of space-based attention with theories of object-based attention.

Five questions to be answered

At the beginning of his paper, Logan focuses on what he considers to be the five key questions that must be addressed by any theory of visual attention. These questions will allow us to reflect on some of the theories we have already met in this chapter. The first question that any theory must consider is "How is space represented?" Space-based theories such as FIT assume that space is represented by a map of locations, with objects represented as points in space. Further, the Euclidean distances between objects is important for space-based attention, for example Eriksen and Eriksen (1974). Object-based theories, by way of contrast, are, according to Logan, unclear about the way in which space is represented. When grouping factors counteract Euclidean distances, for example Driver and Baylis (1989), the theory is object based. Logan argues that as grouping factors, such as proximity, are very important for object-based theories, abandoning Euclidean space seems an odd thing for object-based theorists to do.

Logan's next important question is "What is an object?" This question has no agreed answer. However, although theorists disagree, there is some consensus that objects are hierarchical and can be decomposed into component parts. Remember the example of the tree, the branch or the leaf, when we looked at local and global processing in the last chapter. The next question is "What determines the shape of the spotlight?" Logan says that theorists are generally vague on this matter and must be explicit about what determines spotlight shape, as this "leaves less work for the omnipotent homunculus to do" (p. 604).

The remaining two questions are "How does selection occur within the focus of attention and how does selection between objects occur?" In space-based and object-based theories, selection of everything within the focus of attention is assumed to be processed. Yet the well-known Stroop effect demonstrates that selection can operate within a spatial location. (We shall discuss the Stroop effect in Chapter 9.) The classic Stroop task requires the subject to name the colour of the ink in which a colour name is written. Although there is interference between the two representations of colour, in that the ink interferes with the colour word, selection is possible. So, some other intentional selective mechanism must exist that is not based on spatial representations. Phaf et al. (1990) modelled this in SLAM discussed earlier. The question of how selection between objects occurs is important because theories must explain how attention "knows" which object or spatial location to choose next. Although a cue may indicate a likely target location, for example in Posner's (1980) experiments or bar probe tasks such as Eriksen and Yeh (1985), attention still has to get from the cue to the target. Logan (1995) suggested that one way of doing this conceptually guided selection is to use a linguistic code. This theory is explained in Chapter 9, when we consider the intentional control of behaviour.

CTVA theory is mathematically complex and we shall not go into the maths here. However, in essence, CTVA incorporates CODE theory (Compton and Logan, 1993; van Oeffelen and Vos, 1982, 1983) and TVA (Bundesen, 1990). CODE provides two representations of space: an analogue representation of the locations of items and another quasi-analogue representation of objects and groups of objects. The analogue representation is computed from bottom-up processes that depend entirely on the proximity of items in the display. The representation of objects and groups is arrived at from the interaction between top-down and bottom-up processes. In CODE, location are not points in space, but distributions. The sum of the different items' distributions produces what is called the CODE surface and this represents the spatial array. Top-down processes can alter the threshold applied to the CODE surface. Activations above any given threshold belong to a perceptual group. We have said that within objects grouping is hierarchical, CODE can change levels in the hierarchy by changing the threshold, the lower the threshold, the larger the perceptual group. This changing of the threshold can explain why sometimes items are processed in parallel and at other times not. Logan explains the way in which CODE can account for a variety of data, including the Eriksen effect, but in order to achieve within-object or within-region selection another selective mechanism is required. This is where TVA comes in. Essentially, TVA selects between categorisations of perceptual inputs and assumes two levels of representation. At the perceptual level, representations are of the features of items in the display. At the conceptual level, the representation is of the categorisations of features and items. These two representations are linked by a parameter that represents the amount of evidence that a particular item belongs to a particular category. In TVA, location is not special, it is just another categorisable feature of an item such as shape or colour. Selection is achieved by TVA choosing a particular category or categorisations for a particular item or items. There then ensues a race and the first item or set of items to finish win the race. At the end of the race, both an item and a category have been selected simultaneously, so this theory is both "early" and "late" at the same time.

Does CTVA answer the questions that Logan identified as essential to any theory of visual attention? First, is there explicit detail on the representation of space? In the theory, space is represented in two ways, bottom up on the CODE surface and top down by the imposition of the thresholds that result in perceptual groups. Second, what is an object? According to CTVA, an object is a perceptual group defined by whatever threshold is set by the top-down mechanism. Thus an object may be defined by the changing threshold at different hierarchical levels. Third, how is the shape of the spotlight determined? The spotlight is the above-threshold region of the CODE surface, which depends on both the perceptual input and the threshold set. Fourth, how does selection occur within the area of the spotlight or focus of attention? This is achieved by TVA biasing the categorisation parameter that makes the selection of some categories more likely than others. Last, how does selection between objects happen? This is controlled by top-down language processes and will be discussed further in the chapter on the intentional control of behaviour.

While there are some limitations of CTVA, such as its inability to group by movement or deal with overlapping objects, theories of this kind, although extremely abstract, offer a promising look into the future of cognitive modelling

Summary

For objects to be formed, the attributes that make them up must be accurately combined. Treisman and Gelade (1980) put forward feature integration theory (FIT), in which they proposed that focal attention provided the "glue" that integrated the features of objects. When a conjunction of features is needed to select a target from distractors, search is serial using focal attention, but if a target can be selected on the basis of a single feature, search is parallel and does not need focal attention. Initially, the theory suggested that all conjunctions of features needed integrating if selection were to be possible, but, as time has passed, Treisman has accommodated a variety of data by modifying the theory to include a feature hierarchy and defining features behaviourally as any attribute that allows pop-out. Thus features may include some three-dimensional properties of objects, movement etc. In FIT, information about separable attributes are coded onto their own maps and then are related together via a master map of locations on which focal attention acts. Selected objects also map onto object files that accumulate information about an object and allow access to semantics. Duncan and Humphreys (1989, 1992) suggested that rather than serial or parallel processing depending on whether features need to be combined or not, serial or parallel search will be necessary depending on the ease with which targets and distractors can be segregated, which in turn depends on target/non-target homogeneity and the homogeneity of the distractors. Humphreys and Muller's (1993) model of visual search (SERR) is based on the rejection of perceptually segregated groups in the visual display. In this model, it is objects rather than space that mediate search. FIT can now accommodate perceptual grouping effects with the notion of inhibitory connections from feature maps to the master map of locations, but is still essentially a space-based theory. FIT is more directly concerned with the "binding" problem than Duncan and Humphrey's theory. The binding problem could be explained neurophysiologically by the synchronisation of activity over concurrently active neurons, as suggested by Crick and Koch (1990) and Singer (1994). The idea here is that the brain "knows" what belongs together because of what is concurrently active and this coherent activity could then give rise to conscious experience of the object.

Other approaches to understanding visual attention are via formal mathematical theory, such as CTVA, which is an attempt to combine both space-based and object-based visual attention within one theory. SIAM is an attempt to model the processes that allow objects to be recognised irrespective of their position in the visual field that incorporates a focus of attention and also knowledge network, which allows it to account for object-based attentional deficits.

Further reading

- Bundesen, C., & Shibuya, H. (Eds.). (1995). Visual selective attention. A special issue of the journal *Visual Cognition*. Hove, UK: Lawrence Erlbaum Associates Limited.
- Heinke, D., & Humphreys, G. W. (2004). Computational models of visual selective attention. In G. Houghton (Ed.). *Connectionist models in psychology*. Hove, UK: Psychology Press.

    This paper reviews the main models and shows how they help clarify psychological theories.
- Quinlan, P. (2003). Visual feature integration theory: Past present and future. *Psychological Bulletin*, *129(5)*, 643–673.

    Provides a detailed critical review of the development of FIT and competing theories such as AET.
- Treisman, A. (1993). The perception of features and objects. In A. D. Baddeley and L. Weiskrantz (Eds.). *Attention: Awareness, selection and control. A tribute to Donald Broadbent*. Oxford: Oxford University Press.

    This gives a clear review of the history and development of feature integration theory.
- Treisman, A. (1999). Feature binding, attention and object perception. In G. W. Humphreys, J. Duncan, & A. Treisman (Eds.). *Attention space and action: Studies in cognitive neuroscience*. Oxford: Oxford University Press.

    This gives an overview of FIT and report patient RM.

Auditory and crossmodal attention 5

The nature of sound: Patterns in time

When you read this page you move your eyes along each line taking in the information. The written words are spatially arranged. If necessary, you can make an eye movement and look at the words again. In contrast, when you listen to someone speaking, once a word has been spoken it has gone. Unless the sound pattern is analysed as it is spoken, there is no possibility of hearing it again. So, auditory words are complex patterns distributed in time rather than space. Speech is just one particular, specialised, auditory stimulus, music is another. The environment is filled with sound of all kinds, from the sound we recognise as rain to the hum of a computer. Different sounds can be recognised as pertaining to different objects because they are composed of distinctive combinations of auditory features such as frequency, which we perceive as *pitch*, amplitude, which we perceive as *loudness*, and timbre, or *sound quality*. Most natural objects do not produce pure tones with only one frequency, but have multiple frequencies that combine into the spectrum of a complex sound. The acoustic changes that produce these acoustic features are themselves distributed over time and combine and change over time to provide information about the auditory object that is producing them. For example, we can tell if the rain is heavy or light by the differences in sound made by a large heavy drop and a small light drop and how often the drops are making a sound. Rather than labour the point further, it is evident that auditory information can be attributed to objects and hence objects have auditory features.

Auditory space

Although the acoustic information that gives rise to auditory perception is a pattern distributed over time, the patterns themselves emanate from objects distributed in environmental space. I can selectively listen, or attend to, the rain on the roof or the sound of the keys as I type. I know where these different sounds are coming from and can direct attention to that location. Cues such as interaural time difference (IAT), which is the difference in time that the same sound arrives at each ear, the difference in loudness between the ears, as well as other factors aid sound localisation. Another important difference is that the auditory system receives information from all environmental directions simultaneously. The taking in of acoustic information does not depend on any equivalent to foveation. If we do not wish to see something we can look away. If we do not wish to hear something we cannot close our ears. Selectivity must be achieved another way. For an introductory review of auditory perception, see Styles (2005).

However, we saw in Chapter 2 that early experiments on auditory attention clearly demonstrate that it is possible to attend to one stimulus rather than another. The dichotic listening task utilised our ability to selectively attend to one or other ear. Most of the initial work on attention used auditory stimuli, but research became focused on the early–late debate. While this work did provide evidence on the sort of features that could provide a basis for selectivity other issues remained or were taken up in visual experiments.

In this chapter we shall look at further work on auditory attention and also consider the issue of how auditory and visual information are combined. As is obvious, the environment is not populated with disembodied sounds. A sound is made by some "thing" and it is often important or useful that we know what that "thing" is and where it is. So, in auditory attention, many of the questions we have addressed in sections on visual attention reappear together with the additional problem of crossmodal attention. Much less is known about auditory attention than visual attention and some of what is known is in the realm of technically difficult psychoacoustics. However, there has been a recent resurgence of interest particularly on the question of how attention is involved in selecting between and binding together information from different sensory modalities.

Orienting and focusing auditory attention

To overtly orient visual attention, we move our eyes so that the fovea, which is the part of the retina that codes most detail, cross visual space to focus on the object of current interest. In vision, it is also possible to covertly orient attention without moving the eye, as we saw in Posner's (1980) experiments in Chapter 3, but normally the orienting of visual attention is overt and attention is coincident with fixation. However, with auditory information it is the cochlea and the specialised organs within it that deal with extracting details of the input. (See Moore, 1995 for an overview of the hearing system.) Orienting to a sound must operate differently to visual orienting, first, because of the nature of auditory stimuli and, second, because we cannot move our ears. Although we can orient our head this is only a very gross response. Orienting to an auditory stimulus must rely on selectively directing analysis of some feature of the auditory environment.

Scharf (1998) provides a useful review of the psychoacoustical approach to auditory attention and argues that understanding auditory attention presents a greater challenge than understanding visual attention. He points out that if listening, or paying auditory attention, is an internal act with no apparent peripheral muscular changes, then it is a "wholly cognitive act".

It is well known that both endogenous and exogenous cueing of the position in which a visual target will be presented speeds detection and improves accuracy. Knowing in advance where to direct visual attention allows cortical enhancement of the region of cortex responsible for the processing of stimuli at the cued location (e.g. Posner, 1980). In auditory experiments, attention can be directed to features such as stimulus frequency or to the direction from which a sound comes. We shall discuss a possible mechanism for selective tuning of the auditory system after consideration of some of the experimental data on listener's ability to orient to auditory stimuli.

Orienting attention to frequency

In auditory attention, many studies have measured detection and discrimination when a particular frequency is to be attended. When a listener knows in advance the frequency of an upcoming signal, detection requires a lower threshold for detection. Tanner and Norman (1954) measured a listener's ability to detect a 1000-Hz tone occurring during one of four possible intervals. The listener had to indicate during which of the time periods the signal was detected. The sound level was set such that accuracy was about 65%. Listeners knew the frequency they should be listening for and could therefore endogenously prepare for it. However, after several hundred trials the frequency of the tone was changed to 1300 Hz and detection rate dropped to chance levels. However, as soon as the listeners were given an example of a 1300-Hz tone and told that this was what to listen for performance reverted to 65%. This example shows that auditory attention can be "tuned" to focus on a particular frequency and that this focusing reduces the probability of detecting other neighbouring frequencies. We could think of this effect as similar to focusing the spotlight of visual attention at an expected location.

Greenberg and Larkin (1968) used probe signals at frequencies adjacent to the target frequency to measure the range of frequencies that would be detected when attention was focused on a specific frequency. They found that when listeners focused attention on a 1100-Hz tone only frequencies between 1000 and 1200 Hz were detected. It seems that auditory attention acts as a filter, only passing frequencies with a limited frequency band. This as called a *bandpass filter*. MacMillan and Schwartz (1975) showed that if two frequencies are attended two filters can be set. In another probe signal experiment, Greenberg and Larkin (1968) used a pre-cue to focus attention to a frequency on each trial. When the pre-cue correctly predicted the target frequency, listeners were 90% correct. However, if the target were different from the cue, performance dropped. Even at a difference of 75 Hz percentage correct fell to about 65%. With greater frequency separations performance was almost at chance. Here again, it appears that auditory attention can be oriented to the expected frequency and focused to filter out other frequencies. Figure 5.1 shows the detection rate over range of frequencies centred on an expected 1000-Hz target.

One question that immediately arises is this: Does the filter prevent identification of the signal or does it filter at the response and decision level? Scharf (1998) argues that if listeners hear signals but choose to ignore them because they interpret them as part of the noise signal (in most of these experiments, signals are presented in noise to prevent ceiling effects) then such experiments do not illuminate our understanding of attention. Scharf, Quigley, Aoki, Peachey, and Reeves (1987) provided evidence against what they call the "heard but not heeded" hypothesis. In this experiment, even when listeners were explicitly instructed that targets could be quite different from the expected frequency, and so might be expected to more likely accept a signal as a target rather than noise, performance did not improve. This suggests that the signal was filtered out rather than ignored.

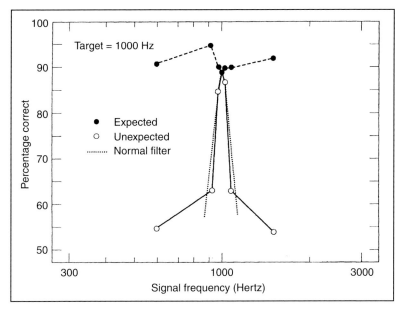

Figure 5.1

Percentage correct detection as a function of signal frequency. The infilled symbols give the percentage correct at each frequency when that frequency was the expected and attended frequency. The dotted line indicates the shape of the internal auditory filter measured in other kinds of masking experiments.

From Scharf, 1998, p. 88, fig. 2.3, In H. Pashler (ed.) *Attention*. Hove, UK Psychology Press, by permission of the publisher.

Dai, Scharf, and Buss (1991), Mondor and Zatorre (1995), and Wright and Dai (1994) all performed a similar probe signal method over a range of different experiments. The overall pattern of results is consistent with the properties of a bandpass filter, which has the effect of producing an attentional filter that only passes frequencies within the attentional band. Performance is at its peak at the target frequency with a sharp decline for frequencies away from the target. Thus auditory attention can be focused on a stimulus dimension to enhance processing of stimuli within the focused region at the expense of stimuli outside that focus.

Orienting attention in space: Detection

Everyday experience suggests that we can easily attend to one of a number of auditory signals on the basis of where it is coming from. However, in everyday situations the sounds that come from different directions are usually not precisely matched in terms of all other auditory features. So, for example, although we can attend to traffic on the left and birdsong on the right, it could be that we are able to selectively attend to either on the basis of some other auditory features rather than direction. Indeed, in the laboratory, a number of experiments have shown that when signals are matched for location, space is a poor basis for selection. A number of studies have measured the effects of valid and invalid location cues on auditory attention, but have found only small or non-existent effects (Buchtel & Butter, 1988; Posner, 1978; Spence & Driver, 1994). Scharf, Canevet, Possamai, and Bonnel (1986), for example, found no difference in detection rates for 1000-Hz tones when they were from the expected or unexpected direction. Although it might have been expected that listeners would orient attention to the expected direction, even when signals were expected to come from a loudspeaker to the right they were detected just as well when they came from a loudspeaker to the left.

However, most of these experiments used weak signals presented in noise and detection rate as the dependent measure. When reaction time is measured to indicate the location of a sound, and the stimuli are well above threshold, it appears that spatial selectivity can have an effect and speeds response to signals presented from the expected direction. Rhodes (1987) surrounded the listeners in her experiment with eight loudspeakers. The task was to name as quickly and as accurately as possible which of the loudspeakers produced a burst of noise. Listeners were told to maintain attention to the speaker that had last produced a noise and were given the probability, either 40% or 60%, that the same speaker would produce that next stimulus. Rhodes found that responses were fastest when the stimulus came from the previously activated location and slower when it came from a different one. In addition, the further away from the previous speaker the second stimulus came, the slower the response. Rhodes interpreted these data as evidence for an auditory analogue of space and that moving attention from one location to another took a time proportional to the distance. A criticism of this experiment, pointed out by Spence and Driver (1994), is that when the same naming response was made in succession, priming could be the cause of the observed facilitation.

In an experiment designed to be similar to visual orienting experiments, Scharf et al. (1986) compared reaction time to signal from an expected direction with those from an unexpected direction. As in Rhodes' experiment the sounds were clearly audible and reaction time the dependent measure, but response priming was not an issue. Listeners were told to attend to the left speaker and were told that although most signals would come from the left, some would come from the right. Each trial started with a warning signal, together with a light signal on the left side. On 80% of trials, the warning was followed by a tone burst, but on the 20% of catch trials, no tone was presented. When a tone was presented, it was only on the left side 75% of the time, the remainder came from the "unexpected" right side. Following the results in visual attention, it might have been expected that when auditory attention was directed to the side away from where the tone arrived, there would be costs. However, there were only small, non-significant effects.

In other experiments using headphones, and in which response priming could not have had an effect, small but significant effects of location cueing have been found by Quinlan and Bailey (1995). In their experiments, localisation was faster and more accurate when the cue was valid than when the cue was invalid. Bedard, Massioui, Pillon, and Nandrino (1993) report similar findings with headphones, but the experiment suffers from the same problem of response priming as that of Rhodes (1987).

Orienting attention in space: Discrimination

When the listener's task is to discriminate between sounds, directional cueing appears to have more of a facilitatory effect. In another experiment, Scharf et al. (1986) asked their participants to respond as quickly and accurately as possible to a 1000-Hz tone, but not to an 800-Hz tone. The procedure was similar to the previous experiment, with listeners instructed to attend to the left, but with signals coming from that side on only 75% of trials. Trials were preceded by a warning signal of a warning tone and a light flash. A second condition reversed directions, with attention to the right and in the control condition the cues came from directly in front of the listener. It was found that there was a 100 msc facilitation for tones coming from the more frequent side when the cue was valid. In the control condition tones were detected more slowly than in those following a valid cue, but more fast than those following an invalid cue. Similar results were found when the task required discrimination between which speaker had produced the tone on the basis of speaker location. The cueing effect was similar for both frequency and location discrimination tasks. This finding, says Scharf (1998), is inconsistent with Rhodes' (1987) prediction that spatial cueing only facilitated spatial discrimination.

The evidence suggests that when a discrimination is required, cueing the location of stimulus produces endogenous orienting of auditory attention that facilitates stimulus discrimination but not stimulus detection. This finding is in accordance with Scharf's view that the auditory system, by virtue of it being constantly open to environmental inputs from all directions simultaneously, provides the information processing system with an excellent early warning system. Detection occurs for all stimuli irrespective of where they come from but once a location is selected, attention can facilitate other processing of the detected stimulus.

Orienting attention in multi-source environments

In the experiments described so far, the sound to be attended was the only signal presented. Arbogast and Kidd (2000) investigated spatial tuning in a situation where many signals were to be selected from. The authors suggest that spatial tuning would be more important in a multi-source environment. In Chapter 2 we met Cherry's (1953) investigation of the "cocktail party problem". Arbogast and Kidd (2000) point out that one of the factors that Cherry identified as a solution to the problem was that the different speakers were at different spatial locations. However, in his dichotic listening experiments, only two messages were presented and the relevant message could be selected on the basis of a binaural cue, that is, one that relies on determining which ear the message arrives at on the basis of interaural time difference or intensity. In a real multi-source environment, this is not such an effective cue. Arbogast and Kidd (2000) review experiments that show listening advantages occur in situations where there is a large amount of "informational masking". Informational masking is thought to be due to uncertainty and reflects central rather than peripheral mechanisms. Kidd et al. (1995) trained listeners to recognise six sound patterns. These patterns were then presented together with either a simple noise mask or a multi-tone informational mask. The spatial separation between the signal and mask was varied and results showed that spatial separation had a much larger effect for the informational mask than the noise mask. These results suggested that a spatially tuned filter would aid a listener in selecting a target source in a multi-source environment.

To test this, Arbogast and Kidd (2000) designed a modification of the probe signal experiment in which accuracy and response time for signal identification was measured in the presence of informational masking. The listener was seated in a soundfield designed to simulate a quiet living room environment, with seven, numbered, speakers arranged around them, as depicted in Figure 5.2.

The task was a two alternative forced choice to determine if the pattern presented was a sequence of rising or falling tones. Accuracy and response time was measured. The trial began with a warning light and the stimulus played 800 mscs after the light. In the control condition, the signal was played at the cued location every time. In the experimental condition, the listener was told to direct attention

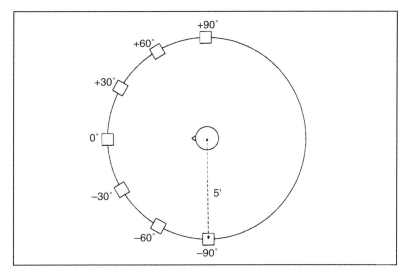

Figure 5.2 Schematic of the soundfield used in Abrogast and Kidd (2000). The listeners head is depicted at the centre of the circle, facing 0 degrees. The speakers are represented by the squares.

Reprinted with permission from Tanya I. Abrogast and Gerald Kidd, Jr, *The Journal of the Acoustical Society of America*, *108*, 1803 (2000). Copyright 2000, Acoustical Society of America.

straight ahead, at 0°, throughout the block of 64 trials. On 75% of trials the signal appeared at 0° but on the remaining 25% the signal (probe) was played randomly from one of the other six speakers. After training on the basic task, the same procedure was repeated with informational masking that had been designed to be similar, but not the same as any of the learned patterns. Results showed a significant decrease in accuracy and a significant increase in reaction time for the unexpected locations relative to the expected locations. However, there was no significant main effect of signal location. This task required pattern discrimination in order to "tune in" to the signal band and the effects found were large in comparison to experiments in quiet environments. In a multi-source environment if a signal arises from an unexpected location the information in the masks together with six possible sources to search make finding the signal more difficult. The authors argue that "an auditory spatial filter is more advantageous in a highly uncertain, multi-source environment than in less complex listening environments" (p. 1809).

Selection from brief multi-element displays

Darwin, Turvey, and Crowder (1972) attempted to replicate Sperling's partial report experiment using auditory stimuli, in what is sometimes called the "three-eared man" experiment. Listeners were presented with three simultaneous lists of words over headphones. One list was presented to the right ear, one to the left ear and a third list sounded as it were located in the middle of the head. Listeners were presented with nine speech items within one second, with the items differentiated by spatial location and semantics. Shortly after the auditory array was presented, recall was required. Listeners were to report as much as they could from the whole display (whole report) or the words from the cued channel. Of course, in Sperling's (1960) visual experiment, all items in the brief visual display could be presented simultaneously. In this auditory version, the temporal nature of sound requires a rapid sequential presentation, so exact equivalence to the visual experiment is not possible. However, despite this difference, a small partial report (PR) advantage was found. Treisman and Rostron (1972) found similar small PR advantages using successive sets of 100 msec tones presented simultaneously over loudspeakers. Holding, Foulke, and Heise (1973) also found a small PR advantage using compressed speech.

These studies provide evidence for a brief, high capacity auditory memory, which decays rapidly. This memory was termed "echoic memory" by Neisser (1967) and is similar to the iconic memory for visual information. The duration of echoic memory is longer than for iconic memory and allows selective report ear by ear, as in the split span experiments discussed in Chapter 2. In everyday life we sometimes ask a speaker to repeat what they just said, but before they answer we tell them, "No, it's OK", because although we thought we missed what was said, we have subsequently retrieved the information from echoic memory. This effect has been shown experimentally by Norman (1968) who interrupted people while they were shadowing one ear and asked them to report what had been on the unattended ear. He found that, for a few seconds, there was information still available on the previously unattended channel. The PR effects found with auditory stimuli are much smaller than those found in vision and Pashler (1997) suggests this may be due, among other things, to the fact that selection by location is far less effective for auditory than visual information. We have already seen that cueing to a spatial location is not very effective in the studies on orienting discussed previously.

Segregating auditory features

When listening in a complex auditory environment we are aware of many overlapping sounds coming from multiple sources. Think of standing in a busy street. There are the sounds of cars, busses, people's footsteps, voices, a clock chiming and so on. However, it is possible to segregate and group these sounds. For example, the traffic can be heard separately from the clock or voices. Auditory perception has the important function of allowing us to decompose this complex auditory scene into its constituent elements. This process is known as "auditory stream analysis" or "auditory streaming" (e.g. Bregman, 1990). It is generally agreed that the acoustic environment is segregated using Gestalt principles of grouping. These principles allow the auditory scene to be divided into different groups depending on a number of featural properties. Deutsch (1982) argues that sounds that are similar are likely to be coming from the same source, while those that are different are likely to be coming from different sources. One obvious way of analysing the auditory scene is to group them according to their apparent location, but as we have seen humans are not very accurate at localising sound. Taken together with the problems of echo and reflected sounds this makes localisation even more problematic. It has been argued that poor localisation is overcome by using pitch as the segregating feature (Bregman, 1981). Sloboda (1999) points out that in natural environments, sounds of the same or similar pitch usually emanate from the same sound source, at least over short durations, and that if pitch does change, it is likely to be only in small or smooth steps rather than large discontinuous steps. He suggests that, in nature, perceived pitch and perceived location "tend to be mutually reinforcing" (p. 156).

The scale illusion

Experimental evidence from studies that set pitch and location in opposition show that listeners will group on pitch rather than location. For example, Deutsch (1975) presented listeners with two simultaneous tone sequences, one to each ear, through headphones. Neither sequence was a melodic scale by itself, but was made up from a major scale, with sucessive tones alternating from ear to ear. The scale was played simultaneously in both ascending and descending order in such a way that when a tone from the ascending scale was in the right ear, a tone from the descending scale was in the left ear. When presented this way the stimuli produce an illusion that there are two melodic lines, moving in contrary motion. When asked to report what they actually heard, listeners reported hearing two smooth streams of sounds that rose and fell in pitch – they heard part of a musical scale rather that alternately high and low notes. The melody produced by the higher tones appeared to be located in one ear, while the melody produced by the lower tone appeared to be located at the other ear. The illusion is a demonstration of the powerful effect of grouping by pitch proximity. The tones are reorganised in auditory space to conform to good continuity of pitch irrespective of where in physical space they emanate from.

Does stream segregation require attention?

The phenomenon of streaming by pitch illustrates how grouping is influenced by relative changes in frequency difference in series of tones. When a single source producing a sequence of tones simply alternates in frequency, one or two auditory streams will be perceived depending on size of the frequency difference and the rate of tone presentation. When the frequency difference is small, or presentation rate is slow, a single stream is heard, which is perceived as a "galloping" rhythm. As the frequency difference increases, a point will be reached when the single stream separates into two. This segregation into streams takes a short while to "build up", a stream that initially sounds like a single stream will only segregate after several seconds. An important question about auditory streaming is whether or not this perceptual analysis requires focal attention or takes place pre-attentively. This has only recently been addressed.

Carlyon, Cusack, Foxton, and Robertson (2001) designed a divided attention experiment to test this. Two tasks were presented, one to each ear. One task involved making a judgement on the number of streams heard, the other task was to discriminate between bursts of sound that were either increasing or decreasing in frequency. For the first 10 seconds of each trial, participants were asked to attend to the frequency discrimination task and, then, after another 10 seconds, make the stream judgement. In comparison to a control condition that only involved stream judgements, the buildup of stream segregation was reduced in the divided attention condition. This result suggests that attention is necessary for auditory streaming. To test this further, Carlyon et al. (2001) conducted another experiment in which both judgements were made on the same tone sequence. In this case, there was no difference between the primary and secondary tasks, presumably because attention had been directed to the stimulus during the primary task.

Although these experiments suggest attention is important for segregating acoustic attributes into streams, MacKen, Tremblay, Houghton, Nicholls, and Jones (2003) argue that it is important to know whether auditory streaming happens without focal attention. In the experiment of Carlyon et al. (2001), the auditory stimuli were always the object of focal attention at some stage of the study. To discover if unattended auditory information is analysed into streams, MacKen et al. (2003) tested effects of streaming without directly asking participants to attend to it. To do this, they used the "irrelevant sound effect", which refers to the interference caused by task-irrelevant sound on recall for visually presented items (e.g. Salame & Baddeley, 1987). Sounds differ in their ability to interfere; in particular, sounds that are constant do not have a disrupting effect, but sounds that have what is called "changing state" do. Given this critical difference between stimuli that do or do not cause disruption, MacKen et al. (2003) reasoned that if auditory streaming can happen pre-attentively, without focal attention, then by manipulating the frequency difference between successive tones in the unattended stimulus, they could influence whether it should form one or two streams. One stream would be producing a changing state and so interfere with recall of visually presented items. However, if the unattended stimulus became segregated it would become two steady streams, cease changing, and so would be less disruptive. This is what the results showed. Listeners had been instructed that the sounds were irrelevant, that they should ignore them and would never be asked about them. Despite this, as the rate of presentation of the tones increased, they increasingly interfered with the recall task up to the point where the streams segregated, but at that point, the interference dropped to the same levels as no sound. Therefore, it appears that despite being outside focal attention, the auditory stimulus was pre-attentively analysed and hence formed into streams.

Combining auditory features

A great deal of work has been directed to understanding the psychological mechanisms involved in combining visual features. Feature integration theory (FIT) (Treisman & Gelade, 1980) is the most influential of these and was discussed in the previous chapter. In comparison, much less is known about feature integration in audition. According to FIT, visual features are combined by reference to a master map of spatial locations, however, we have seen that in audition the ability to locate stimuli in space is poor. Therefore, it is unlikely that a direct translation of FIT to auditory stimuli is feasible.

Woods and Alain (2001) review some of the problems with this and other approaches and point out some problems that make parallel feature search difficult in audition. First, although we have seen that auditory features can be held in echoic memory long enough for a small partial report superiority to be found, Woods and Alain (2001) argue that "the transience of an auditory signal implies that even a rapid serial scan would be faced with the loss of signal integrity" (p. 493). Another reason to reject a direct translation from FIT in vision to auditory stimuli is that a number of studies have shown that response times to conjunctions of features can be faster that feature detection. This is difficult to reconcile with an initial parallel stage of feature registration assumed in FIT. Woods, Alain, and Ogawa (1998) measured the time course of processing for the auditory features of frequency and location and for conjunctions of the two features. Listeners heard rapid sequences of loudness-matched tones of three frequencies presented randomly to the left ear, right ear of centre of head. In frequency conditions, they were asked to respond to tones of a specific frequency, in the location condition, they were to respond to tones at a specific location. In the conjunction condition, they responded only to tones of a designated combination of frequency and location. Responses were faster in the frequency feature conditions, but were also faster in some conjunction conditions than for location alone. This result for the single features is in line with other data showing frequency is a more effective cue than location for attracting and maintaining attentional focus (e.g. Woods, Alain, Diaz, Rhodes, & Ogawa, 2001). There were also differences dependent on tone location with particularly slow location responses to tones between 1500–2500 Hz, which is known to be a particularly difficult range of frequencies to locate (Scharf & Houtsma, 1986). However, the faster responses to conjunctions than individual features is incompatible with any model that assumes parallel search of features prior to conjunction with focal attention. Such a model cannot predict that RT to a conjunction can ever be faster than to one of its component features. Interestingly, Woods et al. (2001) conducted a similar rapid visual presentation experiment and found smaller, but significant, evidence that some visual conjunctions can be faster than feature detection for orientation. They argued that their results suggest the processing of individual features interacts, particularly in the case of auditory stimuli, such that when attention is focused on the more discriminable feature of frequency, this improves feature processing of other features at the same location. This is called facilitatory interactive feature analysis (FIFA).

Woods and Alain (2001) investigated auditory feature processing using event-related potential (ERP) recordings. This grew from some previous studies such as Hansen and Hillyard (1983), who investigated attention to auditory features and conjunctions. In these experiments, participants were to attend to tones with a specified frequency and location, presented together with distractor tones that varied along both frequency and location dimensions. Both dimensions could be easy or hard to discriminate. Hansen and Hillyard (1983) used event-related potential (ERP) to measure attentional effects. ERP recording measures the amplified electrical activity using electrodes attached to the scalp. The response to individual signals can be measured by taking the difference between the background electrical activity and that related to the stimulus event. The ERP can take a number of negative (N) or positive (P) values that relate to stimulus processing. The amplitude and time course of the potentials are also measured. It was found that attentional effects for frequency only occurred for tones presented at attended locations. Hansen and Hillyard proposed a parallel self-terminating model for auditory feature processing.

There is an early parallel stage during which auditory features are analysed until evidence has been accrued along any feature dimension that the stimulus is not a target and then analysis is terminated. Woods, Alho, and Algazi (1994) showed that when listeners attend to a conjunction of two highly discriminable features, ERPs show enhancement of processing for both feature dimensions. These changes are evident at short latencies, immediately following stimulus presentation and are thought to reflect modulation of neural activity in feature specific neurons. In Woods and Alain's (2001) experiment, listeners were asked to respond to tones defined by a conjunction of the three auditory features of location, frequency and duration. The ERP results showed that processing for single target features began at 60 mscs and lasted more than 400 mscs. The authors suggest the duration of single feature processing is evidence for auditory features undergoing "exhaustive feature analysis that occurs in parallel in both space (different features are processed in different locations) and in time (features of successive stimuli can undergo concurrent analysis)" (p. 507). The ERPs showed that when a stimulus contained two or three target features the ERP associated with processing all features of the tone are enhanced. This, they suggest, provides evidence for the FIFA model, in that the combined activation from all features amplifies individual features and enhances detection of the conjunction.

In conditions where a previously ignored frequency became the target frequency on the current trial a negative priming effect was evident. Woods et al. (2001) suggest this is consistent with non-target frequencies being "gated" before full analysis, although it could be that only non-targets of the designated frequencies captured attention and underwent further analysis for location. Woods et al. (2001) suggest that frequency may play a role in auditory selective attention tasks that is analogous to the role of spatial position in visual attention tasks.

Focusing on frequency

We have seen that frequency appears to be a more effective selective cue than location for auditory stimuli. The question to be addressed, then, is how can the detection of frequency be controlled? In many of the experiments we have reviewed, a listener is given a specified frequency to detect. Somehow, that frequency is able to take precedence over others, at least within a narrow bandwidth. The listener is able to focus attention on the target frequency and allow that information to pass through a "filter" while other information is excluded. We have argued several times that setting the focus of auditory attention must be an entirely internal process, as the sensory apparatus of the ear cannot move around the auditory scene in the same way as the eye can move around the visual scene. Therefore, some sort of "tuning in" process would seem appropriate, in the same way as you can tune your radio to the frequency of the channel you wish to listen to.

Scharf (1998) provides a possible explanation for how a sensory filter could be controlled by other cortical structures. So far, we have concentrated on the bottom-up aspects of auditory processing, starting with the stimulus and working toward "later", central cortical processes. Messages from receptors in the cochlea feed afferent signals through the auditory pathways to more specialised auditory areas and the auditory cortex and these higher brain centres have efferent pathways that provide feedback. The olivocochlear bundle (OCB) is a bundle of 1400 efferent nerve fibres that transmit neural information from the auditory centres in the temporal lobe back to the cochlea. This, top-down, neural information may be able to prepare the hair cells on the basilar membrane of the cochlea to be more responsive to one frequency rather than another. So, although auditory selection may be implemented at the receptors, the message that determines the basis of that selectivity has been generated internally. Given a sample of tone to be attended, top-down activation can feedback to enhance processing of the selected frequency.

Evidence that the OCB is involved in selective attention to frequency comes from Scharf, Magnan, and Chays (1997). They tested patients who had their vestibular nerve severed to relieve the symptoms of Mernier's disease. The OCB is incorporated into the vestibular nerve. We have already seen that people can normally selectively attend to a narrow frequency band, for example, Greenberg and Larkin (1968). Scharf et al. (1997) used a modification of Greenberg and Larkin's experiment on the patients. Before their operation, patients behaved like the normal listeners and ignored frequencies outside the target frequency range. However, following the operation, this selectivity was lost and responses were made to signals as far apart as 300 and 3000 Hz.

Scharf (1998) suggests this result can be explained if in normal ears, that have input from OCB, the basilar membrane is tuned to the expected frequency range and other signals are attenuated. He suggests that this selective tuning is:

> [A]chieved by the OCB's innervation of the outer hair cells, which are analogous to a miniature motor system; they contract and dilate when stimulated. Accordingly, auditory selectivity may also involve a kind of motor control remotely akin to that in vision where the oculomotor system directs the fovea toward the attended stimulus. (Scharf, 1998, p. 112)

This ability of OCB to bias the response of the auditory system might be one mechanism that allows us to selectively attend to a specified frequency or a particular voice at the cocktail party.

Other evidence supports the view that OCB can selectively inhibit response to auditory stimuli and could be involved in turning down, or gating, auditory inputs. Such an effect would be useful when an animal wants to focus attention on another sense, say, sniffing the ground or looking for prey. In this case it might be advantageous to temporarily suppress response to auditory signals, and Hernandez-Peon, Scherrer, and Jouvet (1956) demonstrated that when a cat smelled fish or saw a mouse, the response to sounds in the auditory nerve were reduced. It also appears that the OCB is involved in the interaction between visual and auditory stimuli (Igarashi, Alford, Gordon, & Nakai, 1974). Cats that had had an operation to sever the connections of OCB were more distractible by noise in a visual task than cats with intact connections. However, we said earlier that the auditory system could be an important early warning system and to shut it down while attending to other sense data would not necessarily be a good idea. Scharf (1998) suggests that not all auditory information is suppressed, rather that response to loud monotonous sounds is reduced, but response to quiet or novel sounds remains unaffected. It appears that, for audition at least, there are neural mechanisms that can operate according to intention that allow the other senses to be selected in preference.

Crossmodal links in auditory and visual spatial attention

Although a huge amount of research is dedicated to understanding visual attention and auditory attention, we do not inhabit a world of disembodied visual and auditory information. Objects usually have both visual and auditory properties, as well as tactile and olfactory features. While we may give priority, or selectively attend to one sense modality rather than another, for survival it is usually better to be aware of as much sense data as possible. It is important, for example, that we can attribute an auditory message with the person who is speaking it. The sudden onset of a sound will probably make us turn to not only listen, but also look toward it. So, does orienting visual attention in space not only enhance visual processing at the attended location, but also affect attention to other modalities at the same location, and vice versa? First, we shall consider auditory and visual attention.

Most studies have used varieties of Posner's spatial cueing experiments, discussed already. Many studies have investigated crossmodal links in spatial attention between visual and auditory stimuli (e.g. Spence & Driver, 1996, 1997). (See Driver & Spence, 1998 for a review and Schmitt, Postma, & De Haan, 2000.) For example, Spence and Driver (1996) designed a task, illustrated in Figure 5.3. The participants involved fixated on a light at the central location. Four loudspeakers, each with a light in the centre, were arranged in pairs, two to the left and two to the right, with one speaker on each side above the other.

On each trial, participants were told on which side the target was likely to be presented. Direction of gaze was monitored to ensure no eye movements were made and the participants head was clamped to ensure all attention shifts were covert. A single auditory or visual target was then presented on each trial and the participants made a speeded response to indicate whether each target came from the upper or lower row, irrespective of which side the target appears or attention had been directed to. Results showed that when covert attention was directed to the side at which the target was presented the up/down judgements for both visual and auditory target were

Figure 5.3 Schematic view of the position of possible target loudspeakers (shown by ellipses) and target lights (shown as black circles), plus central fixation light in Spence and Driver's (1996, 1997) studies of audiovisual links in covert spatial attention.

Reproduced by permission of the Royal Society of London and Spence. From Driver and Spence, *Phil. Trans. R. Soc. B353*, pp. 1319–1331 (1998).

discriminated better. Even when the participants were expecting a target in one modality and the other modality was most likely to arrive on the other side, there was facilitation for the unexpected modality target. This pattern of results suggests that there are strong crossmodal links between audition and vision in endogenous orienting of covert spatial attention. In another experiment, Spence and Driver (1996) found evidence for the ability to split endogenous covert attention between the visual and auditory modalities.

Spence and Driver (1997) used a similar experimental arrangement to test the effects of peripheral, spatially non-predictive cues on exogenous spatial orienting. The results showed that while auditory cues attract both auditory and visual covert attention, visual cues have no effect on auditory attention. Driver and Spence (1998) explain that an abrupt sound leads to faster judgements for visual (and tactile) events presented near the sound shortly after its onset, showing that "salient auditory events generate rapid cross-modal shifts in covert spatial attention . . . yet we have repeatedly found that peripheral visual cues do not affect auditory judgements (at least when eye-movements are prevented)" (p. 1321). It appears, therefore that there is a difference between the crossmodal attentional effects of voluntary, endogenous attention and involuntary, or reflexive exogenous attention, in that there appear to be no effect of exogenous visual cues on auditory targets. Further, the effects of exogenous cues in cross-modal attention are generally smaller and short lived in comparison to the effects of endogenous cues. This difference in effect may be related to the neurophysiology of the colliculus and Scharf's (1998) suggestion that hearing is an important early warning system and as such must be constantly sensitive to new sounds arriving from different locations, even when we are engaged in another task, for example attending to a visual stimulus location. If exogenous direction of visual attention also drew auditory attention to the same location the capability of the early warning system could be compromised.

The different attentional effects of exogenous and endogenous cues also suggest that rather than a single "supra-modal" attention system that is recruited by either cue, the attentional system is more complex. There appear to be strong crossmodal links, but not for all possible combinations of modality.

Crossmodal attention in vision and touch

When we see or hear an object we may very often want to reach out and touch or grasp it. Orienting to tactile stimuli has also been investigated in a number of studies. Spence, Nicholls, Gillespie, and Driver (1998) demonstrated that touch can also generate crossmodal shifts of exogenous covert spatial attention in a series of three experiments. In the first experiment, the participants were seated at a table in a darkened room, fixated on a small LED straight ahead, with their arms resting on the tabletop. The index finger of each hand was positioned over an aperture through which a vibrotactile stimulus could be presented and held in place by Velcro. Auditory cues were presented from one of two loudspeakers to either side of the listener. The task required the participants to detect whether the tactile stimulus was continuous or pulsed. At the beginning of each trial, an auditory cue was presented from either the left or right loudspeaker and then after a variable delay, the tactile stimulus was presented from either the same side or the opposite side from the auditory cue. Participants were told to ignore the auditory signals and responses were made with foot pedals. Eye movements were monitored to ensure fixation was maintained. This was important as there is evidence that simply fixating the eyes at a target location can speed response to a tactile target, even in darkness (Driver & Grossenbacher, 1996). Results showed that response to the tactile stimulus was fastest when it was preceded by an auditory cue on the same side of space and that the exogenous auditory cue must have also attracted covert tactile attention.

Spence et al. (1998) repeated the experiment, this time using lights rather than speakers, to test the effect of a visual cue on exogenous tactile orienting. Again, participants were told the visual signals were uninformative and they should be ignored. Analysis showed, again, that participants responded significantly faster to tactile targets from the same side as the cue than the opposite side, showing that an exogenous visual cue also attracted covert tactile attention. In their final experiment, Spence et al. (1998) used tactile stimuli as the uninformative cue for visual and auditory stimuli using an experimental design similar to that used by Spence and Driver (1996), described earlier. Participants now had to indicate whether a visual or auditory stimulus presented to the left or right was up or down.

Judgements were faster and more accurate for both auditory and visual targets when they were presented shortly after a tactile stimulus presented on the same side. Spence and Driver argue their results "demonstrate there are extensive cross-modal links between touch, vision and audition in the control of exogenous covert orienting" (p. 552).

Spatial coordinates of crossmodal attention

Driver and Spence (1998) were interested to discover the nature of the spatial representation used in drawing attention from one modality to another. For example, Driver and Spence (1999) give the example of feeling an insect crawling over your hand. It would be useful to be able to brush the insect off, in case it were to bite you, but say your hands were crossed, then your right hand could be in left visual space. The question then is this: Do the crossmodal links allow remapping so that the tactile stimulus draws visual attention to the current location of the stimulated hand irrespective of posture? In Spence and Driver's (1998) experiment, participants held, in each hand, a sponge cube between their thumb and index finger. The cube had one vibrator and a small light at the position of the thumb and a separate light and vibrator at the position of the index finger. (See Figure 5.4.)

We know already that a visual cue will enhance detection of a tactile stimulus at or near the same location, so we would expect a light cue on the left side of visual space to facilitate the processing of tactile stimuli delivered to the left hand. This is the case where the hands are uncrossed in Figure 5.4 (a). However, the question is, what will happen when the hands are crossed, in Figure 5.4 (b)? The answer

Figure 5.4 Illustration of relative hand position in a) the uncrossed condition and b) the crossed condition in a visual-tactile or tactile-visual cueing experiment.

Reproduced by permission of the Royal Society of London and Spence. From Driver and Spence, *Phil. Trans. R. Soc. B353*, pp. 1319–1331 (1998).

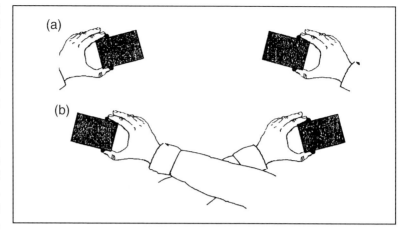

is that a visual cue on the left still facilitates tactile discriminations on that side of space, but now for tactile stimuli delivered to the right hand. This result shows that the spatial mapping of retinal locations has been remapped onto the current position of the hands. The authors suggest that proprioceptive information on body posture influences the attentional interactions between the other modalities and this is updated as the body posture changes.

Visual capture of touch: The rubber gloves illusion

In accordance with the evidence on remapping, Spence, Pavani, and Driver (2000) argue that we use information from touch, proprioception and vision to enable us to know which body part is touched and where in space we are touched, but that when sense data conflict, vision dominates. Spence et al. used an interference task to discover if a flash of light would interfere with where their participants felt a tactile vibration. A small box was held between the thumb and forefinger and the vibration was delivered to the thumb or finger. At the same time as the vibration was delivered, a light flashed beside either the thumb or finger and the task was to judge which digit was touched and ignore the light. Results showed that the light flash interfered with the tactile judgements, but only when it was very close to the hand. Using this interference effect as an indicator of where in space subjects feel a touch, Spence et al. (2000) set up an experiment in which subjects, wearing rubber gloves, could either see their own hands while the touch and light were delivered or could see what appeared to be their own hands, but were, in fact only a pair of rubber gloves (their own hands were hidden directly beneath). The question was, where would the touch be felt: on the real, hidden, hands or the visible rubber hands? It was found that participants begin to feel as though the rubber gloves were their own hands and that the vibrations came from where they saw the rubber hands. The interference effect of the lights moved toward the rubber hands, confirming that where the vibration was felt it had moved toward the rubber hands. Although the subjects knew the false hands were not their own hands, they could not overcome the illusion. Spence et al. (2000) argued that where we feel touch is determined by what we see. Such illusions suggest that vision is the dominant sense and that visual evidence takes precedence over other sensory evidence.

Which sense is dominant?

When participants are asked to make a judgement of the perceptual properties of an object, but the information from the two modalities is conflicting, psychologists can determine which of the senses is dominant. For example, Hay, Pick, and Ikeda (1965) report an experiment in which it is arranged that the observer views one hand through a prism, which has the effect of displacing the visual information on where the hand is located in space. The visual displacement produces conflict between where the hand is seen to be in conflict with the proprioceptive information on where the hand is felt to be. (Proprioception is perception of where our limbs are and is provided by sensors in the joints and muscles.) The participant cannot see their other hand. The task is to point with the unseen hand to the place where the visible, but visually displaced, hand is either felt or seen to be. The accuracy of pointing in these conditions was compared with accuracy when judgements were made only on vision or only on proprioception. It was found that visual information dominates, in that the hand is felt to be where it is seen. Participants resolved the conflicting information from proprioception and vision by deciding to believe their eyes. In a classic study, Rock and Victor (1964) demonstrated that vision completely dominates touch in a matching task where visual and tactile form conflict. Other studies have shown complete or very strong visual dominance for perceptual judgements of size, length, depth and spatial location. In these cases there is said to be "visual capture" of the perceptual event. Contrariwise, observers sometimes make compromise judgements, where one modality does not completely dominate, but only biases the judgement in the other modality. We have seen that orienting cues presented in one modality can affect speed of processing in another modality and it has been shown that the phenomenon of extinction can occur across the modalities. For example, Mattingley, Driver, Beschin, and Robertson (1997) reported a neuropsychological case where a visual stimulus could extinguish a tactile stimulus and vice versa.

Illusory conjunctions between vision and touch

According to feature integration theory (FIT), discussed in Chapter 4, illusory conjunctions occur when focal attention is not directed to an object and so has not conjoined the features present at that location with the "glue" of focal attention. Cinel, Humphreys, and Poli (2002) report a series of experiments that show illusory conjunctions can arise across modalities. Participants in this experiment faced a computer screen on which visual stimuli were displayed and at the same time placed their hands on a table covered by a screen on which tactile stimuli were presented. This arrangement meant that the visual stimuli could be seen but not touched and the tactile stimuli could be touched but not seen. The tactile stimuli were rectangles onto which different textures, such as beans, fur, carpet, were glued. The visual stimuli had three possible shapes, triangle, square or circle, as well as the same surfaces as the tactile stimuli. Visual stimuli were presented only briefly to set accuracy for shape and texture between 75% and 90%. The participant's first task was to name the orientation of the tactile stimulus; this was to make the participant attend to the tactile stimulus sufficiently to determine its orientation, without drawing attention to its texture. The second task was to report the shape and texture of the visual items. A crossmodality conjunction error was deemed to have been made when the participant reported the visual target as having the texture belonging to the tactile stimulus. Cinel et al. (2002) found that conjunction errors, or illusory conjunctions, were made not only within modality, but also *across* modality. In further experiments, they demonstrated that illusory conjunctions are more likely when the tactile and visual stimuli are in the same side of visual space. This evidence is interpreted in terms of sensory dominance and crossmodal biasing of attention and suggests that there is tagging of sensory information across modalities.

Crossmodal interactions: The ventriloquist effect

Visual dominance over audition is also evident in the ventriloquist effect, or illusion, which illustrates how observers mislocate the sounds they hear towards its apparent visual location. When the ventriloquist speaks without moving his own mouth, but synchronises the movements of the dummy's mouth with the words being spoken, it appears that the speech sounds emanate from the dummy. Again this illustrates how conflicting sensory data are resolved in favour of vision. Although auditory cues can be used to localise sound, we also use visual cues to confirm or contradict the auditory information. Normally, if we hear speech coming from a particular direction we expect to see the person who is speaking move their lips, so when the ventriloquist speaks without moving their lips, it is the dummy with the moving mouth that appears to be the source of the sound. A similar illusion is evident in the cinema, where the voices appear to come from the actors speaking on the screen although the sound comes from loudspeakers set around the auditorium. People with normal hearing may not think they engage in lip reading, but when sound and vision are not synchronised, for example in a film, we are immediately aware that the visual information on lip movements is out of phase with auditory information on speech sounds. Related to this, Bertelson and Aschersleben (1998) demonstrated that the ventriloquism illusion breaks down when there is temporal assynchrony between the auditory and visual information. Normally, we expect all sources of sensory information arising from the same location to be integrated. If this integration is not evident, then the cognitive system attempts to resolve this conflict. A good example of distorting the percept to make sense of conflicting information arising from different sensory modalities is the McGurk effect (McGurk & MacDonald, 1976). In their paper, aptly named "Hearing lips and seeing voices", they show that when a visually lipread sound does not match the presented auditory sound the way the sound is heard is modified. In the ventriloquist effect, when a sound is presented in a spatial location that conflicts with the visual evidence on where the sound is coming from, the location of the heard sound is a shift toward its apparent visual source. Vroomen and de Gelder (2004) provide a review of the ventriloquism effect.

Driver (1996) used a dichotic listening task to investigate auditory visual integration. (See Figure 5.5.)

Driver presented participants with two simultaneous auditory messages, each made up from three two-syllable words in random order. The task was to repeat the target triplet of words, e.g. "sunset,

Figure 5.5 Schematic illustration of the apparatus used by Spence and Driver (1996).

Reproduced by permission of the Royal Society of London and Spence. From Driver and Spence, *Phil. Trans. R. Soc. B353*, pp. 1319–1331 (1998).

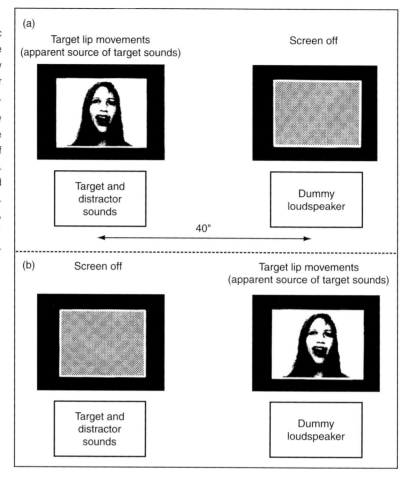

tulip, headline" while ignoring the other triplet, e.g. "music, flooring, pigment". However, the messages were in the same voice, in synchrony, from the same sound source. Therefore, there were no auditory or semantic cues that could be used to segregate the messages. The cue given was visual. A screen showed the speaker's face with the to-be-reported auditory sequence accurately synchronised with the lip and tongue movements. It was expected that lip reading would allow the participant to select the target words. However, we have seen that people tend to locate sounds towards where they see the movements that synchronise with the speech, in the ventriloquist illusion. Driver was interested to discover the effect of moving the location of the sound source away from the "speaking" face. He found a quite remarkable result. Shadowing was better when the sound source was moved away from the speaking face. It was as if, as in the ventrilo-quist illusion, the visual information draws the sound source towards it, allowing better separation of the two auditory messages. This illu-sory separation allowed auditory attention to select the shadowed message more easily. This effect has been suggested to indicate that the integration of sensory data takes place pre-attentively (Driver & Spence, 1998).

The modality appropriateness interpretation

A number of researchers have proposed that the different sensory modalities are specialised to process different kinds of incoming information. So, as vision is especially good for spatial information, audition is good for temporal resolution, then the most appropriate modality will be selected depending on whether the current task required spatial or temporal judgements. Lederman, Thorne, and Jones (1986) found that vision or touch dominated perception depending on the name given to the judgement that was asked for in a sensory conflict experiment. They suggested that vision tends to focus on the spatial aspects of texture, as proposed by Gibson (1950), whereas touch uses texture to judge the surface properties of objects. Lederman et al. (1986) predicted that this difference between what the senses are used for would affect the modality they relied on to make texture judgements. When asked to judge spatial density, vision would predominate, but when asked to judge roughness, touch would dominate. The results confirmed the prediction. When asked to judge roughness, observers relied more heavily on tactile information, but when judgements were on spatial density, vision was relied on. There was not, however, complete domination in each case. The data were consistent with a model in which information from the senses is integrated across the modalities but with the evidence from the modality most appropriate for the current judgement being given more weight.

Recent work by Soto-Faraco, Spence, and Kingstone (2004) investi-gating crossmodal capture in the perceived direction of apparent movement in visual and auditory stimuli shows, for example, that sounds are often responded to as coming from the direction of con-current visual motion, but apparent visual motion was rarely affected by apparent auditory motion. The asymmetry of effects in the results suggests that visual information on movement carries more weight than auditory information on movement. According to the modality appropriateness view, as vision is more accurate in coding spatial properties than audition, in a task that requires motion detection vision dominates and visual evidence will be weighted more heavily than auditory evidence when there is a conflict between modalities. In the experiment of Soto-Faraco et al. (2004), the stimuli were not static, as in the normal ventriloquist illusion, but had apparent motion, still best detected by vision. It is argued that dynamic properties of stimuli are also subject to interactions between the modalities.

Although vision usually dominates hearing when spatial resolution is most important, when time resolution is most important, there is evidence for the auditory capture of vision. We discovered at the start of the chapter that sounds are patterns distributed in time and, hence, analysis of auditory information is crucially dependent on accurate information on time. Morein-Zamir, Soto-Faraco, and Kingstone (2003) investigated whether irrelevant sounds influenced the judgement of temporal order judgements of which light appeared first. Analogous to the spatial ventriloquism used by Driver (1996) to separate auditory messages, Morein et al. (2003) showed that presenting a sound before the first light and after the second light, appeared to pull the perception of the lights further apart in time and improved performance relative to a control condition in which the presentation of the lights and the sounds were simultaneous. A reverse effect was found when the sounds were presented after the first light and before the second light. In this case, the visual stimuli appeared to be pulled together in time. These results produce what is called "temporal ventriloquism", and provides new support for the modality appropriateness hypothesis. What is attended depends on the modality most likely to provide the most accurate information for the intended task. Thus the nature of the task affects which modality is appropriate (see de Gelder and Bertelson, 2003 for a review).

Parietal cortex and crossmodal attention

Behrmann, Geng, and Shomstein (2004) review the role of the parietal lobe in subserving attentional effects across the modalities. In response to the development of ever more sophisticated neuroimaging and brain-recording techniques psychologists are increasingly trying to understand the neural anatomy and architecture that underpins behavioural data. The parietal lobe is "at the crossroads of the brain" (Critchley, 1953). It is located at the junction of the visual, auditory and tactile cortices and is connected to other regions involved with motor response. Therefore it plays an essential role in transforming sensory input into motor output. Functional magnetic resonance imaging (FMRI) studies have shown that the attentional biasing mechanisms of "attentional capture", or bottom-up exogenous orienting, and goal-directed or endogenous orienting involves distinct areas of the parietal lobe. Bottom-up attentional capture for task-relevant stimuli involves the right temporoparietal junction (TPJ). However, when participants are monitoring for a change in either a visual or auditory stimulus presented simultaneously TPJ activation is only evident for a change in the task relevant modality. By the same token, unexpected or novel stimuli irrelevant to any ongoing task activate TPJ irrespective of whether they are visual, auditory or tactile stimuli. This Behrmann et al. (2004) suggest, reflects the "multi-sensory role played by the TPJ" (p. 213). Different regions of parietal cortex, the superior parietal lobule, SPL and the precuneus (PC) become active when the task involves top-down attentional control. In a task where a central, identity cue indicates whether the participants should maintain or shift attention to the contra-lateral side, it was found that there was transient activity in SPL, suggesting this area is the source of a brief attentional control signal that precede an attentional shift. Once attention is shifted to one side or the other, activity on the side of the attended stimulus is higher than that on the unattended side. However, we have seen that there is increasing interest in crossmodal attentional effects and evidence that attending in one modality, particularly vision can enhance processing of stimuli at the same location in another modality. However, a number of studies are revealing the representation of crossmodal representations in another part of parietal cortex, the anterior intraparietal sulcus (aIPS). For example, Macaluso, Eimer, Frith, and Driver (2003) presented visual and tactile stimuli concurrently to one or other side of space following an auditory cue indicating on which side the target was likely to appear. It was found that there was preparatory activation in aIPS following the spatial cue and before stimulus onset for both visual and tactile targets. In addition, they found modality specific activation in primary visual cortex or somatosensory cortex depending on target modality.

Pain and attention

One of the most important functions of the sense of touch is to provide a warning to the cognitive system when the body is sustaining damage. Eccleston and Crombez (1999) propose a cognitive-affective model to account for the way that pain interrupts ongoing activity to demand attention. The model allows pain to capture central processing mechanisms that allow selection of an action to enable us to escape the pain. However, if pain were automatically responded to, that in itself could be dangerous. For example, if you lift a pan of boiling fat and the handle burns your hand, releasing the handle could result in a greater injury. Clearly, any action plan must take account not only of the current pain experience but also of the consequences of making or not making an action. Eccleston and Crombez (1999, p. 357) invoke the concept of attention as a "dynamic mechanism of selection for action". Selection and control of action is the topic of Chapter 8.

While pain can interrupt ongoing activity, our response to it can be affected by cognitive, emotional and motivational factors.

Eccleston and Crombez (1999) review experimental evidence that demonstrates how pain interferes with and interrupts performance on another attention-demanding task. Eccleston (1994) compared the performance of chronic pain patients with pain-free controls on an easy and a difficult attention task. Results showed that patients with high intensity chronic pain performed significantly worse than low intensity chronic pain patients and pain-free controls. Therefore, it appears that pain demands attentional engagement and the interrupting effect of the pain reduces other task performance.

However, responding to pain is only one of the demands for action that the environment makes on us and pain may or not be prioritised as the focus of attention. Fernandez and Turk (1989) examined the effect of distraction on pain perception to discover if diverting attention from pain can relieve chronic pain. In general, it appears that a distraction task must be sufficiently difficult or demanding of attentional processing for there to be an effect. Emotions such as fear or motivation to succeed can be attentionally demanding and some of the variation in the pain experience reported may be due to the distracting effect of emotions demanding attention (Beecher, 1956).

Eccleston (1995) argued that environments in which pain occurs often provide numerous demands and possible interruptions. When a task is interrupted the cognitive system appears to need to return to it and complete it, if at all possible (Gillie & Broadbent, 1989). To maintain coherence of ongoing behaviour in the face of these inter-ruptions attention must be switched between tasks and demands. Using a modification of the intentional, executive switching task used on normal subjects by Allport, Styles, and Hsieh (1994), covered in Chapter 8, Eccleston tested the performance of chronic pain patients. He discovered that the ability to switch between tasks in people suffering high intensity chronic pain is significantly impaired. It appears that chronic pain acts as constant interruption to other ongoing activities and the maintenance of coherent behaviour requires intentional switching between pain and other tasks. Eccleston and Crombez (1999) propose a functional model for the interruption of pain and attention with seven interrelating components:

- the environment
- stimuli arising from the environment
- the sensory system
- action programmes
- a focal task
- threat mediation
- moderating factors.

Before the introduction of a noxious stimulus the system is engaged in a focal task and the initial priority for attentional engagement is to focus on the sensory information related to that task. Other sensory information will be received by the senses, for example, background noise or colours of objects, but these are not the focus of attention. However, if a pain is then sensed the initial task is interrupted by the pain signal. The novel, threatening sensory information breaks through and captures control of action. At the same time, other activities you were previously unaware of, such as maintaining posture and normal breathing, are also interrupted as attention switches to escaping the damage. There are now two competing demands on attentional resources: continue with the initial task and escape the pain. Both tasks can continue but only by rapidly switching between them. As pain repeatedly interrupts and demands attention and action while other possible actions and their consequences need to be monitored, this interruption compromises performance on other tasks.

Event-related potentials and crossmodal attention

Driver, Eimer, Macaluso, and van Velzen (2004) review the neurobiology of spatial attention and argue that the emerging evidence suggests that the effect of attentional preparation in cortical areas prior to the presentation of any stimulus, reveals selective effects far earlier than any proposed in conventional, box-and-arrow-type information processing accounts of attention such as were discussed in Chapter 2. Driver et al. (2004) also discuss event-related potential (ERP) studies on crossmodal spatial attention and the crossmodal sensory modulation effects such as those we have met earlier. They propose that the ERP data show that in studies of endogenous spatial orienting reveals that sensory-specific ERPs, which are generally considered "unimodal", are, in fact, affected by crossmodal attentional constraints. ERP data can plot the time course of brain activity involved in attentional processing: early components reflect sensory-specific processing, while later components reflect decision-related processes. Examination of the changes in ERPs depending on whether participants endogenously cued to attend to one or other or both modality on the same or opposite side of space reveal many cross-modal interactions. In general, it appears that even very early components of stimulus processing, that would generally be considered sensory specific, or "unimodal", are affected when other stimuli are expected in another modality on the opposite side of space. So, Driver et al. argue, this implies that:

> Cross-modal links in endogenous spatial attention can affect perceptual processing that may arise in "unimodal" sensory cortex. This suggests that remote brain areas, each specialising in different modalities, come to focus on a common location together, in a manner consistent with the idea of "integrated attentional function". (p. 280).

Similar effects have been found for exogenous attention.

Summary

Auditory information differs from visual information in that its features are sequentially distributed over time. Unlike foveation in vision, auditory attention cannot be physically moved to survey the environment. However, auditory attention can be oriented to properties of stimuli such as frequency, and listeners can selective tune to frequencies within a narrow band. Outside the bandwidth of selectivity signals are missed (Greenberg & Larkin, 1968). Auditory attention does not appear to benefit very much from orienting cues to the location of an upcoming signal when the task requires detection. However, when listeners must make a discrimination response direction cueing facilitates response. It appears that detection occurs for all stimuli irrespective of location, but once attention is directed to a location discrimination is better. Scharf (1998) suggests this pattern is evidence for the audition acting as an early warning system. Selective report from brief auditory arrays suggests the existence of an "echoic memory" somewhat analogous to iconic memory in vision, but the partial report advantage is much smaller than for vision. Auditory stream analysis and auditory streaming segregate multiple sources of auditory information into perceptual groups and allow sources of complex sounds to be attributed to auditory objects. It appears that auditory segregation is pre-attentive (MacKen et al., 2003).

The data on integration of separate auditory features do not fit well with an auditory analogue of feature integration theory for vision (Treisman & Gelade, 1989). Woods et al. (2001) found some conjunctions of auditory features, such as frequency and location, were faster than feature detection for location alone. This pattern of results suggests individual features interact during processing and that focusing attention on a more easily discriminable feature facilitates processing of other features at the same location. This was called facilitatory interactive feature analysis.

Scharf (1998) suggests that focusing on frequency is achieved by the ability of olivocochlear bundle (OCB) to bias frequency detection in the cochlea. The relation between attentional processes in vision, audition and touch is investigated in crossmodal experiments. Research by Driver and Spence and colleagues has spearheaded this work, which aims to discover how orienting attention in one modality affects attention in another modality. When covert attention is directed to an expected target location both visual and auditory targets are discriminated better, suggesting strong crossmodal links between the visual and auditory modalities in endogenous orienting of spatial attention. However, there appear to be no effects of exogenous visual cues on auditory target detection (Spence & Driver, 1997), which is in accordance with the view that auditory attention acts as an early warning system that must be constantly open to new sounds from all locations. Crossmodal experiments on the relation between other modalities and touch show that touch can also generate crossmodal shifts of spatial attention and that, even when hands are crossed, spatial attention is facilitated to the side of space touched rather than the right or left hand, suggesting a remapping of spatial location according to proprioceptive information on body posture. Illusory conjunction between vision and audition, and vision and touch and crossmodal interactions produce a variety of illusions, such as ventriloquism and the McGurk effect. These interactions suggest the integration of sensory information occurs pre-attentively, and brain-imaging studies implicate several areas of the parietal lobes, in these processes.

Further reading

- Driver, J. & Spence, C. (1999). Cross-modal links in spatial attention. In G. Humphreys, J. Duncan, & A. Treisman, *Attention, space and action*. Oxford: Oxford University Press.

  An integrative overview of crossmodal attention.
- Moore, B. (1994). Hearing. In R. Gregory & A. M. Colman (Eds.). *Sensation and perception*. Harlow: Longman.

  An introduction to basic auditory processes.
- Scharf, B. (1998). Auditory attention: The psychoacoustical approach. In H. Pashler (Ed.). *Attention*. Hove, UK: Psychology Press.

  Provides more details on selective auditory attention.
- Sloboda, J. (2000). *The musical mind: The cognitive psychology of music*. Oxford: Blackwell.

  For those interested not only in hearing but in music, this book covers a range of topics about hearing.

Task combination and divided attention 6

Introduction

Just as there is controversy over the nature of attentional processing in selective attention tasks, psychologists hold a variety of views about the best explanation for human performance in divided attention conditions. When two tasks need to be done at the same time, is attention shared? Are there different attentional mechanisms responsible for different tasks? Different modalities? But what exactly is it that we do "at the same time"? The classic PRP studies by Welford (1952) looked at overlapping tasks, in which one and then another simple stimulus was presented for speeded response. This type of task is the most frequently used in studies of PRP (see Pashler, 1993 for a review). Other tasks, some of which we shall meet here, require subjects to do two tasks at the same time, but on a trial-by-trial basis (e.g. Posner and Boies, 1971). Sometimes, experiments involve the continuous performance of two, quite lengthy, ongoing tasks, Allport, Antonis, and Reynolds (1972), for example. It is possible that these different tasks make quite different demands on the attentional system.

According to original filter theory, there was just one processing channel and therefore task combination could only be achieved by rapid switching of the filter and multiplexing or time-sharing tasks. If it could be demonstrated that two complex tasks that should require continuous attentional processing could be combined without loss of speed or accuracy, then the argument that there was only a single processing channel would have to be abandoned. Allport et al. (1972) asked competent keyboard players to play the piano, sight reading examination pieces that they had not seen before, at the same time as shadowing prose at a rate of 150 words per minute. With only a little practice, Allport and colleagues' subjects were able to perform both tasks in combination as fast and as accurately as they could when they performed them separately. This result was interpreted as evidence against a single channel for attentional processing. Experiments like that of Allport et al. (1972) are not without their critics. Broadbent (1982) points out that it is possible to detect decrements in the performance data when the two tasks are combined. Furthermore, it is extremely difficult to determine whether or not each individual task requires absolutely continuous attentional processing. Broadbent would argue that both shadowing prose and sight reading music are tasks involving stimuli that have a certain amount of redundancy in them. Redundancy is a concept from information theory, which was explained in Chapter 2. What redundancy means is that prose and music contain information that allows the subjects to predict what letter or note is likely to come next. If the subject can predict with some certainty what is likely to come next in either task, then at those moments when predictability of the next word or note is high, attention can be rapidly switched, allowing time sharing between the tasks, rather than simultaneous combination. To be certain that there was no time sharing, both tasks would have to be absolutely continuous and include no redundancy whatsoever. We would also have to be certain that each individual task was being performed at the limit of attentional resources. Only if these conditions were fulfilled for the separate tasks and we could be certain that there were absolutely no decrements in either task when they were performed together could we say that there was no limit to dual task combination.

Single channel or general purpose processing capacity?

Both Welford (1952) and Broadbent (1958) suggested that there was a central bottleneck in processing which limited dual task performance. Other theorists argued that the bottleneck was not due to the structure of the human information processing system, but rather reflected a limited amount of processing "capacity" that could be allocated to a single task or shared between a number of tasks according to priorities. We shall examine some of these theories in a moment. We can see here that while we have one metaphor that likens attention to a resource or capacity or "amount of something", we have the other metaphor in which attention is like a bottleneck where selection has to take place due to the fact that parallel processing must change to serial processing to protect the limited capacity component of the processing system. Although these metaphors are rather different, they are related. If either the attentional resource or capacity that limits the system is of a "general purpose" type, then all tasks that require attention will draw on the same resource or compete at the same bottleneck. This is the concept of a single, general purpose, limited capacity central processor (GPLCP). According to this conception, if the GPLPC is engaged in one mental operation, such as shadowing, then it is not available for another operation, such as sight reading. If one response is being selected, then another response will have to wait until the GPLPC is free.

However, if there are different varieties of resources, or different capacities, that are dedicated to processing different kinds of information, then although there may be specific limits on each variety of resource, there need not be a general limit on task combination. Provided two tasks do not compete at the same time for the same resource there is no reason why they should interfere, unless there is competition at some other common level, such as data extraction. (See Allport, 1980b for a critical review.)

Capacity theories and the human operator

A selective bottleneck in processing is a structural limitation and many of the experiments on selective attention discussed in the previous chapters were concerned with discovering the location of that bottleneck. Although we have seen evidence for selective attention operating at different levels dependent on the task demand the idea of selection at some point in processing remains. However, the amount of information processing that an organism can do at any one time might alternatively be conceived of as being limited by the amount of processing capacity, or processing resources, available to the organism. Human factors research, which is concerned with measuring workload, stress, noise etc. and human performance, clearly suggests that the human information processor is limited in the number and complexity of operations that can be concurrently performed and that in different circumstances task combination is more or less difficult. This difficulty might be moderated by other variables, external to the operator, such as heat or noise, or by variables internal to the operator such as personality, lack of sleep or fear. Revelle (1993) provides a useful review of "non-cognitive" factors that can affect an individual's ability to perform attentionally demanding tasks. Most of these effects are to do with personality and levels of arousal.

Knowles (1963) proposed that the "human operator" could be thought of as having a "pool" of processing resources and that this pool was of limited capacity. If one task demands more of the resources, then there will be less of the pool available to another task. As the first task becomes more and more difficult, more and more resources will be drawn from the pool, resulting in poorer and poorer performance of the secondary task. Note here an important difference from the structural view of attention. Rather than attention being directed to one task at a time, resource or capacity theory allows for attention to be shared between tasks in a graded manner. Moray (1967) pointed out that the adoption of a capacity view of attention did away with the need to assume a bottleneck. Interference between tasks simply arose out of the capacity demands of the tasks and this could appear at any stage in processing.

Kahneman's theory of attention and effort

Kahneman (1973) put forward a theory that likens attention to a limited resource that can be flexibly allocated as the human operator changes their allocation policy from moment to moment. Attention can be focused on one particular activity or can be divided between a number of activities. When tasks are more difficult, more attention is needed. Unlike Broadbent's flowchart of information through a structural system (see Figure 1.1), Kahneman's model is a model of mind. It includes enduring dispositions, momentary intentions and an evaluative decision process that determines the current demand on capacity. Attention here is rather like a limited power supply. If you turn on the rings of a gas cooker and the central heating boiler fires up, the height of the gas jets in the cooker rings goes down. There is only a limited supply of gas to these two appliances and the demand from the boiler reduces the amount of fuel available to the cooker. However, in Kahneman's theory, if we put more "effort" into a task we can do better. (For example during increased demand the gas company might raise the gas pressure in the main supply.) So, the amount of attentional capacity can vary according to motivation. The amount of effort available is also related to overall arousal level; as arousal increases or decreases, so does attentional capacity.

While there are some attractive properties in this model, such as the move away from structural limitations to processing limitations, there are some serious problems with the theory. First, it is known that at low levels of arousal, performance is poor; according to Kahneman this would be because the attentional capacity is low when arousal is low.

As arousal increases, so does performance, up to an optimum level, beyond which further increases in arousal, rather than improving performance, produce decrements. This is known as Yerkes–Dodson law (Yerkes and Dodson, 1908). We have probably all experienced situations in which a little background noise, for example, helps to keep us alert and improves performance, but if the noise becomes extremely loud, we find it impossible to do anything else. If attentional effort were directly related to the arousing effect of the noise, task performance should improve monotonically with the increase in the noise.

Second, defining arousal is very problematic (Revelle, 1993). Third, and possibly this is the most serious problem, how can task difficulty be measured independently (Allport, 1980b)? Kahneman put forward the idea that task difficulty could be determined by the amount of interference on a concurrent task. However, if task difficulty is measured by interference, and interference is an index of difficulty, we have no independent measure. Another problem is that interference between concurrent tasks is said to be non-specific. As capacity is "general purpose", any combination of tasks will result in some decrement in one or other or both tasks. We shall see a little later that there is now ample evidence to suggest that interference between tasks is task specific, for example, McLeod and Posner (1984) and Posner and Boies (1971). For the moment, we shall continue our discussion of capacity theories.

Bourke, Duncan, and Nimmo-Smith (1996) conducted a series of experiments to test central capacity theory. Their participants were engaged in dual tasks and instructed to give priority to one of the tasks over the other. Four tasks were used, designed to be quite different from one another. The tasks were random number generation; prototype learning; a manual task requiring nuts to be screwed up and down bolts; and tone detection. Bourke et al. (1996) reasoned that if the central processing capacity is shared between tasks, then the task that demands most capacity will interfere most when combined with each of the other tasks. Similarly, the task demanding least capacity will interfere least when combined with the other three tasks. Despite these tasks being very different in their apparent processing they all interfered with each other. Importantly, random number generation interfered *most* with all other tasks and tone detection interfered *least*. However, an important finding was that random number generation produced dual task interference irrespective of whether it was designated the primary or secondary task and likewise the tone detection task always interfered least. Bourke et al. (1996) say this experiment provides evidence for a general limiting factor being involved in the dual task decrement, but does not elucidate whether the limit is one of a general pool of processing resources, a limit on central executive processes that control and coordinates concurrent tasks or a general limit on how much information can be processed concurrently by the entire cognitive system.

Measuring resource allocation

Limitations: Data-limited and resource-limited processing

Wickens (1984) prefers the word "resources" over other terms such as "attention", "effort" and "capacity". Attention, he feels, has so many ambiguous meanings as to be meaningless. Effort suggests a motivational variable that does not necessarily have to correlate with performance and capacity suggests some kind of limit rather than a variable amount. Wickens' paper is a useful review of ideas concerning processing resources in attention.

Perhaps the first, best developed theory of resources in attention came from Norman and Bobrow (1975). Norman and Bobrow introduced the idea of a performance resource function (PRF). (See Figure 6.1.) For a single task, resources can be invested up to a point where, no matter how much more resource is invested, performance will not improve. At this point, performance is said to be data limited. There will be a data limitation if the data input is of poor quality, for example when conversations are noisy or print is smudged. Data limitations could also arise in memory. A data limitation cannot be

Figure 6.1 Performance resource functions for tasks differing in practice or difficulty. A = difficult; B = easier or practices; C = higher data limited asymptote.

From Wickens (1984), in Parasuraman and Davies (1984) *Varieties of Attention*, *p. 73.* Copyright (1984). Reproduced with permission of Elsevier and C. Wickens.

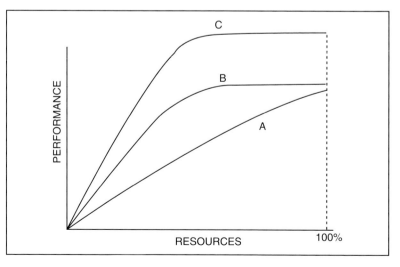

overcome, no matter how much we try. However, if more resources are invested or withdrawn and performance changes accordingly, performance is said to be resource limited.

When two tasks are combined, resources must be allocated between both tasks. Depending on the priorities we set, more or less resource can be allocated to one or other of the tasks. If performance on one task is plotted against performance on the other task, a performance operating characteristic (POC) is obtained. Using POCs it is possible to try to capture resource allocation to each task. The curve of a POC represents the change in level of performance on one task when the level of performance on another concurrently performed task is changed. If the two tasks are resource limited, then there will be a complementary relationship between the two tasks, so that as performance on one task improves there will be a corresponding decline in performance on the other task. Figure 6.2 shows two possible POCs. Curve A shows the case when both tasks share a particular resource. Here diverting resources from Task X results in a corresponding improvement in Task Y. The other POC, curve B, shows a case where this complementary relationship does not hold. This can be interpreted as showing that either Task X and Task Y do not share resources or that the tasks are data limited.

Norman and Bobrow (1975) believed that there were a variety of resources such as "processing effort, the various forms of memory capacity and communication channels" (p. 45). This means that each kind of resource would have to be investigated separately to determine whether or not two tasks were competing for them. Allport (1980b) provides an in-depth analysis and critical review of Norman and Bobrow's (1975) theory. He claims that this theory ends up being as circular as that of Kahneman's (1973). One problem is that, again, there is no independent way of measuring the resource demands made by tasks and whether these resources are from the same or different pools. If two tasks interfere, they are said to be competing for the same resource, if they don't interfere, they are using separate resources or are data limited.

Hirst (1986), too, points out that until resources are better specified, it will be difficult to come up with a good theory of divided attention. He remarks that psychologists are not even clear about whether there is one central resource on which all tasks draw or whether there are multiple resources drawn on by different tasks, e.g. a "visual pool" drawn on by visual tasks and a "verbal pool" drawn on by verbal tasks. Or, possibly, whether there is a combination of specific multiple resources and a central resource!

Figure 6.2 Performance
Operating
Characteristic
representation of (A)
a case in which
resources from a
secondary task on the
abscissa can
compensate for
difficulty changes in
the primary task on
the ordinate; and (B) a
case in which this
reallocation is not
possible.

From Wickens (1984).
Copyright (1984), in
Parasuraman and
Davies (1984)
Varieties of Attention,
p. 80. Copyright
(1984). Reproduced
with permission of
Elsevier and
C. Wickens.

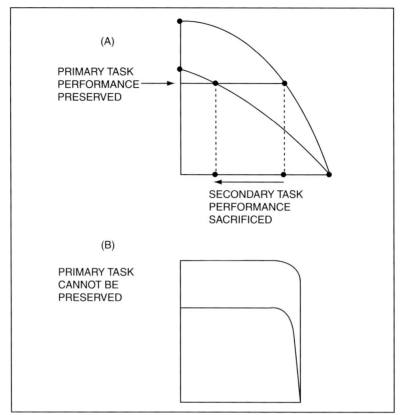

Dual task performance: How many resources?

Let us look at some of the evidence that has led psychologists to think
that resources are shared between tasks or are specific to different
kinds of task. Posner and Boies (1971) asked their subjects to do two
things at once. One task involved letter matching, in which a warning
signal was followed by a letter, e.g., A. After half a second, another
letter was presented and the subject had to judge whether or not the
letters were the same. While responding to the letter-matching task
with their right hand by pressing a key, subjects were also monitoring
for the presentation of an auditory tone. When they detected the tone
they were to press the left-hand key. The auditory signal could be
presented at varying times during the presentation sequence of the
visual task. Posner and Boies (1971) showed that reaction time to the

tones was more or less equal during the parts of the visual task in which the warning signal was presented and during the waiting time before the first letter. This was taken to show that processing the warning signal takes little attention. However, if the tone was presented at the same time as either of the letters, response was slower, but not as slow as when the tone was presented during the interval between letter presentation, i.e., when the subject was attending to the first letter in preparation for response to the second. This experiment could be taken as evidence for a general limit on attentional processing. During the "easy" part of the visual task, attention is free to support the tone detection task; but in the "difficult", part of the visual task, which demands attention, there is less available for tone detection or response. There is, of course, an alternative explanation.

In a clever experimental manipulation, McLeod (1977, 1978) altered just one aspect of Posner and Boies' (1971) task. Rather than responding to the auditory tone by pressing a key, McLeod asked his subjects to say "bip", a response that was completely different from the key press required in the visual matching task. Using these response arrangements, there was no interference between the letter-matching task and tone detection, irrespective of whereabouts in the letter-matching task the tone was presented. So, if the response systems for the two tasks are separated, interference disappears. The result of McLeod's experiment is clearly contrary to a general resource limitation on attentional processing, as the limit here is specific to the type of response required. There appears to be no attentional limit on the subject's ability to perform the letter-matching task and concurrently monitor for a tone, which are in different domains, one visual and one auditory. Taken in conjunction with the Posner and Boies study, it looks as if we are limited in making two similar responses to two different tasks. Multiple resource accounts of attentional capacity proposed there are a number of resources that may be required by a task and that tasks will only interfere in as far as they compete for the same resource (e.g. Navon and Gopher, 1979).

More effects of stimulus response compatibility

McLeod and Posner (1984) carried out further experiments on stimulus response compatibility. They suggested that there is a special class of translations between input and output, i.e., relations between stimuli and responses, in dual task conditions. They tested the effects of different auditory/vocal transformations by combining a number of auditory/vocal tasks with visual/manual pattern matching. The basic method involved two tasks. The first task was a version of the visual letter-matching task used by Posner and Boies (1971) and McLeod (1977). This task was then combined with an auditory task that varied in the nature of the transformation between stimulus and response. We shall look at this experiment in some detail as it is rather interesting.

There were four groups of subjects. Three groups made a vocal response to the auditory task and moved a lever to the left or right depending on whether the letters in the visual task were the same or different. The fourth group, called the modality crossover group, responded manually to the auditory task and made a vocal response "same" or "different" to the visual task. Each group did a different auditory task. Subjects in group 1 were to shadow the auditory stimulus, they heard "up" or "down" and repeated the word. The second group of subjects also heard "up" or "down" but responded by saying a semantic associate, i.e. "high" or "low". The subjects in group 3 heard the word "high" to which they responded "up" or a 400-Hz tone to which they responded "low". The fourth cross-modality group, heard "up" or "down" and responded by moving a lever up or down, remember that this group was making a vocal response to the visual task. Presentation of the auditory stimulus, or probe, was given at six different stages during the visual task. The probe could be given as follows:

1. 700 msec before letter 1
2. 100 msec before letter 1
3. 100 msec after the onset of letter 1
4. 100 msec before letter 2
5. 100 msec after the onset of letter 2
6. 1000 msec after the onset of letter 2.

These six probe positions give three different kinds of dual task trials. For the probe positions 1 and 6, there was no temporal overlap between the two responses. However, when the probe was presented at positions 2 and 3, a response was required for the auditory stimulus during the time in which the first letter was being encoded. If the auditory probe was presented at positions 4 or 5, a response was needed for both tasks simultaneously.

Two main results were clear. First, when the processing demands of the two tasks overlapped in positions 2, 3, 4 and 5, there was inter-ference between tasks. The group doing the semantic auditory task, saying "high" to "up", showed more interference than the shadowing group, but the modality crossover group showed far more interference than the other groups at positions 3 and 4. That is, in the condition when they had to give a verbal response to the visual task at the same time as giving a manual response to the auditory task. The mixed word tone group showed more interference when response was to a tone than to a word. Clearly, performance is very good when the subject simply shadows, or repeats the auditory probe, but is very poor in the modality crossover condition. The shadowing task is "ideomotor compatible" in that the response resembles the stimulus, but McLeod and Posner suggest a different reason for the difference between shadowing and the crossmodality task. They suggest, on the basis of neuropsychological evidence, that there is a "privileged loop", which allows the articulatory programme that is involved in word production to be retrieved by hearing a word. This loop is separate from the rest of the processing system and allows spoken repetition of heard words to proceed without interference from other tasks.

In the modality crossover condition, the subject is prepared, or primed, to make a vocal response to the visual stimulus. However, if the auditory probe arrives while the subject is waiting to do this, the articulatory response to the word is activated via the privileged loop. This then causes interference with the word that the subject is trying to produce in response to the visual task. McLeod and Posner suggest that there is an automatic linking between an auditory input and a vocal response that is always active. If there are other privileged loops between particular inputs and outputs, such as the one proposed here, then it begins to look as if the human information processing system may have multiple channels that relate particular input patterns to overt actions. Interference will only be observed when there is specific competition within channels. This interference will always appear and make some tasks impossible to combine without cost. Shaffer (1975) found that typists could copytype and simultaneously do a shadowing task, but could not audiotype and read aloud. The difficulty here is that when people listen to the auditory message, the privileged loop from those heard words, tends to activate the motor programmes for their pronunciation. If, at the same time, other words, which the subject is trying to read, are also activating their motor programmes there will be interference. However, copytyping can be easily combined with shadowing, because there is a direct route from the shadowed input to speech output which is quite independent of the mapping between the seen words and manual response of copytyping. We will look more closely at skills such as typing, the effects of practice and automaticity and the differences between the performance of experts and novices in Chapter 8.

The psychological refractory period

The psychological refractory period (PRP) has already been put forward as part of the original evidence for a bottleneck in processing. When two signals requiring two responses are presented in rapid secession, so that the second stimulus is presented before response has been made to the first, the second response tends to be delayed. As the onset of the two signals gets closer, so the delay in the response to the second tends to increase. This delay became known as the psychological refractory period. Welford (1952) suggested that this effect was evidence for a limited capacity mechanism that could only process one response decision at a time and was part of the initial evidence for a single channel theory of attention. It was reasoned that a bottleneck at the response decision stage meant that the second response had to "queue" until the first response has been selected. (See Figure 6.3.)

Effect of stimulus response compatibility on PRP

We have already seen that one particularly important factor that influences PRP appears to be the compatibility between the stimulus and the response to be made to it. (Welford, 1967, provides a review of PRP research up to that date.) In the Posner and Boies (1971) study, the keypress response to the auditory tone was not very compatible and would have required a translation from the auditory input to a manual response. McLeod (1978) asked his subjects to say "bip" in response to hearing a "bip", a more compatible response, and the interference disappeared. Greenwald and Schulman (1973) experimented with stimulus response compatibility and PRP. Two signals were presented in rapid succession. The first task was to push a switch in the direction of an arrow, the second task to be performed had either a compatible or incompatible response with its stimulus. In the compatible condition, subjects were to say "one" in response to hearing "one", in the incompatible condition, they were to say "A" when they heard "one". When the stimulus and response were highly compatible there was no refractoriness, but when the response to the second stimulus was incompatible, saying "A" to hearing "one", there

Figure 6.3 A typical PRP procedure. Stimulus 2 (S2) follows stimulus 1 (S1) after a stimulus onset asynchrony (SOA). According to a response queuing account of PRP, selection of the response to the second stimulus (RT2) must wait until the response to S1 (RT1) has been selected.

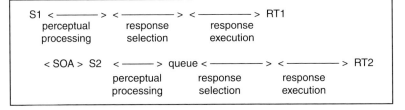

was evidence for a refractory period. Thus in Posner and Boies' experiment refractoriness may be contributing to the observed interference between letter matching and tone detection, because the auditory signal has to be translated to a keypress. In McLeod's experiment, hearing a "bip" and saying "bip" is similar to hearing "one" and saying "one" in the study by Greenwald and Schulman, i.e. no psychological refractory period is found because there is a more direct matching between stimulus and response. Greenwald and Schulman (1973) suggested that when the response to a stimulus was "ideomotor compatible", the feedback from the response resembled the stimulus to which the response was made and tasks of this kind could be combined with other tasks without cost. Pashler (1984) has extended and refined work on PRP and provided strong evidence for a central bottleneck in overlapping tasks. Pashler (1990) investigated refractoriness in an experiment in which subjects were, as is usual in PRP experiments, given two successive stimuli to which they had to respond as fast as possible. However, in one experiment, Pashler (1990) manipulated the similarity between the two stimuli and their responses. The stimuli were an auditorily presented tone requiring a spoken response and a visually presented word requiring a keypress response. Thus, the stimulus response mapping was very similar to the experiment by McLeod (1978), in which no dual task interference was found. Of course, the dual task technique used by Posner and Boies (1971) and McLeod (1978) gives less accurate measures of the relation between the two tasks than can be obtained in a PRP experiment. One of the questions Pashler asked was this: Does the PRP arise because of a central processing bottleneck or because the stimuli and responses are similar? If the bottleneck account is correct, then there will be refractoriness even if the stimuli and their associated responses are quite different. If similarity is the cause, however, there should be no PRP when the stimuli and responses for them are different. Pashler found that even when the stimuli and responses were dissimilar, i.e., the spoken response to the tone and the keypress response to the visual word, there was still a psychological refractory period. Furthermore, in a condition where the subjects did not know the order in which the stimuli would be presented, response to the first stimulus was slower than it was when subjects knew which task would come first. It looks as if the subjects were not able to prepare in advance for both possible stimulus response pairs. Knowing the order of tasks allowed the subjects to get ready for the expected stimulus and its response. The results therefore supported the existence of a processing bottleneck, even when tasks are quite different.

Fagot and Pashler (1992) considered the possibility that the problem people have in making two responses to two stimuli in quick succession, might be due to the difficulty of making responses to two different objects. We have seen already, when we examined visual attention, that there is evidence for attention being allocated to objects. For example, Duncan (1984) showed that two judgements could be made about two attributes of a single object as easily as one. We also saw that attention is allocated to items that form a perceptual group, for example the experiment by Driver and Baylis (1989) who showed that interference in the Eriksen and Eriksen (1974) task was not necessarily spatially based, as letters that moved together (hence forming a perceptual group, or object) exhibited the flanker compatibility effect. These results, together with others from Treisman (e.g. Treisman & Gelade, 1980; Treisman Kahneman, & Burkell 1983), suggest that focal attention is directed to one object at a time and the features of that object are then integrated. We have examined this kind of evidence in Chapter 4. Applying these findings to the PRP experiment, Fagot and Pashler (1992) hypothesised that there were two ways of explaining the occurrence of the bottleneck in processing. One model could be that after an object is identified, focal attention is used to send information about the object to the response decision stage where a response decision mechanism selects all the possible responses for that single object. An alternative model is that the bottleneck can only select one response, but the number of objects is irrelevant. In a series of experiments, Fagot and Pashler asked their subjects to make two separate responses to the attributes of a single object. The results showed that even when the two different responses are to the same object, e.g., name the letter, press a button for the colour, only one response can be selected at a time. However, when asked to make two responses to the same attribute of an object, e.g., name the colour and press a button for the colour, this can be done with only one response selection. Based on other manipulations of stimulus response compatibility, using Stroop stimuli and the Simon effect (e.g., pressing the left button to a stimulus on the right), Fagot and Pashler (1992) concluded that only one response selection operation occurs when subjects make two responses to the same attribute of an object. So the response selection mechanism which was hypothesised to be the location of the bottle-neck can select two responses at once, provided certain condition are met.

A production system model for the bottleneck in PRP

Fagot and Pashler (1992) suggest a straightforward model, based on a production system framework. Anderson's (1983) ACT* is a production system used by computer scientists and is described in Chapter 7. They propose that a model to explain the bottleneck in production system terms would have these properties:

1. Prior to the task being performed, a number of response selection rules are activated. The more rules that are activated the less the individual activation for each rule.
2. Each rule has a condition and an action. When the condition for the action is met, the rule applies and the action is carried out. The higher the activation of the rule, the faster it will be applied.
3. Only one rule can be applied at once.
4. A rule can specify multiple motor responses in its action statement.

In order to find the right action given a particular condition specified by the perceptual input, a code must be generated or retrieved from memory. Fagot and Pashler say the code can be considered as a specification of where to find a description of how to make the response that, their experiments have shown, can be multiple motor actions. They suggest that the bottleneck is at the point of generating the code and only one response can be retrieved at a time. Later mechanisms that look up response specifications and translate them into action are not limited. Overall, Fagot and Pashler believe the evidence is consistent with a bottleneck in processing at the stage where action codes are retrieved and generated. They do, however, point out some problems for the model. In Chapter 2, we looked at the question of early and late selection in visual attention and found evidence in the experiment by Eriksen and Eriksen (1974) for irrelevant letters which flank a target causing interference. This interference was interpreted as evidence for response activation from the distractors conflicting with the response to the target letter. This effect should not happen if only one response can be retrieved from memory at a time, which is what the model just seen suggests. Fagot and Pashler (1992) suggest a way around this paradox. If the system were incapable of implementing two rules at a time because the neural mechanisms that implement the rules cannot settle into two different patterns of activity at the same time, then although two responses could not be made at once, the pattern of activity from redundant inputs could still interfere with the process of settling into one pattern, hence slowing response and producing the Eriksen effect.

The idea that the brain has to resolve conflict to "settle" to a steady state is a consequence of viewing information processing within connectionist frameworks mentioned in Chapter 4 and will be discussed again in Chapter 9. In addition, Carrier and Pashler (1995) showed that "memory retrieval is delayed by central processes in the choice task, arguing that the central bottleneck responsible for dual task interference encompasses memory retrieval as well as response selection" (p. 1339).

Is there bottleneck?

If the PRP is simply due to competition at memory retrieval and response selection it should not matter which task is done first. However, evidence exists that suggests that response order on the previous trial influences response on the next trial, with participants tending to repeat the previous response order. De Jong (1995) examined how the performance of two overlapping tasks is organised and controlled. In De Jong's experiments, subjects were presented with stimuli in unpredictable order. It was found that expected order rather than actual presentation order affected performance, that there was facilitation when task order was repeated on the next trial and that it was the performance of the second task that benefited most when task order was held constant over a number of trials. These effects were greatest at short inter-trial intervals. De Jong (1995) suggests that the results support the notion that overlapping task performance is controlled by a "multi-level control structure that prepares the processing system not only for the immediate processing of the first task but also for a timely and rapid switch to the second task" (p. 21). Although there is evidence that preparation and response selection limit performance in overlapping PRP tasks, De Jong points out that we need to know the relative importance of the limitations on response preparation and the limitations on response selection. We have seen that task similarity effects such as those we discussed in the dual task experiments of Greenwald and Shulman (1973) and McLeod and Posner (1984) suggest that when tasks are highly ideomotor compatible, the limitation on response preparation may be reduced. However, De Jong suggests that this compatibility may equally well demand less of the central channel processing capacity. Recently, Schumacher et al. (2001) have demonstrated near perfect time sharing in a PDP task where the two tasks are compatible in this way. Experiments showed that after only a moderate amount of practice, some participants were able to achieve almost perfect time sharing between tasks. The tasks were arranged in a similar way to those of McLeod (1997), with one task having an auditory–vocal stimulus – response mapping, the other task having a visual–manual stimulus – response mapping. Similar results have been found by Hazeltine, Teague, and Ivry (2002). However, there is an ongoing debate about whether the PRP effect can truly be eliminated when tasks are ideomotor compatible. Lien, Proctor, and Allen (2002) argue that ideomotor compatibility does not eliminate PRP and that the very concept requires clarification before its importance in task combination can be fully understood. Greenwald (2004) disagrees with Lien et al. (2002) and argues that it is possible to empirically demonstrate perfect time sharing; that it is necessary to stress speed of responding to obtain such data; that ideomotor compatibility is not a necessary or sufficient condition to demonstrate perfect time sharing, but when tasks are so compatible, perfect time sharing can be obtained with less practice than when only one task is ideomotor compatible. One interpretation of perfect time sharing is discussed later, when we consider Meyer and Kieras' (1997a, 1997b) account of PRP. This account of PRP suggests that processing capacity might be shared between tasks rather than allocated all or none to one or the other.

Alternative accounts of PRP

We made the distinction between attention as a single channel and attention as a resource at the start of this chapter. As a consequence, there are similar differences in the explanations given for the PRP effect. Tombu and Jolicoeur (2003) compare and contrast different approaches to explaining PRP and put forward their own account for the effect. They distinguish among three major classes of explanation, which the term "structural bottleneck theories", exemplified by Welford (1952) and Pashler (1994); "capacity sharing theories", exemplified by Kahenman (1973) and Navon and Gopher (1979), Navon and Miller (2002); and "strategic bottleneck theories" proposed by Meyer and Kieras (1997a and 1997b).

Structural bottleneck account
Perhaps the most widely accepted account for PRP effects involves the assumption of a structural bottleneck account (Pashler 1994, 1997, Pashler & Johnston, 1989). When two tasks overlap in time both the first and the second task seem to need to use the same mechanism that retrieves the code for response. If this central mechanism is busy processing the information from the first task, the second task simply

had to wait. This wait causes PRP, or refractoriness. The single channel bottleneck account can explain a hallmark property of PRP, that of the interaction between PRP and the time delay between the presentation of the first and second task stimulus as follows. At long stimulus onset asynchronies (SOAs) between task 1 and task 2, task 1 has finished processing at the bottleneck stage by the time the stimulus for task 2 is presented and so there is no competition for processing in the bottleneck and task 2 is not delayed. However, at short SOAs, task 1 is still occupying the bottleneck when task 2 needs to use it and so task 2 processing is delayed until task 1 has finished using bottleneck processes. As SOAs become shorter and shorter, task 2 has to wait longer and longer to use the bottleneck. Because task 1 always has first access to the bottleneck there should be no effect of SOA on task 1.

A strategic bottleneck? Executive control models

Meyer and Kieras (1997a, 1997b, 1999) also proposed a model for dual task performance and PRP. The executive process interactive control (EPIC) model is of skilled performance and uses procedural knowledge. These topics are detailed in Chapter 7. In principle, once a skill is learned, it should be possible to combine it with another skilled task without cost because neither task requires central processing. Dual task interference could therefore arise from two sources. First, the tasks may not be fully proceduralised as a skill and, second, there may be strategic executive control that can optionally postpone some stages of one task while the other is given priority. Any interference is still in a sense due to processing bottlenecks, but where the bottleneck is located in the sequence of information processing is strategically placed by executive control and can therefore be early or late in processing. However, under the right conditions it should be possible to operate strategy in which both tasks could perfectly time share the available processing. Such evidence of perfect time sharing has been found by Schumacher et al. (2001), mentioned earlier. The ability to share time perfectly could be affected by instructions about task priorities and individual preferences in whether participants chose to adopt a cautious, successive, scheduling of tasks or a daring, simultaneous, task schedule. Perfect time sharing is only possible in special conditions and Meyer and Kieras suggest that usually these conditions do not apply, for example, most tasks paired in PRP experiments involve the same input or output processors and so a strategic bottleneck is needed to control input or output. Logan and Gordon (2001) also provide a model called executive control of the theory of visual attention (ECTVA). It is a combination of Bundesen's

TVA theory mentioned in Chapter 2 and another model of response selection by Nosofsky and Palmeri (1997). ECTVA allows tasks to be prioritised and has mechanisms that are involved in control of allocating resources to tasks, setting goals that enable the performance of a particular task and inhibiting unwanted responses. Tombu and Jolicoeur (2003) claim that these adaptive executive control models, although allowing for strategic control, nevertheless still amount to bottleneck accounts.

Capacity-sharing accounts of PRP

According to this class of account, the overlapping tasks in a PRP experiment can, in principle take place in parallel, but rather than a structural bottleneck, there is a limited amount of processing resource (see Kahneman's, 1973 theory and McLeod's, 1977 experiment discussed earlier). As resources are limited, task 1 and task 2 must share these resources. Tombu and Jolicoeur (2003) suggest that as many early PRP experiments gave participants instructions that stressed the importance of task 1 over task 2, most capacity would have been allocated to task 1 and so the results appear to confirm a single channel for processing. In their paper they are able to show mathematically that this is indeed the case. Navon and Miller (2002) also argue that as "the overlapping tasks paradigm is heavily biased in favour of a speedy reaction to the stimulus that appears first, it is not optimal for testing the central bottleneck model" (p. 193).

Tombu and Jolicoeur (2003) have developed a central capacity-sharing model of dual task performance. It assumes that there are stages of processing that are not capacity limited and others that are. The capacity-limited stages are referred to as "central stages". These central stages can process multiple stimuli simultaneously, when tasks overlap in time, but to do this, capacity is shared and the processing of both tasks is slowed down. Only the central capacity stages can share processing over tasks. The other processing stages are termed precentral and post-central. When tasks share the central capacity, each task takes a "sharing proportion" between 0 and 1 of the total capacity. Using calculations based on the total time to perform a task in terms of precentral, central and post-central stage durations, Tombu and Jolicoeur were able to predict how tasks would be affected by a number of parameters. They examined the case where SOAs are long and there is no central overlap between task 1 and task 2, and the case where SOAs are short and task 1 starts with full access to central processing and uses all available capacity. In this case, when task 2 begins to draw on central processing capacity, task 1 and task 2 must share capacity until task 1 has completed central processing. The sharing proportion allocated to each task determines how long central processing takes for each task.

Pashler and Johnston (1989) claimed that central capacity-sharing models could not account for the finding that perceptual factors such as the contrast between the stimulus and its background affected response time to task 2. The argument is that the difficulty of discriminating the task 2 stimulus does not need processing at the bottleneck and should therefore be able to continue while task 1 is being finished. So, at short SOAs prebottleneck processing of task 2 can be done at the same time as task 1 and therefore the difficulty of stimulus discrimination has little influence on task 2 response time. However, when SOA between task 1 and task 2 is longer, the discrimination of the task 2 target cannot begin until it presented and so there no opportunity to get on with prebottleneck processing while task 1 is being processed in the bottleneck. Pashler and Johnston claim this underadditivity between SOA and task difficulty is not predicted by capacity-sharing models. However, Tombu and Jolicoeur argue this prediction only follows if capacity sharing is necessary for all aspects of task processing and show that their model, which assumes only central processing is shared, predicts the same outcome.

Another argument against capacity-sharing models was made by Pashler (1994) based on the different patterns of response time distributions produced by participants in PRP tasks. In particular he suggested that when participants were free to respond to task 1, a tone, and task 2 a letter, in any order they pleased and the tasks were presented at zero SOA, a capacity-sharing account would predict that, on average, the tasks would be given an equal amount of available capacity and so finish at the same time, so the inter-response interval (IRI) between the response to task 1 and task 2 would be small. However, random variations would mean the one task would always finish before the other and so the distribution of RT would be broad and centred on zero. Alternatively, if performance were best characterised by the bottleneck account, Pashler argued, then three different response patterns would emerge depending on the response strategy adopted by participants. Either participants would delay response for one task until the response for the other tasks was known and produce IRS very close together and another type who did not wait and produced a bimodal distribution of responses one to each side of zero. This is what Pashler found. Tombu and Jolicoeur (2003) suggest that this result is not evidence against capacity sharing, because it is well known that the response on the previous trial has a strong influence on the response to the next trial, as for example demonstrated in the experiments by De Jong (1995), discussed previously. Therefore, there will be trial-to-trial variations in central capacity allocation due to biases in response order, which could produce a bimodal distribution, but have nothing to do with whether the processing system has a central shared capacity. A number of other arguments are made that indicate it is very difficult to empirically differentiate between a bottleneck and central capacity-sharing account of PRP. A critical evaluation of the single bottleneck theory is provided by Navon and Miller (2002), appropriately titled "queuing or sharing?" Clearly, there is a lot more work to be done here to discover the true interpretation of the data.

How are tasks controlled in the PRP task?

In his paper, De Jong (1995) also considered the question of how the switch to the second task is accomplished. The voluntary control of task switching is a topic which we will consider in Chapter 8, but here we will note that De Jong suggests that there may be two components of the control operation. First, the retrieval of the rules from memory, followed by a second operation that implements these rules. As De Jong (1995) points out, either of these control components could benefit from advance preparation and affect the PRP effect. More recently, Luria and Meiran (2003) have examined the online control of order in the PRP paradigm. Their central interest is the control of task switching, which is a subject we will discuss in more detail in Chapter 8. However, here we shall focus on the PRP paradigm as a simple task that requires a single switch from task 1 to task 2.

Luria and Meiran (2003) point out that one of the popular accounts of PRP, i.e., that of Pashler (1993, 1994), does not include any account of order control for the tasks in the PRP experiment. However, other accounts, such as that of Logan and Gordon (2001) and Meyer and Kieras (1997a, 1997b) specifically include order control. Luria and Meiran reasoned that if they could demonstrate effects of order in PRP this would differentiate between the competing accounts. Using a task-switching paradigm, in which the order of tasks for the PRP experiments were arranged to require either task repetition from trial to trial or switching from one task to another from trial to trial. It is well documented (see Chapter 8) that when participants have to switch from one task to another there is an increased response time, known as the "switch cost" in comparison to the repeated task condition. When tasks must be switched there is need for online control to prepare or set cognitive system to respond to the different task. While there is currently disagreement over the explanation for switch costs, if the need to switch interacts with PRP effects, particularly SOAs, this would suggest there are components of the PRP task that involve monitoring and controlling the tasks in their order. We saw earlier that De Jong suggested the PRP effect is modulated by task order. Luria and Meiran (2003) compared PRP effects in a number of experiments where they manipulated the order in which pairs of PRP stimuli were presented. In the fixed order condition, the order of tasks was constant, participants always responded to letter then colour, or colour then letter. In this case, the only cost would be within the trial for switching between the letter or colour. In the other conditions participants, switch and no switch the colour then letter and letter then colour trials were randomly mixed. This meant that sometimes the task would be repeated, but on other occasions the opposite task would be required. Visual displays presented the stimuli and a cue was given at various intervals prior to display onset to cue the participants as to which task were to be performed. After the second response was made there was a variable interval before the cue for the next trial. If the effect of the previous task dissipated over time, then with longer intervals between trials, less switch cost should be observed on the next trial. If preparation for task order influences switching costs, then when there is longer interval between the cue for task, switching should also be reduced.

The results of the experiments provided evidence that order information can be activated in advance of task execution, because switching cost was reduced with longer preparation. However, this need for order control interacted with the PRP effect, producing an increased PRP when more control was required. Luria and Meiran (2003) argue that their results require the assumption that some stages in response to the second stimulus are "prolonged by order switching and order mixing. This implies that order control is involved in performance in the PRP paradigm, an effect that cannot be accounted for by Pashler's (1993, 1994) model" (p. 570). In contrast, the results provide support for those models such as EPIC and ECTVA, which incorporate mechanisms that can control task order.

Attentional blink

The PRP task requires people to respond to two successive targets presented close together in time. Another task that presents a rapid sequence of successive targets is the rapid serial visual presentation

(RSVP) task, but rather than only two stimuli, both of which must be responded to, the RSVP task requires the participants to monitor the stream of stimuli, usually letters, and respond as soon as they detect a target. The target is usually differentiated from non-targets by colour and stream of letters are presented at a rate of about 100 mscs per item all at the same location. The usual pattern of results, first reported by Broadbent and Broadbent (1987), is that attentional processing for items that follow the target are impaired for between 200 to 500 mscs. This phenomenon has come to be known as the "attentional blink" (AB). It is as if attention is temporarily unavailable in the same way that vision is briefly cut off when we blink with our eyelids. This means that if target 1 (T1) is identified, and a second target, T2, comes soon afterwards it is likely to be missed, or a different item in the stream reported in error. In RSVP experiments, the position of items in the stream is termed the "lag". An item immediately following T1 is said to be at lag 1, the item next in the stream is at lag 2 etc.

AB has been observed in many experiments using a variety of stimuli and paradigms. For example, Chun and Potter (1995), Raymond, Shapiro, and Arnell (1992); Shapiro, Raymond, and Arnell (1994). The time course of AB can be determined by varying the position in the RSVP stream of the first and second target. The stimulus presented immediately following a target is usually spared, with poorest performance for target 2 occurring when it is presented at lag 2. Detection of the second target gradually improves up to lag 6, when the AB effect disappears. A related effect is repetition blindness (RB), which was mentioned in Kanwisher's (1987) experiment in Chapter 4. RB is an effect in which observers often fail to detect the repetition of an item in a RSVP stream.

The reasons underlying attentional blink and how it relates to RB are not yet fully understood, although a number of theories have been proposed. As for the explanations proposed for the PRP effect, the major distinction between theories depends on whether the information processing system is considered to have a single channel that provides a processing bottleneck, which if occupied with one task cannot begin processing a second task until task 1 has completed bottleneck processing, or whether attentional capacity is viewed as limited processing resource that can be shared between concurrent tasks.

Chun and Potter (2001) suggest that AB is due to capacity limitations in consolidating visual information into working memory and awareness. Expanding on suggestions by Broadbent and Broadbent (1987) they propose that target processing in RSVP has two stages.

Stage 1 codes stimulus features in parallel and processing is not capacity limited. All items in the RSVP stream are identified in stage 1 and have the potential to be immediately identified, but their representations are fragile and will decay or be overwritten by subsequent RSVP stimuli. When a key target feature is detected, the item bearing that feature is entered into a temporary buffer and successful report of the target requires further processing to consolidate the fragile representation into a more stable form. However, this second stage is capacity limited and a subsequent target cannot be consolidated at the same time because the limited capacity stage 2 is still occupied by the previous item. The sparing of the item at lag 1 is explained by assuming that as the first and second items are very close together in time they both gain entry to the buffer before it closes, even though the second item does not possess a target feature and are processed simultaneously. The outcome of stage 2 processing allows the consolidated items to enter short-term memory and become available for recall. Items occurring later in the stream must wait for the bottleneck at stage 2 to clear and this waiting time gives rise to the attentional blink effect.

An alternative account of AB suggests that the effect arises as a consequence of interference because items arriving close together compete for limited-capacity processing resources. Raymond, Shapiro, and Arnell (1992) found that there was no AB effect when the first target was followed by a blank interval or participants were not required to identify the target. They proposed that when a stimulus is presented after the target but before target identification processes are complete, there is interference at the letter recognition stage. Shapiro, Raymond, and Arnell (1994) showed that similarity between targets and distractors was a crucial factor that influenced AB and proposed an interference model of AB based on Duncan and Humphreys' (1989) AET model of visual search, which was explained in Chapter 4. To remind you, AET suggests that selection of a target among distractors depends on the similarity between targets and distractors and the more similar they are to each other, the more difficult target selection becomes. According to Shapiro et al. (1994), the blink is a consequence of competition between multiple items in the RSVP stream and the selection of an incorrect item as the second target. They suggest, following Duncan and Humphreys' model, that target search follows a series of "loosely sequential stages". First, all items in the visual field are initially processed in parallel for visual, spatial and categorical features. Next, the representations are compared with an internal representation, or target template, of target defining features. Finally, when an item is selected as a potential match to the target template it begins to draw on a limited resource of processing capacity for about 500 mscs. Ward, Duncan, and Shapiro (1996) called this the "attentional dwell time". During this dwell time, the perceptual and categorical features of the item are processed into an integrated representation that allows the item to emerge in visual short-term memory (VSTM), from where it can control response. Shapiro et al. (1994) proposed that in order to allow an item to enter VSTM a gate opens, but this gate does not shut immediately and can allow items closely following a target item to enter as well. Items that are presented during the interval when the scarce processing resources are being allocated to a preceding item have to compete for resources. If insufficient resources are available this leads to the second item failing to enter VSTM. As T1 and T2 are selected for entry to VSTM depending on how closely they match their target templates, when distractors share features with targets they will also partially match the target template. This means that increasing similarity between targets and distractors increases the number of items likely to enter VSTM and further competition for resources. Items that fail to capture sufficient attentional resources will be lost in the attention blink.

Recently, Awh, Serences, Laurey, Dhaliwal, van der Jaght, and Dassonville (2004) have challenged both the single channel and the interference account of AB. Using a two target paradigm rather than RSVP, they demonstrated that although an AB effect was found when T1 was a digit and T2 was a letter, there was no AB when T1 was a digit and T2 was a face. They suggested that these data are incompatible with the view that AB results from competition between items for a stage of visual processing, either for a structural bottleneck or for general processing capacity. Rather, it would seem there is one channel that can process the sorts of feature that comprise letters and digits and another channel that can process the sort of configural information necessary to discriminate between faces. Awh et al. (2004) suggest that face processing can proceed during the AB period exerted by a featural process because the face discrimination task could access a processing channel not disrupted by the processing required for the T1 digit task. These findings are more in line with Wickens (1984) multiple resource theory of attention.

Relationship between the psychological refractory period and attentional blink

There are some obvious similarities between PRP and AB. Both show that the ability to attend to the second of two targets presented within about 500 mscs of the first is impaired. Also, as the separation between T1 and T2 increases both PRP and AB effects are progressively eliminated. Further, in both cases it appears that although T2 processing is compromised as a consequence of processing T1, T1 processing is not affected by the requirement to perform a subsequent task. There are, of course, differences. In the typical PRP experiment, only two successive stimuli are presented, as speed of response is the dependent measure, the modality of presentation may be auditory or visual. In the typical AB experiment, many successive visual stimuli are rapidly presented and accuracy of target detection is the dependent measure.

We have seen that there are a variety of theoretical accounts for the PRP effect and the AB effect, but these theories have considered the two effects attributable to different causes. However, given the similarities outlined earlier, is it the case that both effects reflect a common set of underlying limitations in dual task processing? Arnell and Duncan (2002) review both PRP and AB effects and theories and suggest that recent evidence suggests that:

> While different causes have usually been considered for PRP and AB phenomena, recent evidence has supported a unified account based on a single shared restriction on concurrent processing. (p. 105)

Arnell and Duncan point out that while the most common accounts for PRP locate a bottleneck at a response selection stage, typical AB explanations locate the limitation at an early stimulus encoding stage and that AB experiments are specifically designed to examine perceptual rather than response limitations. In order to fully test the relationship between PRP and AB, researchers have started to use a hybrid PRP–AB paradigm in which a speeded response to an auditory stimulus is followed by an unspeeded response to a visual stimulus. Arnell and Duncan refer to such an experimental design as the SA–UV paradigm and results in experiments by Jolicoeur (1998) and Jolicoeur and Dell'Acqua (1998) have shown that a speeded response to an auditory target (T1) reduce accuracy for a following unspeeded visual identification task (T2) and Jolicoeur and Dell'Acqua (1998) have demonstrated the reverse pattern, in which an unspeeded response to a masked visual target at T1 interferes with a speeded response to an auditory target at T2. These results from the hybrid paradigm have led Arnell and Jolicoeur (1999) and Jolicoeur and Dell'Acqua (1998) to theorise that the same serial processing system is involved in both selecting a speeded response (typically, a PRP explanation) and consolidating a trace in short-term memory (typically, an AB explanation). Thus both PRP and AB arise because of a processing queue for a serial processing system that is required for both response selection and memory consolidation. Arnell and Duncan (2002) call this the "shared limitation view" and discuss how such a view relates to bottleneck and capacity sharing accounts of dual task performance such as those we covered earlier in the chapter; in particular, they focus on the argument between a single shared resource (e.g. Kahneman, 1973) and multiple resources (e.g. Allport, 1980b).

Arnell and Duncan (2002) argued that, in order to demonstrate whether resources were shared or whether limitations in dual task performance arose from crosstalk in a multiple resource system, an experimental design was needed that allowed comparison between all possible combinations of speeded auditory and unspeeded visual stimuli. They conducted these experiments and found that, to some extent, the resource limitations underlying PRP and AB are task specific, but there is also evidence of task specific crosstalk interference in the right conditions. In conclusion, it appears there is evidence for both shared and specific resources in the dual task procedures of both PRP and AB and the contribution of the shared resources component can be substantially increased by increasing task demand. Arnell and Duncan (2001) sum up the evidence:

> As so often in psychology, both conflicting views hold good in restricted regions of the task space; the broader picture is that neither accounts for the full range of PRP/AB phenomena. (p. 145)

Summary

Rather than a central bottleneck in information processing, some psychologists proposed that the human operator had a pool of processing resources available, which could be allocated according to task demand (e.g., Kahneman, 1973; Wickens, 1984). Tasks are data limited if no matter how much resource we apply to the task, we cannot improve. Resource-limited tasks are those in which as resources are invested or withdrawn, performance changes accordingly (Norman and Bobrow, 1975). Initial research suggested that there was a general limit on task combination (e.g. Posner and Boies, 1971), but manipulations of the input and output for the two tasks showed that in some cases tasks could be combined without cost (e.g. McLeod, 1977). Other experiments seemed to indicate that complex tasks such as sight reading for piano playing and shadowing could be combined with no apparent decrement in either task (e.g. Allport et al., 1972). These results suggested that rather than a single general purpose channel or general purpose resource, there are a variety of resources, or capacities, that are task specific, and provided that the tasks to be combined are not competing for the same resource or capacity, there will be no dual task interference (McLeod & Posner, 1984). It might be that in dual task combination, for example piano playing and shadowing, measurements are not precise enough to detect a performance decrement. Recent results from experiments on refractoriness by Pashler and colleagues (Carrier & Pashler, 1995; Fagot & Pashler, 1992; Pashler, 1990) suggest that there are attentional limits in memory retrieval, which limits task performance even when tasks are dissimilar. As a response needs to have a code retrieved from memory and only one retrieval can happen at once, response to more than one object is limited. However, objects specify all the responses that can be made to them and so two responses can be made to one object, but when two objects need two responses, this is limited. De Jong (1995) suggests that overlapping tasks are controlled by a multi-level control structure involved not only in the preparation of tasks, but also in switching between them. More recent evidence suggests that in some conditions there can be perfect time sharing between tasks, but there is continuing debate over whether or not ideomotor compatibility can eliminate PRP (Lien et al., 2002; Schumacher et al., 2001). There is also a difference of opinion on whether PRP is best accounted for by a structural bottleneck, a strategic bottleneck (Meyer and Kieras, 1999), or due to capacity sharing (Tombu and Jolicoeur, 2003). Capacity-sharing explanations could involve competition for either specific or shared resources. The phenomenon of attentional blink (AB) has similarities with PRP that might suggest they arise from similar processing limitations. Arnell and Duncan (2001) have argued that there is evidence for both shared and specific resources contributing to both PRP and AB effects, but neither account explains all the data.

Further reading

Most cognitive psychology texts have something on dual task performance. for example:

- Eysenck, M. W. and Keane, M. T. (2000). *Cognitive psychology: A student's handbook* (Chapter 5). Hove, UK: Psychology Press.

- Smyth, M. M., Collins, A. F., Morris, P. E., & Levy, P. (1994). *Cognition in action* (2nd ed., Chapter 5). Hove, UK: Lawrence Erlbaum Associates Limited.

For a more detailed review see:

- Pashler, H. (1993) Dual task performance and elementary mental mechanisms. In D. E. Meyer, & S. Kornblum (Eds.). *Attention and performance, XIV: A silver jubilee*. London: MIT Press.
- Pashler, H. (1998). *The psychology of attention* (Chapter 6). Cambridge, MA: MIT Press.
    This is not an introductory text, but is a useful review of dual task and PRP work over its history.

Automaticity, skill and expertise 7

Introduction

When we first start learning a complex task, such as driving a car, there seem to be too many component tasks involved. We are overwhelmed by the combination of steering, operating the clutch, monitoring the road and changing gear. With practice, less and less conscious effort is necessary. Steering round a corner while operating the clutch and changing gear is accomplished in one operation, often while we converse with the passenger. Clearly, something changes with practice, driving the car seems to be controlled in a very different way by the experienced driver than the learner. The expert can drive while talking, the novice cannot; the expert can control two tasks yet the novice has difficulty with even one. What has been learned by the expert? When driving a new car, the expert may initially switch on the windscreen wipers every time they intend to indicate. It can take many hours of driving the new car before the new configuration of controls is learned. The expert has become able to make many actions such as moving the indicator lever automatically, but when one of these action needs modifying, time and practice is needed all over again. The automatic response has to be deliberately modified, i.e., control has to wrested from the automatic mode by conscious control. So, what is learnt with practice and what can this tell us about the nature of the systems that control information processing?

It looks as if there are two different modes of controlling information processing, "automatic" control and "controlled" control. Automatic control has at least four meanings (Norman & Shallice, 1986): it refers to the way in which some actions are carried out without awareness, for example walking on an even surface; second, it refers to the way in which some actions are initiated without any conscious deliberation, such as sipping a drink while talking; third, attention may be automatically drawn to a stimulus, as in the orienting response to a sudden onset of a visual signal in the periphery (Posner, 1978); fourth, automatic control is used to refer to the cases where tasks can be combined without any apparent interference or competition for processing resources. Controlled processing is deliberate and conscious and can only deal with a limited amount of information at once. When tasks interfere this is usually taken to indicate competition for limited attentional processing resources. Conscious control requires attention, but automatic control does not.

In Chapter 6, we looked at some of the difficulties people have when they try to combine two tasks. We saw that while some tasks could be combined without much difficulty, other tasks were impossible to do together. One explanation for this is that tasks can be combined, provided that the mappings between the input and output systems of one task are independent of the mappings between input and output of the other task. If there is crossover between input and output systems required for both tasks, there will be interference. Examples like this were evident in the studies by McLeod and Posner (1984), Schumacher et al. (2001), and Shaffer (1975). When tasks can be combined successfully, they seem to be controlled automatically and independently, that is, each task shows no evidence of being interfered with by the other and is performed as well in combination as it is alone. However, when the mappings between the stimuli and their responses are not direct, the tasks interfere with each other and a different kind of control is required, one that requires conscious attention and appears to be of limited capacity. Some tasks that interfere when first combined become independent with enough practice. Why is this so?

Learning to do two things at once

Spelke, Hirst, and Neisser (1976) examined the effect of extended practice on people's ability to combine tasks. They gave two students 85 hours of practice spread over 17 weeks and monitored the ways in which dual task performance changed over that period. To begin with, when the students were asked to read stories at the same time as writing to dictation, they found the task combination extremely difficult. Reading rate was very slow and their handwriting was poorly formed. Initially, the students of Spelke et al. showed extremely poor performance, but after six weeks' extended practice their reading rate had increased, they could comprehend the text and their handwriting of the dictated words had improved. Tests of memory for the dictated words showed that the students were rarely able to recall any of the words they had written down. (Note here that this suggests attention is necessary for remembering. In Chapter 2, we discovered that words presented on the unattended channel in a dichotic listening task were not remembered even after repeated presentations (Moray, 1959).) In the experiment of Spelke et al., after even more practice, the students were able to detect rhymes and semantically related words within the dictated lists and finally were able to write down the category to which the dictated word belonged rather than the word itself at the same time as reading the text at normal speed and fully comprehending it!

This dramatic improvement in performance clearly needs an explanation. It looks as if although both tasks needed attention to start with, they did not need it later. Did the tasks become increasingly "automatic" or could attentional "capacity" have increased with practice? How could we tell how much attention is needed for a task or whether the "amount" of attention has increased with practice? Many theories of attention assume that capacity is general purpose and of limited capacity. (We discussed this issue in Chapter 2.) If attentional resources are assumed to be of fixed capacity and general purpose, then certain further assumptions can be made, for example, that if two tasks interfere they are drawing on the same attentional resource. By the same token, with tasks that do *not* interfere, it must be that one or both do not require attention. However, in Chapter 6, we have already seen that tasks that do not interfere in one combination may interfere in another combination. So tasks that appear not to require attention in one case do seem to require it in another case. We have already analysed these problems, but for the moment we must step back in time to examine some influential theories that did assume general purpose limited capacity attentional resources, which were amenable to strategic control by the subject.

Two process theory of attention: Automatic and controlled processing

According to the two process approach, mental processing can operate in two different modes. In "automatic" mode, processing is a passive outcome of stimulation, it is parallel and does not draw on attentional capacity. In "conscious control" mode, mental processing is consciously controlled by intentions and does draw on attentional capacity. Some of the first people to explicitly involve control processes in their theorising were Atkinson and Shiffrin (1968) in their model of memory. Previously, control processes were simply assumed. For example, when we looked at Broadbent's filter model in Chapter 2, did you ask yourself the question "Who sets the filter?" Atkinson and Shiffrin pointed out the importance of understanding not only the structure of the information processing system, but also how it was controlled. While their model was one of memory, it is, in fact, quite similar to Broadbent's model. Information entered the system in parallel, residing in a sensory buffer from which some information was selected for entry into short-term memory. In Atkinson and Shiffrin's model, the selection, rehearsal and recoding of information in short-term memory all required "control" processes. Short-term memory was seen as a "working memory" in which both storage and processing took place. The more demanding the processing was, the less "capacity" would be available for storage and vice versa. We have all experienced the difficulty of trying to solve a mental problem, where as soon as the products of part of the computation become available, we forget what the question was! We just don't seem able to keep all the information in mind at the same time as consciously manipulating it. In this example we can see the close relationship between working memory and conscious attentional control. Recently, Lavie et al. (2004) have shown that loading working memory reduces the ability to ignore distractors in visual search. When high priority targets are in competition with low priority, but salient distractors, cognitive control of visual search is compromised by a concurrent short-term, working memory task. It appears, in this case, that the ability to control the selective filter is reduced when attentional capacity must be allocated to the memory task. We shall discuss these and other experiments in more detail in Chapter 10. For now we shall note the close relationship between attentional control and working memory. Following on from Atkinson and Shiffrin (1968), later modifications of the working memory concept have all included both storage and control aspects (e.g., Baddeley, 1986; Broadbent, 1984). For information in working memory to be "working" it needs manipulation by "the subject" and what the subject does is "control". Atkinson and Shiffrin tell us nothing about this control except that it is something that the subject does. If we are to avoid the homunculus, or little man in the head, we must try and explain the difference between these two kinds of processing in terms of well defined psychological mechanisms. This, as we shall see, is extremely difficult to do. Leaving aside for a moment the problem of determining how control processes operate or are instigated, as this is the subject of the next chapter, let us look at some of the proposed differences between tasks that do or do not require the "subject" or homunculus to take control.

Posner and Snyder (1975) drew the distinction between:

> [A]utomatic activation processes which are solely the result of past learning and processes that are under current conscious control. Automatic activation processes are those which may occur without intention, without any conscious awareness and without interference with other mental activity. They are distinguished from operations that are performed by the conscious processing system since the latter system is of limited capacity and thus its commitments to any operation reduces its availability to perform any other operation.

Posner and Snyder were interested in the extent to which our conscious intentions and strategies are in control of the way information is processed in our minds. We can see from their quotation that they thought the conscious processing system was a general purpose limited capacity system because they say that any attention demand of one task would reduce the amount of attention available for another attention demanding task. Let us look at some the reasons behind Posner and Snyder's ideas.

One of the most widely investigated effects in cognitive psychology is the Stroop effect (Stroop, 1935). Imagine you are presented with the word "BLUE" written in red ink. If our task is to read the word as quickly as possible there is no problem. The word is available immediately and without any apparent effort; it seems to pop into our mind "automatically". However, if our task is to produce the name of the ink colour, red, in this case, response is much slower; subjectively, we feel as if more conscious effort is needed to overcome the tendency to produce the incongruent written word that seems to interfere with naming the ink. This slowing is not simply because colour naming is always slower than word reading, naming a colour patch is much faster than naming the ink in an incongruent Stroop stimulus. What seems to be happening here is that our ability to selectively respond to one aspect of the Stroop stimulus is interfered with by the other. No matter what our conscious intentions are, the written word cannot be completely ignored. The Stroop effect can be found with other kinds of stimuli in which there are (usually) two responses available from the same stimulus. Another example is having to count the number of characters present in a display, when the characters themselves are digits. Usually the Stroop effect is asymmetrical, in the case of colour words written in an incongruent ink colour; the word interferes with the ink naming, but not vice versa. It seems that the word automatically activates its response and although conscious control can prevent the response from being made overtly, there is a time cost while the intended response, ink naming, gains control of overt action. The asymmetry arises because the ink naming is less strongly mapped onto a response and is easily overcome by the stronger mapping of the word to its response. Word reading in adults is an extremely well-learned skill, but in early readers, the effect is not present and may even be reversed. The direction of interference, contrariwise, may depend on task demands. When the task involves deciding if stimuli match physically, judgements are made more quickly for colours than words and, in this case, experiments show that there is more interference from colours on words (Murray, Mastroddi, & Duncan, 1972). However, if the ink colour and word are congruent the word may facilitate vocal colour naming (Hintzman, Carre, Eskridge, Owens, Shaff, & Sparks, 1972).

Posner and Snyder (1975) suggest that there is automatic parallel processing of both features of the stimulus until close to output. Automatic processing cannot be prevented, but conscious attention can be used flexibly. So, while some cognitive operations proceed automatically, others take place under strategic, conscious, attentional control, which is deployed according to the subject's intentions. To test their theory, Posner and Snyder (1975) conducted a series of experiments using a letter-matching task. On each trial, the subject was presented with a priming stimulus, either a letter or a plus sign. The prime was followed by a pair of letters and the task was to decide, as quickly as possible, if the letters were the same or different. There were two basic predictions. First, the prime would automatically activate its representation in memory, so that if the prime were "A" and the pair of letters to be matched were "AA", response would be facilitated because the activation in memory was confirmed. According to their view, if the prime was different to the target, there would be no inhibition produced by this automatic memory activation on other responses. Second, Posner and Snyder predicted that once the subject "invests his conscious attention in the processing of a stimulus" the benefit of pathway activation would be accompanied by a widespread cost or inhibition on other signals. This would account for the fact that subjects do well when they receive an expected stimulus, but perform poorly when an unexpected stimulus arrives. They applied what is called a "cost–benefit analysis" to their data, which measures how much better or worse subjects perform in the experimental conditions relative to a neutral control.

The basic design of the experiment is to precede the target stimulus by either a neutral warning signal, in this case, the plus sign or a non-neutral prime, which should, if attended, bias target processing. The probability that the prime would be a valid cue for the target was manipulated, as it was assumed that the subject would adopt a strategy whereby they invested more or less attention in the prime depending on whether or not they thought it would be a valid predictor of the target. According to the theory, when the subject pays little processing capacity to the prime, a valid cue will automatically produce facilitation but no costs. However, when the subject "actively attends" to the prime, there will be facilitatory benefits from both automatic activation and from conscious attention if the prime is valid, but when the prime is not valid there will be inhibitory costs due to strategic processing.

Results showed that when the prime was a poor predictor of the target there was benefit but no cost. When the prime was of high validity, the benefit accrues more rapidly than the cost. This effect was interpreted as showing that the allocation of conscious attention takes more time than automatic activation. The differential time course of facilitatory and inhibitory effects suggested a real difference between the two kinds of processing.

Shiffrin and Schneider's theory

A general theory involving controlled and automatic processing was proposed by Shiffrin and Schneider (1977), who carried out a series of experiments on visual search and attention. Schneider and Shiffrin (1977) report a series of experiments on visual search using a multiple-frame visual search paradigm. They gave their subjects one, two or four letters as the memory set, presented in advance of each search trial. Then a fixation dot appeared for 500 mscs, followed by a series of 20 frames presented for a fixed time. On each frame there would be either no or one member of the memory set. In different experiments, they manipulated frame time, memory set size and frame size. This same paradigm was also used in the companion paper by Shiffrin and Schneider (1977). In one experiment, performance was tested when subjects had to search for a member of the memory set in visual displays containing one two or four items. Their task was to decide as rapidly as possible whether any of the letters from the memory set were present in the display. The crucial experimental manipulation was the mapping between stimuli and responses. For the "consistent mapping" condition, targets were always consonants and distractors were always digits, i.e., there was a consistent mapping of target and distractors onto their responses. In this case, whenever the subject detected a member of the memory set, in the display, it had to be a target. Performance in the constant mapping condition was contrasted with that in the "varied mapping" condition. In this condition, both the memory set and the distractors were a mixture of letters and digits. Schneider and Shiffrin found a clear difference between performance in the two conditions. With consistent mapping, search is virtually independent of both the number of items in the memory set and the number of items in the display, as if search is taking place in parallel. Shiffrin and Schneider (1977) said this type of performance reflected "automatic processing". However, with varied mapping where the target and distractor set changed from trial to trial, subjects were slower to detect the target and their response times increased with the number of distractors in the display. Search seemed to remain serial. This type of performance was said to be indicative of "controlled processing".

Of course, letters and digits have well-learned responses associated with them, these will have been learnt over years of practice. Shiffrin and Schneider were interested to see if, given enough practice, subjects would develop automatic processing of items divided by a novel, arbitrary distinction. To do this they divided consonants into two sets, B to L and Q to Z. In consistent mapping, only one set of consonants was used to make up the memory set and distractors were always selected from the other set. After over 2100 trials, performance began to resemble that of subjects in the letter/digit experiment. Search became fast and independent of the number of items in the memory set or the number of items in the display. Having had all this practice with one response mapping, subjects were given another 2400 trials in which the mapping between sets was reversed, i.e., letters that were once targets were now distractors and vice versa. There was a dramatic change in performance. In the early stages, subjects were unable to "change set" and performance was very poor, slow and limited by both the memory set size and number of distractors; subjects gave many false alarms. Very gradually subjects began to improve their hit rate and after 2400 trials of reversal training, subjects were performing at the same level as they were after 1500 trials of the original training. It was as if the subjects either had to "unlearn" an automatic attentional response to the previous memory set or overcome some kind of learnt inhibition to the previous distractor set or both before the reversed set could become automatic.

It appears, then, that after extended practice with one consistent mapping between stimulus and response, subjects find it extremely difficult to change to a different stimulus response mapping. However, Shiffrin and Schneider showed that varied mappings, despite extended practice, could easily be altered according to instructions, so the difficulties that subjects experienced in the consistent mapping condition were not simply due to changing from one set to another. From the results of these experiments, it appears that there are indeed two different processes involved in attention: one type of processing that can be quickly adapted by the subject's conscious intentions; and another kind of process that runs off automatically beyond conscious control. This distinction is supported by the results of another experiment by Shiffrin and Schneider. Subjects were asked to attend to some display locations and to ignore others. When a target that had been a member of the consistent mapping set appeared in an irrelevant location subjects were unable to ignore it, there was an attentional "pop-out" effect rather like those we looked at in the chapter on visual search. This intrusion of information from the irrelevant location suggests that automatic processes are operating in parallel over the display, taking in information from both relevant and irrelevant display locations, rather like the parallel feature search in Treisman's feature integration theory. Irrelevant targets from previous varied mapping, control search conditions, did not "pop out", subjects were unaware of them and they did not interfere with target processing. These results were taken as evidence that even under controlled search conditions subjects are not always successful in controlling their attention if an automatic detection is made.

Neuman's critique of two process theory

Neuman (1984) summarises the "primary criteria" of automaticity on which most two process theories agree, under three headings:

1. *Mode of operation.* Automatic processes operate without capacity and they neither suffer nor cause interference.
2. *Mode of control.* Automatic processes are under the control of stimulation rather than under the control of the intentions (strategies, expectancies, plans) of the person.
3. *Mode of representation.* Automatic processes do not necessarily give rise to conscious awareness.

Some "secondary criteria" that do not necessarily define automaticity but that are suggested or implied by some theories are that automatic processes are determined by connections that are either wired in or are learned through practice and that this kind of processing is relatively simple, rapid and inflexible in that it can only be modified by extended practice.

Neuman then goes on to evaluate the data to try and determine whether these criteria are correct and then to specify the functional properties of automatic and non-automatic processes. He argues that it is extremely difficult to demonstrate that a task that appears to be "automatic" does not require attentional capacity. While a task may be "interference free" in one task combination, in a different combination interference may well be found, hence the task now appears to require attention while before it did not. The experiment by Spelke et al. (1976), which we looked at earlier, is one in which there was a constant rule between input and output. Subjects always wrote what they heard and read what they saw. Thus the stimuli were presented in different modalities and one task, the reading, did not require overt response. In this situation, practice can lead to apparent automaticity. However, when both tasks involve similar stimuli, as for example in some of Shiffrin and Schneider's experiments, even well-practised tasks cannot be carried out simultaneously. We saw a similar effect in McLeod's (1977) experiment where changing the response mode affected whether or not there was task interference. Neuman suggests that practice leads to the development of a skill, which "includes a sensory and, at least during practice, a motor response. After practice the response may remain covert, but is still . . . as Schneider and Shiffrin's term correctly suggests . . . an attentional response connected to the particular target stimuli" (p. 269). However, even well-practised tasks will display interference if the responses are similar. Tasks may also interfere, according to Neuman, if the initiation of a new response is required, only when there is a continuous stream of information-guiding action, as in the Spelke et al. study, can apparent automaticity be found. It would seem then that Neuman's analysis throws doubt over the lack of interference criterion.

What about the criterion concerning mode of control? Automatic processes are, according to two process theory, unavoidable; they run off as a consequence of stimuli in the environment, rather than as a consequence of intentions. Evidence from studies of the Stroop effect have been interpreted as demonstrating obligatory processing of the unwanted word name even when the subject was intending to name the ink colour. This is the case when the colour and the word occupy the same stimulus location, i.e., when the word is itself written in a colour. However, Kahneman and Henik (1981) have shown that when the word and incongruent colour are separated, interference is reduced. In the last chapter, we discussed some examples from the literature on visual attention that demonstrated that both grouping factors and spatial separation are involved in the efficiency of selection. Processing of the unwanted stimulus dimension will only be "automatic" within a constrained set of circumstances when the subject's ability to focus attention breaks down. Neuman suggests that distractors produce interference not simply because they are present in the stimulus environment, but because they are related to the intended action. So, Stroop interference may arise because both the ink and the word are related to the currently active task set. We have already seen that the direction of interference may depend on task demands. Stroop interference depends very much on where attention is directed, the task to be performed and what strategies are used. If this is so, then it is the strategic, controlled attention allocation deployed to set up the cognitive system to "respond to colours", which results in the production of interference. Normally, this interference is defined as a result of automatic processes, but we can see here that there is an involvement of intention in automatic processing. Automatic processing is not, therefore, an "invariant consequence of stimulation, independent of a subject's intentions" (p. 270). Despite this evidence, Neuman admits that there probably are situations in which stimulus processing may be unavoidable and outside the control of current intentions.

Neuman believes that automatic processing is not uncontrolled, but rather is controlled *below the level* of conscious awareness. Awareness is one of the key properties of conscious control. But what do we mean by awareness? – or consciousness for that matter? In Chapter 9, we shall look in detail at some definitions of consciousness and some criteria for deciding when people are conscious. In Neuman's analysis there are three kinds of unawareness. He says there are three questions we can ask. First, whether or not brain processes not directly related to ongoing activity are "unaware"; second, whether there are some processes within the execution of a task that may escape awareness; and, third, whether an action as a whole can proceed without awareness. Certainly the answer to the first question is yes. Neuman says, for example, that we are unaware of the contents of long-term memory and the changes that take place during forgetting. We can also answer "yes" to the second question, again Neuman takes an example from memory, the "tip-of-the tongue phenomenon".

When people are given a definition, such as "a far eastern trade vessel", they may be unable to recall the word "sampan" immediately although they feel it is on the "tip of the tongue", they may come up with some candidate answers that they know are wrong, but sound like what they are looking for. After abandoning memory search, the answer suddenly springs to mind, clearly as a result of some ongoing processing activity that has been working below the level of awareness. It is probably the case that the lion's share of information processing takes place at a level below conscious awareness. We are not, for example, able to introspect on the processes that underlie the production of words in sentences we produce, although when the sentence is articulated it appears to make perfect sense. For the main part, we are only aware of the outcome of processing not the working of the underlying processes themselves.

The answer to the third question is also "yes"; whole actions can be carried out without a person being aware. For example, you arrive home having driven along a familiar route, but cannot recall passing the traffic lights. You know you intended to lock the back door but cannot remember doing it, on checking you find that you have. Whether you were *unaware* of carrying out the action at the time or simply forgot that you had done it is difficult to determine, but these "slips of action" (Norman, 1981; Reason, 1979) suggest some failure of whatever system controls and monitors ongoing activity.

Slips of action usually happen during the execution of frequently performed routine activities, that have become "automatic" in Norman and Shallice's (1986) third use of the term. There are few experimental data on whole tasks proceeding outside awareness, however, Neuman cites an experiment similar to that of Spelke et al. (1976), reported by Hirst, Spelke, Reeves, Caharack, and Neisser (1980), in which highly practised subjects became able to read for comprehension at the same time as writing down and understanding dictated sentences of which they had little or no awareness.

The first type of processes really do happen outside awareness but account for only a small proportion of tasks that are usually considered to be automatic according to two process theory. The second type of processes occur in the context of some ongoing activity and must therefore depend to some extent on intention, although many of them may take place with little or no awareness. The third case, where a whole action may happen without awareness, will only happen in particular circumstances, which Neuman likens to the conditions that are a prerequisite for interference free dual task performance.

Neuman proposes a different conception of automaticity. He suggests that the difference between automatic and controlled processing is the level of control required. Actions can only be performed if all the parameters for that action are specified. For example, naming the ink colour of an incongruent Stroop stimulus. To do the action as planned we must select one aspect, the colour not the word, of a particular object. Also we must retrieve specific information, the colour's name rather than its category "colour", then carry out a movement sequence to pronounce the response as quickly as possible. Some parameter specifications are stored in long-term memory, Neuman terms these "skills". Other specifications come from the stimulus itself, but the remaining specifications must come from an attentional mechanism, whose function is "to provide the specifications that cannot be obtained by linking input information to skills" (p. 281). These three sources of constraint work together to guide our actions.

According to Neuman, skills have two functions. First, they specify actions and, second, they help pick up information from the environment. Skilled typists produce very even predictable finger movements (Rumelhart & Norman, 1982); novices do not. Thus the actions of a skilled typist are strongly constrained by their skill. Skilled chess players can encode the arrangement of a chess game very much more quickly than novices (Chase & Simon, 1973). For an expert chess player, the game in progress matches and activates existing schemata in long-term memory, enabling the information to be picked up more quickly. Novices do not have these pre-existing schemata to aid them. When parameters are left unspecified, the action cannot be successfully performed and it is in this case that the attentional mode of parameter specification is needed. Thus, according to Neuman, "a process is automatic if its parameters are specified by a skill in conjunction with input information. If this is not possible, one or several attentional mechanisms for parameter specification must come into play. They are responsible for interference and give rise to conscious awareness" (p. 282). It is clear from Neuman's argument that automaticity is not some kind of process, but something that seems to emerge when conditions are right. The right conditions depend not only on the processing system but also on the situation.

Modelling the Stroop task

Cohen and Huston (1994) and Cohen, Dunbar, and McClelland (1990) produced a connectionist model of Stroop performance. In the model, there are two processing pathways, one for word reading and one for colour naming. The model is trained more on the word reading than colour naming and this results in greater increases in the strength of the connections within the word reading pathway, i.e., there is an asymmetry in connection strength. As a result, when the network is presented with a word, such as "red" written in green ink, it responds more quickly and strongly to "red" than green, just as humans do. However, humans are able to produce the weaker response, albeit more slowly. To model this, the network needs to be able to in some sense inhibit or modulate the stronger response in order to output the weaker one. This is achieved by including a set of input units that are responsive to task demands and represent intended behaviour. (See Figure 7.1.)

Activation of a task demand unit "sensitises" the appropriate processing pathway and "desensitises" the task-irrelevant pathway. This modulation allows the weaker response to ink colour to control output even though the connection strengths are stronger in the word reading pathway. We have already met Singer's (1994) idea that intentional behaviour might be achieved by modulation of activity in cortical areas by the thalamus. So it would seem plausible that the intentional selection of a weak response over a strong one could be achieved the same way in humans.

The SLAM model of Phaf et al. (1990), which was mentioned at the

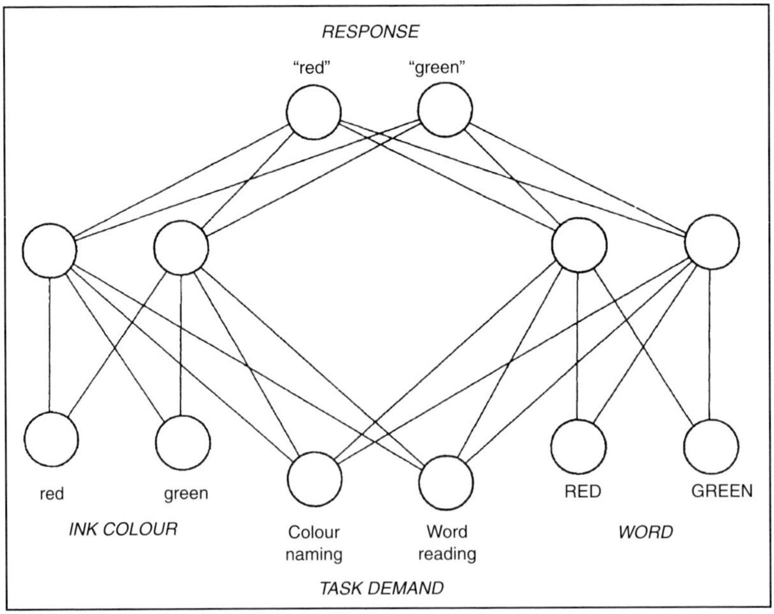

Figure 7.1 Network architecture for the model of the Stroop task. Units at the bottom are input units and units at the top are output (response) units. From Cohen and Huston (1994).

In Umilta and Moskovitch, *Attention and Performance XV*. Copyright MIT Press. Reproduced by permission of the publisher.

end of Chapter 4, also models Stroop performance. Phaf et al. argue that Cohen and colleagues' (1990) model has a problem, because if Stroop interference were a result of differential learning or practice, then we should, by practice, be able to reverse the Stroop effect. In fact, there is some evidence for reduction of Stroop interference with practice (Neill, 1977) and presumably reading is such an overlearnt skill acquired over years, it would take as many years of practice to remove the asymmetry.

MacLeod and Dunbar (1988) directly studied the effect of practice on Stroop interference. They trained subjects to call each of four different shapes by the name of a colour (green, pink, orange, or blue). These shapes could then be presented in a neutral colour, the congruent colour or the incongruent colour and the subjects asked to name either the shape or the colour of the ink. MacLeod and Dunbar discovered that when subjects had been given only a little shape-naming practice, ink colour interfered with shape naming, but not the reverse. At moderate levels of practice shape naming, interference was equal in each task. After extended practice, shape names interfered with ink colour naming, but not the reverse. Thus, increased practice with shape naming systematically increased interference on the naming of ink colour. This is particularly interesting because there was no competing "colour word", as there is in conventional Stroop tasks, and because shape naming never became faster than ink colour naming, so ruling out a "race" model of interference.

In his review of the Stroop effect, MacLeod (1991) concluded that, in general:

> The degree of practice in processing each of the dimensions of a multidimensional stimulus is influential in determining the extent of interference from one dimension to another. The greater the practice in processing a dimension, the more capable that dimension is of influencing the processing of another dimension. (p. 182)

Therefore the reason why one task appears "automatic" is due to the relative strength of the pathways of the two tasks, exactly as modelled by Cohen and Huston (1994) and Cohen et al. (1990).

Attentional control as a skill

We have spent some time examining the criteria for automaticity and discovered that there are a variety of problems with the two process theory. The distinction between automaticity and control is not as clear cut as once thought. Over the years it has proved notoriously difficult to make a clear empirical distinction between these two modes of processing. A more promising approach seems to be to accept ideas like Neuman's, in which there is no clear distinction but a gradation.

Neuman suggested that practice can produce skills that constrain the parameters of actions. When skills do not provide enough specification, attention is needed. Presumably more or less attention will be needed depending on how well or how many parameters are specified by pre-existing skills. Hirst (1986) discusses a rather different kind of skill, that of allocating attention itself, and Gopher (1993) also investigates whether there are skills involved in attentional control. In his paper, Gopher seeks evidence to support the idea that attention management is a skill and that it can be learnt through training. He argues that we would need to show, first, that subjects do actually have the potential to control their allocation of attention and, second, that this potential is not always fulfilled, insofar as subjects may fail to maintain control; and, last, that with appropriate training, difficulties of control can be overcome. In everyday life, we are continually having to perform complex tasks. These require the division, allocation and re-allocation of attention, depending on task demands and our currently active goals and intentions. A good example of this is driving. The driver must divide attention between controlling the car, monitoring the behaviour of other vehicles, watching for traffic signals, following the route, and possibly listening to the radio or having a conversation. If an emergency arises, the driver may stop talking while avoiding an obstruction. Driver behaviour suggests that there is moment by moment priority setting and attentional trade-offs involved in complex task performance. Gopher suggests that we employ strategies to allow us to cope as best as we can with competing task demands within the boundaries of our processing and response limitations. Given that we are able to adopt and execute attentional strategies, Gopher asks two further questions about control. First, to what extent are we consciously aware of the strategies we use and their efficiency? Second, how do we do it? How are changes in attentional strategy implemented? So far we have mentioned many theories and models that have appealed to some kind of control or controlled processing, but the best explanation of how control works is almost invariably to say "that the subject does it". This, of course, is no explanation at all.

While as yet we have not been provided with an explanation for how subjects in experiments actually operate or implement control, we have seen many examples where control is said to be operating. In focused attention experiments, subjects do focus attention as far as they are able within the context of the experiment. In divided attention experiments, subjects are able to divide attention and can do so according to priorities. If you ask subjects to give 70% attention to one task and 30% to another task, they can usually become able to do this. We have looked at performance operating characteristics (POC) in Chapter 6, when we considered resource theories of attention. In tasks like these, subjects allocate more or less attention according to instructions and the tradeoff between tasks is studied. This is a clear example of the manipulation of strategic control. Subjects can also alternately respond to different dimensions of a stimulus. Allport, Styles, and Hseih (1994) showed that subjects can alternately switch attention between the conflicting responses of a Stroop stimulus. In this example, the stimulus provides no clues as to which response the subjects must make. All shifts of attention must be executed by intentional control and, although there may be a time cost of shifting, subjects can do this task successfully. We will examine these experiments in more detail later.

Although we are usually successful in controlling attention, there are plenty of examples of situations where control fails. In the experiments combining writing to dictation while reading, Spelke and colleagues' subjects were unable to divide their attention, at least in the beginning. In Shiffrin and Schneider's experiments, letters that were from the overlearned constant mapping condition could not be ignored, attention was automatically "captured" despite the subjects intentions of control. So, we have as Gopher required, evidence that control is possible, but that it can also fail.

Varieties of skill

We have been discussing attentional control as a skill, but, of course, this is only one kind of skill. One important distinction to make is that between perceptuomotor skills and cognitive skills. Putting a golf ball or playing tennis plainly involve perceptuomotor skills, whereas playing the piano or typing involves rapid skilled motor actions together with cognitive control and planning. Chess or logical problem solving are almost entirely cognitive skills. However, most tasks usually involve both types of skill in that they normally involve at least some cognitive aspects such as planning or problem solving to reach a goal and involve at least some action, even if it is only moving the chess piece or speaking a response. As is evident in the studies of Gopher just described, skilled performance may require not only rapid and accurate motor response, but also strategic, cognitive planning. So, a skill may be classified as motor or cognitive only in terms of the relative degree of each kind of skill involved in task performance. Most everyday activities can be thought of as "cognitive–motor" skills because they involve both aspects.

Skills training

An important question of interest to both pure and applied research is how best to train people to become skilled at complex tasks. Peck and Detweiler (2000) examine training in multi-step tasks to assess the effectiveness of different training techniques. They explain that training techniques can be divided into two broad categories: part task and whole task (Stammers, 1982). Playing the piano is a multi-step task, in that each note must be played in succession, at the right time, for the tune to emerge correctly. The fingers of each hand must be accurately controlled in time and space, not only within each hand, but also between hands. A similar problem is faced by typists, although in this case, provided each key is pressed in the right order, the duration of each press is not so important and the two hands take turns to press their keys rather than press multiple keys at once. Rumelhart and Norman (1982) designed a PDP simulation of a skilled typist. While it might be imagined that the typist programmes each keystroke successively, it is evident that the hands and fingers move in anticipation of what is to be typed next, so that even as a finger on the left hand is typing one letter in the word, the right hand is moving its fingers toward the position of the upcoming letter. These anticipations can lead to errors when sequencing goes wrong for example typing "wodr" rather than "word". This anticipation also has higher level effects, such as typing the wrong letter twice, when a double letter has been programmed to be performed, such as "leeter" rather than "letter", but is applied to the wrong key press. In their PDP typing model, behaviour that appears strictly serial emerges from a complex parallel process operating in a network of excitatory and inhibitory connections. These are learned and strengthened by practice.

Returning to a novice learning to combine the actions of both hands to play a piano piece, this can be done in two ways. The part-task technique involves the learner practising each hand separately before trying to put them together. In this case, attention is allocated to the individual tasks in turn. Alternatively, using the whole-task technique the learner practises the notes for both hands together and, in this case, also learns the strategies necessary to coordinate timing and cope with crosstalk between motor commands for each hand. Detweiler and Landy (1995), among others, have shown that in multi-step tasks, whole-task training produces greater transfer to other concurrent task situations than part training. By transfer, we mean that a skill developed in one situation produces a benefit in performance in a similar, but new, task. However, part-task training reduces cognitive load during learning and it has been suggested that part-training techniques that also provide the opportunity to develop strategies for coping with concurrent task demands should promote the benefits of whole-task training, without overloading the learner.

In his 1993 paper, Gopher also looks at how people can learn to improve their attentional skills by training. One of the tasks used for this training is called the space fortress, which was designed to present the subject with a complex, dynamic environment within the confines of a well-specified (as far as the experimenters were concerned) computer game. The game involved the player in controlling the movements of a spaceship as if they were flying it, at the same time as firing missiles, to try and destroy the fortress. While doing this they must avoid being destroyed themselves. The rules of the game are quite complex and the main aim is to score points.

When players first tried the game their initial response was usually panic. They felt that the demands of the situation were too high, everything happened too fast, too much happened at once and the situation seemed to be out of control. This sounds very like our feeling when we first attempt any complex skill, such as driving a car. After considerable practice, the players began to work out a strategy and performance improved. Without specific training, people would not necessarily work out or adopt an optimal strategy, but Gopher found that if subjects were led through a sequence of emphasis changes for sub-components of the game, similar to the variable priority method used in POC studies, performance could be improved. Subjects were advised to concentrate on one sub-component at a time and only respond to the other components if they could do so without neglecting the component they were to concentrate on. The game remained exactly the same, apart from the introduction of a reward element in that the selected game component received more points. (This was to give subjects positive feedback on their success.) Otherwise, only the allocation of attentional priorities was altered. Four groups of subjects were studied. The control group were given practice but no specific emphasis training, two groups were given emphasis training on just one task component, mine handling or ship control, and the fourth group of subjects were given emphasis training on both, in alternation. The results showed that the group that had received the double manipulation outperformed all other groups, which did not differ from each other. An interesting finding was that although special training finished after six sessions, the improvement in performance continued over the next four sessions to the end of the experiment. This result suggests that after six sessions the double manipulation group "had already internalised their specialised knowledge and gained sufficient control to continue to improve on their own" (p. 315).

The application of this kind of training is demonstrated in another study reported by Gopher, in which Israeli airforce cadets were given training on a modification of the space fortress game. Cadets who drop out often do so because they have difficulty coping with the load of a flight task, dividing and controlling attention. In comparison to a control group, which was given no training on the game, the experimental cadets who were given double emphasis training showed a 30% increase in their actual flight performance. The advantage was largest in the manoeuvres that required integration of several elements. After 18 months, there were twice as many graduates in the experimental group as the control group. Gopher points out that the advantage of game training is not because it is similar to actual flying, because real flying is very much more demanding than the game and the game is not very realistic. What the game does do is train people in the kinds of attentional skills needed in complex situations. Given direct experience with different attentional strategies performance improves and these skills transfer to new situations and different task demands. The skill of attentional control appears to be learned. Gopher suggests that there is a move from controlled application of attentional strategies to automated schemata, where response schemata that have become associated with proficient behaviour become "hardwired". With learning, the attentional strategies that once needed control become automatic.

Peck and Detweiler (2000) report a study comparing training techniques in which participants learnt to control a pretend submarine. To do this they had to monitor and manually adjust the navigation system in the centre of the screen and also monitor and adjust the six peripheral systems displaying information on speed, radar, oxygen etc., that were positioned around the navigation display. There were four conditions: two "pure" conditions, a whole-task condition in which participants had to adjust both systems on each trial; and a part-task condition in which they had to adjust only one system on each trial. The other two conditions involved "forward chaining". In forward chaining, the task is broken down into components. For example, in playing the piano, the first two bars are practised, then the first four bars, then the first six bars, etc. until the whole piece is learned. Chaining provides the opportunity to practise the difficulties of each step of the task in isolation before the next steps are added. Without chaining, the task is more demanding because the difficulties associated with each step are less easily identified. Peck and Detweiler (2000) explain that according to Sweller (1988) learners must trade attentional effort between the resources required to actually perform the task and the resources needed to learn the task. So, the more effort that is needed to perform the task the slower the learning will be. To test this idea, the other two conditions were part task and whole task with concurrent chaining. In the whole task, participants controlled both systems but the number of trials per block gradually increased with training. Those participants trained in the part-task chaining condition first practised one task alone, then the second task was added gradually. After training all participants were tested on the whole task to measure transfer.

It was expected that the part-task training would reduce working memory demands and allow quicker learning and that the pure part-task condition would produce the most accurate training performance because it made the lowest demand on working memory; that the whole-task conditions would demand most from working memory and be least accurate, because of high working memory demand and that part-task chaining would be intermediate. However, with respect to transfer, it was expected that the pure whole-task condition would be best because these techniques should have allowed most opportunities for practising the coping strategies required to deal with competing task demands. The concurrent chaining conditions should have intermediate effects. Results showed that, indeed the pure part-task condition showed best training performance and least transfer performance, while the whole-task and concurrent chaining conditions showed the opposite effect; lower training performance, but better transfer. Importantly, however, due to the experimental design, the number of trials and time spent in training was about 50% less in the chaining conditions than in the pure conditions. So, although participants had had fewer learning opportunities in the chaining conditions, they showed similar transfer. This result shows that when equated for number of trials the chaining techniques provided better transfer than the whole task, suggesting that training techniques that help learners to identify and practise concurrent task relationships are important for effective transfer of these skills to another task. Again, as in Gopher's work discussed earlier, it appears that it is the opportunities provided by practice, rather than the amount of practice that is important and: "In addition the techniques that promote the best training performance do not necessarily promote the best transfer performance" (Peck and Detweiler, 2000, p. 388).

But what about the question of how "control" processing is actually done? Who or what does the controlling? What changes with practice? Gopher's review has demonstrated that people can operate attentional control and improve with training, but it still seems that it is always "the subject" that is in control, rather than a well-specified cognitive mechanism. How do people do it?

Production systems

One theoretical option is that skills, including attentional skills, result from the operation of "procedures". The basic principle underlying production systems is that human cognition can be conceived of as a set of condition–actions pairs called productions. The condition specifies a set of data patterns and if elements matching these patterns are in working memory then the production can apply. So a procedure is a condition–action link between a set of conditions in working memory and data or knowledge stored as schemata in long-term memory. Production systems are widely used in artificial intelligence and can be extremely powerful computational devices. They are expressed as IF . . . THEN correspondence rules, so that IF a condition or set of conditions are active in the working memory part of the system and there is a rule or schema in long-term memory corresponding to the IF conditions, the THEN part of the rule will be executed. New information resulting from the computation is then deposited in working memory leading to a new data pattern and the sequence of IF . . . THEN matching can start again. In his 1984 Maltese Cross model of memory Broadbent tries to avoid the "homunculus" problem of attentional control by proposing a production system architecture rather like ACT*. Rather than the little man in the head, control emerges from the correspondence between input patterns, long-term knowledge and the contents of working memory.

ACT* cognitive architecture

Anderson (1983) provides a theory of cognition based on a production system called ACT*. In ACT*, there are three memories: working, procedural, and declarative. (See Figure 7.2.)

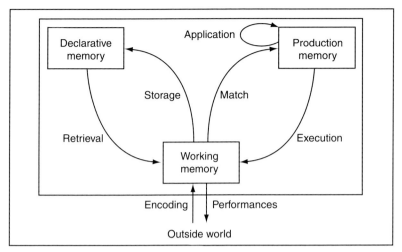

Figure 7.2 ACT*. Overview of the ACT* cognitive architecture. From Anderson (1983).

Reproduced with permission of J. R. Anderson.

Working memory contains the information to which the system currently has access. This comprises information that has been retrieved from long-term memory together with the temporary structures that have arisen from encoding processes and the action of productions. Working memory is, therefore, declarative knowledge, either permanent or temporary that is currently active. (In the human processor, this would be equivalent to the consciously available contents of short-term working memory.) An important distinction made by memory theorists is between declarative knowledge, to which we have conscious access and procedural knowledge, to which we have no conscious access. This distinction between procedural and declarative knowledge is fundamental to ACT*. Working memory is severely limited in the amount of information that can be concurrently represented in it. If all the computational steps involved in human information processing had to be represented in declarative form in working memory, the system would be in danger of overload. However, if only a small amount of task-relevant information needed to be represented in declarative form, the system could run much more efficiently. Provided the declarative system has access to the outputs from productions, there is no need for the productions themselves to open to conscious inspection. Allport (1980a, 1988), like Neuman (1984), suggests that only a very small amount of information processing is available to consciousness and that unconscious processing is the rule rather than the exception. Productions in Anderson's ACT* model run off automatically as a result of pattern matching and only the products of their execution enter working memory.

Learning in production systems

In the initial stages of learning a new task or skill, such as playing chess, people's performance is usually slow and full of mistakes. Novices repeat the rules to themselves and have to work out the implications of each move one at a time. An expert, by way of contrast, can rapidly "sum up" the state of the game and make a good move without seeming to have had a problem to solve at all. On interrogation, the expert may have difficulty in explaining exactly why they made one move rather than another. In contrast to the novice, the expert seems to have poor access to declarative knowledge for the reasons underlying their decision although the expert's performance is much better than that of the novice. According to Anderson's theory, there are three successive stages of learning involved in the acquisition of cognitive skills. In the beginning, learning involves the collection of relevant facts. So, for example, when learning to play chess, we need to know which moves are legal and which pieces move which way. The novice then applies previous experience in problem solving, to work out which is the best move. However, performance is slow and error prone because of the need to activate and retrieve all relevant knowledge into the working memory. When working memory is overloaded, relevant information may be lost and an error result. With more practice, the rules of chess begin to become proceduralised. New productions are formed from the declarative knowledge gained in the initial stages of learning. This proceduralisation frees space in working memory as the knowledge that was once declarative becomes embedded in procedures that do not need to be retrieved in declarative form to be used by the information processing system. So, for example, the rules governing legal moves by different chess pieces are just "known" by the system, the player does not have to keep on retrieving that knowledge into active working memory. The player will also begin to learn that if a particular configuration of pieces is on the board, then making a particular move is likely to produce a good outcome. In the final stages of learning, new procedures are formed from existing productions. This composition of procedures allows complex patterns of IF . . . THEN rules to be complied, so that the IF side of the production can be made up of several clauses, which will THEN produce one or a series of actions. Production rules become strengthened with use, and may become so "automatic" that the information within them is no longer available in declarative form. Experts just "know" the answer to problems and may find it extremely difficult to explain why they come to decisions.

Anderson (1983) uses bridge as an example of procedural learning in ACT*; however, the same kind of learning could be equally well applied to chess. Here are two cases where generalisation takes place in a player who is assumed to already have some procedures that have been compiled by experience. P1, P2 etc. refer to production 1, production 2 etc.:

P1   IF I am playing no trump
        and my dummy has a long suit
    THEN try to establish that suit
        and then run that suit.

P2   IF I am playing spades
        and my dummy has a long suit
    THEN try to establish that suit
        and then run that suit.

These two productions, P1 and P2, will be generalised by ACT* into a different production, P3, by the deletion of a condition clause that was different in each production:

P3   IF my dummy has a long suit
    THEN try to establish that suit
        and run that suit.

More complex generalisation can occur when, rather than deletions, constants are replaced by variables (LVs). Anderson gives another example from bridge:

P4   IF I am playing no trump
        and I have a king in a suit
        and I have the queen in that suit
        and my opponent leads a lower card in that suit
    THEN I can play the queen.

P5   IF I am playing no trump
        and I have a queen in a suit
        and I have a jack in that suit
        and my opponent leads a lower card in that suit
    THEN I can play the jack.

By substituting constants for variables, the generalisation of these two procedures becomes:

> **P6** IF I am playing no trump
> 　　　　and I have LV card 1 in a suit
> 　　　　and I have LV card 2 in the suit
> 　　　　and my opponent leads a lower card in that suit
> 　　THEN play LV card 2.

However, an important fact has been lost by this generalisation. Additional constraints need to be added to capture the fact that the cards are honours and they follow each other. Adding these constraints gives rise to the following production:

> **P7** IF I am playing no trump
> 　　　　and I have LV card 1 in a suit
> 　　　　and LV card 1 is an honour
> 　　　　and I have LV card 2 in the suit
> 　　　　and LV card 2 is an honour
> 　　　　and LV card 1 follows LV card 2
> 　　　　and my opponent leads a lower card
> 　　THEN I can play LV card 2.

This is the rule for playing touching honours in bridge. Once a rule is proceduralised, it can be easily applied to novel situations.

Chase and Simon (1973) carried out a classic study of chess players. They showed that master chess players could memorise the positions of pieces on a chessboard far more quickly than novices, but only when the pieces formed part of a valid game. If the pieces were placed at random, the novices and experts were just the same. It appears that experts perceive board positions in much larger "chunks" than novices. An expert sees the pieces in relational groups, whereas the novice sees each piece individually. In terms of production systems like ACT*, the expert has acquired a whole set of productions in which patterns of pieces on the board specify the conditions for making particular moves, which allows information that matches previous experience to be grouped into a coherent whole. "Random" patterns of pieces do not fit with previous experience and are no easier for the expert than the novice.

Gopher's (1993) experiments on training attentional strategies, he suggests, could be considered in terms of production rules that have aggregated into complex "macro-operators". Because productions run off automatically, skill learning can be viewed as procedure learning. As more and more declarative knowledge becomes proceduralised, there is less and less demand on the conscious, strategic processing that is said to be attention demanding.

Automatic processing and conscious interference in motor skills

Once performance of a skill has become automatic, there is evidence that consciously "thinking" about it can actually reduce efficiency. For example, Beilock, Carr, MacMahon, and Starkes (2002) tested expert golfers' putting performance when they were asked to focus their attention on the components of the process, such as monitoring the club swing and stopping the follow-through, and under a dual task condition in which the golfers putted while doing an auditory tone-monitoring task. It was found that putting performance in expert golfers was better under the dual task condition than under the skill-focused condition. The explanation for this effect is that directing attentional control to the component processes of a well-learned task interferes with the running off of automatic processes. While a skill is being learnt attention needs to be directed to the component processes of the task, but as the skill becomes proceduralised, less and less attention should not be needed for step-by-step execution of the task. As we have seen, skill acquisition involves the development of inte-grated task control structures, such as production rules. In the novice, the rules are held in working memory, but in the expert these rules have become proceduralised, or automatic, and therefore make little demand on attention or working memory. Beilock, Bertenthal, McCoy, and Carr (2004) reasoned that these differences in attentional demands make predictions about the effect of drawing attention to, or away from, the execution of a task in experts and novices. The novice should benefit from attending to the step-by-step components of task execution and be damaged by a concurrent dual task, whereas an expert should show a benefit in the dual task condition because attention would be distracted from interrupting the automatic pro-cessing routines. This is exactly what was found. In a second experi-ment, the novices and experts were placed under time pressure to put as quickly as possible. If the novices were depending on retrieving declarative knowledge into working memory to monitor put per-formance on line, then while focusing their attention on aspects of the skill improves performance, forcing them to put quickly should impair their accuracy. However, if the experts' performance is under the guidance of procedures that are unattended during real-time execution, then forcing them to act quickly should prevent them paying any attention to task control that might disrupt the skill. Again, the results confirmed the predictions; novices were worse under speeded instructions, but experts were more accurate. The authors conclude that although novices benefit from skill–focus conditions, experts benefit from conditions that prevent the deployment of attention to task execution. Participants in this study commented on how they felt their performance was affected. One novice stated the speed instruction "made me rush and not think enough about the task", whereas one expert reported that the speed instructions aided performance because they "didn't let me go into the depth of the actual put". Another expert stated, "The faster I did, the better I did" (p. 378).

Focus of attention in motor skill learning

There are many related findings in support of the idea that the way instructions alter the focus of attention or influence the feedback used by learners can affect motor skill acquisition (Wulf & Prinz, 2001 provide a review). In general, a distinction can be made between directing attention to the body movements being made, an "internal focus of attention", and directing attention to the effects or consequences of the body movements on apparatus or the environment, an "external focus of attention". It is generally found that an external focus results in better learning as measured by retention of the motor skill in comparison to internal focus. Learning advantages for external focus of attention in comparison to internal focus have been found for sport skills such as golf (Wulf, Lauterbach, & Toole, 1999) and tennis (Maddox, Wulf, & Wright, 2000). Wulf, McNevin, and Shea (2001) were interested in the reasons behind the effect of attentional focus on motor skill learning and tested the hypothesis that when performers use an internal focus of attention they constrain, or interfere with, the automatic control processes that normally regulate movement, and that when attention is directed to an external focus the motor system can be allowed to self-organise. This is known as the constrained action hypothesis (McNevin Shea & Wulf, 2003). In their experiment, Wulf et al. (2001) had participants learn to balance on a stabilometer, which is a platform that is unstable. Accuracy of balance can be measured by the degree to which the table is deviated from horizontal. The task was to maintain balance and participants were told to attend either to the movements they made, internal focus, or to external markers linked to the platform, external focus. To discover the attentional demands of the external and internal focus conditions, they introduced a secondary task that measured probe reaction time to an auditory signal responded to by a handheld button. The authors reasoned that the amount of attentional capacity required for the balancing task would be reflected in RT to the auditory probe. That is, if an external focus encourages less conscious control and more automatic control of the motor task, then attention will be freed up for the secondary task, and probe RTs should be faster than under the more attentionally demanding internal focus condition. Results of the experiment revealed that when attention was directed to an external focus, participants made smaller balancing errors, made finer adjustments to their balance and gave faster responses to the auditory probes than the participants in the internal focus condition. It appears that the data are consistent with the constrained-action hypothesis because an external focus of attention promotes a higher level of automaticity and reduces the level of conscious interference in the balancing task. These studies provide evidence on the different attentional control requirements in novices and experts and suggest that attending to skilled performance can produce detrimental effects.

Long-term working memory and skill

Although productions are stored in long-term memory and, as we have already explained, can be run off automatically without any demand on working memory, Ericsson and Kintsch (1995) have argued that the traditional view of the use of memory in skilled activity needs to include a long-term working memory. They say that current models of memory (e.g. Anderson's (1983) ACT*; Baddeley's working memory model (1986)) cannot account for the massively increased demand for information required by skilled task performance. They outline a theory of long-term working memory (LTWM), which is an extension of skilled memory theory (Chase & Ericsson, 1982). The proposal is that in skilled performance, say of chess players, what is needed is rapid access to relevant information in long-term memory. This is achieved by the use of LTWM in addition to short-term working memory (STWM). They suggest that learned memory skills allow experts to use LTM as an extension of STWM in areas where they are well practised. LTWM is basically a set of retrieval structures in LTM. A retrieval structure is a stable organisation made up of many retrieval cues. Load on STWM is reduced because rather than all the retrieval cues having to be held there, only the node allowing access to the whole structure need to be available in STWM. Thus in skilled performance, all the relevant information stored in LTM is rapidly accessible through the retrieval cue in STWM. Indirect evidence for LTWM was found in a series of experiments by Ericsson and Kintsch, in that a concurrent memory task produced virtually no interference on the working memory of experts.

Ericsson and Oliver (1984) and Ericsson and Staszewski (1989) studied the ability of expert chess players to mentally represent a chess game without the presence of a chessboard. Over 40 moves were presented and the chess players' representation of the resulting game position was tested in a form of cued recall task. It was found that their responses were fast and accurate, suggesting a very efficient and accurate memory representation despite the number of moves that had been made, which far exceed the capacity of STWM. The results suggest that the expert chess player is using this additional LTWM to maintain and access chess positions. The ability to perform tasks automatically, therefore, depends on a variety of factors and as we become more expert what we have learnt modifies the way in which tasks are controlled.

Situational awareness, working memory and skill

Sohn and Doane (2003) investigated the roles of working memory capacity and long-term working memory in complex task performance in novice and expert pilots. They test the view of Ericsson and Kintsch (1995) that accessibility to information relevant to a given task increases working memory capacity. In their experiments, Sohn and Doane were interested to discover how WM and LTWM contributed to situational awareness (SA). SA can be defined in terms of the cognitive processes required at three levels (Endsley, 1995): the first level is concerned with perceptual processing of elements in the environment, for example, other aircraft, cockpit warning lights, terrain; the second level is concerned with integrating the perceived situation into meaningful configuration by activating structures stored in LTM; the third level uses goal-relevant activated knowledge to predict the status of the aircraft. Sohn and Doane (2003) reasoned that SA is a demanding cognitive task. Understanding and interpreting flight information from the cockpit instruments should impose a heavy WM load on a pilot. They compared the ability of measures of WM and of LTWM to predict individual performance in the SA task and hypothesised that, according to Ericsson and Kintsch, LTWM skills would reduce the importance of WM capacity in SA task performance.

LTWM skill was measured by a task similar to that used by Chase and Simon (1973) for chess players, but rather than reconstructing meaningful or non-meaningful configurations of a chessboard, participants reconstructed meaningful or non-meaningful cockpit situations incorporating altitude, heading, airspeed etc. WM capacity, as measured by a span task did not differ significantly between novice and expert pilots. The LTWM for experts was significantly greater than that of the novices, but only for the meaningful cockpit situations. This result confirms that the expert knowledge supports more efficient retrieval structures. In the SA task participants viewed consecutive screens that showed a goal description and two consecutive cockpit snapshots. They were asked to judge if an aircraft with the information as displayed in the snapshots would reach the goal state within the next 5 secs. without any further changes in control movements. This task requires prediction of the aircraft's behaviour. The relationship between WM capacity, LTWM skill and SA performance was analysed. It was found that both WM and LTWM contribute to performance on the SA task and also that WM and LTWM skill interacted. It appears that WM capacity has greater effect in low LTWM skill participants, but not for high LTWM skill participants. Therefore, the more expert participants with high levels of LTWM skill appeared not to rely on WM capacity as much as low skill participants and is consistent with the view that LTWM skills reduce reliance on WM capacity during performance of complex cognitive tasks.

Summary

Tasks that start off being very difficult to combine may be combined successfully after extended practice. Initially, both tasks seem to require attention but later seem to proceed quite effectively without it. Posner and Snyder (1975) distinguished automatic processes, which occur without intention, and controlled processes, which are performed by the conscious, limited-capacity processing system and are open to strategic attentional control. The question of what happened with practice was addressed in two papers by Schneider and Shiffrin (1977) and Shiffrin and Schneider (1977), who proposed a general theory of automatic and controlled processing. After extensive practice in constant mapping conditions where targets were always targets and distractors were always distractors, target processing could become automatic. However, in varied mapping conditions where the target distractor relationship changed from trial to trial, so that targets on one trial could be distractors in another, automatic processing never emerged. Neuman (1984) gave a critical appraisal of the distinction between these two hypothetical processes and searches for reliable criteria to distinguish between them. Neuman concludes that automatic processing is not "uncontrolled", but is controlled below the level of conscious awareness. In Neuman's view, a process is automatic if its parameters are specified by the perceptual input and by skills, learned through practice, stored in long-term memory. When it is the case that not all the parameters to control an action are specified by these two sources, then an attentional mechanism provides the specifications that are missing. Rather than a clear distinction, Neuman thinks there is a gradation between so called "automatic" and "controlled" processing. Skills may be largely perceptuomotor or largely cognitive, but most skills are a combination of both types. Attentional control itself has been suggested to be a skill (Gopher, 1993; Hirst, 1986). Subjects can learn to be more effective in complex task combination. Skills training can be taught using whole-task and part-task techniques. Part-task training reduces working memory load, but whole-task training provides more opportunities for learning strategies. Peck and Detweiler (2000) found that the training techniques that produced the greater learning during training did not necessarily produce the greatest transfer effects. Skills and expertise has been modelled in production systems, such as ACT* (Anderson, 1983). In essence, a production system works using sets of IF . . . THEN condition action pairs: IF the condition is met, THEN the rule applies. Through practice, these procedures are entered into procedural memory, which is not open to conscious inspection and will run off automatically. Hence experts are often unable to explicitly give the reason for their decisions. It is possible that experts also use long-term working memory in skilled performance (Ericcson & Kintsch, 1995). Sohn and Doane (2003) studied the contribution of WM capacity and LTWM skill to a SA task and, in line with the view of Ericsson and Kintsch (1995), found that LTWM skill relieved reliance on WM and that expert pilots with better LTWM skills than novices could perform the SA task with less reliance on WM.

Further reading

- Allport, D. A. (1980b). Attention and performance. In G. Claxton (Ed.). *Cognitive psychology: New directions*. London: Routledge & Kegan Paul.

  Although rather old, this chapter is one of the clearest, in-depth critical appraisal of capacity theory, automatic and controlled processing and concurrent task performance.
- Matthews, G., Davies, D. R., Westerman, S. J., & Stammers, R. B. (2000). *Human performance: Cognition, stress and individual difference*. Hove, UK: Psychology Press.

  This book provides excellent coverage of all aspects of skills and factors that affect human performance.

Selection and control of action 8

Asking the right questions

So far, we have seen how different experiments, by virtue of their design, might be considered to be measuring, manipulating or observing different varieties of "attention" in different modalities and tasks. On the "small" scale, some answers may have been found, for example, the minimum "width" of the spotlight (in certain conditions), stimulus dimensions that facilitate selectivity (in certain conditions), how the perceptual display is segregated (in particular conditions) etc.

Psychologists have collected an enormous amount of data, on both "normal" and neuropsychological subjects, driven by particular questions about selectivity, task combination, consciousness and control. All of their questions are, of course, important and there are chapters within this book with such titles. Perhaps we should stop here and consider what we have been looking at. Generally speaking, studies, theories and models address issues about how selection operates and at what level of representation. Are we any nearer to discovering the nature of human performance in specific experimental tasks concerned with "attention"? Possibly, but are we any nearer discovering the general nature of attention? Will we ever? Marr (1982) explained that to find the right answers in psychology, we must ask the right questions. In formulating the right questions, we need to reconsider some fundamental assumptions and take into account what is known about the neurophysiology and neuropsychology of the brain. We have seen that this is important and that, more recently, these types of evidence are being increasingly used. One of the greatest changes in research into attention in the past 10 years has been the development of non-invasive methods of recording the activity of living brain in both normal and brain-damaged people. These studies give insight into the areas of brain involved in different tasks and allow some insight into the time course of attentional processing during these tasks. (See Hillyard, 2000 for a discussion of studying brain function with neuroimaging and Katus & Dale, 1997 for an explanation of the use of electrical and magnetic ERPs in reading mental function.)

According to Marr (1982), the most basic question we should ask is "what is attention for?" and what design considerations might have been selected by evolutionary forces as important for the effective use of a complex brain? Of course, the questions we ask will be modified by our conception of what the brain is like, our "metaphor of mind", together with our interpretation of available data. In the beginning, Broadbent (1958) thought that attention served to protect the hypothetical limited capacity processing system from information overload and, hence, had considered what attention was for. However, the conception of the mind was different then, so although the question was asked, the answer was different. Clearly, it is not simply a case of asking the right question, but also of having the right metaphor of mind.

A paradox

One of the most obvious behaviourial properties of the human information-processing system is that there seems to be a fundamental limit on our ability to do a number of things at once. A classic experiment by Hick (1952) showed that choice reaction time, to a single stimulus, increases with the number of possible alternatives (Hick's law). Simply preparing to respond to signals is costly. Evidence from the psychological refractory period (discussed in Chapters 2 and 6) shows that when two stimuli are presented in rapid succession so that the first stimulus has not been responded to when the second stimulus arrives, response to the second stimulus is slowed. This suggests that the second stimulus must wait until the response to the first stimulus has been selected and provides clear indications of such a limit. At the same time, there is now clear evidence that the brain can process an enormous amount of information simultaneously in parallel over a variety of modality specific subsystems. In fact, Neisser (1976) said there was no physiologically established limit on the amount of information that can be picked up at once. *Here we have a paradox*: The brain is apparently unlimited in its ability to process information, yet human performance is severely limited, even when asked to do two very simple tasks at once.

Metaphors of mind

For early workers, e.g., Broadbent, 1958, 1971, Treisman, 1960, this "bottleneck" suggested a limited capacity system and psychologists were interested to find out where the bottleneck was located. The concept of a bottleneck necessarily implies one "place" where processing can only proceed at a limited rate or a limit in "capacity" to process information. A bottleneck implies a point where parallel processing becomes serial and was originally couched in the metaphor of likening the mind to the old digital computer, which had "buffer storage", "limited-capacity" processing components and whose programs were written as flowcharts in which different "stages" had to be completed before others could begin. Of course, these psychologists knew that the brain was not actually like a digital computer and it is still accepted that writing flowcharts is a good way to conceptualise the component processes that are needed to achieve a processing goal. Indeed, such "flowchart" models are still used, but as a description at what Marr (1982) called the computational level of explanation. At the computational level of description, it does not matter about the rules or algorithms used or the neuronal hardware that implements the rules. Although Deutsch and Deutsch (1963) is often interpreted as a late "bottleneck" model and simply tagged on the end of a list of theories that proposed a structural limit on parallel processing, somewhere between sensory coding and response, in some ways, their ideas are quite modern. Rather than a "model" their paper puts forward a set of considerations, some of which we looked at in Chapter 2. There we explained that a set of multiple comparison processes, which Deutsch and Deutsch proposed could assess the most highly activated signal from among others, seemed computationally impossible in 1963 and led to many people dismissing this view. Deutsch and Deutsch thought that a neuropsychological mechanism involved in selective attention might be found that had connections to and from "all discriminatory and perceptual systems" (p. 88). This idea of a highly connected system did not fit well with a serial computing metaphor.

Over the last 20 years, however, there has been an explosion in the use and development of sophisticated computers that can process information in parallel over multiple processing units, pioneered by Hinton and Anderson (1981), McClelland and Rumelhart (1986) and Rumelhart and McClelland (1986). This "new connectionism", otherwise known as parallel distributed processing (PDP) or artificial neural network approach, has had a profound influence on current metaphors of mind. It would be fair to say that the new metaphor for the mind most currently in favour is that the brain is like (in fact is) a neural network. The principal impact of PDP has been on modelling learning and memory and such models very successfully solve all sorts of previously intractable modelling difficulties. PDP has been successfully applied to show how by damaging a "normal" system a neuropsychological deficit can arise (e.g., Farah, 1988; Hinton & Shallice, 1991) and is also being applied to modelling attention, as we saw in Chapter 4. We know from neurophysiological studies that the brain is a massively parallel, highly interconnected and interactive computing device, with different specialised subsystems designed to selectively respond to particular perceptual events and compute specialised information processing operations (e.g. van Essen & Maunsell, 1983). These processing events do not proceed in a stage-like serial fashion but happen simultaneously, in parallel. Although we may draw flowcharts of information processing, where the "boxes" represent theoretical computational stages or specific modules for processing specific information, we need to remember that the brain is, in fact a simultaneous parallel processing device with many neurons and pathways.

However, it is also important to remember that there are neurons and pathways and brain regions selectively responsive to particular types of information and that as processing progresses in time different brain regions become selectively involved. The parietal lobe, for example, has different regions that are recruited at different times in different aspects of attentional behaviour, as mentioned in the previous chapter.

If the brain is concurrently processing vast amounts of information in parallel perhaps there is a problem to be solved. That problem is how to allow behaviour to be controlled by the right information at the right time to the right objects in the right order. Perhaps the "bottleneck", or change from parallel to serial, happens just before response. The brain processes all information as far as it can in parallel, but at the moment of response, we are limited. This is certainly what the evidence on the psychological refractory period suggests.

Possible functions of attention

Schneider and Deubel (2002) identify two different functions of attention or aspects of processing selectivity. First, there is "selection-for-visual-perception", which they say is usually identified with visual attention and includes the subject matter covered here in Chapters 3 and 4. Although Schneider and Deubel (2002) do not mention auditory attention, we could think of it as being "selection-for-auditory-perception". The second type of selective processing is identified by Schneider and Deubel as "selection-for-spatial-motor-action" and refers to "the fact that simple actions such as grasping an object usually imply the need to select one movement target among other potential targets" (p. 609). Schneider and Deubel (2002) suggest that selection-for-visual-perception is carried out within the ventral visual pathway that computes colour, shape, category and so on, whereas the selection-for-motor-action is computed within the dorsal pathway, responsible for computing the spatial information required for a motor action. The distinction between the ventral and dorsal pathways for visual information processing has been covered in Chapter 4, when we noted the distinction between knowing "what" an object is as opposed to "where" it is or "how" to act on it. This second function of attention identified by Schneider and Deubel was first termed "selection for action" by Allport (1987) and it is to this topic we now turn.

Selection for action

Workers in the field of attention are making increasing use of real-world examples to characterise the kinds of problem faced by a complex brain when interacting with the environment. In 1987 both Allport and Neumann wrote influential papers considering the functional and neurophysiological bases of attentional behaviour. Both propose that the question of what attentional behaviour is for or why it appears the way it does must motivate its explanation. Consider some of Allport's (1987) examples:

> Many fruit are within reach, and clearly visible, yet for each individual reach of the hand, for each act of plucking, information about just one of them must govern the particular pattern and direction of movements. The disposition of the other apples, already encoded by the brain, must be in some way temporarily decoupled from the direct control of reaching, though it may of course still influence the action, for example as representing an obstacle to be reached around, not to be dislodged and so on. A predator (a sparrow hawk, say) encounters a pack of similar prey animals, but she must direct her attack

selectively towards just one of them; the fleeing prey must, with equal speed, select just one among the possible routes of escape. (p. 396)

As Allport (1987) points out, although the senses are capable of encoding information about many objects simultaneously, there is a strict limit on action, in that we can usually only make one action at a time with any effector. Basically, we can only direct our eyes to one place at a time, we can only reach for one apple at a time, we can only run one way or the other. Allport argues that there is a biological necessity for "selection for action" and that there must be:

> [A] mechanism of fundamental importance for the sensory control of action . . . that can selectively designate a subset of the available and potentially relevant information to have control over a given effector system, and can selectively decouple the remainder from such control. This need . . . arises directly from the many-to-many possible mappings between domains of sensory input and of motor output within the very highly parallel distributed organisation of the nervous system. (p. 397)

How are actions controlled?

Neuman (1987) considers this problem. If all potential actions were simultaneously trying to control action, there would be behaviourial chaos. In order to prevent such disorganisation of behaviour, there must be selection and, Neuman argues, it is this need for selection that produces the limit on human performance. The psychological refractory period, for example, may be a functional way of preventing two responses becoming available at once. However, Neuman suggests that there are a variety of selectional problems and consequently a variety of selectional mechanisms are needed: "Hence, 'attention', in this view, does not denote a single type of phenomenon. Rather, it should be viewed as the generic term for a number of phenomena, each of which is related to a different selection mechanism" (p. 374).

To specify how actions are controlled, we need to establish what an action is and if there are different kinds of action. Neuman defines an action as a "sequence of movements that is controlled by the same internal control structure and that is not a reflex" (p. 375). Actions can be adjusted to prevailing conditions, such as opening or closing the grip according to the size of the apple you want to grasp, reflexes cannot. To simplify Neuman's argument, he says that actions are controlled by skills that are stored as nested schemata in long-term memory and skills are used to attain goals. We shall cover the intentional control of behaviour and goal directed action a little later in this chapter. To attain a goal, either one or a combination of skills has to be selected and made available to control the motor apparatus or effector. Neuman states there are two immediate problems to be overcome. The first is to recruit the right effector (e.g., for speaking a response, the vocal apparatus must be recruited, for a button press response, the correct finger of the correct hand must be recruited). The problem of effector recruitment is a major limit on performance, as we have only one pair of hands, only one voice. Skills control the effectors, but different skills do not have different dedicated effectors as the hand or the mouth can be used for a variety of skills. Skills do not provide all the parameters needed to carry out an action. Other parameters are provided by the environment. Neuman's (1984) arguments on skills, dual task performance, automaticity and control were covered in Chapter 7.

Neuman (1987) says that the problem of selecting the right effector at the right time so that only one action is attempted is rather like preventing train crashes on a busy railway network. One way to avoid crashes would be to have a central station monitoring the trains on the tracks, the other would be to have a system where the network was divided into sections and when one train was on a track within the section it automatically set the signals to prevent other trains coming along. He argues that the brain uses the blocking method. This results in a capacity limit, as one ongoing action inhibits all other possible actions. Of course, it would be dangerous to have a blocking mechanism that could not be interrupted by a change in environmental circumstances. Orienting responses to unexpected events that have been processed pre-attentively will break through the block.

Overall, Neuman views attention as an "ensemble of mechanisms" that allow the brain to cope with the problem of selecting appropriate information to control action. The apparent limitation on our abilities is not a result of a limited processing capacity but has evolved to ensure coherent behaviour.

How is selection for action achieved?

In order to achieve efficient selection for action, Allport (1987) stressed the importance of perceptual integration. The attributes of all the possible objects available for action must be properly combined; in the example of picking apples, colour and size will be important for our choice. We discussed perceptual integration in Chapter 4. Provided the attributes belonging together are integrated, the next problem is for the processing system to ensure that all the possible actions are prevented from interfering with each other. This, suggested Neuman, was achieved by blocking. Exactly how selective coupling, decoupling or blocking are achieved is not made entirely clear in either Allport's or Neuman's arguments. The psychological refractory period might be an important reflection of fundamental response limitation and we discussed some underlying reasons for PRP in Chapter 7. We also know that inhibition is important in allowing the selection of one stimulus over another. One way this inhibition manifests itself as negative priming, or a slowing of response relative to the control condition, when the previously ignored object is presented as a target on the next trial.

Negative priming

Priming paradigms have been widely used in cognitive psychology. In the more usual, facilitatory priming experiments, response to a second, probe stimulus is speeded up, if either the same or a semantically associated stimulus is presented first. So, for example, prior experience of a semantically associated word, such as "doctor" speeds up naming or lexical decision to a subsequent related probe word such as "nurse" (Meyer & Schavaneveldt, 1971).

Negative priming has been extensively used by Tipper and his colleagues to explore both the level of processing achieved by "unattended" stimuli and mechanisms of selective visual attention (Allport, Tipper, & Chmiel, 1985; Tipper, 1985; Tipper & Cranston, 1985; Tipper & Driver, 1988). In the original form of the experiment, subjects were presented with pairs of overlapping line drawings and had to name one of them. The target stimulus was specified by colour. So, for example, the subject may be presented with a drawing of a dog in green ink, overlapped by a drawing of a spanner in red ink. As the stimuli overlap, spatial separation is not possible, both stimuli fall in the attended area and the target must be selected on the basis of the colour difference. The relation between the target and distractor stimuli on the first, prime trial and the second target stimulus on the probe trial can be manipulated. So, for example, the target on the prime trial may be repeated as the target on the probe trial; this is called attended repetition. When this happens, response to the probe is facilitated as in the usual priming experiment. The interesting and important negative priming effect is found when the distractor on the prime trial is presented as the target on the immediately following probe trial. Now the probe response is slowed down, relative to a neutral control condition, in which the ignored distractor is unrelated to the probe. The effect is found when stimuli are presented so briefly that although subjects are able to report the target on both prime and probe trials, they are unable to report the distractors. Negative priming is evidence for semantic processing of the unattended stimulus, even though the subjects are unable to report its identity. Further, and more important for the argument here, Tipper reasoned, that in order for the target to be selected, the distractor must be actively inhibited. This inhibition results in a slower response to an identical or categorically related item presented on the probe trial.

Driver and Tipper (1989) used both interference and negative priming as measures of distractor processing. For their first experiment, they used a version of an experiment originally performed by Francolini and Egeth (1980). Francolini and Egeth asked their subjects to count the number of red items in a display consisting of both red and black items. When the red items were digits inconsistent with the counting response, there was interference, but when the black, to-be-ignored items were digits inconsistent with the counting response there was no interference. (This kind of interference is often called the Stroop effect, after Stroop (1935) who first found it using colour words written in consistent or inconsistent colour inks.) Francolini and Egeth (1980) claimed that the lack of interference between the red and black items showed that the unattended stimuli were filtered out at an early stage of processing before any identification had taken place. Driver and Tipper (1989) reasoned that if the unattended items in Francolini and Egeth's experiment were not processed sufficiently to produce interference they could not produce negative priming. To test this, Driver and Tipper presented their subjects with successive pairs of displays where the first (acting as a prime) was of the same type used by Francolini and Egeth. The second display was a probe to measure priming. The relation between the black items in the prime display and the number of red items in the probe display was manipulated so that sometimes the black items in the prime were congruent with the probe response and at other times they were incongruent.

The results were quite clear. Data from the prime trials replicated Francolini and Egeth's results in that the ignored black digits did not interfere with the counting response to the red items. However, although the black digits had produced no interference in the prime trial, they did cause negative priming on the probe trial. Similar experiments in the same paper led Driver and Tipper to conclude that the non-interfering distractors are identified and inhibited. If the demonstration of no interference is not equivalent to demonstrating no processing, then any theoretical interpretation of experiments that rely on this assumption may be flawed. These results suggest that all attributes of a target stimulus are fully processed, but those not required for the selection of action, or response, are inhibited. Thus, the goal of the current task influences which stimulus attributes are allowed to control action.

Tipper, Brehaut, and Driver (1990) found that negative priming can also be produced by moving objects, when subjects have to respond by indicating where an identified object is in a moving display. In the picking apples example described earlier, we assume that the picker and the apple are stationary. Tipper et al. (1990) stress that predators must be able to track the movement of an identified object and use the example of a pike trying to catch a stickleback. There are many sticklebacks present, but one must be selected as the object for action by its relative position within a group. Tipper et al. (1990) show that stimulus identity can control spatially directed action and inhibition can be directed to irrelevant object locations. The phenomenon of negative priming suggests that one way of decoupling potentially relevant objects from the immediate control of action is to inhibit their representations or response mappings.

Levels of representation in selection for action

Tipper, Weaver, and Houghton (1994) have shown that inhibitory mechanisms are goal dependent and that inhibition is directed to different properties of a stimulus depending on which properties of the stimulus are required to control response and how difficult the selection task is. They propose that selection is "dynamic and sensitive to task demands". As selection and inhibition can be shown to operate at a number of levels, it seems likely and Tipper et al. argue that distracting objects are represented at multiple levels, some representations are inhibited while others remain active and the complex effects of distractor information can only be explained if this is the case. Further support for selection operating at different levels and inhibition applying to different features of an object depending on goals or task demands comes from both neurological and normal data. Patients with visual neglect and extinction were discussed in Chapter 4. Neglect is usually considered to be an attentional problem. These patients can name a single object, even if presented to the side of visual space contralateral to their lesion, but when two objects are presented simultaneously, only the object in the "good" side is reportable, the other object is neglected.

Baylis, Driver, and Rafal (1993) examined patients who exhibited visual extinction following unilateral parietal damage. Patients were presented with two coloured letters, one either side of fixation, or with a single letter. Their task was to report the colour or the letter. Baylis et al. found that when two objects were presented simultaneously and either the colours or the letters were the same, extinction was more severe. However, performance appeared to be unaffected by unattended dimensions. When presented with a red O and a green O the patient would report each colour correct in its position, however, when asked to report the letter, they reported only one "O" in the good side and said there was nothing else there. Likewise if colour were repeated over the two stimuli, extinction occurred for the colour. Baylis et al. argued that their patients were exhibiting an exaggerated form of an effect observed in normal people called "repetition blindness" (RB). This effect refers to a reduction in accuracy of a report when two identical stimuli are presented (e.g., Hochhaus & Moran, 1991; Kanwisher, 1987). Kanwisher (1991) found that subjects asked to attend to coloured letters presented in a rapid sequence showed RB for letters of repeated colour, but if the second presentation of a letter had been preceded by a white (i.e., unattended) letter there was no RB. Kanwisher, Driver, and Machado (1995) suggest that RB results from difficulty in combining two identical "types" to their own episodic records ("tokens"). We have already suggested that linking or integrating semantic (type) and episodic (token) information is necessary for conscious report (e.g., Allport 1977; Coltheart, 1980a). Although there is one problem integrating, for example, the identity and location of an object, and this may be necessary for selection for action or conscious report, the type–token problem seems to be particulary troublesome in the case where there are two identical examples of the same type that can only be differentiated by another source of information. Kanwisher et al. (1995) argue that if there is an attentional system responsible for integrating information of type and token, it may be unable to link repeated types to different tokens. They report a series of experiments to see if the extinction effects discovered in patients by Baylis et al. (1993) can be mimicked in normal people. Subjects were presented with pairs of brief, pattern masked, coloured letters. The letters could be the same (repeated) or different (non-repeated) and the colours of the letters could also be repeated or not. Subjects were asked to respond first to the left-hand stimulus and then to the right-hand stimulus. Results showed that, as in the experiment by Baylis et al., repetition of the reported dimension reduced performance on the second report but repetition of the unreported dimension did not. According to Fagot and Pashler (1994), RB may arise because subjects are unwilling or reluctant to repeat a response when they are uncertain if it is correct; if this is the case, then RB is a result of a response strategy. In order to rule this out, Kanwisher et al. (1995) introduced conditions in which subjects had to switch the basis for their response between the first and second stimulus and obtained confidence ratings from subjects about their certainty of the responses they chose. In sum, RB appears to be produced by the repetition of attended dimensions. When different dimensions are relevant for the two responses in the switching attention condition, both attended dimensions affect RB. These results, they argue, rule out a response strategy explanation. The most important implication here, is that the goal of the task influences what is attended and attentional demands will be different in different situations. Kanwisher et al. (1995) and Tipper et al. (1994) all suggest that although unattended dimensions can be excluded from the processes underlying performance of a task, if the previously excluded dimension is subsequently selected for another object, those dimensions can still be accessed and influence later performance. So, the level at which selection takes place for a given task does not necessarily mean that the unselected information is entirely lost to the processing system. It is important to appreciate that this evidence shows how behaviourial goals determine the nature of selectivity, appropriate information is selected or not depending on the task. Schneider and Deubel (2002) proposed that there is a "tight coupling" between selection-for-perception and selection-for-motor-action and provides evidence that goal-driven programming of saccades (eye movements) and programming pointing or reaching movements influence perceptual processing.

Reaching and grasping

In addition to knowing which attributes of an object belong together, whether within or between modalities, unless we are going to be content with just reporting the presence of those objects we need to be able to move to, reach and grasp or perhaps run away from those objects. Let us go back to picking apples. Not only do you have to extend your arm the correct distance in the right direction so that it arrives at the selected apple, but at the same time, your grasp must be adapted to fit the shape of an apple. Think about the difference in grasp needed for an apple as opposed to a blackberry. Of course, the blackberry is smaller and you would need finer control of the fingers to reach it, but once the fruit is reached, still more planning is required. While the apple is hard and heavy, the blackberry is soft and light. If you were to use the same pressure of grip on the blackberry as the apple, the blackberry would be squashed. Quite clearly, many sources of information need to be integrated: not only visual and spatial information from the environment about the colour shape and distance, but also semantic information from memory, about the sensory properties, hard/soft, heavy/light etc. This problem is an example of "multiple constraint satisfaction". We know a little about the planning and control of reaching and grasping in response to visuospatial information from the environment, we know rather less about the way in which other properties are involved in the control of action. Jeannerod (1984) analysed videos of subjects reaching for objects and decided that movements could be analysed into two components: the reach and the grasp. Reaching involves aiming the hand in the right direction and moving it the right distance, the grasp phase begins during the reaching movement and the shape of the grasp depend on the target object. During the grasp phase, the fingers and thumb first open out and then three-quarters of the way through the reaching movement, the grasp begins to close up to fit the object. Smyth, Collins, Morris, and Levy (1994) provide an accessible review of planning and controlling movements.

Controlling actions is specified by so many possible combinations of sizes, distances and object properties that there are an enormous number of possible movements that might be required. This is called the "degrees of freedom problem", which is discussed by Jordan and Rosenbaum (1989). They suggest that one way of reducing the number of degrees of freedom is to have connections between potentially independent systems, so that they work in synergy. Driver and Spence (1994) suggested that the attentional system might rely on spatial synergy, in their crossmodal experiment discussed in Chapter 5. Spatial maps are important for integrating visual features (Treisman, 1999), but "space" is not easy to define according to Rizzolatti, Riggio and Sheliga (1994). There is evidence from studies on monkeys that space can be subdivided. Rizzolatti and colleagues (Rizzolatti & Carmarda, 1987; Rizzolatti & Gallese, 1988; Rizzolatti, Gentilucci, & Matelli, 1985) have demonstrated that lesions indifferent to pre-motor areas can produce different kinds of visual neglect, either to "reaching" space, "oculomotor" space or "orofacial" space. In the first case, the animal makes no attempt to reach for an object; in the second case, the animal will not make eye movements toward objects; in the third case, it will, for example, not lick juice from around the mouth. Clearly, "space", and hence spatial attention, needs to be considered in terms of the kinds of action that are appropriate at different distances. Further, "consciousness" must also be considered to breakdown within the same frames.

We have already seen that in monkeys with visual neglect, space can dissociate into that around the mouth, that within grasping distance and that to which eye movements can be made and that the brain has distinct systems for coding "what" and "where" in vision. From studies of monkey, it is known that the cortical system that knows where objects are connects from the visual cortex to the inferior parietal lobule, which is itself made up of a number of distinct anatomical and functional areas. Rizzolati et al. (1994) review the neuronal properties of the frontoparietal circuits and conclude that different spatial representations are computed in parallel in different cortical circuits. Further, space representation is linked to movement organisation and that the "mechanisms for representing space are different in different circuits and most likely are related to and depend on the motor requirements of the effectors controlled by a given circuit" (p. 235).

Neurons have been found that seem to compute the reaching and grasping components identified in Jeannerod's analysis. Gentilucci and Rizzolatti (1990) identified a brain area that codes the spatial relationship between the target of action and the body and translates it into a pattern of movements. Other areas seem to be selective for different types of grip (Rizzolatti & Gallese, 1988) and other neurons fire to objects of expected size even in the absence of any movement. Interestingly, neurons that code grasping do not code space, so in a sense, while they know what the object is in terms of specifying the grasp, they do not know where the object is. A somewhat analogous case to the what/where problem in vision (see Chapter 3).

Experimental evidence on the selective spatial control of arm movements, for instance, Tipper, Lortie, and Baylis (1992), looked at selective reaching to see if there was evidence for "action-centred attention". Their subjects' task was to press a button if a red light came on next to it. On some trials, a yellow distractor light would come on and the interference effects of this light were studied. The subject's hand was either at the top or the bottom of the board at the start of a trial. If the yellow distractor light came on at the top when the subject's hand was at the top, there was greater interference than if the subject's hand was at the bottom. Similar results were found for left and right. When subjects were to respond with the right hand and the distractor came on the right-hand side, interference was greater than if it was on the left. Likewise, if the left hand was used for response, a distractor on the left had more effect that one on the right. Taking this together with other evidence, Rizzolatti et al. (1994) argue that programming arm movements produces a spatial attentional field that is not dependent on eye movements and "that the same system that controls action is the same system that controls spatial attention" (p. 256). This pre-motor theory of attention proposes that spatial selective attention results from activation of neurons in "spatial pragmatic maps" and the activation of those neurons starts at the same time as the preparation for goal-directed, spatial movements. According to the task, different spatial pragmatic maps may be required and spatial attention can originate in any of the maps. Last, in humans and other primates, the fovea is highly developed and so the oculomotor spatial pragmatic map is usually most important. Schneider and Deubel (2002) propose the visual attention model, (VAM) (Schneider, 1995) as an alternative. The major difference is that VAM assumes that motor processing is a consequence of visual attention processes whereas pre-motor theory assumes that visual attention follows motor processing. However, they admit that there is not yet clear evidence available to differentiate these viewpoints and that for a fuller understanding of how task specifications such as "search for a large red square" are combined to produce attentional effects. They suggest that VAM or pre-motor theory should be combined with an attentional theory such as Bundesen (1990), which we covered in Chapter 2.

The evidence considered here tells us something about spatially directed movements, but the question of how other information, for example, semantics are involved in controlling action is as yet little explored.

Intentional control of actions

In everyday life, we are continually making actions to objects that are inviting, or afford, a variety of appropriate responses. Usually, we make these actions in a goal-directed sequence. For example, when making a cup of tea, the sugar bowl, the milk jug and the cup are all containers into which we can pour things. In one part of the tea-making sequence, we have to be sure to pour tea into the cup and milk into the jug, not vice versa. Later in the sequence, it is appropriate to pour milk into the cup. When distracted, we may make a mistake such as pouring tea into the milk jug. Such "slips of action" have been studied and interpreted as failures of control (Norman, 1981; Reason, 1979). While it is well appreciated that complex behaviour requires some kind of control process to coordinate and organise it, there is, to date, no clear idea of exactly how this is achieved. However, if we ask an experimental subject to do one task rather than another, respond to one aspect of a stimulus and ignore all others, the subject is able to do it. Somehow, the cognitive system can be configured to do one task at one time and another task at another time on the basis of intentions. Thus a major question psychologists have to address is how behaviour is controlled by internal intentional states (endo-genously) rather than by external perceptual states (exogenously). Over the past 10 years an increasing volume of research has addressed the internal control of tasks and we shall examine some of it later in this chapter. Much of the initial evidence concerning intentional behaviour has been gathered from the study of patients who show gross behavioural disorganisation following damage to their frontal lobes. Before we look at theories of control we should consider some of this evidence.

Functional deficits following frontal damage

Disorders of control

At the beginning of the chapter, we noted that, occasionally, we do not do exactly what we planned to do. These errors were termed "slips of action" by Reason (1979). A famous example of such a slip is reported by William James (1890) who went upstairs to change and then discovered himself in bed. We all experience "capture errors" occasionally, but for some patients, these happen all the time. Classical symptoms of frontal lobe damage are deficits in planning, controlling and coordinating sequences of actions. Perhaps the first reported case of frontal lobe damage was the famous Phineas Gage (Harlow, 1868). While working on the railway, an iron rod flew up and punctured the front of Gage's skull. He lived and his cognitive abilities seemed well preserved, but he showed impairment in control, behaving in a generally disinhibited antisocial way. He also showed changes in mood and personality. A recent example of the effects of bilateral frontal damage is given by Esslinger and Damasio (1985) in their patient EVR. Before his operation, EVR had been an accountant, but now was extremely disabled in his day-to-day life, because he was unable to plan and make decisions. He lost a succession of jobs because he could not make financial decisions; even deciding what to buy at the shop or which restaurant to eat in was a major task involving in-depth consideration of brands and prices in the shop or menus, seating plan and management style in the restaurant. As early as 1895 Bianchi hypothesised that the frontal lobes were the seat of coordination of information coming in and out of the sensory and motor areas of the cortex. Bianchi (1922) reports studies of monkeys with frontal lobe lesions. Typically, their behaviour is characterised by disorganised fragmentary sequences that are left incomplete. They make repetitive, aimless movements, such as poking at a spot on the wall and repeatedly make actions that have failed to achieve their goal. Although one must be cautious in generalising from monkey to mankind, the similarity between these experimental monkeys and human patients is close. Luria (1966) introduced the term "frontal lobe syndrome" to describe patients who, following frontal lobe damage, showed similarly disorganised, incoherent, incomplete behaviour.

Difficulty changing mental set

One of the most typical difficulties patients with frontal damage experience is "behaviourial rigidity". Milner (1963) tested a variety of patients' performance on the Wisconsin card-sorting test and discovered that the group of patients with frontal lesions performed much worse than patients with lesions in other parts of the cortex. In the Wisconsin card-sorting test, the subject is given four "key" cards on which there are shapes, such as circles, crosses, stars and triangles; there are different numbers of the shapes on each card and the shapes may be in four different colours. There are then, three different dimensions that might be relevant for sorting the cards: colour, number, shape. The experimenter has a rule "in mind" and the subject has to discover that rule by using a pack of "response" cards that also have groups of coloured shapes on them. Each time the subject places a response card on a key card, they are told whether or not they have sorted according to the rule. Whichever rule is first used by the patient is said to be correct and the patient continues to sort on that rule. After a number of trials, the patient is told that the rule has now changed and they are to try and discover it. This means, of course, that the old rule must no longer be followed and some new categorisation rules must be tried out. Patients with frontal damage were unable to change from their original rule. They showed "perseveration", in that, despite being instructed to stop sorting on the old rule and look for another, they were unable to do so. Sandson and Albert (1984) have called this "stuck in set" perseveration. Milner (1963) suggested that her patients were unable to override the activation of well-learned schema. This idea is supported by the fact that naming the ink colour of a Stroop colour word may be totally impossible in patients with frontal damage. Perret (1974) found that patients with left frontal lesions were unable to inhibit word reading to name the ink colour. Further evidence for these patients being inflexible in their mental set is seen in tests of word fluency. Some of Milner's patients were asked to write down as many four-letter words beginning with a particular letter as they could. Typically, normal output is about 30 or 40 words, but frontal patients are often able to produce only five or six. Not only is the output poor, but also they may repeat words or break the rule by including words of more or fewer than four letters. As is often the case with the Wisconsin card-sorting tasks, while patients are breaking the rule or repeating an incorrect action, they frequently commentate that they are doing the wrong thing, but are unable to prevent themselves from doing it.

Distracted behaviour

Frontal lobe patients are often described as distractible (Rylander, 1939). Shallice (1988b) reviews some of the evidence and concludes that, in general, there is evidence for an increased distractibility in frontal patients, in that they seem to have difficulty in both focusing and maintaining concentration. It seems that, although they have difficulty in shifting mental set, leading to inflexible behaviour, these patients also have difficulty in maintaining mental set or inhibiting unwanted actions. This may be because the frontal lobes are large and subserve a variety of functions.

Baddeley (1986) reports a patient, RJ with severe bilateral frontal lesions, studied by him and Barbara Wilson. RJ was asked to measure out a length of string so that it could be cut later, but immediately picked up the scissors and cut it. Although he knew the string was not to be cut and said "Yes, I know I'm not to cut it," he carried on cutting! This behaviour of RJ is similar to the "utilisation behaviour" of Lhermitte (1983) who reports a patient who having a glass and a jug of water placed in front of them, picks up the jug and pours water into the glass. These errors in patient behaviour are similar to "capture errors" in normal subjects, where an unintended, familiar action happens, for example, going to bed when you go into the bedroom rather than fetching what you went for (James, 1890).

Planning ahead and goal-directed behaviour

Another difficulty frequently found in frontal lobe syndrome is the inability to maintain goal-directed behaviour. Shallice (1982) devised a version of the Tower of Hanoi problem (a standard problem-solving task often used by cognitive psychologists), which he called the Tower of London and was suitable for testing patients as it allowed a graded score. In the Tower of London task there are three different length pegs and three different coloured balls. Initially, there are two balls on the longest peg and one on the middle peg. The goal is to get all the balls in the correct colour order, onto the longest peg, in a specified number of moves. Typically, normal subjects will think through the puzzle before they make their moves, to plan the best course of action. Patients with frontal damage find the Tower of London extremely difficult and Baddeley (1986) reports that RJ was unable to even begin the task. Another planning task is Link's cube (Luria, 1966, reporting Gadzhiev). In this task the subject is given 27 small cubes, with varying numbers of yellow sides. The goal is to construct one large yellow cube from all the small ones. Again, the frontal patient finds this very difficult. It appears that goal-directed behaviours, which require planning or looking ahead, are almost impossible for these patients.

Some neurophysiological characteristics of the frontal regions

The frontal lobes are a generally inhomogeneous area occupying all brain areas forward of the central sulcus. However, some areas can be distinguished: primary motor cortex, pre-motor cortex, Broca's area, medial cortex and prefrontal cortex. The prefrontal cortex can be further subdivided into three regions, each with its own pattern of connectivity: the frontal eye fields, the dorsal lateral cortex and the orbitofrontal cortex. Prefrontal cortex has complex connections with other cortical and subcortical regions. Inputs come from visual, somatosensory areas in parietal cortex and there are inputs from and outputs to caudate, thalamus, amygdala and hypothalamus. It is because the frontal lobes are so complex that such a wide variety of deficits can arise when they are damaged.

In an early study of brain activity, Roland (1985) measured regional changes in metabolism and blood flow in human frontal cortex during a variety of tasks. He found that when behaviour was voluntarily controlled, there was heightened activity in primary motor cortex just prior to the beginning of what Roland calls "brain work". The brain seems to "prepare" the cortical fields expected to be needed for the task. Of most interest, Roland found that the superior prefrontal cortex had a number of areas that were prepared in advance of a variety of different kinds of attentional tasks, but were independent of the modality of input or output. These areas seemed to be particularly involved with preparing and recruiting cortical fields. The anterior part became active in tasks that were given a prior instruction, the middle part was active when attention was being directed or switched and the posterior part of the prefrontal cortex became active when a sequential task was performed. Roland characterises voluntary behaviour as requiring "temporal or sequential changes in motor output" (p. 155) and this behaviour must be preceded by a series of brain events. Reviewing a variety of work, Roland concluded that the midsection of superior prefrontal cortex is important for selective attention and the mechanism underlies selectivity is differential tuning or preparation of cortical fields. Roland found increased metabolism in task-relevant areas with depressed metabolism in areas that might have been expected to interfere with processing: "Control of attention implies that the brain maintains a specific organisation of differentially tuned fields and areas" (p. 164). The midsection of superior prefrontal cortex is most active when "the tuned subset of task related information has to be protected from irrelevant information", as when selection from distractors is required, and when "differential tuning has to be switched from one group of cortical fields and areas to another group" (p. 164), as when tasks are shifted. Roland assumed that cortical tuning must also involve the basal ganglia and thalamus. In the 20 years since Roland's work, many advances have been made in brain imaging and in fractionating the role of the frontal cortex. In general, the findings confirm Roland's suggestions. Passingham (1993) reviewed the role of the frontal lobes and voluntary action using data from monkeys, neuropsychological patients and normal subjects and shows, among other things, how the prefrontal cortex is engaged when new voluntary decisions have to be made. However, the functional architecture of the frontal lobes remains somewhat mysterious. Koechlin, Ody, and Kouneiher (2003), reporting on their imaging studies on the architecture of prefrontal cortex, demonstrated that its functional architecture remains poorly understood. Similarly, Walton, Devlin, and Rushworth (2004), again in an fMRI study comment that: "it has proven extremely difficult . . . to separate functional areas in the frontal lobes" (p. 1259). Given the complexity and variety of behaviours in which frontal lobes are implicated, it is perhaps unsurprising that discovering the functional architecture is a challenging task.

Theories of intentional control: The importance of goals

First, let us consider how control might be achieved in some cognitive models. In the ACT* production system designed by Anderson (1983) and covered in more detail in Chapter 7, a crucial concept is that of goals. Productions require not only the activation of a particular data pattern, but also the activation of a goal. So, for example when presented with a Stroop word, where the colour of the ink is different from the colour word in which it is written, we would be unable to respond alternately to the ink or the word, unless the goal could be changed. In one case, the goal is "Name the ink colour", in the other, it is "Read the word". We have seen that the condition–action link between the word and its name is the stronger because of the asymmetry of interference but nevertheless, it is possible to respond to the ink colour; so in some way the goal "Name the ink" can be set to gain control of action. Once the goal has been set, perhaps by the experimenter's instruction "priming" the system, the weaker production rule can apply, albeit slowly. In human performance, if we name the word in error, this could be interpreted as a failure to maintain the correct goal. Production systems include the concept of goal, but do not specify how the goals are set. However, as soon as we say the "subject" sets the goals, we have returned to the homunculus problem. In the connectionist model of Stroop task performance of Cohen et al. (1990), the model has ways of modulating the pathways by task demand, in order for the "weaker" pathway to output a response.

Duncan (1986, 1993) stresses the importance of goals in the selection of inputs to the information processing system and in directing behaviour. When we discussed Broadbent's (1958) filter theory in Chapter 2, one question left unanswered was "who sets the filter?" In his 1993 paper, Duncan considers this question and proposes that the filter is controlled current goals. That is, the filter will select information that is relevant to ongoing behaviour. He suggests that both experimental and neurophysiological evidence support the idea that control of the selective filter is achieved by a process of matching inputs against an "attentional template", which specifies what information is currently needed. This idea is similar to that of Broadbent (1971) who had, in his refinement of filter theory, proposed two mechanisms, pigeonholing and categorisation, which were able to bias central mechanisms toward one outcome rather than another. (For more explanation on this, see Chapter 2.)

Duncan (1986) argued that in normal activities people set a list of "task requirements". He called this a "goal list". In everyday life, goal lists originate from the environment and needs, whereas in the laboratory they may originate from the experimenter's instructions. Goal lists are used to create "action structures", which are the actions needed to achieve the goals. To produce the necessary action structure from a goal list, Duncan says that people use "means–end analysis", which is a common heuristic useful in problem solving. Basically means–end analysis computes the difference between the current state and the desired end state and makes moves or actions that reduce the difference between where you are now (the present state) and where you would like to be (the goal state). Duncan's overall theory involves three components. First, there must be a store of actions and their consequences; these, he sees as similar to a memory of productions as in ACT*. Second, there is a process by which goals are selected to control behaviour. This proceeds by means–end analysis whereby, third, an action is selected to minimise the difference between the current and the goal state and this process will continue until the mismatch between the states is minimal or nil. In order to keep behaviour coherent it is important that the goal list inhibits other potential actions and allows relevant actions to continue.

Normally, the goal list is maintained until all the actions that make it up are carried out and the goal state is reached. Then, control of behaviour by the goal list is relinquished. According to Duncan, frontal patients have difficulty in setting up, maintaining and using goal lists. This means that either they will not be able to do the task at all or will be easily distracted if the goal list is not maintained. A goal list makes performance of goal-directed actions coherent by inhibiting irrelevant actions. Behaviour will become incoherent if there is no goal list, as irrelevant actions will not be inhibited. Hecaen and Albert (1978) noted that when frontal patients are given instructions, they often have to be repeated several times, that patients often stop half-way into a task and need several verbal prompts before they will continue. This failure to continue a task until the goal is achieved is taken by Duncan (1986) as evidence of the patient's inability to control behaviour by matching current achievement to the goal list.

Further, if a goal list has been set up and the goal reached but then the goal list does not relinquish behaviour, the same behaviour, or perseveration, will occur. Duncan's emphasis on the importance of setting and maintenance of goals in normal behaviour seems well justified and provides a parsimonious account of a variety of apparently inconsistent symptoms found in patients who have suffered frontal damage. For example, how they can exhibit both perseveration and the inability to initiate spontaneous actions is easily explained by the difficulty they have with using goal structures.

Norman and Shallice's model of willed and automatic control of behaviour

Norman and Shallice (1986) propose that there are a number of different kinds of task that require deliberate attentional resources. These tasks, they say, correspond to what William James (1890) called "willed" acts. A willed act involves "an additional conscious element, in the shape of a fiat, mandate or express consent". In contrast, there are other acts, which James called "ideomotor" where we are "aware of nothing between the conception and the execution". The distinction between automatic and controlled processing is made in Chapter 8. Norman and Shallice propose that deliberate attentional resources are required when tasks:

1. involve planning or decision making
2. involve components of trouble shooting
3. are ill-learned or contain novel sequences
4. are judged to be dangerous or technically difficult
5. require overcoming a strong habitual response.

Norman and Shallice attempt to account for a variety of phenomena concerning controlled and automatic behaviour. For example, some action sequences that normally run off automatically can be carried out under conscious control if needed, so deliberate conscious control can suppress unwanted actions and facilitate wanted actions. A classic example here would be the Stroop colour word task that we have looked at several times already. The unwanted action "Name the word" (automatic) can be suppressed (by deliberate conscious control) in order to "Name the colour". This example is one that falls into the "overcoming habitual response" category. Their theoretical framework centres around the idea that we have action schemata in long-term memory that are awaiting the appropriate set of conditions to be triggered. This idea is similar to that of the production system ACT* in that if the conditions are right then the appropriate production will run. However, here it is schemata that will be activated not productions.

Normally, the most strongly activated schema will take control of action. In the Stroop example, this would be the written word. However, for the colour to be named, there must be attentional biasing of the schema for naming the colour that allows the normally weaker response to become the most active schema and gain control of action. There are, then, two sources of activation: one from the stimulus environment, which acts "bottom up", and another that acts "top down", according to the current goal. An important component of the model is a basic mechanism called "contention scheduling". This sorts out conflicting schemata by interactive inhibition and excitation. The operation of this system is similar to the interactive activation model of letter recognition proposed by McClelland and Rumelhart (1981).

Well-learned sequences of behaviour can be represented as a horizontal thread of linear processing, where schemata are activated if they match the triggering conditions in the database or memory. Thus for habitual tasks there is a set of conditions, processing structures and procedures that allow actions to be carried out without any need for deliberate conscious attentional control. However, when there is no pre-existing schema, for example in a novel task, or when some additional control is required, top-down biasing of schemata is provided by the supervisory attentional system (SAS). This biasing operates by the application of additional excitation and inhibition to schemata that changes the probability of selection by the contention scheduling mechanism. This "top-down" biasing by the SAS is called a vertical thread and comes into operation when attentional control is required. (See Figure 8.1.)

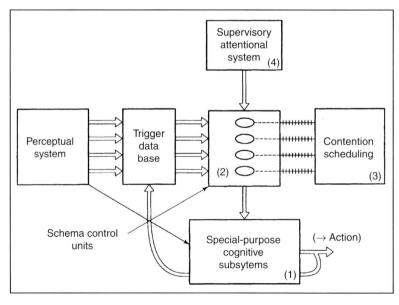

Figure 8.1 The Norman and Shallice model.

Reproduced from (1986). Copyright Oxford University Press. Reproduced by permission of the publisher and the author.

The SAS has been equated with the central executive in Baddeley's (1986) model of working memory. Is this, however, a homunculus by a different name? Baddeley (1986) believes that the "homunculus" can serve a useful purpose provided that we remember it is a way of labelling a problem rather than explaining it and that we continue to work at "stripping away the various functions we previously attributed to our homunculus until eventually it can be declared redundant" (p. 26). Baddeley points out that whether the central executive will prove to be a single unitary system or a number of autonomous control processes is yet to be discovered. Certainly there is good evidence that people act as if they have an SAS and can behave in goal-directed ways, initiating and changing behaviours, apparently "at will".

The symptoms of frontal lobe patients are well explained in terms of Norman and Shallice's (1986) model. Indeed, patient data have provided a large part of the data on which these authors based their ideas. If the SAS is damaged, then it will be unable to bias the schemata that are intended to control action or switch from a currently active schema (current mental set) to a new one. The inability to change the schema that is currently controlling action would produce perseveration errors, as in the Wisconsin card-sorting test. Further, if the SAS is out of action, the schema most strongly activated by the environmental cues will capture control of action, as in RJ cutting string and would explain impulsive, "uncontrolled" behaviour. An interesting point to note here is, that although the patient can tell you what they should be doing, i.e., *not* cutting string, the verbal information has no impact on behaviour. So although at a conscious level the patient "knows" what to do, at another, unconscious level, the information processing system does not "know".

Exploring the voluntary control of tasks

Jersild (1927) is the first person we can find in the literature who investigated "mental set" and "mental shift". In his experiments, Jersild asked his subjects to switch between different calculation tasks, not block by block, as is often the case in experiments, but between elements within the task. For example, subjects were given a list of 25 two-digit numbers and told to add six to the first number, subtract three from the second number, add six to the third and so on. This condition, Jersild called a "shift task". When time to work through the list in the shift task is compared with the mean of both the single tasks, Jersild found a "shift loss" or reduction in efficiency reflected by longer list completion times. This "shift loss" was found to be just over one second per item, which in comparison to many psychological investigations, where every millisecond counts, represents an enormous effect. Spector and Beiderman (1976), whose paper was called "Mental set and mental shift revisited", did more experiments that replicated and extended Jersild's original work. They demonstrated that if subjects had to alternately add three to a number and give a verbal opposite to written words, in mixed lists of letters and numbers, there was no cost of alternation at all, i.e., the mean time taken to perform the pure single tasks was just the same as in the mixed task. In this case, they argue, the stimulus acts as a retrieval cue for the task to be performed on it; you cannot add three to a word or generate the opposite to a number. We could interpret this as showing that the operation to be performed is stimulus driven and therefore no intentional control processes are needed. However, when the stimulus did not unambiguously cue the task to be performed, in lists of all numbers, or all words, they too found large and reliable shift costs and suggested that "changes of set will have a large effect when the selection of appropriate operations requires that one keep track of previously performed operations" (p. 669). Spector and Beiderman are implying here that the cost of shifting is a memory problem rather than a control problem. Clearly, memory must be involved, if we are to make the intended response to the correct stimulus at the appropriate time, but in addition there must also be reconfiguration of the cognitive system to change the mental set that we have remembered as appropriate.

Mental set and mental shift revisited again

Despite these discoveries nothing seems to have been done on this topic for nearly 20 years. In 1994 Allport et al. began further investigations into task switching. For example, in a typical experiment, participants read down a list of Stroop colour words responding alternately with the name of the word and the colour of the ink or to alternately give the number of identical digits in a group or the numerical value of the digit. In Figure 8.2, there are three different lists of stimuli. Using the "uniform digit" list in the figure, you could try to do the task. It is surprisingly difficult, but nevertheless you can do it. Try to respond as quickly as possible, while being slow enough to be accurate.

If you measure the time taken to read down the list doing the same task repeatedly, digit naming is faster than group naming (the Stroop effect); but time to read the list in the alternating condition is much

Uniform digit list	Mixed list	Uniform word list
2 2 2 2	8 8 8 8 8	GREEN
7	BLUE	YELLOW
4 4	1 1 1 1	BLUE
5 5 5	RED	PINK
2	3 3 3 3 3 3	RED
3 3 3 3 3 3	GREEN	BROWN
8 8	6	GREEN
6 6 6 6	YELLOW	BLUE
5 5	3 3	YELLOW

NOTE:
In the experiment, the colour words were written in an incongruent ink colour.

Figure 8.2 Examples of mixed and uniform lists of the type used by Allport et al. (1994).

slower than the average of both single tasks. This slowing in the alternation condition is a demonstration of what we called a "shift cost". Since Allport et al. (1994), there have been many demonstrations of a shift cost in task-switching experiments. It is consistently found that task-switching latencies are slower than task-repetition latencies (e.g. Gopher, Armony, & Greenshpan, 2000; Meiran, 1996; Rogers & Monsell, 1995; Sohn & Carlson, 2000). The switch cost is a very robust phenomenon, but what does it reflect?

Let us consider what is happening when you do this task-alternation experiment in terms of the Norman and Shallice model. The Stroop stimulus is ambiguous, both the number in the group and the digit name enter the perceptual system along the horizontal threads. As digit naming is a more habitual action, the schema for digit naming is triggered. Unless top-down biasing from the vertical system, activated by the SAS, is brought into play, the weaker schema for group naming could not "win" in the contention scheduling system to produce an output. If the responses are to be produced in alternation, according to the task instruction, the control system or SAS must alternately activate/inhibit the immediately relevant/irrelevant task schema. It looks as though this setting and resetting takes time and reflects the operation of a control system. Subjectively, as well, this tasks feels very effortful and you may well agree with Spector and Beiderman that there is also a problem of remembering or keeping a running record of which tasks you are supposed to be doing.

Although there have now been many experiments on task shifting, let us examine one of the first in some detail. Allport et al. (1994) compared task shifting between the different dimensions of Stroop stimuli in conditions where the stimulus did or did not specify the task to be performed on it. One kind of stimuli were traditional Stroop colour words and the other stimuli were groups of numerals, as illustrated in the task you have just done, in which the subjects could respond to either the number of numerals (we call this "group") or to the name of the numeral value (we call this "value"). Two types of list were constructed: "mixed lists" and "uniform lists". In the uniform lists, the stimuli were either all colour words, written in an incongruent ink colour, or all numeral groups, in which the numerosity and individual digit value were incongruent. In mixed lists, the stimuli were alternately colour words written in an incongruent ink colour, or incongruent numeral groups.

When reading uniform lists, participants responded alternately to the colour word and ink colour or to the group size and numeral value. In uniform lists, there is nothing in the stimulus to provide an unambiguous external cue as to which task to perform and so this task must require controlled processing. In the mixed lists, the stimuli are alternately colour words and numeral groups and so should exogenously trigger the appropriate task without the need for endogenous control. List-reading time for shift lists were compared with the average time for each component task alone.

As we already know, colour naming is slower than word naming. It is also the case that group naming is slower than value naming (Fox, Shor, & Steinman, 1971), i.e., in colour words the word is dominant over ink and in numeral groups value is dominant over group. If execution of the non-dominant task involves overcoming interference from the dominant task, then executive control processing should be needed. When subjects have to alternate between the two non-dominant stimulus attributes of ink colour and group, we might therefore expect more biasing to be needed and so a greater shift cost than when alternation is between the dominant attributes of word and value.

The results showed large shift costs, and responses to coloured words were slower than those to the numeral groups. However, the shift cost is the same for both classes of stimuli. In the mixed lists, where responses might have been expected to be stimulus driven, we also observe smaller but still significant shift cost. Note, however, that the shift cost is no greater for the "difficult" shift between non-dominant (colour and group) tasks than for the "easy" dominant (value and word) tasks. The "Stroop" stimuli are slower to respond to, but this is an overall effect that does not increase when alternating. It looks as if "more" control does not result in greater shift costs. Also, the mixed lists, in which according to Spector and Beiderman (1976), we might have expected no shift costs at all, also show a cost of task alternation.

One difference between the experiment reported here and those of Jersild (1927) and Spector and Beiderman (1976) is that our participants performed all tasks in counterbalanced order several times. Sometimes, the target task was name the ink and ignore the word, sometimes the task was ignore the colour and name the word. Previous experimenters had used different groups of subject, so subjects had not recently been responding to stimulus dimensions, which they now had to ignore. So, in another experiment Allport et al. (1994) looked at the effect of consistent stimulus response mapping and its reversal. Two groups of participants were used and all lists were mixed. Remember that in mixed lists the stimuli specify the operation to be performed on them and no intentional control should be needed. The experiment was divided into three blocks of runs. Half the subjects started the first block with the tasks value and word, the other half with group and colour. No mention of the other possible response mappings was made. At the end of the first block of runs, the task was changed. Those participants who had previously been attending to value and word were now to respond to group and colour and vice versa. After the next block of trials, subjects were told to revert to their original tasks.

The results were clear. At the beginning of the first block in the first run, there is an extremely small cost of task shifting, which soon disappeared. However, when the tasks are reversed, so that previous attended dimensions are now to be ignored, there is a large shift cost over the first two or three runs, which settles down to a small but persistent cost. The most interesting comparison is between performance at the beginning of the first block, where participants have not been responding to the to-be-ignored stimulus dimension, and performance at the beginning of block three, where exactly the same task is being performed, but immediately after responding to the alternative dimension. In the first run of block three, there is a very large shift cost of several hundred milliseconds. It seems that the shift cost in mixed lists is not due to the time taken to operate a control process, but is due to interference from the preceding task.

Allport et al. (1994) interpreted these results as reflecting a phenomenon they called task set inertia (TSI), a kind of proactive interference. Proactive interference refers to cases where what you have just been doing interferes with what you do next. TSI suggests that the costs of shifting between tasks is not so much due to the operation of some executive controller, but are the result of the time taken for the information processing system to "settle" to a unique response after the next stimulus has arrived. In terms of the Norman and Shallice model, it is as if the conflict resolution process takes longer to sort out which schema is to win, if conflicting schemata have been recently active.

Allport et al. (1994) also tested the effects of delaying the time between shifts. They hypothesised that if the shift cost represented the time for voluntary, executive control to "set up" the system for task execution, then delaying stimuli for longer than the known shift cost would allow the new stimulus to be responded to immediately it was presented. However, there is no benefit of the wait. The shift cost remained. This result suggests that disengaging from one task must wait until the triggering action of the next stimulus. If this is the case, then what would usually be thought of as a "control" process seems to be stimulus driven, which is one of the major properties of automatic processes.

Using a rapid serial visual presentation (RSVP) task, Allport et al. (1994) asked subjects to monitor rapidly presented words for particular categories. In the shift condition, subjects were given a visual indication (change of location) that they were to stop monitoring for one category, e.g., animals, and change to monitoring for "small things". Data showed that immediately after a criterion shift, subjects were very much less accurate at detection and, more importantly, it took the arrival of between five and seven more words before performance had recovered. By varying the rate of presentation, it was shown that it was the number of items presented and not the passage of time that led to shift cost recovery.

The experiments by Allport et al. (1994) show that what must by any account be considered an act of "will", i.e., doing one task and then another, cannot be controlled entirely from within, endogenously, but is dependent on exogenous triggering from environmental stimuli. You might, of course, want to argue that even though the task requires an environmental trigger, the task must have been set up in the first place. This is exactly what Rogers and Monsell (1995) suggested.

Rogers and Monsell (1995) suggest that task set inertia (TSI) is insufficient to account for the whole phenomenon of the task-shifting data. They propose that changing task set involves at least two components: an initial endogenous process that is done in anticipation of the task; and a second component that is exogenously triggered when the task-relevant stimulus arrives. This second process might well be subject to the kind of proactive interference, or TSI, suggested by Allport et al. (1994), but in addition there must be a stage-like, active process of endogenous task set configuration.

Rogers and Monsell (1995) used an alternating runs paradigm where rather than alternating single tasks within a block of trials, subjects alternated between runs of two trials for the two tasks and were given a cue to remind them which task they were to do. Participants were presented with pairs of characters and had to classify either the digit as odd or even or the letter as a vowel or a consonant by pressing one of two keys. The characters were presented close together, side by side, and the relevant character, which could be neutral or a member of the other stimulus set, was randomly on the left or right of the pair, on the assumption that this would mean the participant would be unable to avoid processing the irrelevant character. For the digit task, only one of the characters was a digit and for the letter task only one of the characters was a letter. When subjects switched between tasks, Rogers and Monsell found the expected shift cost, which Monsell (1996) interprets as reflecting the time for task set reconfiguration (TSR) which is "a process of enabling and disabling connections between processing modules and/or re-tuning the input–output mappings performed by these processes, so that the same type of input can be processed in a different way required by the new task" (p. 135). Although one would expect a subject to reconfigure task set in anticipation of the upcoming task, we have already seen (Allport et al., 1994) that the evidence is that even when the delay between tasks is longer than the longest switch cost, anticipation does not remove the cost of task alternation. Some exogenous "triggering" seems to be necessary.

Rogers and Monsell (1995) find similar results that show anticipation does not eliminate shift costs. When the interval between response to the last task and the next stimulus is randomly varied between 150 mscs and 1.2 secs there is no reduction of shift cost. However, when the preparation time between tasks is kept constant over a whole block of trials, there is a significant reduction in shift costs as the time between tasks is increased up to 500 mscs. Beyond this time there was no further reduction in costs. So although in predictable circumstances shift cost cannot be eliminated, there is evidence that something the subject does, i.e., an endogenous effect, which can reduce switch costs over about the first half second between tasks.

In addition, Rogers and Monsell looked at the effect of crosstalk interference between competing responses. There were two conditions, one, the no-crosstalk condition, where the irrelevant character was always a non-alphanumeric character from a neutral set; and the crosstalk condition, where the irrelevant character was from the neutral set on only one-third of trials. Thus, in the crosstalk condition, there was a character associated with a currently inappropriate task on two-thirds of the trials. In addition, there were congruent and incongruent trials, in which the response button for both the relevant and irrelevant character was the same (congruent) or different (incongruent). Rogers and Monsell found that when stimuli shared attributes with a competing task, both switch and non-switch trials are impaired relative to neutral, they call this the task-cueing effect. They also found that complete suppression of task-irrelevant stimulus response mappings (congruent versus incongruent) was not possible, even if subjects performed accurately, they call this Stroop-like crosstalk. The Stroop-like crosstalk between attributes was less than the task-cueing effect. The task-cueing effects are taken as demonstrating that when a character in the display is associated with the task from which the subject must switch away, switching is much more difficult. Both these interference effects seem to point to exogenously triggered control. So, it seems that both an endogenous and an exogenous component of task switching are involved in producing the time cost of switching between tasks.

Rogers and Monsell (1995) believe their results are generally consistent with Norman and Shallice's (1986) model, described earlier. Activation of schema (or task sets, as Rogers and Monsell prefer to call them) are triggered by external environmental stimuli and this activation is modulated by internal processes that ensure that the appropriate task set wins and the correct action made. They do, however, propose that "substantial elaboration of the metaphor is required to account for the details" (p. 229). These two explanations have been tested and refined but remain the main approaches to explaining shift costs. Rubenstein, Meyer, and Evans (2001) also provide an account similar to that of Rogers and Monsell (1995), but suggest that switch costs arise from a two-stage process: a "goal-shifting" stage that can be activated before the stimulus is presented; and a second "rule activation" stage that begins once the stimulus has arrived.

An important finding in the studies by Allport et al. (1994) and in studies of priming effects on task switching by Allport and Wylie (2000) and Wylie and Allport (2000) is that when measuring individual item shift costs, there is an asymmetry in costs; not all switches are as costly as others. The largest switch cost appears to arise when the shift is from the dominant to the non-dominant task. This counterintuitive finding that it takes longer to switch to a well-learned task could be a reflection of carryover of inhibition from the previous task that had allowed response to the less dominant task. Allport and Wylie (2000) report item-specific priming effects from the stimulus in the previous task, when participants alternated between colour naming and word reading, but a small subset of stimuli that appeared in the word-reading task were also presented as stimuli in the colour-naming task. The items seen before were therefore primed. It was found that there was a greater cost when the stimulus on the switch trial was primed and provides more evidence that switch costs involve a carryover effect from the preceding trial and that a stimulus that has recently been responded to in a previous task may activate the task set stored in memory with which it was recently associated. So, if a stimulus was previously associated with task A and is subsequently presented on a switch trial that requires task B, the presentation of the stimulus still triggers task set A. This is an extension to the TSI explanation of switch costs. These results are difficult to explain if switch costs reflect the time taken to prepare task set for the upcoming task. However, Monsell, Yeung, and Azuma (2000) have found examples when the switch cost is greater to the easier task, that is, the switch asymmetry is reversed, which challenges the account by Allport and colleagues.

Task switching: A PDP model

In order to try and resolve some of the argument over how to account for the behavioural data on task switching, Gilbert and Shallice (2002) have developed a PDP model of task switching. In the introduction to their model they provide a useful summary of the main task-switching experiments, results and theoretical interpretations that their model must capture. Gilbert and Shallice summarise the evidence for what they call "the task carryover account" from Allport and colleagues, which comprises asymmetric switch costs and item-specific costs. This is good evidence for the main cause of costs being due to inhibition required to perform previous tasks and that this carryover is item specific. Evidence for what Gilbert and Shallice (2002) call "the exogenous control process account" comes from the fact that the switch cost remains even when there is a preparation time longer than any switch cost and that examples of reverse switch costs can be found where the switch from less dominant to more dominant tasks is greater. These data cannot easily be accounted for by carry-over effects, but can easily be explained by a process of TSR at the start of a switch trial. In particular, Gilbert and Shallice (2002) pick out the disagreement over the explanation for the improvement in RT from the first to the second trial of a run following a switch trial, which Monsell et al. (2000) believe cannot be accounted for in the Allport and Wylie (2000) account.

To test this argument, Gilbert and Shallice designed a PDP computational model with the properties proposed by the task carryover account. The model simulates word reading and colour naming of Stroop stimuli and is based on an earlier model for Stroop reading by Cohen and Huston (1994) and Cohen et al. (1990), which is described in Chapter 7. The architecture of the task switching model is shown in Figure 8.3.

There are two pathways, one for reading words and one for naming colours, and in each pathway, there are three input units for

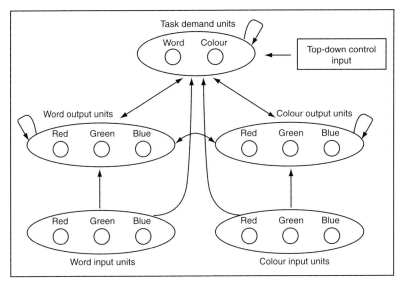

Figure 8.3

Architecture of Gilbert and Shallice's (2002) PDP model of task switching.

Reprinted from Gilbert and Shallice 2002, *Cognitive Psychology, 44*, p. 306, by permission of Elsevier. Copyright 2002.

the three different colours. So, each possible response "red", "green" and "blue" is represented twice, once in each pathway. For each input unit, there is a connection to its corresponding output unit. It is arranged that the connection strengths from input to output is stronger for the word-reading than the colour-naming pathway to mimic the human condition where reading word is better learnt than colour naming. The model relies on interactive activation and activation passes between units along their connection. The network iterates for a number of cycles during which the network collects evidence on the basis of the activation strength of the input units. As soon as the evidence reaches a fixed threshold, the trial is terminated and the number of cycles can be taken to represent reaction time. In order for the model to be able to perform either word reading or colour naming, the model also has "task demand" units, which, when activated, send top-down positive activation to the output units of their associated pathway and inhibitory activation to the output units of the opposing pathway. There are many more details of how the model operates, but we shall not concern ourselves with these here.

Performance of the task-switching model

First, the model accurately predicts performance in non-switch blocks of word reading and colour naming, i.e., it simulates the Stroop effect. This property is important as the basis for moving onto how the model behaves when "asked" to switch tasks. Next, the model was tested using mixed blocks in an alternating runs task like that used by Rogers and Monsell (1995). The model produces switch costs and these are limited to the first run of the block, just as Rogers and Monsell (1995) found. However, the switch cost is also asymmetrical, being much larger for the word than the colour task, as reported by Allport and Wylie (2000) and Allport et al. (1994). Observing how the model produces these costs shows that the task demand units take longer to reach the activation level necessary to facilitate the intended task and inhibit the unintended task. This occurs for two reasons. First, at the start of the trial the task demand unit is the wrong sign (e.g., positive when it needs to be negative) and this produces a carryover effect from one task to the next. Second, the model has a learning mechanism and the task demand units have to overcome what has been learnt from performing the task already on the same item. When the task changes, this leads to item-specific effects. The model also produces asymmetric switch costs, for both the stronger to the weaker task and from the weaker to the stronger task, and reverse Stroop effects. It also simulates the effect of preparation time in reducing switch costs.

Overall, the model designed to implement the task carryover theory is able to reproduce an impressive number of empirical finding on switch costs. Importantly, the model simulates these effects without any need for any additional processes on switch trials of the type suggested by Monsell et al. (2000), Roger and Monsell (1995) or Rubenstein et al. (2001). The authors explain that: "The model has these properties as a result of its architecture and general processing principles rather than as a result of the specific parameter values that were chosen" (p. 33). Gilbert and Shallice (2002) go on to compare the PDP model with Norman and Shallice's (1986) model that we discussed earlier. In the PDP model, "precisely the same processes occur on switch and non-switch trials. The only difference between the two types of trial is in the initial state of the network. Thus the switch cost does not measure the duration of any distinct process" (p. 35). It appears that a model base on the task carryover account can explain the behaviour data to an impressive degree.

Comparison with Norman and Shallice

Although, they say, the Norman and Shallice (1986) model was not designed to account for task switching, it has a "great deal in common" with the new account of the control of tasks. The schemata that control tasks can be selected in one of two ways, either by contention-scheduling process that selects the most active schema triggered by the environment to control action or if one task is to be carried out in the face of competition, by top-down biasing from the SAS. The schemata correspond to the task demand units, the environmental triggering corresponds to the connections between the stimulus input units and the task demand units, while the SAS corresponds to the top-down input to the task demand units. One important difference is that in the Norman and Shallice model, the SAS only comes into play when non-routine behaviour is required. In the PDP model there is no distinction between routine and non-routine behaviour and therefore can be said to have a single "action-controlling hierarchy".

Summary

People have begun to consider the question of what attention is for. The brain is known to be a massively parallel computational device in which many varieties of information are concurrently available from different parts of the system. In order to maintain coherent behaviour, some of this information needs to be combined for response while other subsets need to be "ignored" to allow selection for action. Two influential papers, Allport (1987) and Neuman (1987) put forward the ideas behind "selection for action". The idea is that we must consider the functional and neuropsychological bases of attentional behaviour, for example, when picking apples, what is demanded of the system and how might attention guide behaviour? Allport proposed that the control of action necessitated a fundamentally important mechanism that could allow relevant information to control behaviour and decouple irrelevant information from interfering. In Neuman's view attention is an "ensemble of mechanisms" that allow the brain to cope with the problem of selection for action and that the apparent limit on attention has evolved to allow coherent behaviour. Numerous studies have shown the negative priming effect: Tipper et al. (1990, 1994) have shown that stimuli that are not to control behaviour are inhibited and that this inhibition can be at different levels of representation depending on the task being performed. In everyday life, information need to be coordinated across different modalities. Driver and Spence (1994) demonstrated synergy between visual and auditory stimuli, suggesting that spatial attention does not operate independently for the different modalities, which would help us to interact effectively with the environment. Attention also seems important in motor movements such as reaching and grasping, remembering and planning.

In order to interact with the environment in a goal-directed manner, we have to be able to select which response is appropriate at any given moment. Most stimuli have a number of possible actions that are appropriate to them, but depending on circumstances we may sometimes choose one action and sometimes choose another. Patients with damage to their frontal areas show gross disorganisation of behaviour. They exhibit a bewildering variety of symptoms, from behavioural rigidity to extreme distractibility. Planning ahead and goal-directed behaviour is compromised, patients often being unable to start or complete a task. Duncan (1986) believes these patients have difficulty setting up and using goal lists. Duncan has argued for the importance of setting up goal lists that are designed to meet our desires and needs. Goal lists are used to create action structures that are set up using the problem-solving heuristic of means–ends analysis. For goals to be achieved other potential actions have to be inhibited. Norman and Shallice (1986) have a theory in which the activation or inhibition of task-relevant schema, or actions, can be intentionally controlled by a supervisory attentional system (SAS). This system can bias the schema that are needed for intended actions so that instead of the action that would normally be most active capturing control, the intended action can be made. The SAS has been equated with the central executive of working memory (Baddeley, 1986). If the SAS were damaged, behaviour would degenerate in the manner observed in frontal patients. Experiments on the control of task switching in normal participants (e.g., Allport et al., 1994; Rogers & Monsell, 1995) have shown that when a stimulus is ambiguous, or there is competing task information in the display, there is a large and reliable cost of intentionally switching from one task to another. This shift cost seems to depend on how recently the irrelevant task has been performed. However, even when the time between tasks is increased to be far longer than any shift cost, shift cost is not eliminated. Allport et al. interpreted the shift cost as the time required for conflict (or task set inertia), to be resolved after the next stimulus has arrived. Rogers and Monsell (1995) argue for an endogenous process that reconfigures the task set (TSR) as well as an endogenous process that acts as a trigger. The agent responsible for setting and shifting task may not be part of a single, unitary central executive, but one of a number. Logan (1995) thinks that visual spatial attention could be voluntarily controlled by linguistic descriptions that activate conceptual representations that can be translated into actions. Priming effects on task switching were studied by Allport and Wylie (2000). Larger switch costs are found when switching into the dominant task and this effect suggests that there is a carryover of inhibition on the dominant task from the previous trial and that it is this inhibition that has allowed the less dominant task to be performed. However, contrary evidence has been found by Monsell et al. (2000). Gilbert and Shallice (2002) developed a PDP model of task switching and demonstrated that a model based on the carryover account can explain most of the data.

Further reading

- Allport, A. (1993). Attention and control: Have we been asking the right questions? A critical review of twenty five years. In D. E. Meyer, & S. Kornblum. *Attention and Performance, XIV: Synergies in experimental psychology, artificial intelligence and cognitive neuroscience. A Bradford Book.* Cambridge, MA, MIT Press.
- Gilbert, S. J., & Shallice, T. (2002). Task switching: A PDP model. *Cognitive Psychology, 44,* 297–337.

   In the preview to the model, data and experiments on task switching are reviewed.
- Monsell, S. (1996). Control of mental processing. In V. Bruce. *Unsolved mysteries of the mind.* Hove, UK: Lawrence Erlbaum Associates Limited.

   This is an excellent chapter reviewing the controversies surrounding the mystery of control.
- Norman, D. E., & Shallice, T. (2000). Attention to action: Willed and automatic control of behaviour. In M. S. Gazzaniga (Ed.). *Cognitive neuroscience: A reader.* Oxford: Blackwell.

   This is a really quite approachable paper that lays out the evidence for their theory together with more details of how it works.

The nature and function of consciousness 9

Attention and consciousness

At the beginning of this book, we said that we did not have a simple definition of attention and tried to illustrate the wide variety of situations to which the term "attention" is applied in everyday usage. However, despite this lack of clarity, we set off on our journey through experiments that were said to be about "attention", hoping that as we went along we would discover, if not what "attention" is, at least some of its varieties. We journeyed through selective attention, the movement and allocation of attention, attention to objects, selection for action, divided attention, skill, automaticity and control etc. Along the way we met theories designed, successfully or otherwise, to account for all these "attentional" tasks. Finally, we have arrived at the end of the book to find ourselves engaged in a debate on the nature and function of consciousness. How did this happen? Well, when we quoted William James (1890) at the beginning of the first chapter, I only gave a part of what he said, which was "Everyone knows what attention is". However, James continued:

> It is the taking possession by the mind, in clear and vivid form, of one out of what would seem several simultaneously possible objects or trains of thought. Focalisation, concentration, of consciousness are of its essence. It implies withdrawal from some things in order to deal effectively with others. (pp. 403–404)

Within this statement, James refers to the selectivity of attention, its apparently limited nature and brings consciousness into the explanation. Although William James reflected carefully on attention and consciousness, as long as we have no agreed definition for either "attention" or "consciousness", or for any of their varieties, we are in danger of trying to explain something we do not properly understand in terms of something else that we do not properly understand. For example, we have talked about "conscious control", "intentional control", "willed behaviour", all implying conscious attentional involvement. We have explained the acquisition of skill by saying that, with practice, "attention" is not required and the performance of aspects of the skill become "automatic" or "unconscious". Within the chapters of this book, we shall probably have been as guilty of this as anyone else of using these terms as if one could explain the other. There is, however, a growing body of knowledge that is refining our conceptions of attention, as we have seen in the previous chapters. Also we are beginning to understand what consciousness is, how it arises and what it might be for. In addition, the relationship between attention and consciousness is being considered in the way that James appreciated so long ago. Some of this evidence has come from studies of neuropsychological patients, but evidence is also available from experiments on neurological intact participants. It is with these studies we shall begin.

Evidence from normal subjects

In Chapter 7, the distinction was made between processes that do and do not seem to require attention, i.e., between automatic and controlled processing. One of the major differences between automatic and controlled processing is that controlled processing is, by definition, said to be open to strategic, conscious control whereas automatic processing takes place outside consciousness. So, here we find consciousness implicated in explanations of attentional processing. Although we may become aware of the outcome of automatic processes, we are unable to consciously inspect the processing leading up to that outcome. By this account, it sounds as if the difference between conscious and unconscious processing corresponds very closely to the distinction made between controlled/automatic processing. Some theorists have indeed tried to equate attentional processes with consciousness or awareness. But, be aware that there is more than one meaning or interpretation of what is meant by the term "conscious" or "consciousness". We will return to arguments over the nature of and function of consciousness after we have considered some experiments in which the fate of unattended (unconsciously processed?) information is examined. Despite the problems associated with deciding what we actually mean by conscious and unconscious processing, there is a large literature on the fate of unattended information, where experimenters usually take the term "unattended" to mean "unaware" or "without conscious identification".

In our discussion of the early–late debate in Chapter 2, we saw that the ability of unattended information to bias responses given to attended information was taken as evidence for extensive pre-attentive (automatic, unconscious) processing. That is, prior to the selective, attentional stage, where information became consciously available, unconscious information processing was producing subliminal semantic priming effects. These results were taken as evidence for "late" selection.

Over the years there has been a continuous debate about the validity of experiments said to prove semantic activation without conscious identification (SAWCI). There is argument about the best methodology to use, which criteria should be chosen to determine consciousness or awareness in the subject and the right kind of thresholding techniques. Studies of SAWCI and unconscious perception have been undertaken using a variety of experimental paradigms, but as the unconscious is, by any definition, unable to be reported, all these paradigms involve looking for indirect evidence of unconscious processing.

Dichotic listening tasks

In this paradigm subjects are presented with two messages, one to each ear. They are instructed to repeat back or "shadow" one message and ignore the other. Rather than repeat a number of experiments that we have already discussed in Chapter 2, let us take one experiment as an example. Corteen and Wood (1972) had conditioned their subjects to expect an electric shock in association with particular words to do with "the city". Then, in a dichotic listening experiment while subjects shadowed the attended message, some of the shock associated words were presented on the unattended channel. Although subjects claimed to be unaware of anything on the unattended channel, they showed a clear galvanic skin response not only to the shock-associated words but also to semantic associates of shock words. This result seemed to provide good evidence that the unattended message, although unconscious, was nevertheless processed to a semantic level. However, this experiment does not replicate easily. For instance, Wardlaw and Kroll (1976) did exactly the same experiment using Corteen and Wood's procedure, but were unable to find the same effect. They suggested that subjects in Corteen and Wood's experiment may have sometimes been aware, albeit briefly, of the unattended message. Unless we can be absolutely certain that subjects never become aware of the unattended channel, the dichotic listening task cannot provide a sufficiently well-controlled experiment on which to base arguments about unconscious processing.

Parafoveal vision experiments

Another way of controlling conscious awareness of visual stimuli is to manipulate the focus of visual attention. It is assumed that unless focal attention is directed to a stimulus it will not become consciously available. Experiments using stimuli presented in the parafovea are conceptually similar to dichotic listening experiments. Here the subject is instructed to focus attention on a central visual stimulus and to ignore any other stimuli that are presented toward the parafovea. Here again, let us look at one example. Underwood (1976) claimed to have demonstrated the unconscious, automatic semantic processing of unattended words that flanked a target. Each target word was flanked by other words that, although the subject was unable to explicitly report them, were shown to bias the semantic interpretation of the attended word. So, for example an ambiguous target word like "palm" might be interpreted as to do with trees or hands depending on what the unattended meaning was. This result was taken to suggest that the semantic information in the unattended stimuli was processed outside conscious awareness. Other researchers have shown that the semantics of unattended words in the periphery can influence the processing of fixated words, in the absence of eye movements. Lambert, Beard and Thompson (1988) and Lambert and Voot (1993) showed that when an abrupt onset distractor appeared for 30 mscs in the periphery, response to the target was slowed by a semantically related distractor.

Visual masking experiments

Some of the most striking examples of apparently "unconscious" processing of word meaning comes from studies using backward visual masking. In some experiments the subject is shown a word immediately followed by a pattern mask and asked to guess what the word was, e.g., Allport (1977). Allport found that even when subjects could not report the meaning of the word, they would sometimes produce interesting errors, when forced to guess. Given the word "jazz" the subject might respond "blues", indicating that although there was no conscious perception of the stimulus, its semantics had been accessed. The subject was unable to determine exactly which of the semantically activated meanings corresponded to the stimulus word, because the pattern mask prevented the possibility of integrating the physical, episodic features of the stimulus with the meaning. (See the section on iconic memory in Chapter 2.) The subject was therefore unaware that the stimulus had been presented and was only left with semantic activation on which to base a guess. Without any feeling of confidence, the guess turned out to be a "semantic paralexia". Similar errors are made by patients with deep dyslexia (Coltheart, 1980b).

Unless we have a conscious experience of a stimulus, we are unlikely to try and act on it and both Allport (1977) and Coltheart (1980a) have suggested that it is the act of integrating physical and semantic information that gives rise to conscious awareness and confident report. These arguments were discussed in more detail in Chapter 3, when we looked at the way information about "what" and "where" a stimulus is appear to dissociate in iconic memory experiments. The visual masking experiments used to test for SAWCI are in a sense extreme versions of iconic memory experiments. In some iconic memory experiments the subject is shown a brief backward masked stimulus array (supra-liminally) and the limits of report tested. In experiments on SAWCI, the procedure is just the same except the stimulus duration is so short that the stimulus is subliminal. If the stimulus duration is such that there is no time for any perceptual integration, there will be no possibility for a confident report. Although there may have been semantic activation of "what" the stimulus was, any information about "where" it was has been disrupted by the mask. Hence there can be semantic activation, without conscious identification. Umilta (1988) suggests that the role played by consciousness is to allow voluntary organisation of unconscious operations that are going on in our minds. He proposes that "voluntary control over cognitive processes depends on the phenomenal experience of being conscious" (p. 334). Without this phenomenal experience we would not be able to act on otherwise unconscious processes. There are a variety of neurological syndromes that illustrate this. For example, patients with blindsight, visual neglect and amnesia all provide evidence that information is available within the processing system, but is below the level of conscious awareness. With careful testing, this information can be shown to influence behaviour. We shall evaluate the evidence from patient data at the end of this chapter.

If, in normal subjects, there really is semantic activation from stimuli that we are unable to report, then we should be able to look at the effect of that activation on a subsequent task. There have been a number of experiments that have attempted to use the semantic activation from unreportable words to prime subsequent stimuli. In these experiments, the first (prime) stimulus is presented very rapidly, usually in a tachistoscope, and immediately followed by a mask. The speed with which the mask follows the stimulus can be set such that the subject is not even able to determine if a word were presented at all, let alone what the word was. Subsequent presentation of another word (the probe) at a supra-liminal level is usually used to test for any effects of the first word on the second. This priming paradigm has produced some of the most controversial experiments in the SAWCI literature. Under these conditions, there seems to be little possibility that the subject could pay any conscious attention to the first, priming stimulus, even if they tried, so we can be more certain that any effects are due to "unconscious" processing. Of course, there is always the problem of determining what exactly we mean by "unconscious" and the difficulty of setting the prime mask duration so that we can be sure that the subject really was "unconscious". We will discuss these problems in more detail after we have looked at some examples of visual masking experiments, said to demonstrate SAWCI.

Marcel (1980, 1983) has provided some of the most controversial data on high level information processing below the level of conscious awareness. Using an associative priming paradigm based on that of Meyer and Shavaneveldt (1971), Marcel presented his subjects with a masked prime and then measured how long it took for the subjects to make a lexical decision. Lexical decision tasks involve asking subjects to say as quickly as possible whether the letter string they see is a word or not. In normal, supra-liminal conditions, a prime such as BREAD will facilitate the lexical decision for an associated word like BUTTER, but will not facilitate an unassociated word such as NURSE. Marcel's priming stimuli were masked so severely that the subject could not detect their presence on more than 60% of trials. Would the same results be found in this subliminal condition? When the primes were masked by a pattern mask, there was evidence of facilitation, i.e., BREAD primed BUTTER, just as in supra-liminal experiments. However, when the mask was a random noise mask, there was no priming. This is taken as evidence for two different kind of masking (see Turvey, 1973 for a review); one produced by the noise mask, which degrades the stimulus input "early" in processing and another kind produced by the pattern mask. Marcel proposed that the pattern mask does not prevent the automatic, unconscious access to stored semantic knowledge, but does prevent perceptual integration and hence access to consciousness. This argument is similar to the one made by Allport (1977) and Coltheart (1980a).

In another experiment, Marcel looked at the Stroop effect. Here he presented his subjects with colour patches in which a colour word was written. Remember that with normal Stroop stimuli the colour word interferes with colour patch naming. Subjects were individually tested for the stimulus mask onset assynchrony (SOA) where they were able to detect the presence of the word 60% of the time and then, using that SOA, subjects were asked to name the colour patches with the word superimposed on them. Marcel found that there was the typical Stroop interference effect, even though the words were not reportable. This looks like further good evidence for the unconscious processing of word meaning. However, there are problems. Why did Marcel choose a criterion of 60% rather than chance, which would be 50%? How do we know that when a subject says they cannot detect a stimulus they are really telling the truth? Some subjects may be more or less willing to say there is or is not a stimulus there so what does it mean to ask a subject "Are you sure you couldn't see anything?"

Holender's critique

Holender (1986) provided an extensive, critical and sceptical review of experiments that claim to provide evidence for semantic activation without conscious identification (SAWCI). He concluded that both dichotic listening and parafoveal vision experiments were unsuitable for demonstrating SAWCI. To be certain that there is no chance of the subject having any possibility of conscious knowledge of the stimulus under test it is not safe to rely on the subject voluntarily ignoring it. In dichotic listening experiments, subjects may indicate that they were unaware of the ignored message when questioned afterwards, but it could be that they were temporarily aware at the time but rapidly forgot. As SAWCI effects are typically small, it is possible that just the occasional "switch" to the unattended channel could be enough to give a significant result. The same is true in parafoveal vision experiments. Here the words presented in the periphery may occasionally be attended and the experimenter would have no way of testing this. Quite rightly, Holender suggests that, if we are to find good evidence for SAWCI, it will come from experiments using visual masking. Under severe pattern masking, a stimulus can be rendered unreportable because of data limitation (Norman & Bobrow, 1975) (see

Chapter 6), so no matter how hard the subject tries, they are unable to report the stimulus. While it is that case that there have been many experiments in the dichotic listening and parafoveal vision paradigms that could be demonstrating SAWCI, uncertainty over when the biasing stimuli were or were not in some sense consciously processed means we must be cautious when interpreting the results.

The question of thresholds

Cheesman and Merikle (1984) argued that two kinds of threshold should be considered: subjective and objective. At the subjective threshold, the experimenter has to rely on the subject's own subjective report of whether or not the prime was seen and subjects may vary in their confidence and willingness to report. Objective thresholds are those that can be set independently and objectively by the experimenter. Furthermore, a threshold should be set at statistical chance and many trials are needed to avoid the threshold changing with practice. Merikle and Daneman (2000) and Merikle, Smilek, and Eastwood (2001) review the evidence for perception without awareness and the main methodological approaches used.

The question of what we mean by "conscious" is crucial to interpreting and explaining data. There have been two general approaches. The first is to simply rely on the participants' self-report. Dixon (1981) advocated asking the subject if they were "consciously aware" of the stimulus. If the subject says they were not consciously aware, then that is taken as the evidence for lack of subjective awareness, by definition. However, the other approach, first advocated by Eriksen (1960), is that awareness is the ability to make a discriminatory response. Thus, if the subject reports lack of awareness, but nevertheless is able to make a discriminatory response, the subject is objectively aware. According to Eriksen, the subject is only unconscious of the stimulus when they are unable to make a discrimination response. Despite the difference in definition, Merikle and Daneman (2000) now suggest that "both approaches may be assessing the same underlying subjective awareness of perceiving" (p. 1295).

Subjective versus objective measures of awareness

Cheesman and Merikle (1985) criticised the experiments of both Allport (1977) and Marcel (1983). They suggest that the semantic errors in Allport's study could have arisen by chance and unless it is known how many semantic errors might be expected to occur by chance, we cannot take his evidence as reflecting unconscious semantic processing. Later attempts to replicate Allport's experiment by Ellis and Marshall (1978) found approximately the same number of semantic errors. However, when the error responses were randomly assigned to masked words to establish baseline levels of semantic association, the proportion of semantic errors remained the same. Therefore it would appear that Allport's results could have been due to chance association rather than true semantic errors. Further problems are demonstrated in an experiment by Fowler, Wolford, Slade, and Tassinary (1981), who showed that response strategies were an important factor in priming experiments. Fowler et al. replicated one of Marcel's (1983) experiments in which, subjects were asked to decide:

1. which of two alternatives were more similar in meaning to a masked word
2. which of two words was more graphemically similar to a masked word
3. whether a word or a blank field had been presented.

Marcel had manipulated SOA and monitored accuracy. He found that presence–absence decisions were less accurate than either the graphemic or semantic judgements and as SOA decreased, the graphemic judgements reached chance levels before semantic judgements. Marcel interpreted these data as evidence for unconscious word recognition. Fowler et al. were able to produce exactly these results, but then proceeded to run the same experiment again, but without presenting any words before the mask. Subjects were asked to make the same decisions about the similarity between the first stimulus (which, of course, did not exist) and the subsequently presented word. Fowler et al. found a similar pattern of results without there being any words presented for comparison. These effects were interpreted as evidence that response strategies, in the absence of any perceptual experience, could give rise to better than chance performance. However, there was a small difference, in that when words were actually present in the pre-mask phase, semantic judgements were slightly more accurate than when no words were presented. So, although not all of Marcel's effects could be due to response strategies, at least some could be explained in those terms. Cheesman and Merikle suggest that unless response strategies can be eliminated from an explanation of subliminal semantic priming, there will always be problems with this type of experiment.

Another problem, according to Cheesman and Merikle (1985) is that of determining the criterion for chance performance and Marcel used subjective rather than objective thresholds. Cheesman and Merikle looked at Stroop colour–word priming in an experiment similar to Marcel's, but used an objective threshold, where subjects were unable to give a discriminatory response between the colour words in a forced choice test. The SOA at which forced choice accuracy reached chance was shorter than that at which subjects were subjectively aware of the stimulus. Using the objective threshold as their criterion, Cheesman and Merikle found no evidence for unconscious processing of the colour words, i.e., there was no Stroop interference. As performance on the threshold task increased towards perfect performance, the amount of Stroop interference also increased. However, between the objective threshold and the subjective threshold, there was evidence for Stroop interference. Cheesman and Merikle argue that in Marcel's study, although subjects were not subjectively aware of the masked stimuli, they would have shown a discriminatory response on forced choice. In line with this argument they propose that it is important to make an explicit distinction between objective and subjective thresholds in order to account for the relationship between word recognition and consciousness. In their experiments, they only found evidence for both conscious and unconscious processing above the objective threshold. Below that level, there was no evidence, either direct or indirect, that the information had been processed at all. Once the stimulus is processed sufficiently for discrimination responses to be made, the subjects may still be phenomenally unaware, but there is evidence for perceptual processing below the level of subjective awareness. The subjective threshold is, according to Cheesman and Merikle, the "transition between unconscious and conscious processing". It is the point in perceptual processing when a stable, integrated percept is formed that allows conscious report and phenomenal awareness. At the objective threshold no perceptual records have been formed, but at the subjective threshold "sufficient" information has been accumulated for stable integrated percepts to be formed. Thus sensitivity to perceptual events can be found below the subjective threshold, although subjects claim to be unaware of them.

Priming below the objective threshold

According to Cheesman and Merikle (1985), once the objective threshold has been reached there can be no possibility of finding semantic priming effects, because there are simply no perceptual records on which it could be based. Kemp-Wheeler and Hill (1988) agree that there is an important distinction to be made between the objective and subjective threshold, but suggest that Cheesman and Merikle's results do not provide sufficient evidence to prove there is no semantic priming below objective threshold. Picking up and modifying a number of methodological problems in the Cheesman and Merikle work, Kemp-Wheeler and Hill (1988) were able to demonstrate that semantic priming effects can be found when pattern masked primes were presented 10% below objective detection threshold. Kemp-Wheeler and Hill (1988) criticised the four choice identity discrimination procedure used by Cheesman and Merikle in which subjects were to say which of four pattern masked colour words had been presented. They say that identity discrimination does not assess detection threshold and, furthermore, there are strong colour preferences when people are asked to produce colour names in free association. Simon (1971) found that 52% of college men gave "blue", 11% gave "red", 10% "green", 8.5% "brown", 5.5% "purple" and 3% "yellow". This biasing to produce responses may have meant that when Cheesman and Merikle were setting thresholds and subjects were in a state of great uncertainty as they approached "objective" threshold, the SOA may have been reduced more than necessary. Although Cheesman and Merikle told their subjects that all four colours were equally probable, Trueman (1979) found that even when subjects were told about colour preferences, this did not eliminate response bias.

Although critical of Cheesman and Merikle, Kemp-Wheeler and Hill accept the criticisms made of other work, such as Marcel's. They suggest that for really good evidence to be found for priming at objective threshold it is necessary to:

- use detection rather than identity discrimination to determine thresholds
- demonstrate non-discriminative responding at threshold using Merikle's (1982) criteria
- demonstrate that the magnitude of any priming effect is not significantly related to detection performance.

Merikle's (1982) criteria are statistical guidelines involving the use of confidence limits to ensure that the response distribution is no different to chance and all types of responses category are used. Kemp-Wheeler and Hill carefully and individually measured the objective criterion and set prime mask SOA 10% below that level.

They used the "d" measure from signal detection theory to correlate with the priming effects of found and sophisticated statistical analysis. They used dichoptic and binocular presentation and were careful to equate lighting conditions during threshold setting and during the experiment, in case light adaptation was different between threshold setting and the experiment (Purcell, Stewart, & Stanovitch, 1983). In sum, they believed that they were able to demonstrate (in very strict conditions, meeting as far as possible any criticism that could be made) that semantic priming could be found below the objective threshold. More recently, Dagenbach, Carr, and Wilhelmsen (1989) and Greenwald, Klinger, and Liu (1989) have reported subliminal priming given certain (usually different) conditions are met.

Inattentional blindness

In the studies we have discussed so far, researchers have tried to eliminate the possibility of participants devoting any attention to stimuli and then tested to see if there is any evidence for processing of those stimuli without conscious awareness. However, there are other experiments in which participants are not told to ignore anything and no special steps such as masking or threshold setting are taken to ensure the critical stimuli are "unattended". Despite this, stimuli are apparently not "seen". Some examples we have met before are attentional blink (AB) and repetition blindness (RB), discussed in Chapter 8. In both cases, participants try to do the tasks, but fail to become aware of stimuli due to temporal limitations on attention.

Mack and Rock (1998) studied another phenomenon called "inattentional blindness". They manipulated attention by requiring participants to focus attention on one part of a display. Participants are not told to ignore anything, but the test is to discover if an unexpected, unattended stimulus is processed outside the attentional focus. The experimental task required the participants to judge which arm of a cross was the longest. The presentation sequence was a 1500 mscs fixation display; a 200 mscs presentation of a large cross in one quadrant of the display field followed by a 500 mscs blank field. This sequence was repeated for two trials, but on the third trial as well as the large cross there was a word located in the centre of the display. When asked if they had seen anything other than the cross, 60% of participants were "blind" to the fact that a word had been there or that the display was in any way different to the others. To discover if the word to which the participants were apparently blind had undergone any processing, Mack and Rock (1998) tested for priming using forced choice recognition and word stem completion. On both measures of priming, there was evidence that the word that could not be "seen" influenced participants' performance. In comparison to the control group, which had not been shown any word and which chose the word on 4% of trials by chance, 47% of participants chose the word to which they were "blind" in the forced choice task and 36% used it in stem completion. This result appears to provide evidence of semantic activation of words that are not available for conscious report and that without attention visual objects such as words do not reach a form of representation that can be reported.

Rees, Russell, Frith, and Driver (1999) used functional imaging to determine the level of processing achieved by unattended words in an inattentional blindness experiment. The question Rees et al. wanted to resolve was whether the words were simply not perceived, a true inattentional blindness, or whether the words were perceived but rapidly forgotten, an inattentional amnesia. We know from some of the earliest studies on divided attention that words presented on the unattended channel are not remembered, e.g., Cherry, 1953, but also that in some cases an "unattended" word can produce priming, e.g., Lewis, 1970, discussed earlier. However, we have also seen that there are criticisms, such as those by Holender (1986) of the procedures used to eliminate attention being allocated to the so-called "unattended" items. In an inattentional blindness experiment, participants can be in a position where a word is actually on fixation, yet is apparently not attended. Rees et al. (1999) used an RSVP procedure to present their participants with a rapid serial stream of letter strings superimposed onto a rapid stream of pictures. Participants were told to attend to either the letters, which were green, or the pictures, which were red, in any particular stream and to detect any repetitions. Rees et al. reasoned that if selecting the target stream (letters or pictures) was sufficiently demanding, attention would be fully occupied by monitoring the target stream, leaving no attention available for processing the irrelevant, non-target stream. Based on previous brain-imaging studies that had identified networks in the left hemisphere responsible for word processing, they measured brain activity in response to letter strings when they were in the unattended stream. Results showed that when attention was fully engaged in monitoring for a repetition in the stream of pictures, there was no activity in the areas of left hemisphere normally active when words are processed and that whether or not the words were familiar or meaningless strings made no difference in brain activity. From this result, it appears that when attention is fully occupied it is an inattentional blindness that occurs, not an inattentional amnesia, and that even when familiar words are presented on fixation, without attention meaningful words go unrecognised. Rees et al. (1999) do not suggest that their participants were blind to the presence of the letters while monitoring the picture stream, but they were blind to the difference between words and random strings. They report that the "phenomenal experience" while doing the task is that there are both red pictures and green letters concurrently present, but there is only awareness for the identities of items in that attended stream. It appears, then, that we can become consciously aware of a subset of object properties, such as the features that distinguish letters from pictures and colour, but without attention, but the meaning is not processed at all. This is reminiscent of the finding of some of the earliest experiments we met, where it was demonstrated that physical information but not semantic information was available without attention. What is new here, is that functional brain imaging allows us to observe what the brain is actually doing and so there is no argument about what level of processing has been achieved by the unattended stimulus.

Change blindness

In the phenomenon of change blindness, people quite often fail to detect quite gross changes in an object or scene when the change occurs after a brief blank interval or while attention is diverted. Blackmore (2001) says: "The phenomenon of change blindness calls into question the very world we think we experience" (p. 524). She explains that when we view a scene such as looking out of a window, we have the impression that we take in and are aware of most of the details present, such as the trees, the sky, flowers etc. We would expect to notice if the scene changed. However, there are quite striking examples of people's inability to detect major changes in the environment. Blackmore, Belstaff, Nelson, and Troscianko (1995) demonstrated when participants are shown a picture that is then changed during a brief blank interval or during a movie cut, they find detecting the difference difficult. They are apparently blind to the change. Perhaps more startling is the result of an experiment by Simons and Levin (1998) who engaged participants in a conversation with one person and then, during a short distraction period, swapped the original person for a different one. Half the participants did not notice the change in the very person they were talking to. In applied situations, this inability to detect change could be catastrophic, for example in airtraffic control, where changes are frequent and attention may often be shifted from one display to another. DaVita, Obermayer, Nugent, and Linville (2004) demonstrated change blindness while operators were to manage critical events in a combat display that involved monitoring changes among only eight items on 15% of trials equivalent to guessing.

Rensink (2002) reviews change blindness and five aspects of visual change detection: what is meant by a change; methodological approaches; the role of focused attention in change blindness; how change blindness aids understanding of visual perception; and, finally, current limits to understanding change detection. He argues that the concept of what is meant by a change requires careful definition, especially that change refers to a transformation over time of a single structure, but difference applies to a lack of similarity between two structures. Further, it is important to differentiate between a structure that is external, i.e., the scene itself, and the internal representation of that scene. When these definitions are applied, not all experiments claiming to show change blindness actually do so. Rensink also reviews methodological approaches. The studies by Blackmore et al. (1995) and Simons and Levin (1998) described previously can be considered "one-shot" experiments, since the change is made only once in each trial and minimises the role of eye movements and long-term memory, methodologically they are also quite like real life. Rensink (2002) argues that as change blindness can be found in such a wide range of conditions it must be the case that the mechanisms underlying it must be central to the way we perceive the world around us and this central mechanism is focused attention. Remember that change blindness only occurs when attention is momentarily withdrawn from the original stimulus. Normally an abrupt change in a visual scene would capture attention, just like a peripheral cue in Posner's (1980) orienting experiments. However, without focused attention being exogenously summoned by the change, the change goes unnoticed. Thus, suggests Rensink, rather than focal attention explaining change blindness, change blindness may help us understand what focused attention, of the sort proposed by Treisman and Gelade (1980) is and does. After a review of evidence, Rensink (2002) suggests that focal attention does not construct general purpose representation of the whole scene, rather it constructs a more specific representation relevant to the ongoing task. Thus focused attention produces a stable representation of only one object at a time, as it is needed; see also Shapiro (2000). However, Smilek, Eastwood, and Merikle (2000) argue that attention is not only guided by focal attention, which is slow and serial, but also by unattended changes in the display. Participants had to detect changes involving either a large or small number of features, in displays containing between four and 16 items. It was reasoned that if preattentive processes were involved in guiding focused attention to the changed location, they should speed response and the search slope for RT against display size would be shallower than that predicted by a strictly serial search with focal attention alone. This prediction was confirmed and Smilek et al. (2000) concluded that unattended changes can guide focal attention.

Whatever the underlying mechanisms for change blindness are, it appears, subjectively, that all the objects in a scene are concurrently available, but they are not. Blackmore (2001) says we are misled, because, if we need to know about another object in the scene, we look again to check on it. So, while it appears that all the scene is available, the scene itself is acting as an external memory giving the illusion of viewing the whole scene. According to Rensink (2000): "This idea of a stable, general purpose internal picture accords nicely with subjective experience. It does not, however, accord quite so nicely with objective fact" (p. 1469). People are not only blind to changes in a scene, but also deaf to auditory changes. Vitevitch (2003) had demonstrated that participants engaged in shadowing tasks failed to detect changes to the attended voice. Evidently, our conscious experience of the world around us is at odds with the results of change detection experiments.

Differences between conscious and unconscious processing

Chalmers (1996) argues that being conscious of a stimulus allows the information perceived to be used for the basis of action, but unconsciously processed information results only in automatic reactions that cannot be consciously controlled. This distinction suggests that there should be qualitative differences between the outcome of consciously and unconsciously perceived information. Arising from this is an alternative, and more recent, approach to understanding conscious and unconscious processing that tries to discover differences between the consequences of conscious and unconscious processed stimuli. Merikle and Daneman (2000) argue that such studies provide stronger evidence than an approach that only attempts to demonstrate unconscious perception. In a number of studies such differences have been found. For example, Cheesman and Merikle (1985) manipulated the percentage of trials on which

Stroop colour words were congruent and incongruent. They found that above the subjective threshold, interference effects indicated strategic processing by the subjects, in that when there was a high probability that the word and colour would be congruent, inconsistent stimuli showed greater interference than normal. However, when the stimuli were presented below subjective threshold, interference effects were independent of the probability that colour and word would be congruent. These results suggest there are qualitative differences between the processing operations that can be carried out on stimuli presented above and below the subjective threshold of conscious awareness. Conscious processing is open to strategic manipulation, but unconscious processing is not. In these results, there seems to be a parallel between the conscious/unconscious distinction and the controlled/automatic distinction. Another example is provided by Marcel's (1980) experiments. Although Cheesman and Merikle (1984) criticised Marcel for using subjective thresholds, they were able to use another of his experiments to provide further evidence for the qualitative difference between conscious and unconscious processing by assuming Marcel used the subjective threshold. Marcel presented his subjects with three successive letter strings and asked them to make lexical decisions to the first and third stimuli. On some trials, the second letter string was a polysemous word, for example "PALM", and was either masked or unmasked. As an index of which meaning of the polysemous word had been accessed, Marcel had measured lexical decision time to the third letter string. When there was no masking and all three words were clearly visible, lexical decisions to the third word in a list like TREE–PALM–WRIST were slower than lexical decision for the third word in unrelated lists like CLOCK–RACE–WRIST. Thus, in the first list, TREE had biased PALM to be interpreted as "palm tree", not as "palm of the hand". This then slowed response to WRIST relative to the unrelated case. Lexical decisions were fastest to the third word in lists like HAND–PALM–WRIST when the meaning of the third word was consistent with the first. This pattern of results suggests that when all the words are consciously available to the subjects, the initial word in a list biases which meaning is accessed by the following word.

When the second word in the list was pattern masked to the point where subjects claimed to be unable to detect it, quite different results were obtained. Now all the meanings of the polysemous word seemed to be activated; lexical decisions to WRIST were equally facilitated whether they were in the sequence TREE–PALM–WRIST or HAND–PALM–WRIST, in comparison to an unrelated list like

CLOCK–RACE–WRIST. These results from Marcel's (1980) experiment demonstrate a clear, qualitative difference between the kinds of processes initiated in conscious and unconscious processing. Another example of a qualitative difference between detected and undetected stimuli is given by Merikle and Reingold (1990). They argue that: "If stimulus detection is an adequate measure of conscious awareness then any dissociation between stimulus detection and another measure of perception is sufficient to demonstrate perception without awareness" (p. 574). Subjects were presented with either words, non-words or a blank field, which was pattern masked. First, subjects make a detection decision and then make a forced choice recognition decision. Merikle and Reingold found that when subjects were unable to detect a non-word, no evidence of processing was found but when the stimulus was a word, even when subjects were unable to detect it, they were better than chance on the subsequent forced choice recognition test. Thus, there were different patterns of results for words and non-words and only words which had pre-existing memory representations were able to support recognition. When subjects were able to detect the stimuli there was no difference between words and non-words. This dissociation, they argue, show that "the detect and non-detect states are qualitatively different" (p. 582). and therefore stimulus detection can be used as a measure of conscious awareness.

In another study Debner and Jacoby (1994) presented pattern masked words at either short (50 mscs) or long (150 mscs) SOAs. At the short SOA, most words were not consciously perceived and, at the longer SOA, most words were consciously perceived. Immediately after presentation of the masked word, participants were asked to complete a word stem, with any word that came to mind, but not the word that had just been presented. So, for example, if the word that had just been presented was "dough", and the word stem was "dou" the participant could complete the word stem with "double" or "doubt", but not "dough". At short SOAs, participants were not able to exclude the first word from their stem completions, but with the longer SOAs they could. Merikle and Daneman (2000) argue these results are consistent with the view that unconsciously perceived words produce "automatic reactions that cannot be controlled by the perceiver. In contrast, consciously perceived information allows individuals to guide their actions so that they are able to follow instructions" (p. 1300). Further evidence for this qualitative distinction is reviewed by Merikle et al. (2001).

There is so much evidence and counterevidence, argument and

counterargument over the existence of unconscious perception and SAWCI, how are we to determine the truth? Why do some experimenters find evidence and others do not? Research on "unconscious perception" is controversial and apparently inconclusive. Possibly some of the best evidence comes from patients who have suffered brain damage.

Evidence from neuropsychology

While there are numerous difficulties in determining whether or not normal subjects are aware or conscious of a stimulus at the time of presentation, patients with specific forms of neurological damage are never able to report certain stimuli, no matter how hard they try or how long the stimulus duration is. Studies on neuropsychological patients provide more evidence for the importance of "consciousness" in normal behaviour as well as evidence that stimuli that cannot be overtly recognised are, in fact, processed outside consciousness. In the literature, there are a number of striking examples of the way in which attention and consciousness can break down following brain damage. Cognitive neuropsychologists study the behaviour of these patients in order to try and understand not only the damaged system, but also the normal cognitive system. Apart from throwing light on the processes underlying normal information processing, studies of patients demonstrate selective impairments of different varieties of consciousness.

One of the most important assumptions that cognitive neuropsychologists make is that the human brain is "modular". This assumption stems from the very influential ideas of Marr (1976) and Fodor (1983). In a modular system, large and complicated computations are achieved by lots of "modules". These modules perform particular processing operations on particular, domain-specific, kinds of information. Together, they form the whole system, but each module acts as an independent processor for its own particular purpose. Fodor (1983) argues that modules are innately specified, hardwired and autonomous in that the functioning of the module is not under conscious control. In a modular system, the failure of one module does not prevent the other remaining modules from working. Such a system would seem advisable in terms of survival, we would be in deep trouble if damage to one small part of the brain resulted in all of the rest of the undamaged brain ceasing to work. Not only is a modular system a sensible design, but there is good evidence that when patients suffer local damage to particular brain regions, only certain computational functions are lost. If we assume attention and consciousness are important cognitive processes or states, then it seems likely that cognitive neuropsychology may throw a light on them. Further, if there are varieties of attention and consciousness, we might expect to find patients who show deficits in just one or other variety.

Farah (1994) reviews disorders of perception and awareness following brain damage. She considers the relation between conscious awareness and other brain mechanisms and classifies the theoretical position occupied by consciousness in the view of a number of other authors. According to Farah, some psychologists give consciousness a "privileged role". For example, Shacter, McAndrews, and Moscovitch (1988), who propose that the conscious awareness system is separate from the modules that process other, domain-specific information in the brain. According to this view, consciousness may almost be considered another "module" that can become dissociated from the rest of the modules responsible for perception, cognition and action. Schacter et al. (1988) call their model DICE (dissociated interactions and conscious experience).

Another view, which Farah considers as giving consciousness a privileged role, is that proposed by Gazzaniga (1988). Gazzaniga suggests that the conscious/non-conscious distinction is related to which cerebral hemisphere is responsible for information processing of particular tasks. The left hemisphere has language and is "conscious", whereas the right hemisphere does not have language and is "unconscious". Unconscious processing occurs when perceptual representations fail to access the language areas of the left hemisphere. Again, rather like the DICE model, consciousness can become disconnected from other processing. Farah (1994) categorises another set of theories about consciousness together because they put forward the view that consciousness is a "state of integration among distinct brain systems". Kinsbourne's integrated field theory sees consciousness as a state of the brain that arises when all the concurrently active modality-specific information is mutually consistent. Normally, these systems will produce an integrated conscious output, but brain damage may result in a situation where processes become disconnected and do not form an integrated consciousness. In this state, there can be a dissociation between processes and consciousness. Without the integrated state, there can be processing but no conscious experience of that processing. The importance of binding and perceptual integration has arisen already in our discussion of change blindness and in several chapters. In Chapter 5, possible mechanisms for perceptual integration were discussed, for example, Treisman's (1993) feature integration theory and Singer's (1994, 2004) theory of temporal synchrony.

Similar views were put forward by Crick and Koch (1990) who consider that consciousness of visual stimuli arises from the binding together of different separately represented visual properties of a stimulus. Damasio (1990) has also theorised that "binding" gives rise to conscious awareness. In her review, Farah (1994) points out that in all the cases just examined, consciousness must be all or nothing, it is disconnected or not, domains are integrated or not. However, she argues that there is evidence for consciousness being a "graded property". The most popular metaphor for the brain in current psychology is that of a neural network and we know from studies of artificial neural networks that information in this kind of system can be represented by partial activation. Farah argues that evidence from patients suggests a relationship between the "quality" of a patient's perceptual representation and the likelihood that they will have a consciousness of that percept. We shall pick up this notion of graded conscious experience as we examine some of the neurological disorders.

Blindsight

The term blindsight is used to describe patients who have lesions in their visual cortex that give rise to apparent blindness in part of their visual field. If you ask the subject if they can see anything in the "blind" field, they report that they cannot. However, if the subject is induced to play a "game" in which, despite not "seeing" anything, they are asked to guess about the presence or absence of events in the "blind" field, it is clear that discriminatory responses are being made.

The first report of a patient who exhibited this phenomenon was by Poppel, Held, and Frost (1973). They found that although patients had severe damage to primary visual cortex, they were nevertheless able to move their eyes to the location of a light presented to the "blind" field. A region of blindness caused by damage to visual cortex is called a scotoma. Patients reported no phenomenal awareness of any light falling on the scotomatous region. It was as if eye movements were directed in response to the light, but below the level of conscious awareness. Soon after this initial report, Weiskrantz, Sanders, and Marshall (1974) began in-depth studies of what they called "blindsight".

Weiskrantz et al. (1974) investigated a patient, DB, who had been operated on for persistent migraine. Part of the right hemisphere was removed, particularly striate cortex, and part of the calcarine cortex on the right-hand side. Not surprisingly, DB exhibited a post-operative hemianopia affecting most of the left visual field; over time this blind area contracted to just the lower left quadrant. DB was shown to be able to make eye movements or point to the object he claimed he could not see. DB believed he was guessing, but in fact was surprisingly accurate. DB is not unique; several other similar patients have been reported. Stimuli in the "blind" field can be discriminated on a number of attributes, horizontal/vertical, simple shapes, moving/not moving, "X" or "O" (Weiskrantz, 1988).

Although DB is a well-documented case study, there is evidence for significant variations in preserved abilities between subjects. Most patients can detect and localise light sources and some can detect shape, direction of movement, flicker and line orientation. Occasionally colour vision is preserved (Stoerig & Cowey, 1990). These authors examined the sensitivity of blindsight patients to light of different wavelengths. It was discovered that the spectral sensitivity function for the patients was the same shape as that for normal subjects but the threshold for detection was higher. Thus, colour discriminations could be made, although the patients were phenomenally unaware of the colours. More recent studies by Marzi, Tassarini, Aglioti, and Lutzemberger (1986) have demonstrated response priming effects where, like normal subjects, patients with blindsight respond more rapidly to two stimuli rather than one, even when one of those stimuli falls in the blind field.

It is clear then, that these patients have preserved psychological capacities to process and discriminate environmental stimuli, but they have lost the ability to "know" about them and therefore to make voluntary actions in response to them. This lack of knowledge is severely disabling for the patient because the information available to the brain is not available to the patient's awareness. Stimuli are being processed, but do not reach consciousness. The subject has no confidence in their guesses and remains phenomenally unaware of the stimuli presented. Weiskrantz (1993) believes that the phenomenon of blindsight is difficult to talk about without using the term "unconscious". Is the patient with blindsight similar to the normal subject who is shown a very brief, pattern masked stimulus that they fail to acknowledge but nevertheless show evidence of processing (e.g., Marcel, 1983)? Weiskrantz believes not. There are conditions in which DB, for example, can, in fact, detect stimuli in the blind field better than in the good field. However, at the same visual location form is detected in the good field better than in his blind field, so normal vision and blindsight cannot be the same.

Visual neglect

We have already met visual neglect, extinction and simultanagnosia, in Chapter 4. Evidence of unconscious processing of extinguished stimuli was discovered in several studies, e.g., Volpe, LeDoux, and Gazzaniga (1979) and Berti et al. (1992). In these studies, extinguished stimuli can be shown to have reached a high level of processing, but as the patients were not conscious of the outcome of this processing, they were unable to overtly report the extinguished stimuli. Farah (1994) proposed that extinction occurs because the representations achieved in the damaged field are not strong enough to integrate properly with information from the good field into a "new" integrated brain state and, consequently, the representation in the good field dominates. Presumably, when there is no competing representation in the good field, the weakened representation is able to give rise to a stable brain state and so support conscious awareness. Some other theoretical explanations that can account for not only normal visual attention, unilateral neglect, but also simultanagnosia and extinction, also involve the argument that attentional behaviour is a result of an integrated brain state. Duncan (1999) proposes a distributed view of attentional functions in which "generally, attention is seen as a widely distributed state, in which, several brain systems converge to work on different properties and action implications of the same, selected object" (p. 126). The hypothesis is that the multiple sources of information activating different brain systems responsive to visual input are subject to competitive processing. If one source of information is enhanced, than another is inhibited and the most active pattern of activity gains dominance, or control. Following consideration of lesion studies, Duncan proposes that the attentional bias observed in unilateral neglect and the phenomenon of extinction can be explained in terms of damaged areas losing the competition to dominate processing. Duncan argues that lateral bias is a widespread consequence of lateralised brain injury and that right parietal lesions are not the sole predictor of bias in neglect, simultanagnosia and extinction.

Another approach to explaining neglect that relates to more general, non-lateralised attentional deficits has been proposed by Robertson and Manly (1999). According to this view, there is evidence to suggest that the right hemisphere is more important for sustaining attention than shifting it and that contributions to neglect, extinction and simultanagnosia may result from a more general effect of arousal, impaired spatial attention and reduced attentional capacity.

Prosopagnosia

Prosopagnosic patients have a deficit that renders them unable to overtly recognise familiar faces. To them, all faces are unfamiliar. Even the patient's family, friends and the patient's own face in a mirror cannot be named. However, given the person's voice, or biographical details, the person can be identified. Despite the inability to recognise faces, prosopagnosics can be shown to have unconsciously processed the faces that they are unable to overtly recognise. For example, skin conductance changes when the patient views a familiar face (Bauer, 1984). De Haan, Young, and Newcombe (1987a; 1987b) report studies on their prosopagnosic patient, PH. Although PH could not recognise people from their faces, he could recognise them from their names. De Haan et al. wanted to discover if there would be interference between written names and faces. If the face of a personality was presented together with the written name of that person, this was called the "same" condition. If the name was different from the face, but both the face and the other person's name were from the same category, say politicians, this was called the "related" condition. The "unrelated" condition used a face from one category, say a politician, and the name from another category, for example a television personality. PH was told to judge as quickly as possible whether each name belonged to a politician or a television personality. There was more interference in the incongruent condition, that is, when the face of a politician was presented together with the name of a television personality. Normal people show the same pattern of interference, because both the face and the name access semantics automatically. As the same pattern of interference is observed in people who cannot overtly name a face, the face must have accessed its semantic representation, which interferes with overt naming of the incongruent written word. Clearly then, despite their inability to overtly recognise faces, prosopagnosic patients show evidence of covert, unconscious face recognition. This deficit of "access consciousness", as Young and Block (1996) call it, is very selective.

Some prosopagnosic patients are able to achieve overt recognition of faces in certain circumstances. De Haan, Young, and Newcombe (1991) showed that if enough semantic activation is provided, by giving multiple exemplars of the semantic category, PH is sometimes able to overtly recognise a face. This result is consistent with the idea that overt conscious recognition requires activation to rise above a threshold. Below threshold activation is sufficient to allow priming or interference but insufficient to endow the subject with overt recognition. Above threshold, overt recognition is achieved.

Thus, as Farah (1994) suggested, it looks as if consciousness is a graded property and that such effects could be (are) easily modelled in neural networks.

Amnesia

While patients with amnesia are often considered to have lost the ability to learn new information, this would be an oversimplification of the facts. One of the most famous amnesics is HM reported by Milner (1966). Although HM was only able to learn six new words following his operation, he was able to show improvement on tasks such as the pursuit rotor task, which involves hand–eye coordination, despite not being able to recall ever having done the task before. Many amnesic patients have been studied, for a review (see Parkin, 1996). The difference between learning words and learning skills might be explained in terms of declarative and procedural memory, which we met when we considered ACT* in Chapter 8. Squire (1987) proposed that amnesics have a selective loss of declarative memory, which is where episodic and semantic memories are stored. Learning new words, a semantic task, or recalling that a test has been done before, which relies on episodic memory, is impaired, but performance and learning on a procedural task, like pursuit rotor, unimpaired. Schacter (1987) thought that the procedural/declarative distinction was unsatisfactory, as there was no independent measure of whether a task involved procedural or declarative memory, except to test the patient and see if they could do the task or not. Schacter suggested that memory tasks should be defined in whether or not a task demands access to explicit or implicit memory for accurate performance. Explicit memory is required for any task that requires intentional, deliberate, conscious recall of the previous learning experience, for example a personal experience or a word. An implicit memory task does not need the previous learning experience to be explicitly recalled, in fact in tasks like pursuit rotor and other skills, it simply is not possible, either in normal people or amnesic patients to describe explicitly what is being "done"; this information is unconscious and cannot be made conscious. (See Schacter, 1989 for a discussion and review.)

While skills like eye–hand coordination are preserved, so too are other effects that do not rely on conscious access to stored information. Amnesics demonstrate repetition and semantic priming, by stimuli that they are unable to recall (see Parkin, 1997 for a review). In the section on normal subjects, we discussed the difficulty in demonstrating that priming had taken place below the level of conscious awareness. With amnesics, this is easy, as they can never recall the priming stimulus. Despite this inability to consciously recall the prime, response to following stimuli is influenced by the relation between the prime and probe, giving clear evidence for unconscious processing that effects or modifies subsequent overt actions. In some sense, then, the processing system has "remembered" previously presented information, but this information has not accessed consciousness. The same type of effect was evident in the experiments on prosopagnosics, where we saw that faces which could not be overtly recognised influenced word naming.

Visual form agnosia

Milner and Goodale (1995) report the case of patient DF, who has bilateral damage to the lateral occipital cortex. She is not able to accurately report the location of objects in space, discriminate between different objects or describe object properties such as their shape, size or orientation. Despite not appearing to have any conscious experience of perceiving objects in space, DF not only reaches accurately for objects, but also shapes her hand appropriately for the shape of object to be grasped, although she does not scale the size of the grasp. So, despite having no apparent ability to describe the shape of objects, DF acts on these objects as if that knowledge is available. Remember, in Chapter 3, we saw that Milner and Goodale (1995) suggested two cortical streams for processing visual information: a ventral stream that is involved in the analysis of "what" objects are and a dorsal stream involved in the guidance of actions or "how" to act on an object in space. A possible explanation for the dissociation between what DF can consciously report and how she acts is that conscious experience is mediated by the ventral "what" pathway but skilled action is mediated by the dorsal stream and that the dorsal stream can act independently. In neurologically intact people, the ventral pathway allows the formation of conscious representations that can then be used to guide visuomotor actions such as reaching and grasping.

The mind's best trick?

Wegner (2003) suggests that although we have a powerful subjective experience of being consciously in control of our actions, this may be an illusion. One way this illusion could arise is if both the thought, or intention to act, and the action itself are caused by the same underlying processes. Because the thought and the action are normally contingent, we think and then act, this does not necessarily mean that the thought caused the action. Wegner suggests that we experience conscious will when we infer that our thought causes action. Figure 9.1 shows Wegner's conception of the relationship between the apparent and actual causal paths in the experience of conscious will.

He suggests that: "If conscious will were an illusory add-on to action, we could explain all the odd cases where action and conscious will do not properly coincide" (p. 65). In the case of DF, just discussed, it appears that action can proceed quite independently from conscious control. Other examples of actions occurring outside conscious control are evident in patients with alien hand syndrome associated with split brain patients. Parkin and Barry (1991) report patient MP who, following destruction of the anterior part of the corpus callosum (the connection between the two cerebral hemispheres), frequently

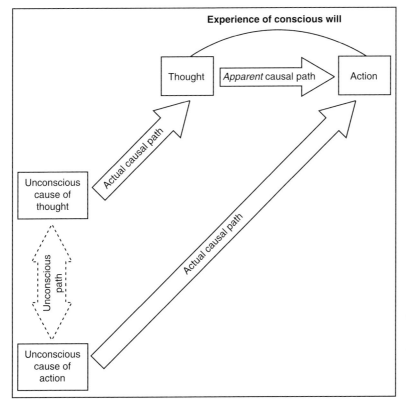

Figure 9.1 The experience of conscious will according to Wegner (2003). The person infers an apparent causal path from thought to action, but the actual causal paths are not present in the person's consciousness.

Reprinted from Wegner 2003, Trends in *Cognitive Sciences*, Vol. 7, No. 2. p. 66, by permission of Elsevier.

experienced the problem of her left hand reaching out and doing things that were in opposition to what she intended. For example, the left hand would undo buttons just done up by the right hand. Packing a suitcase would take a long time because as fast as the right had filled the case, the left hand would remove them. It appears as if the alien hand has a mind of its own and is performing voluntary actions without the patient having any experience of intentional or conscious control over it.

Libet (1985) asked people to hold their arm out in front of them and, then, whenever they felt like it, move a finger. If you do this yourself you will feel as though you make the conscious intention and then flex your finger. However, when electrodes are placed on the scalp over the motor area to record the electrical activity in motor cortex, Libert showed, readiness activity in motor cortex preceded the movement by about 500 mscs and that when participants were asked to recall the position of a clock at the moment they became aware of their intention to make the movement, their awareness followed the readiness potential by 300–400 mscs. Therefore, although participants became aware of the intention to move prior to actually making the movement, this awareness actually occurred after the initial activity in motor cortex. This result implies that consciousness intention follows rather than precedes the processes involved in making a movement.

In other experiments, Wegner and Wheatley (1999) have shown that participants attribute actions to their own free will even when they have not made the action themselves. Using a modified Ouija board, Wegner and Wheatley had two participants place their finger onto a computer mouse on a small board covered with small pictures. While music was being played, the mouse moved around the board according to small difference in force exerted by the two people's fingers. Then, when the music stops, the mouse had to be stopped at one of the pictures. Normally, the mouse would stop at a position determined equally by both participants, but in some conditions, one of the participants was a confederate and forced the stopping place. When asked how certain they were that they had chosen the stopping place themselves, participants who had, in fact, been forced, were sure they had freely chosen it themselves. So, the experience of free will is not a reliable indication of the cause of an action in this case either.

However, Kelley and Jacoby (1990) argued that we cannot distinguish between what they call conscious control and automatic control by simply asking people whether they intended to do something or not, because intention is an attribution that may follow behaviour as well as direct it. When we feel the intention to stand up, for example, this feeling of intention may be following the beginning of the action rather than preceding it. That is to say we may attribute our action to an intention, when, in fact, this was not so. By interpreting our actions in terms of intentions, it gives us the feeling of having rational, meaningful behaviour. Thus it may be dangerous to assume that the subjective experience of free will is evidence for its existence and if this is the case, then the distinction between automatic and controlled processing that relies on "the subject" applying strategic control is immediately blurred.

Returning to Wegner (2003): After reviewing the evidence, he concludes that the mind's own system for computing the relationship between thought and action is not a reliable guide to causation and that in a number of circumstances it can be misled. So, to determine the real link between conscious thought and voluntary action, experiments need to be done that take account of this unreliability and that the experience of conscious will cannot be the basis for a causal explanation.

But what is consciousness?

It is one matter to talk about the experience of conscious thought or explain neuropsychological deficits by saying that these patients have selectively lost "consciousness". It is another matter to explain why it is that "conscious" processes have been lost or what it is that normally allows these unconscious levels of processing to give rise to conscious experience. Shallice (1988a) says that "the existence of consciousness is one of the greatest, if not the greatest, of the unsolved problems of science" (p. 305). So far we have talked about conscious and unconscious processing as if we knew what this distinction meant. At the subjective threshold, a normal subject reports phenomenal awareness of a stimulus and can act on it with confidence. A patient with blindsight has no awareness of stimuli that they can be shown to have knowledge of. Prosopagnosics and amnesics have no "conscious" representation or phenomenal awareness of stimuli that can be shown to affect their judgements. But what is this "phenomenal awareness", does it have a function and how can we determine if someone else is or was phenomenally aware? Could we make a machine that is conscious? Is consciousness of one kind or does it come in a variety of forms?

Over the past 20 years consciousness has come back into the field of psychological enquiry and two important books, Marcel and Bisiach (1988) and Davies and Humphreys (1993), review influential thinking on the subject. Both are collections of essays by psychologists and philosophers and the fact that both disciplines have important contributions to make emphasises the fact that psychology has its roots in philosophy and that "consciousness" was one of the most important issues for early psychologists such as William James and Sigmund Freud. As it became increasingly clear that consciousness was difficult to define and study it was temporarily "banned" by the behaviourists. However, as psychologists rejected behaviourism, consciousness began to creep back into psychology, both as an explanatory term (albeit one difficult to define) and as the basis for a subject's experimental reports. Increasingly, more and more psychologists have begun to try to account for some kinds of "consciousness" in information-processing terms, including Shallice (1972) and Norman and Shallice (1986), whose model we looked at in the last chapter. In their model, consciousness was hypothesised as being involved in intentional control. Other theorists, including Allport (1977), Coltheart (1980a) and Marcel (1983), have proposed that consciousness is the outcome of some kind of perceptual integration or stabilisation. This early idea fits well with suggestions by Crick and Koch (1990), who advocate a neurophysiological approach to consciousness. Their suggestion is that what consciousness does is make available the results of underlying neuronal computations, which have become linked together by synchronous neural activity. As different parts of the brain are specialised for the processing of different information, there is the problem of combining the different sources of information together, for example, the semantics of a word with its perceptual properties. One way of solving the "binding problem" would be by synchronising activity over the groups of neurons that are related to the same object. We considered one theory in Chapter 4, put forward by Singer (1994, 2004), who proposed a neurobiological explanation of binding, attention and consciousness.

There is neither time nor space in a book such as this to give an exhaustive review of current thinking on consciousness. The interested reader should refer to the reading list at the end of the chapter for more ideas. Here, we look at just a few views to give a flavour of the area.

Much of the debate centres on what precisely is meant by the term "consciousness". Baars (1997) believes there is still room for improvement in clarifying the concept of consciousness "because it is so often conflated with co-occurring but distinguishable terms" (p. 363). He asks "Is 'attention' the same as 'consciousness'? How is consciousness related to 'working memory (WM)' and 'perception'?"

(p. 363). Baars suggests that the difference in normal language usage between "looking" and "seeing", "touching" and "feeling" etc. illustrates the distinction between selecting an experience and being conscious of the selected event. So, we look in order to see; we touch in order to feel. Operationally, attention and consciousness are also different. Attention increases the likelihood of selection, consciousness implies that the experience can be reported or some voluntary action can be made. However, see Allport's (1988) argument later. In sum, Baars (1997) argues that the term "attention" applies to the selection and maintenance of conscious events and is distinguishable from consciousness itself. He further argues consciousness is involved in "all working memory input, output and voluntary operations" (p. 369) and suggests that working memory depends on the fundamental features of consciousness. He takes Crick and Koch's (1990) suggestion for a kind of "working awareness", and has shown that the concept of a "global workplace" model of conscious functioning, in which consciousness is itself a workspace, can account for all the functions usually assigned to working memory. He calls consciousness "the publicity organ of the brain, one that is used to access all of its functions. If this is the case, then attention mechanisms exist to control access to this publicity organ, the bright spot on the stage of consciousness" (p. 370). Although Baars (1997) attempts to refine the concepts of attention, consciousness, perception and working memory, he does not delve into differentiating kinds of consciousness. Others have tried to do this.

Criteria for consciousness

The pitfalls and problems associated with determining criteria for different uses of the term conscious is eloquently discussed by Allport (1988). We have seen that the trouble with experimenting on normal subjects is that we need some criterion for establishing whether or not the subjects were consciously aware or not of the stimulus that was presented. What could we use for a criterion? Allport (1988) considers three possible options, all of which he finds to be seriously flawed. First, he considers the criterion of potential action. With much qualification of his arguments, Allport suggests that if a person were "aware" of an event, then they should be able, in principle, to respond to or act on that event. Of course, if the subjects choose not to overtly respond to the event, we have no way of knowing if they were aware of it or not. By this definition, we would then have no way of knowing if they were conscious or unconscious of that event. Allport discusses other possible behavioural indicators of awareness that might be useful for determining a person's state of awareness. Some of these are involuntary, for example, pupil dilation, an autonomic response. Such involuntary indicators often "tell" us something different from what the person is telling us verbally, for example, when someone is lying, involuntary indicators may "give them away". So, Allport argues, the proposal that awareness can be indexed by voluntary actions immediately runs into another problem. He concludes that there may be no behavioural indicators that can be reliably used to determine awareness.

The next criterion for "conscious awareness" that Allport examines is whether the subject can remember an event. When a person can recall an event, then it may be possible to say that the person was aware of that event. However, what if they are *unable* to recall an event? They may have been aware at the time, but have forgotten by the time you question them. There are further problems with the memory criterion, in that we often exhibit absent-mindedness. We perform actions, presumably in response to the environment or internal goals, but do not remember doing them, does this mean we are not aware of these actions or the events that triggered them? How about the confidence criterion, proposed by Cheesman and Merikle (1985), which we discussed earlier with respect to SAWCI experiments? The problem here is how much confidence is required for the acknowledgment of an event.

Overall, then, it seems that there are a variety of indicators that suggest that there is no unique form of consciousness, rather, a variety of forms that may be indicated in different ways. We shall see this most clearly when we review neurological patients in the next section. Perhaps, Allport suggests, "consciousness" is related to selection for action and that objects selected for action are likely to form an episodic memory, which can be recovered explicitly. Objects that are not directly selected for action are only "in some sense" conscious. This idea, however, does not seem to explain how objects that are selected for action, acted on and integrated into a coherent routine, for example, lifting the sugar spoon and adding sugar in tea, may be done twice or not at all. We may have been "conscious" in one sense, but do not have a retrievable episodic memory of our action that we can subsequently report.

Despite the difficulty of defining consciousness and ascertaining its presence or absence, there are psychologists who believe that psychology cannot ignore "phenomenal awareness". Marcel (1983, 1988) believes that consciousness is central to mental life and, as psychology is the science of mental life, ignoring it would reduce psychology to cybernetics or biology. In their experiments, psychologists generally ask people to perform tasks that rely on a report based on a conscious percept. "Press a button as soon as you see a red light", "Do you hear a high or low pitched tone" and so forth. Thus, Marcel argues, the data derived in experiments are based on phenomenal experience. Unless the subject has a conscious experience of the stimulus, they are unwilling to make a response. Here again, we see how important it is that the subject has confidence in their experience if they are to make a voluntary action.

Shallice (1988a) agrees that consciousness is important because we rely on the phenomenal experience of our subjects in psychology experiments and because these experiments also depend on the subjects understanding the task instructions. As we treat subjects as if they were "responsible conscious agents" (p. 307), we are acknowledging something about what it is to be conscious. He suggests that a useful way of approaching the problem might be to try and make a link between information processing and experiential accounts of the same events. Shallice's (1988a) version of the flow of information between control systems included two additional modules to Norman and Shallice (1986): the language system and an episodic memory. However, within this model the problem arises as to what exactly corresponds to consciousness. Shallice identifies five levels within the model that might be candidates: input to the language system; the processing carried out by the SAS; the selection of schemata, the operation of some particular component of the system; or the episodic memory module. Shallice argues that is not easy to decide which part of the system might correspond to consciousness, first, because a definition of consciousness have not yet been worked out (Shallice lists 14 possible varieties in his paper); second, the information processing models are too loosely specified; and last, because as information processing involves so many subsystems, it is difficult to know which ones are critical for producing awareness. Shallice suggests that attempting to find a one-to-one correspondence between any component of the information-processing system and consciousness would be misguided. Rather, control could be shared between subsystems and, as the control structures would be operating on information from the same schemata, "there would be a coherent pattern of control over all other subsystems, which is shared between those control systems that are active. Might not this shared control be the basis for 'consciousness'?" (p. 327). We have met the idea that coherence between subsystems might be important for conscious experience at the beginning of our discussion of consciousness. As patterns of coherence might differ, so might conscious experience.

The conscious/unconscious distinction

Umilta (1988) discusses the proposition with which we started this chapter, i.e., that the conscious/unconscious distinction corresponds to the controlled/automatic distinction, along with four other propositions about the disputed nature of consciousness. Like attention, "consciousness", "awareness", or the combined term "conscious awareness" has proved difficult to define and is, by its very nature, very difficult to experiment on. Let us examine Umilta's arguments. First, he discusses the notion that consciousness is equivalent to our phenomenal experience of what is going on in the limited capacity "central processor" (e.g. the supervisory attentional system proposed by Norman and Shallice, 1986 or the central executive, Baddeley, 1986). Remember, this central processor is said to be in control of attention allocation and contention scheduling of other unconscious processes. As we have said before, this idea is virtually the same as the homunculus and does not get us very far with respect to clearer understanding.

Second, Umilta discusses the proposition that while controlled processing is under the control of the central processor, automatic processing proceeds without central processor control. However, there is evidence, that the central processor does influence "automatic" processes in that these can run off as a consequence of consciously activated goal states. Third, Umilta discusses whether attention and consciousness are synonymous. He says that although the properties of attention and consciousness appear similar in that they are both said, among other things, to be limited capacity, slow, serial processes and active in working memory, they are, in fact, conceptually different. Crucially, consciousness uses attention to control "lower order cognitive processes" (Umilta, 1988, p. 343). We are able to have the intention to attend to something, thus, as intention is the precursor of allocating attention, they cannot be the same thing. Last, Umilta considers what self-awareness is. He says that this kind of consciousness gives us a feeling of being in control of our mind.

Could a machine be conscious?

Johnson-Laird (1983, 1988) points out that this ability for self-awareness is crucial for the formation of intentions. Intentions are based on models of "what the world would be like" if you did so-and-so. Without some awareness of the possible outcomes, planning actions and making decisions would be severely impaired. Self-awareness also allows us to know what we know, this is called metacognition. If I ask you the name of the fifth king of Norway, you will probably "know" immediately that you do not have this knowledge. Contrariwise, if I ask you the name of the fifth king of England, you might think that it is possible that you know the answer and begin a memory search. Naming the fifth day of the week is trivial; you know immediately that you have that knowledge. Knowing what we know depends on having access to the system's capabilities.

In his computational analysis of consciousness, Johnson-Laird argues that one way of solving the problem of what consciousness might be is to consider what would be necessary to produce a computer that had a high level model or awareness of its own operations. First, Johnson-Laird assumes that "consciousness is a computational matter that depends on how the brain carries out certain computations, not on its physical constitution" (p. 358). As the physical constitution is irrelevant to the explanation, any being endowed with consciousness might be explained this way. In terms of Marr's (1982) levels of explanation, we are concerned here only with the computational level. That is, to describe "what" needs to be computed, not the physical hardware that actually "does" the computing.

According to Johnson-Laird, there are four problems that any theory of consciousness must solve. The problem of awareness: any theory must account for the difference between information that can and information that cannot be made available to awareness, i.e., the difference between the conscious and unconscious. The second problem is that of control: in Johnson-Laird's conception, this is equivalent to will power and differs between individuals. The third and fourth problems are ones that we discussed earlier, self-awareness and intention. Self-awareness, metacognition and intentions all depend on the same computational mechanism. The computational system that Johnson-Laird proposes is like the brain in that it is hierarchical and parallel. At the highest level in the hierarchy is the operating system, or working memory, which is relatively autonomous, but does not have complete control over all the other processes. The contents of the operating system/working memory are conscious but all other levels in the hierarchy are not. The operating system needs to be conscious so that it can construct a mental model of itself and how it is performing. Johnson-Laird takes the example of visual perception. The visual system sends data about the locations and identities of an object, then the operating system uses other procedures to construct a model of itself perceiving the world. Now the working memory has a model embedded within a model. This "embedding" of models could in principle continue ad infinitum, you can be aware that you are aware that you are aware, etc. Once a computation system can represent itself and what it knows, it can display self-awareness or be "conscious", make plans and exhibit intentional behaviour. While all this seems promising, we have no idea what a machine that had a high level model of itself would be like. The operating system still sounds rather like a homunculus, but with a clearer description of what it needs to do. Norman (1986) gives thoughtful consideration to the problem of control in PDP computer networks.

Phaf, Mul, and Walter (1994) consider what kind of system could create conscious experience out of unconscious activation and suggest that conscious processing should be added to the general capabilities of PDP models. Some connectionist models of attention were described at the end of Chapter 5, where we considered how information concerning different attributes of an objects are combined. Phaf et al. propose that for conscious experience to arise, there must be an explicit construction process based on the process responsible for sequential recursive reasoning and for temporarily joining together active representations in working memory. They suggest that the articulatory loop would be a suitable candidate for this. Working memory is not generally mentioned in PDP models, long-term memory is considered to be the slowly changing weights within the network and short-term memory the currently decaying activation (Grossberg, 1980).

Phaf et al. (1994) describe an extension to their CALM model, which has a sequentially recurrent network (SeRN), or external rehearsal loop, which feeds back single localised activations, or chunks, to unconnected nodes in the input module for CALM, so that the chunks do not interfere with one another. This model simulated serial position effects in short-term memory as well as primacy and recency effects. In addition, they claim to show that all the requirements of consciousness can be met within connectionist models, although, of course, you could never determine if their model were conscious or not! The external rehearsal loop in SeRN is just one module in their model and activation in other modules must be transformed if it is to enter the loop. Activations that cannot, or do not, reach the recursive loop are unable to be part of the construction process that Phaf et al. (1994) propose is involved in conscious experience.

A dissociable module for conscious experience can explain how processing in one part of the system can proceed without conscious awareness. It seems unlikely, however, that the recursive loop can be the sole explanation for conscious experience, especially if this is equated with the articulatory loop component of working memory. When the articulatory loop is fully occupied with, for example a digit span task, subjects are still able to perform logical reasoning (Hitch & Baddeley, 1976) and are conscious of doing so.

So, from the preceding discussion it is evident that there may be many varieties of consciousness. We must, however be alert to the problem of using "consciousness" in any form of its meaning, to explain another phenomenon, unless we can explain the phenomenon of consciousness itself.

Summary

Experiments that claim to demonstrate semantic activation without conscious awareness have been criticised on a number of counts by Holender (1986). Dichotic listening and parafoveal vision tasks are suspect, because they rely on the subject doing what they are told, that is, to ignore some stimuli, that might become available if attention shifted. Experiments using visual stimuli and backward pattern masking are more reliable, for example, Marcel (1980,1983) because no stimuli have to be ignored. However, the problem here is that the parameters of the experiment have to be arranged so that the subject cannot consciously report the visually presented primes. Argument has centred on how best to determine whether or not the subject was consciously aware, and what in fact it means to be "consciously aware". Cheesman and Merikle (1984) proposed there were two thresholds: subjective and objective. They claimed that most experiments showing SAWCI had used the subjective threshold and that below this, at the objective threshold, no semantic effects would be found. Some studies have shown SAWCI at or below the objective threshold (Kemp-Wheeler & Hill, 1988). In conditions where people should be perfectly able to "see" stimuli, there are a number of phenomena that illustrate the difficulty of encoding and being aware of environmental changes. Mack and Rock (1998) were apparently "blind" to stimuli outside the focus of attention and Rees et al. (1999) found that letters to which participants were "blind" did not activate areas of the brain expected to encode semantic properties, although they had phenomenal experience of the physical properties in the display, such as colour. Change blindness (Rensink, 2000) is the inability to detect gross environmental changes and suggests that attention only constructs the environmental scene on a needs-must basis, so if attention is diverted and a change occurs, this is not detected because the scene was never fully represented in the first place. Blackmore (2001) believes we are misled into believing we are viewing a stable representation of visual space – it is only an illusion; change blindness shows our conscious experience is at odds with the data. Wegner (2003) suggests the subjective experience of conscious control is an also illusion. Perhaps the most convincing evidence for processing without conscious awareness and for dissociations of consciousness comes from neuropsychological patients. Reviewing the evidence on blindsight, visual neglect, prosopagnosia and amnesia, there are a surprising number of selective dissociations between perceptual processing and conscious awareness, as well as good evidence for semantic activation and learning outside consciousness. A further issue is the problem of what we mean by consciousness and whether psychologists should be concerned with it. Consciousness is seen by different people as having different properties, aspects and functions. It is difficult to provide a coherent summary because, really, there is not one. However, a number of people (e.g., Marcel, 1988; Shallice, 1988a, 1988b) have pointed out that although "consciousness" may be difficult to define, it must have a place in psychology, because we use data from "consciously aware" subjects. The notion of some kind of stable brain state being responsible for the emergence of phenomenal awareness seems to have support from a number of quarters, as is evident in Shallice's ideas on coherence between control subsystems, Allport's suggestion of behavioural integration and Crick and Koch's theory of neural synchronisation. Baars (1997) suggests that consciousness is a workplace in which attended information is made available.

Further reading

- Blackmore, S. (2001) State of the art: Consciousness. *The Psychologist*, *14*, 322–325.
    An accessible introduction to the problems of consciousness.
- Davies, M. & Humphreys, G. W. (Eds.). (1993). *Consciousness: Readings in mind and language*. Oxford: Blackwell.
- Marcel, A. J. & Bisiach, E. (Eds.). (1988). *Consciousness in contemporary science*. Oxford: Oxford University Press.
    Dissociations.

- Parkin, A. (1996). *Explorations in cognitive neuropsychology*. Oxford: Blackwell.
- Velmans, M. (2000). *Understanding consciousness*. London: Routledge.
- Young, A. W. & Block, N. (1996). Consciousness. In V. Bruce (Ed.). *Unsolved mysteries of the mind*. Hove, UK: Lawrence Erlbaum Associates Limited.

This provides an easily accessible overview of biological, psychological, philosophical and neurophysiological thinking on consciousness.

References

Abrogast, T. L., & Kidd, G. (2000). Evidence for spatial tuning in information masking using the probe-signal method. *Journal of the Acoustical Society of America*, *108*, 1803–1810.

Adams, M. J. (1979). Models of word recognition. *Cognitive Psychology*, *11*, 136–176.

Albert, M. L. (1973). A simple test of visual neglect. *Neurology*, *23*, 658–664.

Allport, A. (1987). Selection for action: some behavioural and neurophysiological considerations of attention and action. In H. Heuer, & A. F. Sanders (Eds.). *Perspectives on perception and action.* Hillsdale, NJ: Lawrence Erlbaum Associates, Inc.

Allport, A. (1988). What concept of consciousness? In A. J. Marcel, & E. Bisiach (Eds.). *Consciousness in contemporary science*. Oxford: Oxford University Press.

Allport, A. (1989). Visual attention. In M. I. Posner (Ed.). *Foundations of cognitive science. A Bradford book*. Cambridge, MA: MIT Press.

Allport, A. (1993). Attention and control: Have we been asking the wrong questions? A critical review of twenty-five years. In D. E. Meyer, & S. M. Kornblum (Eds.). *Attention and performance, XIV: Synergies in experimental psychology, artificial intelligence and cognitive neuroscience. A Bradford book*. Cambridge, MA: MIT Press.

Allport, A., & Wylie, G. (2000). "Task-switching". Stimulus-response bindings and negative priming. In S. Monsell, & J. Driver (Eds.). *Attention and performance, XVII: Control of cognitive processes* (pp. 35–70). Cambridge, MA: MIT Press.

Allport, A., Styles, E. A., & Hseih, S. (1994). Shifting intentional set: Exploring the dynamic control of tasks. In C. Umilta, & M. Moscovitch (Eds.). *Attention and performance, XV: Conscious and nonconscious information processing*. Cambridge, MA: MIT Press.

Allport, D. A. (1977). On knowing the meaning of words we are unable to report: The effects of visual masking. In S. Dornic (Ed.). *Attention and performance, VI*. Hillsdale, NJ: Lawrence Erlbaum Associates, Inc.

Allport, D. A. (1980a). Attention and performance. In G. Claxton (Ed.). *Cognitive psychology: New directions*. London: Routledge & Kegan Paul.

Allport, D. A. (1980b). Patterns and actions. In G. Claxton (Ed.). *Cognitive psychology: New directions*. London: Routledge & Kegan Paul.

Allport, D. A., Antonis, B., & Reynolds, P. (1972). On the division of attention: A disproof of the single channel hypothesis. *Quarterly Journal of Experimental Psychology*, *24*, 25–35.

Allport, D. A., Tipper, S. P., & Chmiel, N. R. J. (1985). Perceptual integration and post-categorical filtering. In M. I. Posner, & O. S. M. Marin (Eds.). *Attention and performance, XI*. Hillsdale, NJ: Lawrence Erlbaum Associates, Inc.

Anderson, J. R. (1983). *The architecture of cognition*. Cambridge, MA: Harvard University Press.

Arnell, K. M., & Duncan, J. (2002). Separate and shared resources of dual-task in stimulus identification and response selection. *Cognitive Psychology, 44,* 105–147.

Arnell, K. M., & Jolicoeur, P. (1999). The attentional blink across stimulus modalities: Evidence for central processing limitations. *Journal of Experimental Psychology: Human Perception and Performance, 25,* 630–648.

Atkinson, R. C. and Shiffrin, R. M. (1968). Human memory a proposed system and control processes. In K. W. Spence, & J. D. Spence (Eds.). *The psychology of learning and motivation* (Vol. 2). New York: Academic Press.

Avebach, E., & Coriell, A. S. (1961). Short-term memory in vision. *Bell System Technical Journal, 40,* 309–328.

Awh, E., Matsukura, M., & Serences, J. T. (2003). Top-down control over biased competition during covert spatial orienting. *Journal of Experimental Psychology: Human Perception and Performance, 29,* 52–63.

Awh, E., Serences, J., Laurey, P., Dhaliwal, H., van der Jaght, T., & Dassonville, P. (2004). Evidence against a central bottleneck during the attentional blink: Multiple channels for configural and featural processing. *Cognitive Psychology, 48,* 95–126.

Baars, B. J. (1997). Some essential differences between consciousness, attention perception and working memory. *Consciousness and Cognition, 6,* 363–371.

Baddeley, A. D. (1986). *Working memory.* Oxford: Oxford University Press.

Balint, R. (1909). Über die Selbstwahrnehmung der Herderknarkungen des Gehirns durch den Kranken bei Rindentaubheit. *Archive Psychiatrie Nervenkrasse, 32,* 86–111.

Banks, W. P., Larson, D. W., & Prinzmetal, W. (1979). Asymmetry of visual interference. *Perception and Psychophysics, 25,* 447–456.

Bauer, R. M. (1984). Autonomic recognition of names and faces in prosopagnosia: A neuropsychological application of the guilty knowledge test. *Neuropsychologia, 22,* 457–469.

Baylis, G., Driver, J., & Rafal, R. (1993). Visual extinction and stimulus repetition. *Journal of Cognitive Neuroscience, 5,* 453–466.

Beck, J. (1966). Effect of orientation and of shape similarity on perceptual grouping. *Perception and Psychophysics, 1,* 300–320.

Bedard, M. A., Massioui, F., Pillon, L., & Nandrino, J. L. (1993). Time for reorienting of attention: A pre-motor hypothesis of the underlying mechanism. *Neuropsychologia, 31,* 241–249.

Beecher, H. K. (1956). Relationship of significance of wound to pain experienced. *Journal of the American Medical Association, 161,* 1609–1613.

Behrmann, M. (1996). Neglect dyslexia: Attention and word recognition. In M. J. Farah, & G. Ratcliff (Eds.). *The neuropsychology of high-level vision* (pp. 173–214). Hillsdale, NJ: Lawrence Erlbaum Associates, Inc.

Behrmann, M., & Moskovitch, M. (1994). Object centred neglect in patients with unilateral neglect: Effects of left right coordinates of objects. *Cognitive Neuroscience, 6,* 1–16.

Behrmann, M., & Tipper, S. P. (1994). Object-based attentional mechanisms: Evidence from patients with unilateral neglect. In C. Umilta, & M. Moscovitch (Eds.). *Attention and performance, XV: Conscious and nonconscious information processing.* Cambridge, MA: MIT Press.

Behrmann, M., Geng, J. J., & Shomstein, S. (2004). Parietal cortex and attention.

Current Opinion in Neurobiology, 14, 212–217.

Beilock, S. L., Carr, T. H., MacMahon, C., & Starkes, J. L. (2002). When paying attention becomes counterproductive: Impact of divided versus skill-focused attention on novice and experienced performance of sensorimotor skills. *Journal of Experimental Psychology: Applied, 8,* 6–16.

Beilock, S. L., Bertenthal, B. I., McCoy, A. M., & Carr, T. H. (2004). Haste does not always make waste: Expertise, direction of attention, and speed versus accuracy in performing sensorimotor skills. *Psychonomic Bulletin and Review, 11,* 373–379.

Berger, R. C., & McLeod, P. (1996). Display density influences visual search for conjunctions of movement and orientation. *Journal of Experimental Psychology: Human Perception and Performance, 22,* 114–121.

Bertelson, P., & Aschersleben, G. (1998). Automatic visual bias of perceived auditory location. *Psychonomic Bulletin and Review, 5,* 482–489.

Berti, A., Allport, A., Driver, J., Deines, Z., Oxbury, J., & Oxbury, S. (1992). Levels of processing for visual stimuli in and "extinguished" field. *Neuropsychologia, 30,* 403–415.

Bianchi, L. (1985). The functions of the frontal lobes. *Brain, 18,* 497–530.

Bianchi, L. (1922). *The mechanism of the brain and the function of the frontal lobes.* Edinburgh: Livingstone.

Bisiach, E., & Luzatti, C. (1978). Unilateral neglect of representational space. *Cortex, 14,* 128–133.

Bjork, E. L., & Murray, J. T. (1977). On the nature of input channels in visual processing. *Psychological Review, 84,* 472–484.

Blackmore, S. J. (2001). The state of the art: Consciousness. *The Psychologist, 14,* 522–525.

Blackmore, S. J., Belstaff, G., Nelson, K., &

Troscianko, T. (1995). Is the richness of our visual world an illusion? *Perception, 24,* 1075–1081.

Bouma, H. (1970). On the nature of input channels in visual processing. *Nature, 226,* 177–178.

Bourke, P. A., Duncan, J., & Nimmo-Smith, I. (1996). A general factor in dual task performance decrement. *Quarterly Journal of Experimental Psychology, 49A,* 525–545.

Bregman, A. S. (1990). *Auditory scene analysis.* Cambridge, MA: MIT Press.

Bregman, A. S. (1981). Asking the "what for" question in auditory perception. In M. Kubovy, & J. R. Pomerantz (Eds.). *Perceptual organisation.* Hillsdale, NJ: Lawrence Erlbaum Associates, Inc.

Briand, K. A., & Klein, R. M. (1987). Is Posner's "beam" the same as Treisman's "glue"? On the relationship between visual orienting and feature integration theory. *Journal of Experimental Psychology: Human Perception and Performance, 13,* 228–241.

Broadbent, D. E. (1952). Listening to one of two synchronous messages. *Journal of Experimental Psychology, 44,* 51–55.

Broadbent, D. E. (1954). The role of auditory localisation in attention and memory span. *Journal of Experimental Psychology, 47,* 191–196.

Broadbent, D. E. (1958). *Perception and communication.* London: Pergamon Press.

Broadbent, D. E. (1971). *Decision and stress.* London: Academic Press.

Broadbent, D. E. (1982). Task combination and selective intake of information. *Acta Psychologia, 50,* 253–290.

Broadbent, D. E. (1984). The Maltese Cross: A new simplistic model for memory. *Behavioural and Brain Sciences, 7,* 55–68.

Broadbent, D. E. (1985). A question of levels: Comment on McClelland and Rumelhart. *Journal of Experimental Psychology: General, 114,* 189–192.

Broadbent, D. E., & Broadbent, M. H. (1987). From detection to identification: Response to multiple targets in rapid serial visual presentation. *Perception and Psychophysics*, *42*, 105–113.

Bruce, V. (Ed.). (1996). *Unsolved mysteries of the mind: Tutorial essays in cognition*. Hove, UK: Lawrence Erlbaum Associates Limited.

Buchtel, H. A., & Butter, C. M. (1988). Spatial attention shifts: Implications for the role of polysensory mechanisms. *Neuropsychologia*, *26*, 499–509.

Bundesen, C. (1990). A theory of visual attention. *Psychological Review*, *97*, 523–527.

Bundesen, C., & Shibuya, H. (Eds.). (1995). Visual selective attention: A special issue of the journal *Visual Cognition*. Hove, UK: Lawrence Erlbaum Associates Limited.

Campion, J., Latto, R., & Smith, Y. M. (1983). Is blindsight an effect of scattered light, spared cortex and near-threshold vision. *Behavioural and Brain Sciences*, *3*, 423–447.

Carlson, N. R. (1994). *Physiology of behaviour* (5th ed.). Needham Heights, MA: Allyn & Bacon.

Carlyon, R. P., Cusack, R., Foxton, J. M., & Robertson, I. H. (2001). The effects of attention and unilateral neglect on auditory stream segregation. *Journal of Experimental Psychology: Human Perception and Performance*, *27*, 115–127.

Carramazza, A., & Hillis, A. E. (1990). Spatial representation of words in the brain implied by studies of a unilateral neglect patient. *Nature*, *346*, 267–269.

Carrier, L. M., & Pashler, H. (1995). Attentional limits in memory retrieval. *Journal of Experimental Psychology: Learning Memory and Cognition*, *21*, 1339–1348.

Castiello, U., & Umilta, C. (1992). Splitting focal attention. *Journal of Experimental Psychology: Human Perception and Performance*, *18*, 837–848.

Chalmers, D. (1996). *The conscious mind*. New York: Oxford University Press.

Chase, W. G., & Ericsson, K. A. (1982). Skill and working memory. In G. H. Bower (Ed.). *The psychology of learning and motivation* (Vol. 16, pp. 1–58). New York: Academic Press.

Chase, W. G., & Simon, H. A. (1973). Perception in chess. *Cognitive Psychology*, *4*, 55–81.

Cheesman, J., & Merikle, P. M. (1984). Priming with and without awareness. *Perception and Psychophysics*, *36*, 387–395.

Cheesman, J., & Merikle, P. M. (1985). Word recognition and consciousness. In D. Besner, T. G. Waller, & G. E. MacKinnon (Eds.). *Reading research: Advances in theory and practice* (Vol. 5). New York: Academic Press.

Cherry, E. C. (1953). Some experiments on the recognition of speech with one and two ears. *Journal of the Acoustical Society of America*, *25*, 975–979.

Chun, M. M., & Potter, M. C. (1995). A two-stage model for multiple target detection in rapid serial visual presentation. *Journal of Experimental Psychology: Human Perception and Performance*, *21*, 109–127.

Chun, M. M., & Potter, M. C. (2001). The attentional blink within and across modalities. In K. Shapiro (Ed.). *The limits of attention: Temporal constraints in human information processing* (pp. 20–30). Oxford: Oxford University Press.

Cinel, C., Humphreys, G. W., & Poli, R. (2002). Cross-modal illusory conjunctions between vision and touch. *Journal of Experimental Psychology: Human Perception and Performance*, *28*, 1243–1266.

Cohen, G. (1989). *Memory in the real world*. Hove, UK: Lawrence Erlbaum Associates Limited.

Cohen, J. D., & Huston, T. (1994). Progress in the use of interactive models for understanding attention and performance. In C. Umilta, & M. Moscovitch (Eds.). *Attention and performance, XV: Conscious and nonconscious information processing. A Bradford book*. Cambridge, MA: MIT Press.

Cohen, J. D., Dunbar, K., & McClelland, J. L. (1990). On the control of automatic processes: A parallel distributed processing account of the Stroop effect. *Psychological Review*, *97*, 332–361.

Coltheart, M. (1972). Visual information processing. In P. C. Dodwell (Ed.). *New horizons in psychology 2*. London: Penguin.

Coltheart, M. (1980a). Iconic memory and visible persistence. *Perception and Psychophysics*, *27*, 183–228.

Coltheart, M. (1980b). Deep dyslexia: A review of the syndrome. In M. Coltheart, K. Patterson, & J. C. Marshall (Eds.). *Deep dyslexia*. London: Routledge & Kegan Paul.

Coltheart, M. (1984). Sensory memory: A tutorial review. In H. Bouma, & D. G. Bouwhuis (Eds.). *Attention and performance, X: Control of language processes*. Hillsdale, NJ: Lawrence Erlbaum Associates, Inc.

Compton, B. J., & Logan, G. D. (1993). Evaluating a computational model of perceptual grouping by proximity. *Perception and Psychophysics*, *53*, 403–421.

Conway, A. R., Cowan, N., & Bunting, M. F. (2001). The cocktail party phenomenon revisited: The importance of working memory capacity. *Psychonomic Bulletin and Review*, *8*, 331–335.

Corbetta, M., Meizen, F. M., Shulman, G. L., & Petersen, S. E. (1993). A PET study of visual spatial attention. *Journal of Neuroscience*, *13*, 120020–120026.

Corteen, R. S., & Dunn, T. H. (1973). Shock associated words in a nonattended message: A test for momentary awareness. *Journal of Experimental Psychology*, *94*, 308–313.

Corteen, R. S., & Wood, B. (1972). Autonomous responses to shock associated words in an unattended channel. *Journal of Experimental Psychology*, *94*, 308–313.

Crick, F. (1984). Function of the thalamic reticular complex. *Proceedings of the National Academy of Science USA*, *81*, 4586–4590.

Crick, F., & Koch, C. (1990). Towards a neurobiological theory of consciousness. *Seminars in the Neurosciences*, *2*, 263–275.

Crick, F., & Koch, C. (1992). The problem of consciousness. *Scientific American*, *9*, 111–117.

Critchley, M. (1953). *The parietal lobes*. London: Hafner Press.

Dagenbach, D., Carr, T. H., & Wilhelmsen, A. (1989). Task induced strategies and near-threshold priming: Conscious influences on unconscious perception. *Journal of Memory and Language*, *28*, 412–443.

Dai, H., Scharf, B., & Buss, S. (1991). Effective attenuation of signals in noise under focused attention. *Journal of the Acoustical Society of America*, *89*, 2837–2842.

Damasio, A. R. (1990). Synchronous activation in multiple cortical regions: A mechanism for recall. *Seminars in the Neurosciences*, *2*, 287–296.

Darwin, C. J., Turvey, M. T., & Crowder, R. G. (1972). An auditory analogue of the Sperling partial report procedure: Evidence for brief auditory storage. *Cognitive Psychology*, *3*, 255–267.

Davies, M., & Humphreys, G. W. (1993). *Consciousness: Readings in mind and language*. Oxford: Blackwell.

DaVita, J., Obermayer, R., Nugent, W., & Linville, J. M. (2004). Verification of the change blindness phenomenon while managing critical events in a combat display. *Human Factors*, *46*, 205–218.

De Fockert, J. W., Rees, G., Frith, C. D., & Lavie, N. (2001). The role of working memory on selective attention. *Science, 291 (5509)*, 1803–1806.

De Gelder, B., & Bertleson, P. (2003). Multisensory integration, perception and ecological validity. *Trends in Cognitive Sciences, 7(10)*, 460–467.

De Haan, E. H. F., Young, A., & Newcombe, F. (1987a). Face recognition without awareness. *Cognitive Neuropsychology, 4*, 385–415.

De Haan, E. H. F., Young, A., & Newcombe, F. (1987b). Faces interfere with name classification in a prosopagnosic patient. *Cortex, 23*, 309–316.

De Haan, E. H. F., Young, A., & Newcombe, F. (1991). A dissociation between the sense of familiarity and access to semantic information concerning familiar people. *European Journal of Cognitive Psychology, 3*, 51–67.

De Jong, R. (1995). The role of preparation in overlapping-task performance. *Quarterly Journal of Experimental Psychology, 48A*, 2–25.

Debner, J. A., & Jacoby, L. L. (1994). Unconscious perception: Attention, awareness and control. *Journal of Experimental Psychology: Learning, Memory and Cognition, 20*, 304–317.

Desimone, R., & Duncan, J. (1995). Neural mechanisms of selective visual attention. *Annual Review of Neuroscience, 18*, 193–222.

Detweiler, M. C., & Landy, D. H. (1995). Effects of single- and dual-task practice in acquiring dual task skill. *Human Factors, 37*, 193–211.

Deutsch, D. (1975). Two-channel listening to musical scales. *Journal of the Acoustical Society of America, 57*, 1156–1160.

Deutsch, D. (1982). Grouping mechanisms in music. In D. Deutsch (Ed.). *The psychology of music*. New York: Academic Press.

Deutsch, J. A., & Deutsch, D. (1963). Attention, some theoretical considerations. *Psychological Review, 70*, 80–90.

Dick, A. O. (1969). Relations between the sensory register and short-term storage in tachistoscopic recognition. *Journal of Experimental Psychology, 82*, 279–284.

Dick, A. O. (1971). On the problem of selection in short-term visual (iconic) memory. *Canadian Journal of Psychology, 25*, 250–263.

Dick, A. O. (1974). Iconic memory and its relation to perceptual processing and other memory mechanisms. *Perception and Psychophysics, 16*, 575–596.

Dixon, N. F. (1971). *Subliminal perception: The nature of the controversy*. New York: McGraw-Hill.

Dixon, N. F. (1981). *Preconscious processing*. New York: John Wiley & Sons, Inc.

Downing, C. J., & Pinker, S. (1985). The spatial structure of visual attention. In M. I. Posner, & O. S. M. Marin (Eds.). *Attention and Performance, XI*. Hillsdale, NJ: Lawrence Erlbaum Associates, Inc.

Driver, J. (1996). Enhancement of selective listening by illusory mislocation of speech sounds due to lip reading. *Nature, 381*, 66–68.

Driver, J. (2001). A selective review of selective attention research from the past century. *British Journal of Psychology, 92*, 53–78.

Driver, J., & Baylis, G. C. (1989). Movement and visual attention: The spotlight metaphor breaks down. *Journal of Experimental Psychology: Human Perception and Performance, 15*, 448–456.

Driver, J., & Grossenbacher, P. G. (1996). Multimodal spatial constraints on tactile selective attention. In T. Inui, & J. McClelland (Eds.). *Information integration in perception and communication: Attention and performance XVI*. Cambridge, MA: MIT Press.

Driver, J., & Halligan, P. W. (1991). Can visual neglect operate in object centred co-ordinates? An affirmative case study. *Cognitive Neuropsychology, 8*, 475–496.

Driver, J., & McLeod, P. (1992). Reversing visual search asymmetries with conjunction search of movement and orientation. *Journal of Experimental Psychology: Human Perception and Performance, 18,* 22–33.

Driver, J., & Spence, C. J. (1994). Spatial synergies between auditory and visual attention. In C. Umilta, & M. Moscovitch (Eds.). *Attention and performance, XV: Conscious and nonconscious information processing.* Cambridge, MA: MIT Press.

Driver, J., & Spence, C. J. (1998). Cross-modal links in spatial attention. *Philosophical Transactions of the Royal Society of London, B, 353,* 1319–1331.

Driver, J., & Spence, C. (1999). Cross-modal links in spatial attention. In G. W. Humphreys, J. Duncan, & A. Treisman (Eds.). *Attention, space and action: Studies in cognitive neuroscience* (pp. 130–149). Oxford: Oxford University Press.

Driver, J., & Tipper, S. P. (1989). On the non-selectivity of selective seeing: Contrasts between interference and priming in selective attention. *Journal of Experimental Psychology: Human Perception and Performance, 15,* 304–314.

Driver, J., Davis, G., Ricciarelli, P., Kidd, P., Maxwell, E., & Baron-Cohen, S. (1999). Gaze perception triggers reflexive visuospatial orienting. *Visual Cognition, 6,* 509–540.

Driver, J., Eimer, M., Macaluso, E., & van Velzen, J. (2004). In N. Kanwisher, & J. Duncan (Eds.). *Functional neuroimaging of visual cognition: Attention and Performance, XX* (pp. 267–299). Oxford: Oxford University Press.

Duncan, J. (1980). The locus of interference in the perception of simultaneous stimuli. *Psychological Review, 37,* 272–300.

Duncan, J. (1984). Selective attention and the organisation of visual information. *Journal of Experimental Psychology: General, 113,* 501–517.

Duncan, J. (1986). Disorganisation of behaviour after frontal lobe damage. *Cognitive Neuropsychology, 3,* 271–290.

Duncan, J. (1993). Selection of input and goal in the control of behaviour. In A. D. Baddeley, & L. Weiskrantz (Eds.). *Attention: Awareness selection and control. A tribute to Donald Broadbent.* Oxford: Oxford University Press.

Duncan, J. (1999). Converging levels of analysis in the cognitive neuroscience of visual attention. In G. W. Humphreys, J. Duncan, & A. Treisman (Eds.). *Attention, space and action.* Oxford: Oxford University Press.

Duncan, J., & Humphreys, G. W. (1989). Visual search and visual similarity. *Psychological Review, 96,* 433–458.

Duncan, J., & Humphreys, G. W. (1992). Beyond the search surface: Visual search and attentional engagement. *Journal of Experimental Psychology: Human Perception and Performance, 18,* 578–588.

Eccleston, C. (1994). Chronic pain and attention: A cognitive approach. *Journal of Clinical Psychology, 33,* 535–547.

Eccleston, C. (1995). Chronic pain and attention: An experimental investigation into the role of sustained and shifting attention in the processing of pain. *Behavioural Research Therapy, 33,* 391–404.

Eccleston, C., & Crombez, G. (1999). Pain demand attention: A cognitive affective model of the interruptive function of pain. *Psychological Bulletin, 125,* 356–366.

Egeth, H. E., Jonides, J., & Wall, S. (1972). Parallel processing of multi-element displays. *Cognitive Psychology, 3,* 674–698.

Ellis, A. W., & Marshall, J. C. (1978). Semantic errors or statistical flukes? A note on Allport's "On knowing the meaning of words we are unable to report". *Quarterly Journal of Experimental Psychology, 30,* 569–575.

Ellis, A. W., & Young, A. W. (1988). *Human cognitive Neuropsychology.* Hove,

UK: Lawrence Erlbaum Associates Limited.

Ellis, A. W., Flude, B. M., & Young, A. W. (1987). Neglect dyslexia and the early visual processing of letters in words. *Cognitive Neuropsychology*, 4, 439–464.

Ellis, R., & Humphreys, G. W. (1999). *Connectionist psychology: A text with readings*. Hove, UK: Psychology Press.

Endsley, M. R. (1995). Toward a theory of situational awareness in dynamic systems. *Human Factors*, 37, 32–64.

Ericsson, K. A., & Kintsch, W. (1995). Long-term working memory. *Psychological Review*, 102, 211–245.

Ericsson, K. A., & Oliver, W. (1984, November). *Skilled memory in blindfold chess*. Paper presented at the annual meeting of the Psychonomic Society, San Antonio, TX.

Ericsson, K. A., & Staszewski, J. (1989). Skilled memory and expertise: Mechanisms of exceptional performance. In D. Klahr, & K. Kotovsky (Eds.). *Complex information processing: The impact of Herbert A.Simon* (pp. 235–267). Hillsdale, NJ: Lawrence Erlbaum Associates, Inc.

Eriksen, B. A., & Eriksen, C. W. (1974). Effects of noise letters upon the identification of a target in a non-search task. *Perception and Psychophysics*, 16, 143–149.

Eriksen, C. W. (1960). Discrimination and learning without awareness: A methodological survey and evaluation. *Psychological Review*, 67, 279–300.

Eriksen, C. W. (1995). The Flankers task and response competition: A useful tool for investigating a variety of cognitive problems. *Visual Cognition*, 2, 101–118.

Eriksen, C. W., & Collins, J. F. (1969). Visual perceptual rate under two conditions of search. *Journal of Experimental Psychology*, 80, 489–492.

Eriksen, C. W., & Murphy, T. D. (1987). Movement of attentional focus across the visual field: A critical look at the evidence. *Perception and Psychophysics*, 42, 299–305.

Eriksen, C. W., & Rohrbaugh, J. W. (1970). Some factors determining the efficiency of selective attention. *American Journal of Psychology*, 83, 330–343.

Eriksen, C. W., & Shultz, T. (1979). Information processing in visual search: A continuous flow conception and experimental results. *Perception and Psychophysics*, 25, 249–263.

Eriksen, C. W., & St. James, J. D. (1986). Visual attention within and around the field of focal attention: A zoom lens model. *Perception and Psychophysics*, 40, 225–240.

Eriksen, C. W., & Yeh, Y-Y. (1985). Allocation of attention in the visual field. *Journal of Experimental Psychology: Human Perception and Performance*, 11, 583–597.

Eriksen, C. W., Pan, K., & Botella, J. (1993). Attentional distribution in visual space. *Psychological Research*, 56, 5–13.

Esslinger, P. J., & Damasio, A. R. (1985). Severe disturbance of higher cognition after bilateral frontal ablation: Patient EVR. *Neurology*, 35, 1731–1741.

Estes, W. K. (1972). Interaction of signal and background variables in visual processing. *Perception and Psychophysics*, 12, 278–286.

Estes, W. K. (1974). Redundancy of noise elements and signals in visual detection of letters. *Perception and Psychophysics*, 19, 1–15.

Eysenck, M. W., & Keane, M. T. (2005). Cognitive psychology: A student's handbook (5th ed.). Hove, UK: Psychology Press.

Fagot, C., & Pashler, H. (1992). Making two responses to a single object: Implications for the central attentional bottleneck. *Journal of Experimental Psychology: Human Perception and Performance*, 18, 1058–1079.

Fagot, C., & Pashler, H. (1994). Repetition blindness: Perception of memory failure? *Journal of Experimental Psychology: Human Perception and Performance, 21*, 275–292.

Farah, M. (1990). *Visual agnosia: Disorders of object recognition and what they tell us about normal vision. A Bradford book.* Cambridge, MA: MIT Press.

Farah, M. (1994). Visual perception and visual awareness: A tutorial review. In C. Umilta, & M. Moscovitch (Eds.). *Attention and performance, XV: Conscious and nonconscious information processing.* Cambridge, MA: MIT Press.

Farah, M. J. (1988). Is visual imagery really visual? Overlooked evidence from neuropsychology. *Psychological Review, 95*, 307–317.

Fernandez, E., & Turk, D. C. (1989). The utility of cognitive coping strategies for altering pain perception: A meta-analysis. *Pain, 38*, 123–135.

Fodor, J. A. (1983). *Modularity of mind.* Cambridge, MA: MIT Press.

Folk, C. L., Remington, R. W., & Johnston, J. C. (1992). Involuntary covert orienting is contingent on attentional control settings. *Journal of Experimental Psychology: Human Perception and Performance, 18*, 100–1040.

Folk, C. L., Remington, R. W., & Wright, J. H. (1994). The structure of attentional control: Contingent attentional capture by apparent motion, abrupt onset and colour. *Journal of Experimental Psychology: Human Perception and Performance, 20*, 317–329.

Fowler, C. A., Wolford, G., Slade, R., & Tassinary, L. (1981). Lexical access with and without awareness. *Journal of Experimental Psychology: General, 110*, 341–362.

Fox, E. (1995). Pre-cuing target location reduces interference but not negative priming from visual distractors. *Quarterly Journal of Experimental Psychology, 48A*, 26–41.

Fox, L. A., Schor, R. E., & Steinman, R. J. (1971). Semantic gradients and interference in naming colour, spatial direction and numerosity. *Journal of Experimental Psychology, 91*, 59–65.

Francolini, C. M., & Egeth, H. E. (1980). On the nonautomaticity of "automatic" activation: Evidence of selective seeing. *Perception and Psychophysics, 27*, 331–342.

Friesen, C. K., & Kingstone, A. (1998). The eyes have it! Reflexive orienting is triggered by nonpredictive gaze. *Psychonomic Bulletin and Review, 5*, 490–495.

Gazzaniga, M. S. (1988). Brain modularity: Towards a philosophy of conscious experience. In A. J. Marcel, & E. Bisiach (Eds.). *Consciousness in contemporary science.* Oxford: Oxford University Press.

Gazzaniga, M. S. (Ed.). (2000). *Cognitive neuroscience: A reader.* Oxford: Blackwell.

Gentilucci, M., & Rizzolatti, G. (1990). Cortical motor control of arm and hand movements. In M. A. Goodale (Ed.). *Vision and action: The control of grasping.* Norwood, NJ: Ablex.

Gibson, J. J. (1950). *The perception of the visual world.* Boston: Houghton-Mifflin.

Gilbert, S. J., & Shallice, T. (2002). Task switching: A PDP model. *Cognitive Psychology, 44*, 297–337.

Gillie, T., & Broadbent, D. E. (1989). What makes interruptions disruptive? A study of length, similarity and complexity. *Psychological Research, 50*, 243–250.

Goldberg, M. E., & Wurtz, R. H. (1972). Activity of superior colliculus in behaving monkey. II. Effect of attention on neuronal responses. *Journal of Neurophysiology, 35*, 560–574.

Goodale, M. A., & Milner, A. D. (1992). Separate visual pathways for perception and action. *Trends in Neuroscience, 15*, 20–25.

Gopher, D. (1993). The skill of attentional control: Acquisition and execution of attentional strategies. In S. Kornblum, & D. E. Meyer (Eds.). *Attention and performance, XIV: Synergies in experimental psychology, artificial intelligence and cognitive neuroscience. A Bradford book.* Cambridge, MA: MIT Press.

Gopher, D., Armony, L., & Greenshpan, Y. (2000). Switching tasks and attentional policies. *Journal of Experimental Psychology: General, 129,* 308–339.

Graves, R. S. (1976). Are more letters identified than can be reported? *Journal of Experimental Psychology: Human Learning and Memory, 2,* 208–214.

Gray, C. M., & Singer, W. (1989). Stimulus specific neuronal oscillations in the cat visual cortex: A cortical functional unit. *Proceedings of the National Academy of Science, USA, 86,* 1698–1702.

Gray, J. A., & Wedderburn, A. A. (1960). Grouping strategies with simultaneous stimuli. *Quarterly Journal of Experimental Psychology, 12,* 180–184.

Greenberg, G., & Larkin, W. (1968). Frequency-response characteristics of auditory observers detecting signals of a single frequency in noise: The probe-signal method. *Journal of the Acoustical Society of America, 44,* 1513–1523.

Greenwald, A. G. (2004). On doing two things at once: IV. Necessary and sufficient conditions: Rejoinder to Lein, Proctor and Ruthruff (2003). *Journal of Experimental Psychology: Human Perception and Performance, 30,* 632–636.

Greenwald, A. G., & Shulman, H. G. (1973). On doing two things at once: II. Elimination of the psychological refractory period. *Journal of Experimental Psychology, 101,* 70–76.

Greenwald, A. G., Klinger, M. R., & Liu, T. J. (1989). Unconscious processing of dichotically masked words. *Journal of Experimental Psychology: General, 110,* 341–362.

Grossberg, S. (1980). How does the brain build a cognitive code? *Psychological Review, 87,* 1–51.

Haecen, H., & Albert, M. L. (1978). *Human neuropsychology.* New York: Wiley Interscience.

Hansen, J. C., & Hillyard, S. A. (1983). Effects of stimulation rate and attribute cueing on event related potentials during selective auditory attention. *Psychophysiology, 21,* 394–405.

Harlow, J. (1868). Recovery after severe injury to the head. *Publications of the Massachusetts Medical Society, 2,* 327–336.

Harris, J. E., & Morris, P. E. (Eds.). (1984). *Everyday memory, actions and absentmindedness.* New York: Academic Press.

Hasher, L., & Zacks, R. T. (1979). Automatic and effortful processes in memory. *Journal of Experimental Psychology: General, 108,* 356–388.

Hay, J. C., Pick, H. I., & Ikeda, K. (1965). Visual capture produced by prism spectacles. *Psychological Science, 2,* 215–216.

Hazeltine, E., Teague, D., & Ivry, R. B. (2002). Simultaneous dual-task performance reveals parallel response selection after practice. *Journal of Experimental Psychology: Human Perception and Performance, 28,* 527–545.

Hebb, D. O. (1949). *The organisation of behaviour.* New York: Wiley Interscience.

Hecaen, H., & Albert, M. L. (1978). *Human neuropsychology.* New York: John Wiley & Sons.

Heinke, D., & Humphreys, G. W. (1999). Modelling emergent attentional properties. In D. Heinke, G. W. Humphreys, & A. Olson (Eds.). *Connectionist models in cognitive neuroscience – the 5th neural computation and psychology workshop* (pp. 240–251). University of Birmingham, England: Springer Verlag.

Heinke, D., & Humphreys, G. W. (2003). Attention, spatial representation and visual neglect: Simulating emergent attention and spatial memory in the selective attention for identification model (SIAM). *Psychological Review, 110,* 29–87.

Hernandez-Peon, R., Scherrer, H., & Jouvet, M. (1956). Modification of selective activity in cochlear nucleus during "attention" in unanesthetized cats. *Science, 123,* 331–332.

Hick, W. E. (1952). On the rate of gain of information. *Quarterly Journal of Experimental Psychology, 4,* 11–26.

Hillyard, S. A. (2000). Electrical and magnetic brain recordings: Contributions to cognitive neuroscience. In M. S. Gazzaniga (Ed.). *Cognitive neuroscience: A reader.* Oxford: Blackwell.

Hinton, G., & Anderson, J. R. (1981). *Parallel models of associative memory.* Hillsdale, NJ: Lawrence Erlbaum Associates, Inc.

Hinton, G., & Shallice, T. (1991). Lesioning an attractor network: Investigations of acquired dyslexia. *Psychological Review, 98,* 74–95.

Hintzman, D. L., Carre, F. A., Eskridge, V. L., Owens, A. M., Shaff, S. S., & Sparks, M. E. (1972). "Stroop" effect. Input or output phenomenon. *Journal of Experimental Psychology, 95,* 458–459.

Hirst, W. (1986). The psychology of attention. In J. E. LeDoux, & W. Hirst (Eds.). *Mind and brain: Dialogues in cognitive neuroscience.* Cambridge: Cambridge University Press.

Hirst, W., Spelke, E. S., Reeves, C., Caharack, G., & Neisser, U. (1980). Dividing attention without alternation or automaticity. *Journal of Experimental Psychology: General, 109,* 98–117.

Hitch, G. J., & Baddeley, A. D. (1976). Verbal reasoning and working memory. *Quarterly Journal of Experimental Psychology, 28,* 603–631.

Hochhaus, L., & Moran, K. M. (1991). Factors in repetition blindness. *Journal of Experimental Psychology: Human Perception and Performance, 17,* 422–432.

Holding, D. H., Foulke, E., & Heise, R. L. (1973). Brief storage of compressed digits. *Journal of Experimental Psychology, 101,* 30–34.

Holender, D. (1986). Semantic activation without conscious identification in dichotic listening, parafoveal vision and visual masking: A survey and appraisal. *Behaviour and Brain Sciences, 9,* 1–66.

Hommel, B., Pratt, J., Colzato, L., & Godijn, R. (2001). Symbolic control of visual attention. *Psychological Science, 12,* 360–365.

Humphreys, G. W. (1981). Flexibility of attention between stimulus dimensions. *Perception and Psychophysics, 30,* 291–302.

Humphreys, G. W., & Bruce, V. (1989). *Visual cognition: Computational, experimental and neuropsychological perspectives.* Hove, UK: Lawrence Erlbaum Associates Limited.

Humphreys, G. W., & Heinke, D. (1998). Spatial representation and selection in the brain: Neuropsychological and computational constraints. *Visual Cognition, 5,* 9–47.

Humphreys, G. W., & Muller, H. J. (1993). Search via recursive rejection (SERR): A connectionist model of visual search. *Cognitive Psychology, 25,* 43–110.

Humphreys, G. W., Romani, C., Olson, A., Riddoch, M. J., & Duncan, J. (1994). Non-spatial extinction following lesions of the parietal lobe in humans. *Nature, 372,* 357–359.

Igarashi, M., Alford, D. R., Gordon, W. P., & Nakai, V. (1974). Behavioural auditory function after transection of crossed olivo-cochlear bundle in the cat: II. Conditioned visual performance with intense white noise. *Acta Otalaryngol* (Stockholm), *77,* 311–317.

James, W. (1890). *The principles of psychology.* New York: Holt.

Jeannerod, M. (1984). The timing of natural prehension movements. *Journal of Motor Behaviour, 16,* 235–254.

Jeannerod, M. (1997). *The cognitive neuroscience of action.* Oxford: Blackwell.

Jersild, A. T. (1927). Mental set and shift. *Archives of Psychology, 9* (all).

Johnson, J. C., & McClelland, J. (1976). Experimental tests of a hierarchical model of word recognition. *Journal of Verbal Learning and Verbal Behaviour, 19,* 503–524.

Johnson-Laird, P. N. (1983). A computational analysis of consciousness. *Cognition and Brain Theory, 6,* 499–508.

Johnson-Laird, P. N. (1988). A computational analysis of consciousness. In A. J. Marcel, & E. Bisiach (Eds.). *Consciousness in contemporary science.* Oxford: Oxford University Press.

Johnston, W. A., & Dark, V. J. (1986). Selective attention. *Annual Review of Psychology, 37,* 43–75.

Johnston, W. A., & Heinz, S. P. (1979). Depth of non-target processing in an attention task. *Journal of Experimental Psychology, 5,* 168–175.

Jolicoeur, P. (1998). Modulation of the attentional blink by on-line response selection: Evidence from speeded and unspeeded Task-sub-1 decisions. *Memory and Cognition, 26,* 1014–1032.

Jolicoeur, P., & Dell'Acqua, R. (1998). The demonstration of short-term consolidation. *Cognitive Psychology, 36,* 138–202.

Jonides, J. (1981). Voluntary versus automatic control over the mind's eye. In J. Long, & A. Baddeley (Eds.). *Attention and performance, IX* (pp. 187–203). Hillsdale, NJ: Lawrence Erlbaum Associates, Inc.

Jonides, J., & Gleitman, H. (1972). A conceptual category effect in visual search: O as a letter or a digit. *Perception and Psychophysics, 12,* 457–460.

Jordan, M. J., & Rosenbaum, D. A. (1989). Action. In M. I. Posner (Ed.). *Foundations of cognitive science.* Cambridge, MA: MIT Press.

Kahneman, D. (1973). *Attention and effort.* Englewood Cliffs, NJ: Prentice Hall.

Kahneman, D., & Chajczyk, D. (1983). Tests of the automaticity of reading: Dilution of Stroop effects by colour-irrelevant stimuli. *Journal of Experimental Psychology: Human Perception and Performance, 9,* 497–509.

Kahneman, D., & Henik, A. (1981). Perceptual organisation and attention. In M. Kubovy, & J. R. Pomerantz (Eds.). *Perceptual organisation.* Hillsdale, NJ: Lawrence Erlbaum Associates, Inc.

Kahneman, D., & Treisman, A. M. (1984). Changing views of attention and automaticity. In R. Parasuraman, & D. R. Davies (Eds.). *Varieties of attention.* Orlando, FL: Academic Press.

Kanwisher, N. (1987). Repetition blindness: Type recognition without token individuation. *Cognition, 27,* 117–143.

Kanwisher, N. (1991). Repetition blindness and illusory conjunctions. *Journal of Experimental Psychology: Human Perception and Performance, 17,* 404–421.

Kanwisher, N., Driver, J., & Machado, L. (1995). Spatial repetition blindness is modulated by selective attention to colour or shape. *Cognitive Psychology, 29,* 303–337.

Katus, M., & Dale, A. (1997). Electrical and magnetic readings of mental functions. In M. D. Rugg (Ed.). *Cognitive neuroscience.* Hove, UK: Psychology Press.

Kelley, C. M., & Jacoby, L. L. (1990). The construction of subjective experience: Memory attributions. *Mind and Language, 5,* 49–61.

Kemp-Wheeler, S., & Hill, A. B. (1988). Semantic priming without awareness:

Some methodological considerations and replications. *Quarterly Journal of Experimental Psychology, 40A*, 671–692.

Kidd, G. Jr., Mason, C. R., Rohtla, T. L., & Deliwala, P. S. (1995). Release from masking due to spatial separation of sources in the identification of non-speech patterns. *Journal of the Acoustical Society of America, 104*, 422–431.

Kinsbourne, M., & Warrington, E. K. (1962). A variety of reading disability associated with right hemisphere lesions. *Journal of Neurology, Neurosurgery and Psychiatry, 25*, 339–344.

Klein, R. M. (1988). Inhibitory tagging system facilitates visual search. *Nature, 334*, 430–431.

Knowles, W. B. (1963). Operator loading tasks. *Human Factors, 5*, 151–161.

Koechlin, E., Ody, C., & Kouneiher, F. (2003). The architecture of cognitive control in the human prefrontal cortex. *Science, 302(5648)*, 1181–1185.

Kramer, A. F., Tham, M. P., & Yeh, Y-Y. (1991). Movement and spatial attention: A failure to replicate. *Perception and Psychophysics, 17*, 371–379.

Laberge, D. (1983). Spatial extent of attention to letters and words. *Journal of Experimental Psychology: Human Perception and Performance, 9*, 371–379.

Laberge, D. (2000). Networks of attention. In M. S. Gazzaniga (Ed.). *The new cognitive neurosciences* (pp. 711–724). Cambridge, MA: MIT Press.

Laberge, D., & Buchsbaum, J. L. (1990). Positron emission tomography measurements of pulvinar activity during an attention task. *Journal of Neuroscience, 10*, 613–619.

Laberge, D., Brown, V., Carter, M., Bash, D., & Hartley, A. (1991). Reducing the effect of adjacent distractors by narrowing attention. *Journal of Experimental Psychology: Human Perception and Performance, 17*, 65–76.

Lackner, J. R., & Garrett, M. F. (1972). Resolving ambiguity: Effect of biasing context in the unattended ear. *Cognition, 1*, 359–372.

Lambert, A. J., & Voot, N. (1993). A left visual field bias for semantic encoding of unattended words. *Neuropsychologia, 31*, 67–73.

Lambert, A. J., Beard, C. T., & Thompson, R. J. (1988). Selective attention, visual laterality, awareness and perceiving the meaning of parafoveally presented words. *Quarterly Journal of Experimental Psychology, 40A*, 615–652.

Langton, S. R. H., & Bruce, V. (1999). Reflexive visual orienting in response to the social attention of others. *Visual Cognition, 6*, 541–567.

Langton, S. R. H., & Bruce, V. (2000). You must see the point: Automatic processing of cues to the direction of social attention. *Journal of Experimental Psychology: Human Perception and Performance, 26*, 747–757.

Lavie, N. (1995). Perceptual load as a necessary condition for selective attention. *Journal of Experimental Psychology: Human Perception and Performance, 21*, 451–468.

Lavie, N., & Tsal, Y. (1994). Perceptual load as a major determinant of the locus of selection in visual attention. *Perception and Psychophysics, 56*, 183–197.

Lavie, N., Hirst, A., de Fockert, J. W., & Viding, E. (2004). Load theory of selective attention and cognitive control. *Journal of Experimental Psychology: General, 133*, 339–354.

Law, M. B., Pratt, J., & Abrahams, R. A. (1995). Colour-based inhibition of return. *Perception and Psychophysics, 57*, 402–408.

Lederman, S. J., Thorne, G., & Jones, B. (1986). Perception of texture by vision and touch. Multidimensionality and intersensory integration. *Journal of Experimental Psychology: Human Perception and Performance, 12*, 169–180.

Lewis, J. L. (1970). Semantic processing of unattended messages using dichotic listening. *Journal of Experimental Psychology, 85*, 225–228.

Lhermitte, F. (1983). Utilisation behaviour and its relation to lesions in the frontal lobes. *Brain, 106*, 237–255.

Libet, B. (1985). Unconscious cerebral initiative and the role of conscious will in voluntary action. *Behaviour and Brain Sciences, 8*, 529–566.

Lien, M-C., Proctor, R. W., & Allen, P. A. (2002). Ideomotor compatibility in the psychological refractory period effect: 29 years of oversimplification. *Journal of Experimental Psychology: Human Perception and Performance, 28*, 396–409.

Livingstone, F., & Hubel, D. H. (1987). Psychophysical evidence for separate channels for the perception of form, colour, movement and depth. *Journal of Neuroscience, 7*, 3416–3468.

Livingstone, M. S., & Hubel, D. H. (1988). Segregation of colour, form, movement and depth: Anatomy, physiology and perception. *Science, 240*, 740–749.

Logan, G., & Gordon, R. (2001). Executive control of visual attention in dual-task situations. *Psychological Review, 108*, 393–434.

Logan, G. D. (1996). The CODE theory of visual attention: An integration of space-based and object-based attention. *Psychological Review, 103*, 603–649.

Luna, D., Marcos-Ruiz, R., & Merino, J. M. (1995). Selective attention to global and local information: Effects of visual angle, exposure duration and eccentricity on processing dominance. *Visual Cognition, 2*, 183–200.

Luria, A. R. (1966). *Higher cortical functions in man*. London: Tavistock.

Luria, R., & Meiran, N. (2003). Online order control in the psychological refractory period paradigm. *Journal of Experimental Psychology, 29*, 556–574.

Macaluso, E., Eimer, M., Frith, C. D., & Driver, J. (2003). Preparatory states in cross-modal spatial attention: spatial specificity and possible control mechanisms. *Experimental Brain Research, 149*, 62–74.

McClelland, J. L., & Rumelhart, D. E. (1981). An interactive activation model of context effects in letter perception: Part 1. An account of basic findings. *Psychological Review, 85*, 375–407.

McClelland, J. L., & Rumelhart, D. E. (Eds.). (1986). *Parallel distributed processing: Explorations in the microstructure of cognition. Volume 2: Psychological and biological models. A Bradford book.* Cambridge, MA: MIT Press.

McClelland, J. L., Rumelhart, D. E., & Hinton, G. E. (1986). The appeal of parallel distributed processing. In D. E. Rumelhart, & J. L. McClelland. *Parallel distributed processing: Explorations in the microstructure of cognition* (Vol. 1, pp. 2–44). Cambridge, MA: MIT Press.

McGurk, H., & MacDonald, J. (1976). Hearing lips and seeing voices. *Nature, 264*, 746.

Mack, A., & Rock, I. (1998). *Inattentional blindness*. Cambridge, MA: MIT Press.

McKay, D. G. (1973). Aspects of the theory of comprehension, memory and attention. *Quarterly Journal of Experimental Psychology, 25*, 22–40.

MacKen, J. M., Tremblay, S., Houghton, R. J., Nicholls, A. P., & Jones, A. M. (2003). Does auditory streaming require attention? Evidence from attentional selectivity in short-term memory. *Journal of Experimental Psychology: Human Perception and Performance, 29*, 43–51.

MacLeod, C. M. (1991). Half a century of research on the Stroop effect: An integrative review. *Psychological Bulletin, 109*, 163–203.

MacLeod, C. M., & Dunbar, K. (1988). Training and Stroop-like interference: Evidence for a continuum of automaticity. *Journal of Experimental*

Psychology: Learning Memory and Cognition, 14, 137–154.

McLeod, P., & Driver, J. (1993). Filtering and physiology in visual search: A convergence of behavioural and neurophysiological measures. In A. D. Baddeley, & L. Weiskrantz (Eds.). *Attention: Awareness selection and control. A tribute to Donald Broadbent.* Oxford: Oxford University Press.

McLeod, P., & Posner, M. I. (1984). Privileged loops from percept to act. In H. Bouma, & D. G. Bouwhuis (Eds.). *Attention and performance, X: Control of language processes.* Hillsdale, NJ: Lawrence Erlbaum Associates, Inc.

McLeod, P. D. (1977). A dual task response modality effect: Support for multi-processor models of attention. *Quarterly Journal of Experimental Psychology, 29,* 651–667.

McLeod, P. D. (1978). Does probe RT measure central processing demand? *Quarterly Journal of Experimental Psychology, 30,* 83–89.

MacMillan, N. A., & Schwartz, M. (1975). A probe-signal investigation of uncertain frequency detection. *Journal of the Acoustical Society of America, 58,* 1051–1058.

McNevin, N. H., Shea, C. H., & Wulf, G. (2003). Increasing distance of an external focus of attention enhances learning. *Psychological Research, 67,* 22–29.

Maddox, D., Wulf, G., & Wright, D. L. (2000). *The effects of an internal versus external focus of attention on the learning of a tennis backhand.* Unpublished manuscript, Texas A&M University, USA. Cited in Wulf, G., McNevin, N., & Shea, C. H. (2001). The automaticity of complex motor skill learning as a function of attentional focus. *Quarterly Journal of Experimental Psychology, 54,* 1143–1154.

Marcel, A. J. (1980). Conscious and preconscious recognition of polysemous words: Locating the selective effects of prior verbal context. In R. S. Nickerson (Ed.). *Attention and performance, VII.* Hillsdale, NJ: Lawrence Erlbaum, Associates, Inc.

Marcel, A. J. (1983). Conscious and unconscious perception: An approach to the relations between phenomenal experience and perceptual processes. *Cognitive Psychology, 15,* 238–300.

Marcel, A. J. (1988). Phenomenal experience and functionalism. In A. J. Marcel, & E. Bisiach (Eds.). *Consciousness and contemporary science.* Oxford: Oxford University Press.

Marcel, A. J., & Bisiach, E. (1988). (Eds.). *Consciousness in contemporary science.* Oxford: Oxford University Press.

Marr, D. (1976). Early processing of visual information. *Philosophical Transactions of the Royal Society of London, B, 207,* 187–217.

Marr, D. (1982). *Vision.* San Francisco: Freeman.

Martin, M. (1979). Local and global processing: The role of sparsity. *Memory and Cognition, 7,* 479–484.

Maruff, P., Danckert, J., Camplin, G., & Currie, J. (1999). Behavioural goals constrain selection of visual information. *Psychological Science, 10,* 522–525.

Marzi, C. A., Tassarini, C., Aglioti, S., & Lutzemberger, L. (1986). Spatial summation across the vertical meridian in hemianopics: A test of blindsight. *Neuropsychologia, 24,* 749–758.

Mattingley, J. B., Driver, J., Beschin, N., & Robertson, I. H. (1997). Attentional competition between the modalities: Extinction between touch and vision after right hemisphere damage. *Neuropsychologia, 35,* 867–880.

Maylor, E. (1985). Facilitatory and inhibitory components of orienting in visual space. In M. I. Posner, & O. S. M. Marin (Eds.). *Attention and Performance,*

XI. Hillsdale, NJ: Lawrence Erlbaum Associates, Inc.

Meiran, N. (1996). Reconfiguration of processing mode prior to task performance. *Journal of Experimental Psychology: Learning Memory and Cognition, 22*, 1423–1442.

Merikle, P. M. (1980). Selection from visual persistence by perceptual groups and category membership. *Journal of Experimental Psychology: General, 109*, 279–295.

Merikle, P. M. (1982). Unconscious perception revisited. *Perception and Psychophysics, 31*, 298–301.

Merikle, P. M., & Daneman, M. (2000). Conscious vs. unconscious perception. In M. S. Gazzaniga (Ed.). *The new cognitive neurosciences* (pp. 1295–1303). Cambridge, MA: MIT Press.

Merikle, P. M., & Reingold, E. M. (1990). Recognition and lexical decision without detection: Unconscious perception? *Journal of Experimental Psychology: Human Perception and Performance, 16*, 574–583.

Merikle, P. M., Smilek, D., & Eastwood, J. D. (2001). Perception without awareness: Perspectives from cognitive psychology. *Cognition, 79*, 115–134.

Mewhort, D. J. K. (1967). Familiarity of letter sequences, response uncertainty and the tachistoscopic recognition experiment. *Canadian Journal of Psychology, 21*, 309–321.

Mewhort, D. J. K., Campbell, A. J., Marchetti, F. M., & Campbell, J. I. D. (1981). Identification, localisation and "iconic memory": An evaluation of the bar-probe task. *Memory and Cognition, 9*, 50–67.

Meyer, D., & Kieras, D. (1997a). A computational theory of executive cognitive processes and multiple-task performance: Part 1. Basic mechanisms. *Psychological Review, 104*, 3–65.

Meyer, D., & Kieras, D. (1997b). A computational theory of executive cognitive processes and multiple-task performance: Part 2. Accounts of a psychological refractory-period phenomena. *Psychological Review, 104*, 749–791.

Meyer, D., & Kieras, D. (1999). Precis to a practical unified theory of cognition and action: Some lessons from EPIC computational models of human multiple-task performance. In D. Gopher, & A. Koriat (Eds.). *Attention and Performance, XVII: Cognitive regulation of performance. Interaction of theory and application* (pp. 17–88). Cambridge, MA: MIT Press.

Meyer, D. E., & Schavaneveldt, R. W. (1971). Facilitation in recognising pairs of words: Evidence of a dependence between retrieval operations. *Journal of Experimental Psychology, 90*, 227–234.

Miller, J. (1991). The flanker compatibility effect as a function of visual angle attentional focus, visual transients and perceptual load: A search for boundary conditions. *Perception and Psychophysics, 49*, 270–288.

Milner, A. D., & Goodale, M. A. (1995). *The visual brain in action*. New York: Oxford University Press.

Milner, B. (1963). Effects of different brain lesions on card sorting. *Archives of Neurology, 9*, 90–100.

Milner, B. (1966). Amnesia following operation on the temporal lobes. In C. W. M. Whitty, & O. L. Zangwill (Eds.). *Amnesia*. London: Butterworth.

Mondor, T. A., & Zatorre, R. J. (1995). Shifting and focusing auditory spatial attention. *Journal of Experimental Psychology: Human Perception and Performance, 21*, 387–409.

Monsell, S. (1996). Control of mental processes. In V. Bruce (Ed.). *Unsolved mysteries of the mind: Tutorial essays in cognition*. Hove, UK: Lawrence Erlbaum Associates, Inc.

Monsell, S., Yeung, N. P., & Azuma, R. (2000). Reconfiguration of task-set: Is it easier to switch to an easier task? *Psychological Research, 63*, 250–264.

Moore, B. C. J. (1995). *Hearing*. San Diego, CA: Academic Press.

Moray, N. (1959). Attention in dichotic listening: Affective cues and the influence of instructions. *Quarterly Journal of Experimental Psychology, 11*, 56–60.

Moray, N. (1967). Where is capacity limited? A survey and a model. *Acta Psychologia, 27*, 84–92.

Morein-Zamir, S., Soto-Faraco, S., & Kingstone, A. (2003). Auditory capture of vision: Examining temporal ventriloquism. *Cognitive Brain Research, 17*, 154–163.

Morton, J. (1969). Interaction of information in word recognition. *Psychological Review, 76*, 165–178.

Morton, J. (1979). Facilitation in word recognition: Experiments causing change in the logogen model. In P. A. Kohlers, M. Wrolstead, & H. Bouma (Eds.). *Processing of visible language* (Vol. 1). New York: Plenum Press.

Mountcastle, V. B., Lynch, J. C., Georgopoulos, A., Sakata, H., & Acuna, C. (1975). Posterior parietal association cortex of the monkey: Command functions for operations within extrapersonal space. *Journal of Neurophysiology, 38*, 871–908.

Mozer, M. C. (1987). Early parallel processing in reading: A connectionist approach. In M. Coltheart (Ed.). *Attention and Performance, XII: The psychology of reading*. Hillsdale, NJ: Lawrence Erlbaum, Associates, Inc.

Mozer, M. C. (1988). *A connectionist model of selective attention in visual attention* (Tech. Rep. CRG-TR-88-4). Toronto: University of Toronto, Department of Computer Science.

Mozer, M. C., & Sitton, M. (1998). Computational modelling of spatial attention. In H. Pashler (Ed.). *Attention* (pp. 341–393). Hove, UK: Psychology Press.

Muller, H. J., & Found, A. (1996). Visual search for conjunctions of motion and form: Display density and asymmetry reversal. *Journal of Experimental Psychology: Human Perception and Performance, 22*, 122–132.

Muller, H. J., & Maxwell, J. (1994). Perceptual integration of motion and form information: Is the movement filter involved in form discrimination? *Journal of Experimental Psychology: Human Perception and Performance, 20*, 397–420.

Muller, H. J., & Rabbitt, P. M. A. (1989). Reflexive orienting of visual attention: Time course of activation and resistance to interruption. *Journal of Experimental Psychology: Human Perception and Performance, 15*, 315–330.

Murray, D. J., Mastroddi, J., & Duncan, S. (1972). Selective attention to "physical" versus "verbal" aspects of coloured words. *Psychonomic Science, 26*, 305–307.

Navon, D. (1977). Forest before trees: The precedence of global features in visual perception. *Cognitive Psychology, 9*, 353–383.

Navon, D., & Gopher, D. (1979). On the economy of the human processing system. *Psychological Review, 86*, 214–255.

Navon, D., & Miller, J. (2002). Queuing or sharing? A critical evaluation of the single bottleneck notion. *Cognitive Psychology, 44*, 193–251.

Neisser, U. (1967). *Cognitive psychology*. New York: Appleton Century Crofts.

Neisser, U. (1976). *Cognition and reality*. New York: W.H. Freeman.

Neuman, O. (1984). Automatic processing: A review of recent findings and a plea for an old theory. In W. Printz, & A. Sanders (Eds.). *Cognition and motor processes*. Berlin: Springer.

Neuman, O. (1987). Beyond capacity: A functional view of attention. In H. Heuer, & A. F. Sanders (Eds.). *Perspectives on selection and action*. Hillsdale, NJ: Lawrence Erlbaum Associates, Inc.

Norman, D. A. (1968). Towards a theory of memory and attention. *Psychological Review, 75*, 522–536.

Norman, D. A. (1981). Categorization of action slips. *Psychological Review, 88*, 1–15.

Norman, D. A. (1986). Reflections on cognition and parallel distributed processing. In A. M. Aitkenhead, & J. M. Slack (Eds.). *Issues in cognitive modelling*. London: Laurence Erlbaum Associates Limited.

Norman, D. A., & Bobrow, D. G. (1975). On data-limited and resource-limited processes. *Cognitive Psychology, 7*, 44–64.

Norman, D. A., & Shallice, T. (1986). Attention to action: Willed and automatic control of behaviour. In R. Davison, G. Shwartz and D. Shapiro (Eds.). *Consciousness and self-regulation: Advances in research and theory*. New York: Plenum.

Nosofsky, R., & Palmeri, T. (1997). An exemplar bases random walk model of speeded classification. *Psychological Review, 104*, 266–300.

Olshausen, B., Anderson, C. H., & Van Essen, D. C. (1993). A neurobiological model of visual attention and invariant pattern recognition based on dynamic routing of information. *Journal of Neuroscience, 13*, 4700–4719.

Pardo, J. V., Pardo, P. J., Janer, K. W., & Raichle, M. E. (1990). The anterior cingulate cortex mediates processing selection in the Stroop attentional conflict paradigm. *Proceedings of the National Academy of Science of the USA, 87*, 256–259.

Parkin, A. J. (1996). *Explorations in cognitive neuropsychology*. Oxford: Blackwell.

Parkin, A. J. (1997). *Memory and amnesia*. Oxford: Blackwell.

Parkin, A. J., & Barry, C. (1991). Alien hand sign and other cognitive deficits following ruptured aneurysm of the anterior communicating artery. *Behavioural Neurology, 4*, 167–179.

Pashler, H. (1984). Processing stages in overlapping tasks. Evidence for a central bottleneck. *Journal of Experimental Psychology: Human Perception and Performance, 10*, 358–377.

Pashler, H. (1990). Do response modality effects support multi-processor models of divided attention? *Journal of Experimental Psychology: Human Perception and Performance, 16*, 826–842.

Pashler, H. (1993). Dual-task interference and elementary mental mechanisms. In D. E. Meyer, & S. M. Kornblum (Eds.). *Attention and performance, XIV: Synergies in experimental psychology, artificial intelligence and cognitive neuroscience. A Bradford book*. Cambridge, MA: MIT Press.

Pashler, H. (1994). Dual task interference in simple tasks: Data and theory. *Psychological Bulletin, 16*, 220–224.

Pashler, H., & Johnston, J. (1989). Chronometric evidence for central postponement in temporally overlapping tasks. *Quarterly Journal of Experimental Psychology, 41A*, 19–45.

Pashler, H. E. (1997). *The psychology of attention. A Bradford book*. Cambridge, MA, MIT Press.

Passingham, R. E. (1993). *The frontal lobes and voluntary action*. Oxford: Oxford University Press.

Patterson, K. E., & Wilson, B. (1990). A ROSE is a ROSE or a NOSE: A deficit in initial letter recognition. *Cognitive Neuropsychology, 7*, 447–477.

Peck, A. C., & Detweiler, M. C. (2000). Training in multi-step tasks. *Human Factors, 42*, 379–389.

Perenin, M. T., & Vighetto, A. (1988). Optic ataxia. A specific disorder in visuo-motor coordination. In A. Hein, & M. Jeannerod (Eds.). *Spatially oriented behaviour*. New York: Springer.

Perret, E. (1974). The left frontal lobe of man and the suppression of habitual responses in verbal categorical behaviour. *Neuropsychologia, 12,* 323–330.

Petersen, S. E., Robinson, D. L., & Morris, J. D. (1987). Contributions of the pulvinar to visual spatial attention. *Neuropsychologia, 25,* 97–105.

Petersen, S. E., Fox, P. T., Miezen, F. M., & Raichle, M. E. (1988). Modulation of cortical visual responses by direction of spatial attention measured by PET. *Association for Research in Vision and Ophthalmology.* p. 22 (abstr.).

Phaf, R. H., van der Heijden, A. H. C., & Hudson, P. T. W. (1990). SLAM: A connectionist model for attention in visual selection tasks. *Cognitive Psychology, 22,* 273–341.

Phaf, R. H., Mul, N. M., & Wolters, G. (1994). A connectionist view on dissociations. In C. Umilta, & M. Moscovitch (Eds.). *Attention and performance, XV: Conscious and nonconscious information processing. A Bradford book.* Cambridge, MA: MIT Press.

Poppel, E., Held, R., & Frost, D. (1973). Residual visual function after brain wounds involving the central visual pathways in man. *Nature, 243,* 2295–2296.

Posner, M. I. (1978). *Chronometric explorations of mind.* Hillsdale, NJ: Lawrence Erlbaum Associates, Inc.

Posner, M. I. (1980). Orienting of attention. *Quarterly Journal of Experimental Psychology, 32,* 3–25.

Posner, M. I. (1993). Attention before and during the decade of the brain. In D. E. Meyer, & S. M. Kornblum (Eds.). *Attention and Performance, XIV: Synergies in experimental psychology, artificial intelligence and cognitive neuroscience. A Bradford book.* Cambridge, MA: MIT Press.

Posner, M. I. (Ed.). (2004a). *Cognitive neuroscience of attention.* New York, Guilford Press.

Posner, M. I. (2004b). The achievement of brain imaging: Past and future. In N. Kanwisher, & J. Duncan (Eds.). *Functional neuroimaging of visual cognition: Attention and performance, XX.* Oxford: Oxford University Press.

Posner, M. I., & Badgaiyan, R. D. (1998). Attention and neural networks. In R. W. Parks, D. S. Levine, & R. D. Badgaiyan. *Fundamentals of neural network modelling* (pp. 61076). Cambridge, MA: MIT Press.

Posner, M. I., & Boies, S. J. (1971). Components of attention. *Psychological Review, 78,* 391–408.

Posner, M. I., & Cohen, Y. (1984). Components of visual orienting. In H. Bouma, & D. G. Bouwhuis (Eds.). *Attention and Performance, X* (pp. 531–556). Hillsdale, NJ: Lawrence Erlbaum Associates Inc.

Posner, M. I., & Dehaene, S. (2000). Attentional networks. In M. S. Gazzaniga (Ed.). *Cognitive neuroscience: A reader.* Malden, MA: Blackwell.

Posner, M. I., & Petersen, S. E. (1990). The attentional system of the human brain. *Annual Review of Neuroscience, 13,* 25–42.

Posner, M. I., & Snyder, C. R. R. (1975). Attention and cognitive control. In R. L. Solso (Ed.). *Information processing and cognition: The Loyola Symposium.* Hillsdale, NJ: Lawrence Erlbaum Associates, Inc.

Posner, M. I., Snyder, C. R. R., & Davidson, B. J. (1980). Attention and the detection of signals. *Journal of Experimental Psychology: General, 109,* 160–174.

Posner, M. I., Walker, J. A., Friedrick, F. J., & Rafal, R. D. (1984). Effects of parietal injury on covert orienting of visual attention. *Journal of Neuroscience, 4,* 1863–1874.

Poulton, E. C. (1953). Two-channel listening. *Journal of Experimental Psychology, 46,* 91–96.

Poulton, E. C. (1956). Listening to overlapping calls. *Journal of Experimental Psychology, 52,* 334–339.

Pratt, R. A., & Abrahams, J. (1995). Inhibition of return to successively cue spatial locations. *Journal of Experimental Psychology: Human Perception and Performance, 21,* 1343–1353.

Pratt, R. A., & Abrahams, J. (1996). Spatially diffuse inhibition affects multiple locations: A reply to Tipper, Weaver and Watson (1996). *Journal of Experimental Psychology: Human Perception and Performance, 22,* 1294–1298.

Pratt, R. A., & Hommel, B. (2003). Symbolic control of visual attention: The role of working memory and attentional control settings. *Journal of Experimental Psychology: Human Perception and Performance, 29,* 835–845.

Printzmetal, W. (1981). Principles of feature integration in visual perception. *Perception and Psychophysics, 30,* 330–340.

Purcell, D. G., Stewart, A. L., & Stanovitch, K. K. (1983). Another look at semantic priming without awareness. *Perception and Psychophysics, 34,* 65–71.

Quinlan, P. (2003). Visual feature integration theory: Past present and future. *Psychological Bulletin, 129,* 643–673.

Quinlan, P. T., & Bailey, P. J. (1995). An examination of attentional control in the auditory modality: Further evidence for auditory orienting. *Perception and Psychophysics, 57,* 614–628.

Rafal, R., & Posner, M. I. (1987). Deficits in human spatial attention following thalamic lesions. *Proceedings of the National Academy of Science, 84,* 7349–7353.

Ramachandran, V. S. (1988). Perceiving shape from shading. *Scientific American, 259,* 76–83.

Raymond, J. E., Shapiro, K. L., & Arnell, K. M. (1992). Temporary suppression of visual processing in an RSVP task: An attentional blink? *Journal of Experimental Psychology: Human Perception and Performance, 18,* 849–860.

Raymond, J. E., Shapiro, K. L., & Arnell, K. M. (1995). Similarity determines the attentional blink. *Journal of Experimental Psychology: Human Perception and Performance, 21,* 653–662.

Reason, J. (1979). Actions not as planned: The price of automatization. In G. Underwood, & R. Stephens (Eds.). *Aspects of consciousness* (Vol. 1). London: Academic Press.

Rees, G., Russell, C., Frith, C. D., & Driver, J. (1999). Inattentional blindness versus inattentional amnesia for fixated but ignored words. *Science, 286,* 2504–2507.

Remington, R. W., & Folk, C. L. (2001). A dissociation between attention and selection. *Psychological Science, 12,* 511–515.

Rensink, R. A. (2000). Seeing, sensing and scrutinising. *Vision Research, 40,* 1469–1487.

Rensink, R. A. (2002). Change detection. *Annual Review of Psychology, 53,* 245–477.

Revelle, W. (1993). Individual differences in personality and motivation: "Non-cognitive" determinants of cognitive performance. In A. D. Baddeley, & L. Weiskrantz (Eds.). *Attention: Awareness selection and control. A tribute to Donald Broadbent.* Oxford: Oxford University Press.

Rhodes, G. (1987). Auditory attention and the representation of spatial information. *Perception and Psychophysics, 42,* 1–14.

Richards, G. (1996). *Putting psychology in its place.* London: Routledge.

Rizzolatti, G., & Carmada, R. (1987). Neural circuits for spatial attention and unilateral neglect. In M. Jeannerod (Ed.). *Neurophysiological and neuropsychological aspects of spatial neglect*. Amsterdam: North Holland.

Rizzolatti, G., & Gallese, V. (1988). Mechanisms and theories of spatial neglect. In F. Boller and J. Grafman (Eds.). *Handbook of neuropsychology* (Vol. 1). Amsterdam: Elsevier.

Rizzolatti, G., Matelli, M. (2003). Two different streams from the dorsal visual system: Anatomy and functions. *Experimental Brain Research, 153*, 146–157.

Rizzolatti, G., Gentilucci, M., & Matteli, M. (1985). Selective spatial attention: One centre, one circuit or many circuits. In M. I. Posner and O. Marin (Eds.). *Attention and performance, XI*. Hillsdale, NJ: Lawrence Erlbaum Associates Inc.

Rizzolatti, G., Riggio, L., & Sheliga, B. M. (1994). Space and selective attention. In C. Umilta, & M. Moscovitch (Eds.). *Attention and performance, XV: Conscious and nonconscious information processing. A Bradford book*. Cambridge, MA: MIT Press.

Robertson, I. H., & Manly, T. (1999). Sustained attention deficits in time and space. In G. W. Humphreys, J. Duncan, & A. Treisman (Eds.). *Attention space and action*. Oxford: Oxford University Press.

Robertson, L. C., Lamb, M. R., & Knight, R. T. (1988). Effects of lesions of temporal parietal junction on perceptual and attentional processing in humans. *Journal of Neuroscience, 8*, 3757–3769.

Rock, I., & Victor, J. (1964). Vision and touch: An experimentally created conflict between the two senses. *Science, 143*, 594–596.

Rogers, R. D., & Monsell, S. (1995). Costs of a predictable switch between simple cognitive tasks. *Journal of Experimental Psychology: General, 124*, 207–231.

Roland, P. E. (1985). Cortical organisation of voluntary behaviour in man. *Human Neurobiology, 4*, 155–167.

Rolls, E. T., & Baylis, G. C. (1986). Size and contrast have only small effects on the responses of face neurons in the cortex of the superior temporal sulcus of the monkey. *Experimental Brain Research, 65*, 38–48.

Rubenstein, J., Meyer, D. E., & Evans, J. E. (2001). Executive control of cognitive processes in task switching. *Journal of Experimental Psychology: Human Perception and Performance, 27*, 763–797.

Rumelhart, D., & Norman, D. (1982). Simulating a skilled typist: A study of skilled cognitive-motor performance. *Cognitive Science, 6*, 1–36.

Rumelhart, D. E., & McClelland, J. L. (1986). Parallel distributed processing: Explorations in the microstructure of cognition. Volume 1: Foundations. Cambridge, MA: MIT Press.

Rylander, G. (1939). *Personality changes after operations on the frontal lobes: A clinical study of 32 cases*. Copenhagen: E. Munksgaard.

Salame, P., & Baddeley, A. D. (1987). Noise, unattended speech and short-term memory. *Ergonomics, 89*, 63–77.

Sandson, J., & Albert, M. L. (1984). Varieties of perseveration. *Neuropsychologia, 22*, 715–732.

Santee, J. L., & Egeth, H. E. (1980). Interference in letter identifications: A test of feature specific inhibition. *Perception and Psychophysics, 27*, 321–330.

Santee, J. L., & Egeth, H. E. (1982). Do reaction time and accuracy measure the same aspects of letter recognition? *Journal of Experimental Psychology: Human Perception and Performance, 8*, 489–501.

Schacter, D. L. (1987). Implicit memory: History and current status. *Journal of Experimental Psychology: Learning Memory and Cognition, 13*, 501–518.

Schacter, D. L. (1989). Memory. In M. I. Posner (Ed.). *Foundations of cognitive science. A Bradford Book*. Cambridge, MA: MIT Press.

Schacter, D. L., McAndrews, M. P., & Moscovitch, M. (1988). Access to consciousness: Dissociations between implicit and explicit knowledge in neuropsychological syndromes. In L. Weiskrantz (Ed.). *Thought without language*. Oxford: Oxford University Press.

Scharf, B. (1998). Auditory attention: The psychoacoustical approach. In H. Pashler (Ed.). *Attention*. Hove, UK: Psychology Press.

Scharf, B., & Houtsma, A. J. M. (1986). Audition II: Loudness, pitch, localisation, aural distortion, pathology. In K. R. Boff, L. Kaufman, & J. P. Thomas (Eds.). *Handbook of perception and human performance: 1. Sensory processes and perception* (pp. 15–60). New York: John Wiley & Sons, Inc.

Scharf, B., Canevet, G., Possamai, C., & Bonnel, A. (1986). *Some effects of attention in hearing*. Paper presented at the 18th International Congress on Audiology (p. 202). Prague: (Cited in Scharf (1998).)

Scharf, B., Quigley, S., Aoki, C., Peachey, N., & Reeves, A. (1987). Focused auditory attention and frequency selectivity. *Perception and Psychophysics, 42*, 215–223.

Scharf, B., Magnan, J., & Chays, A. (1997). On the role of the olivocochlear bundle in hearing: Sixteen case studies. *Hearing Research, 103*, 101–122.

Schmitt, M. J. M., Postma, A., & De Haan, E. H. F. (2000). Interactions between exogenous auditory and visual spatial attention. *Quarterly Journal of Experimental Psychology, 53A*, 105–130.

Schneider, W., & Shiffrin, R. M. (1977). Controlled and automatic human information processing: I. Detection, search and attention. *Psychological Review, 84*, 1–66.

Schneider, W. X. (1993). Space-based visual attention models and object selection: Constraints problems and possible solutions. *Psychological Research, 56*, 35–43.

Schneider, W. X. (1995). VAM: A neuro-cognitive model for visual attention, control of segmentation, object recognition and space-based motor action. *Visual Cognition, 2*, 331–375.

Schneider, W. X., & Deubel, H. (2002). Selection for perception and selection for spatial motor action are coupled by visual attention: A review of recent findings and new evidence from stimulus driven saccade control. In W. Prinz, & B. Hommel (Eds.). *Attention and Performance XIX: Common mechanisms in perception and action*. Oxford: Oxford University Press.

Schumacher, E. H., Seymour, T. L., Glass, J. M., Fencsik, D. E., Lauber, E. J., Kieras, D. E., & Meyer, D. E. (2001). Virtually perfect time sharing in dual-task performance: Uncorking the central bottleneck. *Psychological Science, 12*, 101–108.

Shaffer, L. H. (1975). Multiple attention in continuous verbal tasks. In P. M. A. Rabbitt and S. Dornic (Eds.). *Attention and Performance V*. New York: Academic Press.

Shallice, T. (1972). Dual functions of consciousness. *Psychological Review, 79*, 383–393.

Shallice, T. (1982). Specific impairments of planning. *Philosophical Transactions of the Royal Society of London, B, 298*, 199–209.

Shallice, T. (1988a). Information processing models of consciousness. In A. J. Marcel and E. Bisiach (Eds.). *Consciousness in contemporary science*. Oxford: Oxford University Press.

Shallice, T. (1988b). *From neuropsychology to mental structure*. Cambridge: Cambridge University Press.

Shallice, T., & Warrington, E. K. (1977). The possible role of selective attention in acquired dyslexia. *Neuropsychologia, 15,* 31–41.

Shannon, C. E., & Weaver, W. (1949). *The mathematical theory of communication.* Urbana, IL: University of Illinois Press.

Shapiro, K., Raymond, J. E., & Arnell, K. M. (1994). Attention to visual pattern information produces the attentional blink in rapid serial visual presentation. *Journal of Experimental Psychology: Human Perception and Performance, 20,* 357–371.

Shapiro, K. L. (2000). Change blindness: Theory or paradigm. *Visual Cognition, 7,* 83–91.

Shapiro, K. L. (2001). *The limits of attention: Temporal constraints on human information processing.* Oxford: Oxford University Press.

Shiffrin, R. M. (1988). Attention. In R. C. Atkinson, G. Lindzey, & R. D. Luce (Eds.). *Stevens handbook of experimental psychology. Vol. 2. Learning and cognition* (2nd ed.) (pp. 738–811). New York: John Wiley & Sons, Inc.

Shiffrin, R. M., & Schneider, W. (1977). Controlled and automatic information processing: II. Perception, learning, automatic attending and a general theory. *Psychological Review, 84,* 127–190.

Shulman, G. L., Remington, R. W., & McLean, J. P. (1979). Moving attention through visual space. *Journal of Experimental Psychology: Human Perception and Performance, 5,* 522–526.

Simon, W. E. (1971). Number and colour responses of some college students: Preliminary evidence of the blue and seven phenomenon. *Perception and Motor Skills, 33,* 373–374.

Simons, D. J., & Levin, D. T. (1998). Failure to detect change to people during real world interaction. *Psychonomic Bulletin and Review, 4,* 644–649.

Singer, W. (1994). The organisation of sensory motor representations in the neocortex: A hypothesis based on temporal coding. In C. Umilta, & M. Moscovitch (Eds.). *Attention and performance, XV: Conscious and nonconscious information processing. A Bradford book.* Cambridge, MA: MIT Press.

Singer, W. (2004). Timing as coding space in the cerebral cortex. In N. Kanwisher and J. Duncan (Eds.). *Functional neuroimaging if visual cognition: Attention and performance XX.* Oxford: Oxford University Press.

Sloboda, J. A. (1999). *The musical mind: The cognitive psychology of music.* Oxford: Oxford University Press.

Smilek, D., Eastwood, J. D., & Merikle, P. M. (2000). Do unattended changes facilitate change detection? *Journal of Experimental Psychology: Human Perception and Performance, 26,* 480–487.

Smyth, M. M., Collins, A. F., Morris, P. E., & Levy, P. (1994). *Cognition in action* (2nd ed.). Hove, UK: Lawrence Erlbaum Associates, Inc.

Sohn, M-A., & Carlson, R. A. (2000). Effects of repetition and foreknowledge in task-set reconfiguration. *Journal of Experimental Psychology: Learning Memory and Cognition, 26,* 1445–1460.

Sohn, W-S., & Doane, S. M. (2003). Roles of working memory capacity and long-term working memory skill in complex task performance. *Memory and Cognition, 31,* 458–466.

Soto-Faraco, S., Spence, C., & Kingstone, A. (2004). Cross-modal capture: Congruency effects in the preparation of motion across sensory modalities. *Journal of Experimental Psychology: Human Perception and Performance, 30,* 330–345.

Spector, A., & Beiderman, I. (1976). Mental set and mental shift revisited. *American Journal of Psychology, 89,* 669–679.

Spelke, E., Hirst, W., & Neisser, U. (1976). Skills of divided attention. *Cognition, 4,* 215–230.

Spence, C., & Driver, J. (1994). Covert spatial orienting in audition: Exogenous and endogenous mechanisms. *Journal of Experimental Psychology: Human Perception and Performance, 20,* 555–574.

Spence, C., & Driver, J. (1996). Audiovisual links in endogenous covert spatial attention. *Journal of Experimental Psychology: Human Perception and Performance, 22,* 1005–1030.

Spence, C., & Driver, J. (1997). Audio-visual links in exogenous covert spatial orienting. *Perception and Psychophysics, 59,* 1–22.

Spence, C., & Driver, J. (Eds.). (2004). *Crossmodal space and crossmodal attention.* Oxford: Oxford University Press.

Spence, C., Nicholls, M. E. R., Gillespie, N., & Driver, J. (1998). Cross-modal links in exogenous covert spatial orienting between touch, audition and vision. *Perception and Psychophysics, 60,* 544–557.

Spence, C., Pavani, F., & Driver, J. (2000). Cross-modal links between vision and touch in covert endogenous spatial attention. *Journal of Experimental Psychology: Human Perception and Performance, 26,* 1298–1319.

Sperling, G. (1960). The information available in brief visual presentations. *Psychological Monographs, 74,* 498 (all).

Sperling, G., & Melchner, M. J. (1978). Visual search, visual attention and the attention operating characteristic. In J. Requin (Ed.). *Attention and Performance, VII.* Hillsdale, NJ: Lawrence Erlbaum Associates, Inc.

Squire, L. (1987). *Memory and brain.* New York: Oxford University Press.

Stammers, R. B. (1982). Part and whole practice in training for procedural tasks. *Human Learning, 1,* 185–207.

Stoerig, P., & Cowey, A. (1990). Wavelength sensitivity in blindsight. *Nature, 242,* 916–918.

Stoffer, T. H. (1993). The time course of attentional zooming: A comparison of voluntary and involuntary allocation of attention to the levels of compound stimuli. *Psychological Research, 56,* 14–25.

Stroop, J. R. (1935). Studies of interference in serial-verbal reaction. *Journal of Experimental Psychology, 18,* 643–662.

Styles, E. A. (2005). *Attention perception and memory: An integrated introduction.* London: Routledge.

Styles, E. A., & Allport, D. A. (1986). Perceptual integration of identity, location and colour. *Psychological Research, 48,* 189–200.

Sweller, J. (1988). Cognitive load during problem solving: Effects on learning. *Cognitive Science, 12,* 257–285.

Tanner, W., & Norman, R. (1954). The human use of information: II. Signal detection for the case of an unknown parameter. *Transactions of the Institute of Radio Engineering, Professional Group on Information Theory, 4,* 222–227.

Tipper, S. P. (1985). The negative priming effect: Inhibitory effects of ignored primes. *Quarterly Journal of Experimental Psychology, 37A,* 571–590.

Tipper, S. P., & Behrmann, M. (1996). Object-centred not scene-based visual neglect. *Journal of Experimental Psychology: Human Perception and Performance, 22,* 1261–1278.

Tipper, S. P., & Cranston, M. (1985). Selective attention and priming: Inhibitory and facilitatory effects of ignored primes. *Quarterly Journal of Experimental Psychology, 37A,* 591–611.

Tipper, S. P., & Driver, J. (1988). Negative priming between pictures and words: Evidence for semantic analysis of ignored stimuli. *Memory and Cognition, 16,* 64–70.

Tipper, S. P., Brehaut, J. C., & Driver, J. (1990). Selection of moving and static objects for the control of spatially based attention. *Journal of Experimental Psychology: Human Perception and Performance, 16,* 492–504.

Tipper, S. P., Driver, J., & Weaver, B. (1991). Object-centred inhibition of return of visual attention. *Quarterly Journal of Experimental Psychology, 43A*, 289–298.

Tipper, S. P., Lortie, C., & Baylis, G. C. (1992). Selective reaching: Evidence for action-centred attention. *Journal of Experimental Psychology: Human Perception and Performance, 18*, 891–905.

Tipper, S. P., Weaver, B., & Houghton, G. (1994a). Behavioural goals determine inhibitory mechanisms of selective attention. *Quarterly Journal of Experimental Psychology, 47A*, 809–840.

Tipper, S. P., Weaver, B., Jerreat, L., & Burak, A. (1994b). Object-based and environment-based inhibition of return. *Journal of Experimental Psychology: Human Perception and Performance, 20*, 478–499.

Tipper, S. P., Weaver, B., & Watson, F. L. (1996). Inhibition of return to successively cued spatial locations: Commentary on Pratt and Abrahams (1995). *Journal of Experimental Psychology: Human Perception and Performance, 22*, 1289–1293.

Tombu, M., & Jolicoeur, P. (2003). A central capacity sharing model of dual task performance. *Journal of Experimental Psychology: Human Perception and Performance, 29*, 3–18.

Townsend, V. W. (1973). Loss of spatial and identity information following a tachistoscopic exposure. *Journal of Experimental Psychology, 8*, 113–118.

Treisman, A. (1969). Strategies and models of selective attention. *Psychological Review, 76*, 282–299.

Treisman, A. (1986). Features and objects in visual processing. *Scientific American*, November, 106–115.

Treisman, A. (1988). Features and objects: The fourteenth Bartlett memorial lecture. *Quarterly Journal of Experimental Psychology, 40A*, 201–237.

Treisman, A. (1993). The perception of features and objects. In A. D. Baddeley, & L. Weiskrantz (Eds.). *Attention: Awareness selection and control. A tribute to Donald Broadbent*. Oxford: Oxford University Press.

Treisman, A. (1999). Feature binding, attention and object perception. In G. W. Humphreys, J. Duncan, & A. Treisman (Eds.). *Attention, space and action: Studies in cognitive neuroscience*. Oxford: Oxford University Press.

Treisman, A., & Schmidt, H. (1992). Illusory conjunctions in the perception of objects. *Cognitive Psychology, 14*, 107–141.

Treisman, A., Kahneman, D., & Burkell, J. (1983). Perceptual objects and the cost of filtering. *Perception and Psychophysics, 33*, 527–532.

Treisman, A. M. (1960). Contextual cues in selective listening. *Quarterly Journal of Experimental Psychology, 12*, 242–248.

Treisman, A. M. (1964a). Monitoring and storage of irrelevant messages in selective attention. *Journal of Verbal Learning and Verbal Behaviour, 3*, 449–459.

Treisman, A. M. (1964b). Verbal cues, language and meaning in selective attention. *American Journal of Psychology, 77*, 206–219.

Treisman, A. M. (1964c). Effect of irrelevant material on the efficiency of selective listening. *American Journal of Psychology, 77*, 533–546.

Treisman, A. M. (1964d). Selective attention in man. *British Medical Bulletin, 20*, 12–16.

Treisman, A. M., & Gelade, G. (1980). A feature-integration theory of attention. *Cognitive Psychology, 12*, 97–136.

Treisman, M., & Rostron, A. B. (1972). Brief auditory storage: A modification of Sperling's paradigm applied to audition. *Acta Psychologia, 36*, 161–170.

Trueman, J. (1979). Existence and robustness of the blue seven phenomena. *Journal of General Psychology, 101,* 23–26.

Tsal, Y. (1983). Movements of attention across the visual field. *Journal of Experimental Psychology: Human Perception and Performance, 9,* 523–530.

Turvey, M. T. (1973). On peripheral and central processes in vision: Inferences from information processing analysis of masking with patterned stimuli. *Psychological Review, 80,* 1–52.

Turvey, M. T., & Kravetz, S. (1970). Retrieval for iconic memory with shape as the selection criterion. *Perception and Psychophysics, 8,* 171–172.

Umilta, C. (1988). The control operations of consciousness. In A. J. Marcel, & E. Bisiach (Eds.). *Consciousness in contemporary science.* Oxford: Oxford University Press.

Underwood, G. (1976). Semantic interference form unattended printed words. *British Journal of Psychology, 67,* 327–338.

Ungerleider, L. G., & Mishkin, M. (1982). Two cortical systems. In D. J. Ingle, M. A. Goodale, & R. J. W. Mansfield (Eds.). *Analysis of visual behaviour.* Cambridge, MA: MIT Press.

van der Heijden, A. H. C. (1981). *Short-term visual information forgetting.* London: Routledge & Kegan Paul.

van der Heijden, A. H. C. (1993). The role of position in object selection in vision. *Psychological Research, 56,* 44–58.

van der Heijden, A. H. C. (2004). *Attention in vision.* Hove, UK: Psychology Press.

van Essen, G. W., & Maunsell, J. H. R. (1983). Hierarchical organisation and functional streams in the visual cortex. *Trends in Neuroscience, 6,* 370–375.

van Oeffelen, M. P., & Vos, P. G. (1982). Configurational effects on the enumeration of dots. Counting by groups. *Memory and Cognition, 10,* 396–404.

van Oeffelen, M. P., & Vos, P. G. (1983). An algorithm for pattern description on the level of relative proximity. *Pattern Recognition, 16,* 341–348.

Vitevitch, M. S. (2003). Change deafness: The inability to detect changes between two voices. *Journal of Experimental Psychology: Human Perception and Performance, 29(2),* 333–342.

Volpe, B. T., LeDoux, J., & Gazzaniga, M. S. (1979). Information processing of visual stimuli in the "extinguished" field. *Nature, 228,* 722–724.

Volpe, B. T., LeDoux, J., & Gazzaniga, M. S. (2000). Information processing of visual stimuli in the "extinguished" field. In M. Gazzaniga (Ed.). *Cognitive neuroscience: A reader.* Malden, MA: Blackwell.

von der Malsburg, C. (1985). Nervous structures with dynamical links. Bunsenges. *Physical Chemistry, 89,* 703–710.

Von Wright, J. M. (1969). Selection in visual immediate memory. *Quarterly Journal of Experimental Psychology, 20,* 62–68.

Von Wright, J. M. (1970). On selection in immediate memory. *Acta Psychologia, 33,* 280–292.

Vroomen, J., & de Gelder, B. (2004). Perceptual effects of cross-modal stimulation: Ventriloquism and the freezing phenomenon. In G. Calvert, C. Spence, & B. E. Stein (Eds.). *Handbook of multi-sensory processes.* Cambridge, MA: MIT Press.

Walton, M. E., Devlin, J. T., & Rushworth, M. F. S. (2004). Interactions between decision making and performance monitoring within prefrontal cortex. *Nature Neuroscience, 7,* 1259–1265.

Ward, R., Duncan, J., & Shapiro, K. L. (1996). The slow time course of visual attention. *Cognitive Psychology, 30,* 79–109.

Wardlaw, K. A., & Kroll, N. E. A. (1976). Automatic responses to shock associated words in a non-attended message: A failure to replicate. *Journal of Experimental Psychology: Human Perception and Performance, 2,* 357–360.

Watson, J. B. (1919). *Behaviorism*. New York: John Wiley & Sons, Inc.

Wegner, D. M. (2003). The mind's best trick: How we experience conscious will. *Trends in Cognitive Sciences*, 7, 65–69.

Wegner, D. M., & Wheatley, T. P. (1999). Apparent mental causation: sources of the experience of will. *American Psychologist*, 54, 480–492.

Weiskrantz, L. (1988). Some contributions of neuropsychology of vision and memory to the problem of consciousness. In A. J. Marcel and E. Bisiach (Eds.). *Consciousness and contemporary science* (pp. 1183–1189). Oxford: Oxford University Press.

Weiskrantz, L. L. (1986). *Blindsight: A case study and implications*. Oxford: Oxford University Press.

Weiskrantz, L. L. (1993). Search for the unseen. In A. Baddeley and L. L. Weiskrantz (Eds.). *Attention: Selection, awareness and control. A tribute to Donald Broadbent*. Oxford: Oxford University Press.

Weiskrantz, L. L., Sanders, M. D., & Marshall, J. (1974). Visual capacity in the hemianopic visual field following a restricted occipital ablation. *Brain*, 97, 709–728.

Welford, A. T. (1952). The psychological refractory period and the timing of high speed performance: A review and a theory. *British Journal of Psychology*, 43, 2–19.

Welford, A. T. (1967). Single channel operation in the brain. *Acta Psychologia*, 27, 5–22.

Wickens, C. D. (1984). Processing resources in attention. In R. Parsuraman, & D. R. Davies (Eds.). *Varieties of Attention*. Orlando, FL: Academic Press.

Wolfe, J. M., & Pokorny, C. W. (1990). Inhibitory tagging in visual search: A failure to replicate. *Perception and Psychophysics*, 48, 357–362.

Wood, N., & Cowan, N. (1995). The cocktail party phenomenon revisited: How frequent are attention shifts to one's name in an irrelevant auditory channel? *Journal of Experimental Psychology, Learning Memory and Cognition*, 2, 255–260.

Woods, D. L., & Alain, C. (2001). Conjoining three auditory features: An event-related brain potential study. *Journal of Cognitive Neuroscience*, 13(4), 492–509.

Woods, D. L., Alho, K., & Algazi, A. (1994). Stages of auditory feature conjunction: An event-related brain potential study. *Journal of Experimental Psychology: Human Perception and Performance*, 22, 81–94.

Woods, D. L., Alain, C., & Ogawa, K. H. (1998). Conjoining auditory and visual features during high-rate serial presentation: processing and conjoining two features can be faster than processing one. *Perception and Psychophysics*, 60, 239–249.

Woods, D. L., Alain, C., Diaz, R., Rhodes, D., & Ogawa, K. H. (2001). Location and frequency cues in auditory selective attention. *Journal of Experimental Psychology: Human Perception and Performance*, 27, 65–74.

Wright, B. A., & Dai, H. (1994). Detection of unexpected tones with short and long durations. *Journal of the Acoustical Society of America*, 95, 931–938.

Wulf, G., & Prinz, W. (2001). Directing attention to movements enhances learning: A review. *Psychonomic Bulletin and Review*, 8, 648–660.

Wulf, G., Lauterbach, B., & Toole, T. (1999). Learning advantages of an external focus of attention in golf. *Research Quarterly for Exercise and Sport*, 70, 120–126.

Wulf, G., McNevin, N., & Shea, C. H. (2001). The automaticity of complex motor skill learning as a function of attentional focus. *Quarterly Journal of Experimental Psychology*, 54A, 1143–1154.

Wylie, G., & Allport, A. (2000). Task switching and the measurement of "switch costs". *Psychological Research, 63*, 212–223.

Yantis, S., & Johnston, J. C. (1990). On the locus of visual selection: Evidence from focused attention tasks. *Journal of Experimental Psychology: Human Perception and Performance, 16*, 135–149.

Yerkes, R. M., & Dodson, J. D. (1908). The relation of strength of stimuli to rapidity of habit-information. *Journal of Comparative Neurology and Psychology, 18*, 459–482.

Young, A. W., & Block, N. (1996). Consciousness. In V. Bruce (Ed.). *Unsolved mysteries of the mind*. Hove, UK: Lawrence Erlbaum Associates, Inc.

Zeki, S. (1980). The representation of colours in the cerebral cortex. *Nature, 284*, 412–418.

Zeki, S., Watson, J. D. G., Leuck, C. J., Friston, K. L., Kennard, C., & Frackowiak, R. S. (1991). A direct demonstration of functional specialisation in human visual cortex. *Journal of Neuroscience, 11*, 641–649.

Author index

Abrahams, R.A., 61
Abrogast, T.L., 126
Acuna, C., 55
Aglioti, S., 276
Alain, 131, 132, 134
Albert, M.L., 68, 231, 236
Alford, D.R., 135
Algazi, A., 133
Alho, K., 133
Allen, P.A., 169
Allport, A., 3, 10, 13, 14, 80, 86, 148,
     199, 219–221, 225, 240–245, 247, 250,
     253, 285
Allport, D.A., 39, 88, 153–155, 157,
     179, 205, 222, 258, 261, 262, 284
Anderson, C.H., 111
Anderson, J.R., 167, 178, 179, 204–208,
     211, 217, 235
Antonis, B., 153, 154
Aoki, C., 122, 124
Armony, L., 242
Arnell, K.M., 175, 176, 178
Aschersleben, G., 143
Atkinson, R.C., 185–186
Avebach, E., 30–32
Awh, E., 59, 63, 65, 177
Azuma, R., 248, 250

Baars, B.J., 284–285
Baddeley, A.D., 131, 186, 211, 232,
     233, 288, 291
Badgaiyan, R.D., 55
Bailey, P.J., 117, 125
Balint, R., 77, 99, 239
Baron-Cohen, S., 58
Barry, C., 280

Bash, D., 48
Bauer, R.M., 278
Baylis, G., 225
Baylis, G.C., 72, 100, 108, 113, 166, 226,
     228
Beard, C.T., 258
Beck, J., 92
Bedard, M.A., 125
Beecher, H.K., 148
Behrmann, M., 75, 76, 109–110, 146–147
Beiderman, I., 240, 243
Beilock, S.L., 209
Belstaff, G., 268, 269
Berger, R.C., 95
Bertelson, P., 1431
Bertenthal, B.I., 209
Berti, A., 71, 277
Bertleson, P., 146
Beschin, N., 142
Bianchi, L., 231
Bisiach, E., 71, 74, 283, 292
Bjork, E.L., 44, 50
Blackmore, S.J., 268, 269, 270, 292
Block, N., 278, 293
Bobrow, D.G., 158, 159, 261
Boies, S.J., 157, 160, 161, 164
Bonnel, A., 124, 125
Botella, J., 48
Bouma, H., 63
Bourke, P.A., 157
Bregman, A.S., 129
Brehaut, J.C., 224
Briand, K.A., 92, 93
Broadbent, D.E., 9, 11, 16, 17, 20, 21,
     25, 31, 36, 37–40, 65, 154, 175, 186,
     216, 217, 235

113, 137–139, 143, 149, 152, 166, 227, 267, 268
Dunbar, K., 195, 196, 197
Duncan, J., 1, 11, 12, 13, 37, 59, 93, 94, 105, 107, 176, 177, 179, 235–237
Duncan, S., 187
Dunn, T.H., 36

Eastwood, J.D., 262, 272
Eccleston, C., 147–149
Egeth, H.E., 42, 46, 222
Eimer, M., 147, 149
Ellis, A.W., 109, 263
Endsley, M.R., 212
Ericsson, K.A., 211, 212
Eriksen, B.A., 44–48, 50, 52, 72, 113, 167
Eriksen, C.W., 32, 44–48, 50, 52, 63, 65, 66, 84, 87, 113, 114, 230
Eskridge, V.L., 187
Esslinger, P.J., 230
Estes, W.K., 45
Evans, J.E., 250
Eysenck, M.W., 41

Fagot, C., 166, 226
Farah, M., 218, 274, 277, 279,
Fencsik, D.E., 168, 170, 174
Fernandez, E., 148
Findlay, J.M., 56
Fitts, P.M., 9, 10, 11, 14, 52, 54, 55, 61, 67–69, 81, 86, 109, 114, 121, 157, 160–165, 168, 184, 187
Flude, B.M., 109
Fodor, J.A., 273
Folk, C.L., 58, 59
Foulke, E., 128
Found, A., 95
Fowler, C.A., 263
Fox, E., 223
Fox, L.A., 243
Fox, P.T., 55
Foxton, J.M., 130
Frackowiak, R.S., 86
Francolini, C.M., 222
Friedrick, F.J., 69

Friesen, C.K., 58
Friston, K.L., 86
Frith, C.D., 51, 52, 147, 267, 268
Frost, D., 275

Gallese, V., 227, 228
Garrett, M.F., 36
Gazzaniga, M.S., 70, 71, 274, 277
Gelade, G., 86, 89, 90, 109, 131, 166, 269
Geng, J.J., 146–147
Gentilucci, M., 227, 228
Georgopoulos, A., 55
Gibson, J.J., 150
Gilbert, S.J., 248–250, 253
Gillespie, N., 138, 139
Gillie, T., 148
Glass, J.M., 168, 170, 184
Gleitman, H., 46
Godijn, R., 58, 61
Goldberg, M.E., 55
Goodale, M.A., 86, 280
Gopher, D., 169, 171, 198, 200–202, 208, 242
Gordon, R., 170, 173
Gordon, W.P., 135
Graves, R.S., 31
Gray, C.M., 101
Gray, J.A., 25
Greenberg, G., 122, 135
Greenshpan, Y., 242
Greenwald, A.G., 164, 165, 168, 266
Grossberg, S., 101
Grossenbacher, P.G., 138

Halligan, P.W., 74, 75
Hansen, J.C., 132, 133
Harlow, J., 230
Hartley, A., 48
Hay, J.C., 141
Hazeltine, E., 169
Heacen, H., 236
Hebb, D.O., 101
Heinke, D., 111, 114
Heinz, S.P., 3, 41
Heise, R.L., 128

Held, R., 275
Henik, A., 193
Hernandez-Peon, R., 133
Hick, W.E., 216
Hill, A.B., 265
Hillis, A.E., 109
Hillyard, S.A., 132, 133, 215
Hinton, G., 217
Hinton, G.E., 102
Hintzman, D.L., 187
Hirst, A., 40, 41, 50, 52, 186
Hirst, W., 159, 184, 185, 192, 194, 198
Hitch, G.J., 291
Hochhaus, L., 225
Holding, D.H., 128
Holender, D., 261–262, 267
Hommel, B., 58, 61
Houghton, G., 73, 224, 226
Houghton, R.J., 130, 131
Houtsma, A.J.M., 132
Hseih, S., 13, 148, 199, 240–245, 250
Hubel, D.H., 85
Hudson, P.T.W., 103, 104, 114, 196
Humphreys, G.W., 12, 28, 77, 78, 93,
    94, 105, 107, 111, 142, 176, 283, 292
Huston, T., 196

Igarashi, M., 135
Ikeda, K., 141
Ivry, R.B., 169

Jacoby, L.L., 272, 282
James, W., 1, 9, 43, 230
Janer, K.W., 55
Jeannerod, M., 77
Jerreat, L., 73
Jersild, A.T., 239, 242
Johnson-Laird, P.N., 288, 289
Johnston, J., 169, 172
Johnston, J.C., 48, 58
Johnston, W.A., 37, 41, 91
Jolicoeur, P., 169, 171, 172, 178
Jones, A.M., 130, 131
Jones, B., 145
Jonides, J., 46, 56

Jordan, M.J., 227
Jouvet, M., 133

Kahneman, D., 9, 43, 48, 49, 92, 156,
    159, 169, 171, 179
Kanwisher, N., 225, 226
Kataus, M., 216
Keane, M.T., 41
Kelley, C.M., 282
Kemp-Wheeler, S., 265
Kennard, C., 86
Kidd, G., 126
Kidd, Jr., G., 126
Kidd, P., 58
Kieras, D., 168, 169, 170, 173, 174
Kingstone, A., 58, 145, 146
Kinsbourne, M., 109
Kintsch, W., 211, 212
Klein, R.M., 81, 92, 93
Klinger, M.R., 266
Knight, R.T., 67
Knowles, W.B., 156
Koch, C., 100, 101, 275, 284, 285
Koechlin, E., 234
Kouneiher, F., 234
Kramer, A.F., 72
Kravetz, S., 30
Kroll, N.E.A., 257

Laberge, D., 48, 56, 64, 70
Lackner, J.R., 36
Lamb, M.R., 67
Lambert, A.J., 258
Landy, D.H., 201
Langton, S.R.H., 58
Larkin, W., 122, 135
Latto, R., 275
Lauber, E.J., 168, 170, 174
Laurey, P., 177
Lauterbach, B., 210
Lavie, N., 40, 41, 49, 50–52, 65, 92, 98,
    186
Law, M.B., 61
Lederman, S.J., 145
LeDoux, J., 70, 71, 277

Rohrbaugh, J.W., 32, 47, 84
Rohtla, T.L., 126
Roland, P.E., 233
Rolls, E.T., 100
Romani, C., 77, 78
Rosenbaum, D.A., 227
Rostron, A.B., 128
Rubenstein, J., 250
Rumelhart, D.E., 102, 103, 105, 195, 200, 217, 238, 250
Rushworth, M.F.S., 234
Russell, C., 267, 268
Rylander, G., 232

Sakata, H., 55
Salame, P., 131
Sanders, M.D., 276
Sandson, J., 231
Santee, J.L., 42
Schacter, D.L., 274, 279
Scharf, B., 121–125, 152
Schavaneveldt, R.W., 222, 260
Scherrer, H., 133
Schmidt, H., 91
Schmitt, M.J.M., 136
Schneider, W., 189, 191
Schneider, W.X., 113, 218, 219, 226, 229
Schor, R.E., 243
Schumacher, E.H., 168, 170, 184
Schwartz, M., 122
Serences, J.T., 59, 63, 65, 177
Seymour, T.L., 168, 170, 184
Shaff, S.S., 187
Shaffer, L.H., 163, 184
Shallice, T., 9, 13, 84, 183, 194, 232, 237–239, 248–250, 253, 283, 284
Shannon, C.E., 18
Shapiro, K.L., 175, 176, 177, 269
Shea, C.H., 210
Sheliga, B.M., 227–229
Shibuya, H., 117
Shiffrin, R.M., 1, 5, 66, 185, 186, 189, 186
Shomstein, S., 146–147
Shulman, G.L., 55, 67, 265
Shulman, H.G., 164, 165, 168

Shultz, T., 87
Simon, H.A., 195, 208, 212
Simon, W.E., 265
Simons, D.J., 269
Singer, W., 99, 100, 101, 196, 275, 284
Sitton, M., 111
Slade, R., 263
Sloboda, J.A., 129, 152
Smilek, D., 262, 269, 270, 272
Smith, Y.M., 275
Smyth, M.M., 181, 227
Snyder, C.R.R., 9, 52, 54, 187, 188
Sohn, M-A., 242
Sohn, W-S., 212
Soto-Faraco, S., 145, 146
Sparks, M.E., 187
Spector, A., 240, 243
Spelke, E., 184, 185, 192, 194
Spelke, E.S., 194
Spence, C., 133, 137–139, 140, 141, 143, 152, 227
Sperling, G., 27–29, 41, 48, 55, 128
Squire, L., 279
Stammers, R.B., 200
Stanovitch, K.K., 266
Starkes, J.L., 209
Staszewski, J., 212
Steinman, R.J., 243
St.James, J.D., 47
Stewart, A.L., 266
Stoerig, P., 276
Stoffer, T.H., 67
Stroop, J.R., 187, 222
Styles, E.A., 13, 41, 79, 148, 199, 240–245, 250
Sweller, J., 203

Tanner, W., 121
Tassarini, C., 276
Tassinary, L., 263
Tanner, W., 121
Teague, D., 169
Tham, M.P., 72
Thirne, G., 145

Thompson, R.J., 258
Tipper, S.P., 61, 73, 75, 76, 97, 222, 224, 226, 228
Tombu, M., 169, 171, 172
Toole, T., 210
Townsend, V.W., 32, 41
Treisman, A., 2, 43, 48, 89–92, 109, 117, 274
Treisman, A.M., 11, 23, 25, 86, 89, 90, 131, 166, 269
Tremblay, S., 130, 131
Troscianko, T., 268, 269
Trueman, J., 265
Tsal, Y., 49, 62
Turk, D.C., 148
Turvey, M.T., 30, 127, 260

Umilta, C., 64, 259, 288
Underwood, G., 256
Ungerleider, L.G., 85

van der Heijden, A.H.C., 20, 88, 103, 104, 114, 194, 196
van der Jaght, T., 177
van Essen, D.C., 111
van Essen, G.W., 218
van Oeffelen, M.P., 113, 114
van Velzen, J., 149
Victor, J., 141
Viding, E., 40, 41, 50, 52, 186
Vighetto, A., 77
Vitevitch, M.S., 270
Volpe, B.T., 70, 71, 277
von der Malsburg, C., 100
Von Wright, J.M., 30
Voot, N., 258
Vos, P.G., 113, 114
Vroomen, J., 143

Walker, J.A., 69

Wall, S., 46
Walton, M.E., 234
Ward, R., 177
Wardlaw, K.A., 257
Warrington, E.K., 84, 109
Watson, F.L., 61
Watson, J.B., 2
Watson, J.D.G., 86
Weaver, B., 61, 73, 224, 226
Weaver, W., 18
Wedderburn, A.A., 25
Wegner, D.M., 280, 282, 283
Weiskrantz, L.L., 275, 276
Welford, A.T., 15, 40, 153, 154, 164, 169
Wheatley, T.P., 282
Wickens, C.D., 158, 160, 177
Wilhelmsen, A., 266
Wilson, B., 110
Wolfe, J.M., 61
Wolford, G., 263
Wolters, G., 290
Wood, B., 36, 257
Wood, N., 22
Woods, D.L., 131, 132, 133, 134
Wright, B.A., 123
Wright, D.L., 210
Wright, J.H., 58
Wulf, G., 210
Wurtz, R.H., 55
Wylie, G., 247, 250

Yantis, S., 48
Yeh, Y-Y., 63, 72, 114
Yerkes, R.M., 157
Yeung, N.P., 248, 250
Young, A.W., 109, 278, 293

Zatorre, R.J., 123
Zeki, S., 86

Subject index

Dichotic listening, 16, 22, 23, 35–36, 120, 143, 257
Divided attention and task combination, 154–169
Dual tasks, 153–163, 194–195, see Task combination, 153–173

Early–late debate, 11, 24, 25, 31, 86–88, 115, 154, 194, 217, 257
    criticisms of, 22–24
    resolution of, 48–50
    visual attention, 34–39, 45–52
early selection models, 20–24
Effort theory of attention, 7
Endogenous/exogenous attention, see Orienting and cues
Eriksen task, 44–48
    flanker compatibility effect, 45–48
    goal dependent interference effects, 58–60
    perceptual load, 49–50
Event related potentials (ERP), 132, 133, 149–150, 216
Executive control theories of visual attention (EPIC, ECTVA), 170–171, 174
Expert performance, 206–207, 209–210
Extinction, 70–71, 77–78

Feature integration theory
    in vision, 86–89, 95–99
    in audition, 128–130, 131–134, 142
Feature search, 90, 101
Features, 89, 128–129
Filter theory of attention, 19–21, 153
Filter setting, 134
Filtering tasks
    auditory, 16–22
    definition, 43–44
    movement, 95–97
    post-categorial, 88
    see also Feature integration theory
Flanker compatibility effect (FCE), 45–48, 72–75
    see also Eriksen task

Focal attention, see Attentional spotlight and Feature integration theory
    in skill learning, 210–211
Frontal lobe damage, 230–234
    and executive control, 50, 51, 231–234

Galvanic skin response, 36
Gestalt principles
    in vision, 72
    in audition, 129
Goals, 8, 60, 125, 221, 236
    behavioural, 226
    directed behaviour, 226
    lists, 235–236
    maintenance, 236
    planning, 236
    selection, 235
    sequences, 229
    shifting, 247

Hear but not heeded hypothesis, 122
Homunculus problem, 5, 10, 204
Human factors, 155–156

Iconic memory, 28, 87
Ideo-motor acts, 237
    compatibility, 168
Ignored information
    in audition, 257–258
    in vision, 258–261
    see also Semantic activation without conscious identification (SAWCI)
Illusory conjunctions, 92
    in crossmodal attention, 142
    see also feature integration theory
Individual differences in selective attention, 51–52
Information processing theory and approach, 3, 17–19
Inhibition
    between visual features, see lateral masking

in schema control, 222
in selection for action, 77
in selection in SIAM, 111–112
in selection in SLAM, 103–104
of response, 222
of return to locations, 61–62
of return to objects, 73
see also negative priming
Interference
and negative priming, 222–224
dual-task, 209
feature or response level, 45
in selection for action, 223
in skills, 209–210
see also Stroop effect
Interruption of tasks, 148

Late selection theory, 24–32
Lateral masking, 44–46, 84, 126
Load theory, 40, 49, 50, 97
Local and global processing, 66
Location
auditory, 121–134
visual codes, 32–35, 84–85
see Feature integration theory
see what and where in vision
Logogens, 26, 27

Masking, 28, 32, 87
and conscious awareness, 258, 260
lateral, 44–46, 84, 126
selective, 190–191
Memory
amnesia, 279–280
and controlled and automatic
processing, 169, 186
echoic, 128
for attended information, 8
for intention, 8, 240
iconic, 87
integration of sematic and episodic,
87
and perceptual integration, 219–221
retrieval in skill, 210
semantic, 36, 285

set, 189–191
working memory, 51, 52, 185–186
and consciousness, 284–285, 289,
291
and dual tasks, 186, 204–206
and executive control, 237–238
load and interference effects,
51–52
long term working memory,
211–213
Mental set, 4, 190–191, 231–232, 240
changing in patients, 231–232
in normal subjects, 239–249
see also Switching and shifting set
Mernier's disease, 135
Metaphors of mind, 3, 17, 217–218
Mislocation and migration errors, 84
Modality appropriateness, 145–146
Modularity, 273

Negative priming, 222–224

Object
auditory, 119
files, 89, 97
frames, 89
see also Feature integration theory
Object based effects
of attention, 73
inhibition of return, 73
in SIAM, see SIAM
visual neglect, 68, 73–75
Olivocochlear bundle, 134–136
Orienting
auditory attention, 121–126
covert/overt, 56–57
cross-modality, 136–137
endogenous/exogenous, 54–57,
137, 138, 149, 150
in neglect, see visual neglect
neurological bases, 54–56
reflexive/voluntary, 59
symbolic control of, 57–59
touch, 138–139
visual attention, 52–56

neglect of, see Visual neglect
spatial representation, 113–114
spatial position and attention
spatial pragmatic maps, 227–228
Split-span technique, 20, 22, 25
Stream segregation, 130–131
Stroop effect
    asymmetry of, 188
    automatic processing, 187, 195, 237
    control of, 237, 240–243
    dilution, 49
    goal activation, 237, 247–248
    modelling, 196–197
    practice, 195–197
    unconscious priming, 261
Supervisory attentional system (SAS),
    237–239, 287
Switching and shifting attentional set
    attentional control of, 173–174,
        190–191
    modelling, 248–250
    and pain, 149
    SIAM, 112
    task set inertia, 244–248
    task set reconfiguration, 244–248

Tachistoscope, 28
Texture segregation, see Feature
    integration theory, and
    Attentional engagement theory
Thresholds, 264–266
    attenuator model, 27
    detection, 270–272
    objective and subjective, 262–264,
        271
    setting, 256, 266
Tip-of-the-tongue phenomenon,
    193–194
Top-down processes, 4, 27, 56, 59, 238
Touch, 145
Tower of Hanoi, 233

Unattended information, 35–36
Unconscious processing
    in agnosia, 279
    in amnesia, 250
    in blindsight, 275–276
    and masking, 258
    in prosopagnosia, 278–279, 283
    in visual extinction, 70–71, 77–78
    in visual neglect, see Visual neglect
    see also Semantic activation
        without conscious
        identification (SAWCI)
Utilization behaviour, 232

Varied mapping, 190
Ventriloquist effect, 143
Visual capture, 141, 199
Visual extinction, 70–71, 77–78
Visual masking, see masking
Visual neglect, 68, 75–76, 94, 109, 224,
    225, 227, 277
    dyslexia, 84
    in Balint's syndrome, 77–78
    of imagined space, 71
    of objects, 69, 72
Visual search, see Feature integration
    theory (FIT) and Attentional
    engagement theory
Voluntary control, 189–209, 229–249
    disorders of, 230–234
    willed acts, 237–239
    see also the homunculus problem

What and where in visual processing,
    32, 34, 84, 85, 99, 219, 259–260, 280
    neurophysiological evidence,
        85–88, 280
    unconscious processing and
        SAWCI, 259
Wisconsin card sorting task, 231
Working memory, see memory